to BUTTER BEANS BLACKBERRIES

BUTTER BEANS to BLACKBERRIES

recipes from the southern garden

RONNI LUNDY

north point press

a division of farrar, straus and giroux

new york

North Point Press
A division of Farrar, Straus and Giroux
19 Union Square West, New York 10003

Copyright © 1999 by Ronni Lundy
Distributed in Canada by Douglas & McIntyre Ltd.
Printed in the United States of America
Designed by Debbie Glasserman
First edition, 1999

Library of Congress Cataloging-in-Publication Data

Lundy, Ronni.
    Butter beans to blackberries : recipes from the southern
garden / Ronni Lundy. — 1st ed.
        p.   cm.
    Includes index.
    ISBN 0-86547-547-4 (alk. paper)
    1. Cookery, American—Southern style.   I. Title.
TX715.2.S68L8497   1999
641.5975—DC21   98-44304
Every effort has been made to secure the right to reprint previously published material in this book.

Grateful acknowledgment is made to the following for the right to reprint previously published material:

Billy C. Clark: Excerpt from the essay "Leatherbritches" first appearing in *Savory Memories* from the University Press of Kentucky, copyright © 1998 by Billy C. Clark.

Tony Early: Excerpt from the essay "A Worn Path" first appearing in *The Oxford American,* issue no. 19, copyright © 1997 by Tony Earley.

HarperCollins Publishers, Inc.: Excerpt from *Divine Secrets of the Ya-Ya Sisterhood* by Rebecca Wells, copyright © 1996 by Rebecca Wells.

Houghton Mifflin Company: Excerpt from *The Ballad of the Sad Café* by Carson McCullers, copyright © 1987, Houghton Mifflin Company.

Alfred A. Knopf Incorporated: Excerpt from *In Pursuit of Flavor* by Edna Lewis, copyright © 1988 Edna Lewis.

Time-Life Books Inc.: Excerpts from *Foods of the World: American Cooking: Southern Style* by Eugene Walter and the Editors of Time-Life Books, copyright © 1971 Time-Life Books Inc.

University of North Carolina Press: Excerpt from *Bill Neal's Southern Cooking* by William F. Neal, copyright © 1985 by the University of North Carolina Press.

Photographs on pages 132, 158, 168, 178, 188, 200, 212, 234, 284, 302, 312

Copyright © 1999 by John Nation.

Small photographs of Southern homes copyright © 1999 by Dawghaus Photography.

Contents

At the Table ix

Introduction xi

ABOUT:

Butter Beans 3

Crowder Peas 21

Soup Beans, Red Beans, and the Humble
     Peanut 37

Green Beans 53

Sallet Greens 77

Corn 95

Grits 109

The Spring Garden 119

Tomatoes 133

Cucumbers and Melons 149

Okra 159

Irish Potatoes 169

Eggplant 179

Bell Peppers 189

Squash 201

Sweet Potatoes 213

Roots 225

Mountain Mushrooms 235

HoneyBells, Ruby Reds, Calamondins, and
     Other Citrus 251

Peaches, Mayhaws, Quinces, and Bananas 271

Apples 285

Figs, Plums, and Scuppernongs 303

Strawberries and Blueberries 313

Blackberries 327

Things to Order 338

Places to Go 341

Farm Markets 343

Index 345

CONTENTS

Growing up in a city (further removed in time than in actual distance from the mountains my ancestors had called home), I nevertheless marked my calendar by the rituals of the garden. Autumn arrived on the first damp evening I came home from school to find the windows of the kitchen steamed by the pot likker in which a mess of kale had simmered all day on the back of the stove. Winter was marked by the first dinner of soup beans and cornbread dished up with a slice of raw onion on the side and was underscored when my aunt sent a tall and spicy apple stack cake for the holidays. Spring was begun with more greens, these tender and cooked quickly, though still strongly seasoned, and served with a slim green onion laid across the top of the bowl; and spring ended with the very first harvest of tart strawberries, which filled our house with a perfume to make a child dizzy with anticipation.

And summer?

In my family we have a ritual dinner served in the heart of every summer, though I never thought of it as such until a few years ago. The foods are as specific and their preparation as prescribed as those for Passover: fresh corn is cut, then "milked" from the cob with the edge of a spoon and simmered in a cast-iron skillet with butter, cream, salt, and pepper; white half-runner beans and small, creamy white potatoes in their jackets are braised slowly all day on the back of the stove; deep-red and warm-yellow tomatoes are laid out in thick slabs on a china plate turning translucent with age; cucumbers not much bigger than a grown man's thumb are sliced, salted, and chilled in a glass dish with ice cubes on top; coleslaw is made the painstaking way my mother always made it, with hand-slivered cabbage; trimmed green onions are served standing tall in a water glass or mug; a jar of chow-chow or some other hot homemade relish is passed on the side; something from the garden is dredged in seasoned cornmeal and fried in a black cast-iron skillet—green tomatoes or okra, maybe; and always there is a pan of hot cornbread and a pitcher of iced tea with sugar melted in it and lemon on the side.

We ate this meal around my great-aunts' round oak table on the screened-in back porch when we went for summer vacations to Corbin, Kentucky, where I was born. We ate it in the summer around my parents' round oak table in Louisville (where my family had moved for work), using produce brought up in washtubs and bushel baskets by the aunts and uncles and cousins from back home. We prepare this meal and eat it around that same oak table every summer now, using produce brought in to the farmers' markets scattered throughout town.

Like a Passover meal, this one has its ritual litany: we recite all the names of friends and relatives dead or living (but not here) who would have savored this dish or that as it makes its way around the table. We eat until our bellies are full and then eat on until our souls are satisfied as well. And then we take deep breaths and make room for cobbler of blackberries or peaches, or homemade ice cream, and, of course, the watermelon that has been chilling in a tub of ice water or in the bottom of the refrigerator all day.

Through it all, through the years, the people around the table tell stories that are brought to mind (like Proust's remembrances) by the taste or smell of foods first savored and sniffed ages and ages ago. And in the dark, as the crickets sing and the fireflies come out to tempt the children away from the table, we remember who we are.

On a summer evening some years ago, two of the South's most celebrated writers, William Faulkner and Katherine Anne Porter, were dining together at a plush restaurant in Paris. Everything had been laid out to perfection; a splendid meal had been consumed, a bottle of fine burgundy emptied, and thimble-sized glasses of an expensive liqueur drained. The maître d' and an entourage of waiters hovered close by, ready to satisfy any final whim.

"Back home the butter beans are in," said Faulkner, peering into the distance, "the speckled ones."

Miss Porter fiddled with her glass and stared into space. "Blackberries," she said wistfully.

—Eugene Walter, *Foods of the World:*
American Cooking: Southern Style (1971)

This story begins in Atlanta, Georgia, in the autumn of 1995 at a banquet table at the Ritz-Carlton Hotel with John and Ann Egerton on either side of me. We are there for a national food writers' conference, one which has focused on the abundance and history of Southern food and so has been, for the most part, a blissfully tasty celebration.

"Being a Southerner is itself a celebration," popular Atlanta chef and caterer Tim Patridge had said in a panel just the day before. "Especially when I go to New York. Do I ever love to get back . . . and eat."

We have been reveling in such chauvinism in the realm of cooking as the Southern foods that have been dished up to our colleagues from around the country have provoked oohs and ahhs and, sometimes, even outright surprise.

"I thought all you people ate were grits and fried chicken," one writer from the Northwest said to me as we marveled over the delicate nuttiness of tiny pink-eyed peas nestled on a bed of tangy mustard greens. The flavor was so exquisite, I found it easy to hold my tongue and simply smile.

In fact, we've eaten our way through a half dozen varieties of greens prepared in that many different ways; an array of tiny beans and field peas; corn soup, corn relish, corn cakes, corn pudding, and roasted corn; coulis of fresh tomatoes, blackberries, peaches, and beets; sweet potatoes mashed, baked, casseroled, and fried; a mountain of pork ribs and vast vats of fresh roasted oysters; buttery boiled and salted peanuts; regional delicacies from pan-fried

"Midmorning in that house at the corner of Bayou and Conti Streets was a kind of mad levee, a morning party like those held by King Louis XIV of France, when people were received and the day's events were discussed. My grandmother would install herself in a rocking chair on the high back porch to glance at the morning Mobile Register, shell beans and sip a lemonade or iced tea. And hold court."

—Eugene Walter, *Foods of the World: American Cooking: Southern Style* (1971)

quail to Coca-Cola cake, and more. We have had foods as they have been prepared by Southern cooks for centuries and foods prepared by a new generation of Southern cooks in fresh but still-rooted ways.

Almost every bite has been a celebration—except, of course, this one particular meal, which is taking the "nouveau" of its nouveau Southern designation way too seriously. We have begun inauspiciously with a precious small offering of field peas, minimally seasoned and cooked so little that they crunch at every bite.

"Has a law been passed that says you can't cook beans until they're done anymore?" whispers John, the author of *Southern Food* (University of North Carolina Press, 1993), the veritable Bible of our regional cuisine.

"Is there a law that says we can't have salt on the table?" murmurs Ann.

Salt, it turns out, is in fact forbidden by the chef, who apparently doesn't trust mere diners with such a heady option as

flavor-to-taste. We coax and cajole our waiter, who eventually brings us one tiny crystal shaker shrouded in a napkin, which he surreptitiously passes to John below the table's edge. We take pains to hide it as it is gratefully passed around our table of eight and then spirited over to the imploring diners at the table next to ours.

While we try to season and rearrange the arch menu items into some semblance of dinner, we do what Southerners have done forever when faced with less than palatable food. We recollect the great foods we have eaten before.

"Have you ever had lady cream peas?" I ask, having just recently discovered this Deep-South delicacy when my neighbor brought me a small bag of dried ones—the perfect memento from his trip to New Orleans.

Everyone sighs with delight and Ann tells me that I have to try them fresh, because the flavor is even more enchanting. And then John tells about going to the Asheville, North Carolina, farm market one summer and being amazed at the great long lines of folks snaking through the Quonset huts to buy a mess of just-in creasy beans (also called greasy beans or cut-shorts).

We sing the praises of speckled butter beans and speculate on the mysterious sallet peas that all of us have heard about but never tasted. I pine for slow-simmered white half-runners, while John admits he's partial to Kentucky Wonders.

We grin, drunk on savory memories, and then I confide: "I've been thinking lately about writing a book about nothing but Southern beans and field peas."

"That would be such a good book," John says at once.

And together Ann and I sigh. "Nobody would buy it."

"Maybe not," John says. "But it would be a real good book to have."

The idea simmered for a time on the back of the stove. It was that other venerable and peripatetic Southern food scribe, the late Eugene Walter, who made it all come together.

I met Eugene at a book fair featuring Southern writers in Montgomery, Alabama, in October of 1991. I didn't know anything about his literary (and lively) past or his then latest book, *Hints and Pinches* (Longstreet Press, 1991), but did know the moment I saw him that he was outrageous and great fun.

Small in height but huge in stage presence, he dominated an authors' cocktail party. His profile would have been leonine—regal nose, shock of white hair swept straight back—but for the wild mischief that sparkled behind thick black glasses. He teased his audience with the caginess of an old cat, spinning one tempting anecdote after another. (Alas, his best—about how, in his twenties, he made his way from Mobile to a back stage on Broadway to get a "relic" from Tallulah Bankhead—cannot be told in a family cookbook.)

After two days of speeches, sales, and cocktail parties, we swapped books and promised to meet again. He signed my copy of *Hints and Pinches* "your garlicky ole Mobile Uncle Eugene." I felt blessed.

Just how blessed I didn't realize until I got home and settled in to read his amazing compendium of recipes and lore about herbs, spices, and plants, including dozens of Southern favorites from benne (sesame) seeds to kudzu. More than a delight to read, it became an essential reference for my food library; and it sent me out in search of more of his work. I found a very worn copy of his novel *Love You Good, See You Later* at the library and ordered a copy of *The Untidy Pilgrim*, the winner of the 1954 Lippincott Award for fiction, from a local bookstore.

From the jacket blurbs I discovered that Eugene had been born in Mobile and was touring with his own marionette company by his teens. He made his way to New York, then Paris, then Rome, spending thirty years in Europe writing libretti; articles for the *Paris Review, The Atlantic Monthly, Harper's,* and *Vogue*; an operetta version of *Alice in Wonderland*; and the song "What Is a Youth?" for Franco Zefferelli's *Romeo and Juliet*. He also popped up in a couple of Fellini films. But most important, for me at least, Eugene was the author of the classic Time-Life tome, *American Cooking: Southern Style* (1971).

Even if I hadn't heard its reputation from food friends already, I'd have been compelled to track it down simply because the food references in his stories and novels were so rich, specific, and tempting. Here's one from a page I dog-eared in *The Untidy Pilgrim*:

"Did y'all go hunting for possum-grapes?"

"Lord, possum grapes, I haven't even thought of them for a hundred years!"

"Little black ones way up in the tops of trees—they's oodles and oodles of them in Sophia County."

"Don't I know it! We don't have them this close to the Gulf; plenty of bullises and scuppernongs, though."

"And chufers!" I cried.

"Omigod, *chufers!*" bellowed Acis and we both nearly fell out laughing. I don't know why, the sound of chufers, I guess.

"Y'all must be getting real hungry," came Ada's voice as she sidled into the room. "Anybody so concerned over chufers. Well, supper will be tereckly."

Anybody so concerned over chufers had to have crammed a wealth of information on Southern foods into that Time-Life volume, but coming by the book seemed for a while to be impossible. Out-of-print, it showed up in several used-book stores I checked as I traveled around the country, but always as one volume in a whole set. None of the dealers I talked to was willing to break up a set. I couldn't believe my luck, then, when I found it on a shelf, by itself, at the used-book store just up the street from my house. The owner blanched at the $6.50 price when I took it to the counter. "We never ever get single volumes of this," he said. "Somebody's marked it wrong. You got yourself a treasure."

And indeed I had. As I read through Eugene's remarkable travelogue, this lit-

any of love to the traditions of Southern hospitality and food, I felt, as I often do with most true books about the South, that I was inhabiting a place both real and imagined.

Eugene had left the South to write. It was food that literally brought him back, to write this book about Southern cooking. In the process, he rediscovered not only the land he came from but the best parts of it that still inhabited himself. His journey made me think of my own in writing about Southern food and culture.

But I was still eaten up with the idea of a book on Southern beans, although every time I seriously began to research, I found myself distracted by the likes of chufers, mayhaws, or cymlings. I thought I knew a lot about the varieties of Southern fruits and vegetables, but the more I read and asked around, the more it seemed that every region had its secret prize and that every generation had devised a new, delicious way to prepare it.

Then, in *American Cooking: Southern Style,* I found the anecdote that begins this volume, the one about Faulkner and Katherine Anne Porter pining in Paris for speckled butter beans and blackberries. It pleased me so much, seemed so essentially Southern, that I typed it into my word processor file on the spot. Later that night the words came back to me in that drowsy cusp just before sleep.

"That's it!" I thought, coming straight out of bed. "Not a book about beans, but one about Southern beans and berries and fruits and squash and the whole garden of treasures that every Southerner remembers and loves but hardly ever sits down to write about."

And so this book began in earnest.

I've not told that Paris anecdote to a single Southerner who didn't identify with it. For some it isn't the speckled butter beans of Faulkner's Deep South, but mountain shuck beans, or the sivvy beans of Charleston, or the lady cream peas of Montgomery, Mobile, and New Orleans. Or instead of the tang of blackberries, it's the musky nectar of scuppernongs or the sugary-drip-down-the-chin liquor of real Georgia peaches. But for all of us, the epiphany is the same: there are certain fruits and vegetables we grew up with, modest in appearance but potent in taste, that have no peer and are capable of stirring in us the deepest and most powerful longings for home.

Songs have been written about the crisp fried chicken and tangy country hams of the South; volumes about her pies, cakes, cornbread, and biscuits. Books on barbecue alone could fill a king's pantry. But get any born-and-raised Southerner to reminisce about the dishes remembered best and longed for most, and you will hear a surprising, delicious, and passionate litany of the native vegetables and fruits of the South.

Beans alone could fill a volume with recipes and stories about succulent purple speckled butter beans, pink-eyed peas, soup beans, crowders, lady cream peas, shuck beans, shell-out beans, creasy or greasy beans, sallet peas, peanuts, and white half-runners. Their earthy, buttery flavors—accented not only by the seasoning they've cooked in but, so it seems, by

the very soil in which they've grown—are subtle, distinctive, and so evocative that years and years after last tasting them, transplanted Southerners still long to roll those unique flavors around their tongues again.

When I wrote my first cookbook, *Shuck Beans, Stack Cakes, and Honest Fried Chicken* (Atlantic Monthly Press, 1991), and included a recipe for the creamy, rich speckled butter beans I'd eaten as a child, I soon found myself getting requests like this one from a native of the Tennessee hills transplanted in Dayton, Ohio: "Please, *please* tell me the company that packs these beans frozen. My grocer says he has never heard of them, but if you will tell me where to find them, I will make sure that he gets them in stock, for there is nothing in this world so good as the taste of speckled butter beans and cornbread."

The shuck beans of the title, tender white half-runners which have been hand-strung and dried (also called leatherbritches, and an ancient and labor-intensive winter staple of mountain South), are so prized that the handful of folks who still dry them can sell them for a ransom, as much as $40 for a pound.

Every man, woman, and child seems to have a favorite from the Southern bean patch, beloved not just for the flavor but also for the rituals: stringing the beans on the front porch in the morning, or gathering around big wooden tables to prepare bushels of beans for canning or drying for the winter.

And it isn't simply beans we are passionate about.

> *"Gumbo born and gumbo bred*
> *Tabasco follies fuzz my head.*
> *South is my blood and south my bone*
> *So haply formed on pork and pone.*
> *Incan, African move in me.*
> *You say 'South? Where can it be?'*
> *Chewing my sugar cane, I repeat:*
> *'Why, in all we like to cook and eat.' "*
>
> —Eugene Walter, *Foods of the World:*
> *American Cooking: Southern Style* (1971)

Corn is sacred food in this region, fried, in fritters and soups, boiled fresh from the stalk, roasted wrapped in bacon, dried and made into hominy, grits, and meal for the holy cornbread. Also revered are the greens: collards, poke, turnip, dock, lamb's quarters, crow's toes, kale, dandelion, creases, cress, and spinach. Hot peppers and pungent onions, from Vidalias to the tiny, spring green onions to the boisterous ramp, are prized.

This is the land of okra—fried, simmered, or stewed in dishes such as gumbo (which gets its name from an African word for the vegetable) or Limpin' Sally, a distaff version of Hoppin' John. Eggplant, summer squash (from yellow crooknecks to mirlitons to pattypans), tomatoes (red, yellow, purple, and green), radishes, and cucumbers all hold places of honor on the Southern table, and come in many guises.

Apples are the mainstay of the mountain South, including the elusive Grimes Golden, Arkansas Black, Mutsu, Braeburn, tiny green June apples, and Lady apples—each with its own special use in the kitchen, from drying to cooking slow to make thick, fragrant apple butter.

Muscadines, blackberries, Georgia peaches, pawpaws, mayhaws, figs, strawberries, dewberries, watermelons, honeydews, cushaws, and Florida oranges are the stuff of jams, pickles, wines, and preserves. Some show up in pies (regular and fried), grace shortcakes, or fill the centers of magnificent cakes. But they serve also as accents and undercurrents to more serious dishes, compote with pork and chicken in the old days, coulis with grits and greens in more modern interpretations.

And though the rest of the world has persisted in believing that we Southerners know how to cook these earthly treasures in only one of two tasty ways (simmered long and slow or breaded and quick-fried), the truth is that for centuries we have used them in dishes that reflect the range of cuisines that are our heritage, from American Indian to African, West Indian, Spanish, German, French, Irish, English, and on.

"A Southerner's insistence on the finest, freshest vegetables comes naturally," Bill Neal wrote in Bill Neal's *Southern Cooking* (The University of North Carolina Press, 1985). "Almost everyone had a garden, or at least access to one (I know lawyers who are still paid in produce). City dwellers had reliable farmers who called at home early each morning with dew-laden pickings. One had a vegetable man, period, though the best were hard to come by. A farmer would check and cross-check the references of any potential customer. Those who proudly sold to the Sartorises did not call on the Snopeses. One's social standing could be accurately charted by knowing from whom one bought one's produce."

How you prepared these vegetables could be an indication of where you came from and of where you stood in the community. From plantation times on, wealthier Southerners, who had "help" in the kitchen, savored foods that took much time and labor to prepare and often used rare or exotic ingredients. For the most part, black and poorer white folks made magnificence from meager stores by relying on foods that they could make quickly or leave to simmer on the back of the stove while they worked hard all day. What the two cuisines shared was a common store of homegrown resources and a common love of intense and satisfying flavor.

The cooking of the South is diverse, ranging from the delicately spiced melanges of Creole coastal cuisine to the more straightforward down-home slow-simmer style prevalent in the highland mountains. It is nearly impossible to define by specific cooking techniques, spices, or ingredients, although to paraphrase: You'll know it when you eat it.

Both John and Eugene researched their classic Southern food books on the road, traveling the South to taste the food firsthand and to talk face-to-face with the people who made it, grew it, and ate it. I decided that I, too, would make as many trips as I could to the varied parts of the region to taste for myself what was there. Over three years, I made more than a dozen forays through the South to discover not only the legacy of things past but also the finest examples of the recent renaissance in Southern cooking.

For this book I've surveyed the foods of Kentucky, Virginia, West Virginia, Maryland, North and South Carolina, Georgia, Florida, Alabama, Mississippi, Louisiana, Arkansas, and parts of Texas. Not all these states would be included in every political or social definition of the South, but in terms of foodways, they form a whole.

I was a little apprehensive at first. Through the early 1990s my experiences with restaurant interpretations of the cooking of the "New South" had generally been as odd and unsatisfying as the nouveau dinner described earlier. To be sure, there were hidden treasures scattered around the South, like Jocelyn's in Ocean Springs, Mississippi, where traditions were gently updated, and Louis's Restaurant and Bar, where Louis Osteen forged solid new territory with panache. But for the most part, the first wave of New South cooking seemed to be trying to translate into California or New York trends a tradition that needed to be explored and celebrated on its own terms.

By the mid-1990s, however, a new generation of Southern cooks seemed to be coming into its own. Confident now of their own skill, and surer of their personal taste, these cooks began to return to their roots. Unlike the postwar generation before them, they were less interested in convenience foods and processed products. More like their grandparents, great-grandparents, and great-great-grandparents, they looked to the harvest of the land around them for resources and inspiration. In that harvest they discovered a richness of flavor and a diversity of pleasures to rival the finest gourmet items from anywhere in the country or the world: salt-cured country ham as delectable as that of Parma; sun-ripened dried Shenandoah Valley tomatoes with a sweetness of flavor unmatched by California's or Italy's best; fresh-pressed cider with the mingled medley of half a dozen tart, tangy, or honeyed local varieties; dusky sweet sorghum syrup; sugary mild Vidalia onions; juice-oozing Carolina, Georgia, or Alabama peaches; and sharp, winy berries plucked from wild, briar-filled vines.

In the past, many Southern cookbooks have dealt lightly with the traditions of the Southern garden table, in part because the preparation of such dishes seems deceptively simple and the foods themselves (bowls of pureed pattypan squash flavored with broken bits of bacon, big pots of field peas simmered with ham hock or salt pork) have been perceived as too common or humble to be of interest beyond the region. As we have learned more about what is good for us to eat, however, we have realized that such dishes not only are pleasurable to our senses but can be important to our health and well-being, too.

In the past, the remarkable diversity of Southern garden products was also often neglected in Southern cookbooks, simply because this produce was so difficult to come by outside of the region. What was

the point of celebrating the glory of sivvy beans if you could eat them only in Charleston? What was the hope of convincing Yankees of the delicate allure of okra when the only kind they were apt to ever taste slid slimily from a can?

In recent years, however, as we have become more conscious of the glory of regional American foods, and as such foods have become more and more available to us—not just through special orders but in markets around the country and in our own gardens—our interest in discovering that which is singular and special in regional harvests has grown as well.

What is happening in the South, as in other parts of the country (northern California, Washington State, and the berry fields of Michigan, for instance) is a vigorous revival of interest in locally grown produce specific to the region. And as the produce of the South, in all its tempting diversity and with all its captivating fragrance and flavor, becomes better known (through travel, word of mouth, and the work of inspired chefs like those whose recipes appear here), the products themselves are becoming more widely available as well. Witness the Vidalia onion, once known only to those who visited Vidalia, Georgia, but now spreading its sweet savoriness in supermarkets across the map.

When I began this book, the most common plaint I heard from serious Southern cooks, both home and professional, was that one simply couldn't *find* the old, flavorful varieties of beans, corn, tomatoes, and berries. But in just the past three years, the realm of specialty growers, local farm markets, and mail-order suppliers has burgeoned.

Between 1994 and 1996 alone, the number of farm markets nationally surged from a modest 655 to an impressive 2,410, according to U.S. Department of Agriculture tallies. Along with the usual berries, corn, and tomatoes, Southern growers are increasingly finding success with heirloom varieties, prized regional favorites such as McCaslan or cut-short beans, and produce grown organically. Some have even branched out into mail order. And while you'll find many such sources listed in this book, it has been a pleasurable frustration to me that even more are coming along faster than I can keep up with them.

But the deepest pleasure I experienced as I researched this book came in finding, again and again, that generosity of spirit which has come to be known as Southern hospitality. Cooks, writers, suppliers, and devotees swapped stories and shared food with me in person, and traded recipes and leads by phone. The tastes and techniques they introduced me to were often as distinctive as the many variations of Southern accents that I heard. And yet the dishes and stories were variations on one overriding theme. All of us shared a passion for the harvest of the region and for the flavors we remembered from childhood. And all of us were determined that tradition would, indeed, rise again.

---

*"**In my childhood** we ate, my father remarked, 'as if there were no God.' "*
—Katherine Anne Porter

BUTTER BEANS

Classic Southern Butter Beans

Jerry's Speckled Butter Beans

Speckled Butter Beans and Country Ham in Lemon Velouté

Wylie's Butter Bean and Shoepeg Salad

Simple Succotash

Virginia Corn Cakes with Butter Bean Ragout

Winter Succotash

It was likely June when Faulkner and Porter had their historic conversation. At least that's when the butter beans, the speckled ones, come in around Mississippi, Faulkner's home. Wylie Poundstone, the chef at King Cotton Produce Company, a combination produce market and restaurant in Montgomery, Alabama (see Places to Go, page 341), says, "It takes a while for butter beans to grow, but if the weather cooperates, we can have them from June right on through the fall." Bob Gulsby, one of the four owners of King Cotton says, "As long as we've got 'em, we'll ship 'em fresh to anybody who wants to order."

Those who do are often transplanted Southerners longing for the taste of a vegetable as common as July fireflies where they grew up, but hardly known elsewhere. My experience has taught me that asking for butter beans north of the Mason-Dixon is apt to get you a bowl of thick soup made from very large, dried lima beans. It's tasty, but a bit on the brackish side and doesn't have the sweet, creamy flavor of a Southern butter bean at all.

The term "butter bean" is used to refer to lima beans, which fall roughly into three categories. First it refers to fresh limas, with the most prized being those with beans of the "baby" variety—small (about the size of your thumbnail) and very tender. Such beans can be found throughout the United States either fresh (in season), frozen, or canned.

Second, a distinction is made in many regions of the South between this already small lima bean and even smaller ones. These smaller beans may go by different colloquial names. They are known as butter peas in the Montgomery area but may be called "sieve" beans in other parts of Alabama or the South. This is also the bean prized as the "sivvy" of Charleston and the surrounding Low Country area of South Carolina. Joe Kemble, assistant professor of horticulture at Auburn University, says the common names are a corruption of the more proper name, sieva bean. Sivvy beans are prized for their sweetness but, alas, don't ship well.

Third, the speckled butter bean is a variety of lima with a colored, mottled skin—usually a deep purplish brown and green, or black and green. Speckled butter beans have a creamier texture and more buttery flavor than their green lima cousins. I, like my mother before me, watch religiously for speckled butter beans in the very brief period in the summer when they may show up shelled and fresh in the produce department of local supermarkets. Although the farmers in this part of Kentucky don't grow them commercially, speckled butter beans are a summer staple in farm markets throughout the deeper South, and if you drive the non-interstate highways in June, you are apt to see hand-lettered signs on the side of the road proffering "fresh speckled butter beans—just in." Most commonly, though, I come by these beans frozen, and sold throughout the year at supermarkets here. They are very nearly as tasty frozen as they are fresh.

Like sieva beans, speckled butter beans sometimes go by colloquial names. For instance, Wylie Poundstone says lots of folks around Montgomery call them rattlesnake beans. And elsewhere a lima variety with cream and maroon speckled skin is called the Christmas bean.

Technically, you can interchange the more widely available baby lima beans for the speckled butter beans in most recipes, but the flavor will be different. All of the beans are delicious, however, and, as Wylie says, "You can do *so* much with them. They're some of the most versatile vegetables in the Southern kitchen."

Remember to go easy on seasonings when you cook butter beans, since it's the beans' own subtle flavor which you want to emphasize.

Classic Southern Butter Beans
SERVES 6 TO 8

This is the fundamental recipe for fresh shelled butter beans. If you're accustomed to limas cooked in very little liquid (seasoned with a pat of butter and dash of salt on the way to the table), this may seem like a lot of water for cooking, but you want the dish to yield some sweet pot likker to be sopped up by Real Cornbread (page 103). If you're eating Low Country–style, serve the beans over rice.

2 quarts water
1 ham hock
6 cups (about 2 pounds) fresh shelled
   baby lima or speckled butter beans
salt

In a large pan, bring the water and ham hock to a boil. Cook, partially covered, at a low boil for about 30 minutes, to season the water. Add the beans and bring the water back to a boil, then turn down the heat and simmer, partially covered, for 30 minutes to 1 hour (see The Time It Takes, below), until the beans are tender and creamy inside. Remove the hock and add salt to taste. Serve immediately or keep refrigerated for 2 to 3 days. Reheat thoroughly before serving.

Note: *Frozen speckled butter beans or baby lima beans may be used. When you add them to the water, use a wooden spoon to gently break apart clumps.*

the time it takes

Southerners cook butter beans anywhere from 30 minutes to a couple of hours. The choice depends somewhat on the size and freshness of the beans (the larger or older they are, the longer they take to reach tenderness). Some folks like butter beans just at the point when the inside is tender but the skin still pops when bitten. Unless you are making a salad or relish with the beans, I think that's missing the point. Perfect butter beans are cooked until the insides are quite creamy—the reason for the "butter" in their name.

In most of the recipes for butter beans here, you will find estimated cooking times with a wider variance than is usual in a cookbook. Experiment until you discover what degree of tenderness you prefer; and be aware that even the same type and size of bean will take a different amount of time to cook from one batch to another, depending on the freshness of the beans. If you want to serve butter beans for a dinner that requires precision timing, cook them to doneness a day or two before, refrigerate them, and reheat thoroughly at serving time.

MAIL ORDER

The folks at King Cotton Produce in Montgomery, Alabama, will ship fresh butter beans or crowder peas (including the elusive lady cream peas or purple-hull peas) in the continental United States. Call for prices and availability. (See Things to Order, page 338.) If they don't have butter beans in stock, it's worth asking what's fresh and shippable. If you're in town, be sure to stop by at lunchtime so you can get a taste of Wylie Poundstone's good Southern cooking as well.

If you want to experiment with bean varieties by growing your own, Southern Exposure Seed Exchange in Earlysville, Virginia, specializes in heirloom seeds with an emphasis on Southern varieties. Its catalog offers more than half a dozen pole lima beans, ranging from the Aubrey Deane, a pre-1890 family heirloom from Greene County, Virginia, to the Worchester Indian Red Pole, reported to be of Native American origin. See Things to Order, page 338.

Jerry's Speckled Butter Beans
SERVES 4

My mother loved to cook frozen speckled butter beans in the winter when their rich, creamy texture and nutty flavor were salve to the soul. We made many a meal of these beans, her mashed potatoes (page 171), and Real Cornbread (page 103), and thought ourselves supremely well fed.

2 cups water
16-ounce package frozen speckled
    butter beans
2 tablespoons butter
2 tablespoons half and half
salt

In a pan with a lid, bring the water to a boil and add the butter beans, stirring gently with a wooden spoon to separate. When the water returns to boiling, reduce the heat, cover, and simmer for 30 to 35 minutes, until the beans are tender. (You may need to add a little water near the end of the cooking time to keep the beans from sticking, but you want most of the water to cook away.) Add the butter and

You Can't Get Theirs from Here

Andrea Limehouse of Limehouse Produce in Charleston, South Carolina, says the region's famed sieva (generally referred to as "sivvy") bean is, in fact, just a very, very small baby lima.

"They range from the size of the nail of your little finger to no bigger than the nail of an index finger," Andrea says. But while she concedes that sivvy beans are biologically the same as baby limas, gastronomically, she swears, they are far superior—and generations of Low Country South Carolinians agree.

"Oh, they are wonderful. They're sweet as sugar and they make the most delicious liquor. They just taste fresher than the lima beans from somewhere else. And you can get them machine-shelled, but that does stress them. The real purists around here only use sivvy beans which have been hand-shelled."

So what would account for this better flavor?

"Well you know, this used to be called 'South Carolina: The Iodine State,' " Andrea says. "Because of the large amount of iodine in the water, this is purported to be a great vegetable-growing state. And it's true that certain vegetables here just have a better taste."

Alas, Limehouse Produce won't ship sivvy beans elsewhere. "They're actually quite fragile," Andrea says. "They don't keep up well in the heat at all, and it's quite warm during the seasons."

That's right, seasons. Fortunately for travelers with Charleston on the itinerary, sivvy beans have not one, but two seasons: June to August and late September to November. (Andrea warns that in recent years, however, the fall crop has not been good because of excessive rain.) If you are looking to buy a mess of sivvy beans while in town, you can't do better than to drop by Limehouse Produce (see Places to Go, page 341).

If you want to try to take some home, Andrea says, they freeze "very, very well. You really should never blanch them. Some people here just literally throw them in the freezer. I like to put mine in a little water, just enough to cover. When you cook them up later, they are very nearly as delicious as they are fresh."

You can cook the beans the way the locals do (see page 6) and serve them with rice. John Taylor, dean of Low Country cooking, says sivvy beans and rice are typically served with corn relish. Real Cornbread (page 103) is perfect for sopping up the pot likker.

allow it to melt, then add the half and half and stir. Cover and simmer for another 5 minutes, then add salt to taste.

Speckled Butter Beans and Country Ham in Lemon Velouté SERVES 6 TO 8

I never thought I'd taste a dish with butter beans as blissfully perfect as my mother's, but this one is its peer, with a velvety texture and the perfect marriage of complementary flavors in the beans, tart sauce, and tangy ham.

BUTTER BEANS
2½ cups water
5 cups fresh or frozen speckled butter beans
¼ pound country ham with fat removed, cut in small pieces

LEMON VELOUTÉ
1½ cups chicken stock
3 tablespoons butter
3 tablespoons flour
2 tablespoons freshly squeezed lemon juice
salt

In a heavy pan, bring the water to a boil and add the butter beans. (If using frozen beans, use a wooden spoon to gently break up clumps.) When the water returns to a boil, turn the heat down and let the beans simmer for about 45 minutes, or until the skins are tender and the insides creamy, and most of the water has boiled off.

While the beans are simmering, make the lemon velouté. In a small pan, heat the chicken stock. Fill the bottom of a double boiler with water, and bring to a boil. Meanwhile, in the top of the double boiler, set directly over low heat, melt the butter and whisk in the flour. Cook, whisking, for five minutes, then slowly whisk in the hot stock. Place over the boiling water and cook for 45 to 50 minutes, stirring occasionally to keep a crust from forming on top.

When the beans are done, add the country ham pieces and cook until the ham is just warmed. Meanwhile, remove the velouté from the heat, add the lemon juice, and salt to taste. Remove the beans from the heat, pour the velouté over the beans, and mix well. Serve immediately.

STEAM BEANS

If you should luck upon a crop of fresh sivvy beans or butter peas still in their pods, and they are truly fresh and very young, you may want to try something my friend Don Nobles of Montgomery, Alabama, recommends: "I've had butter peas steamed still in their little pods when they are very, very young. Just steamed for a few minutes until they're tender, and then served with salt and butter. They've a flavor in between an English pea and a snow pea. Truly splendid!"

MAiL ORDeR

A few years ago, I was fortunate enough to feast on a meal prepared by the marvelous Italian chef Giuliano Bugialli. As we waited for the antipasto to arrive, the delightful gentleman sitting next to me decided to tell me about the legendary Parma ham which was coming. First he described plump pigs feeding on chestnuts and whey in the rolling hills of northern Italy, then the care taken in the seasoning of the ham, and finally the picture of these beautiful rose-brown objects hanging in open windows, their salt-cure enhanced by the naturally briny air of the nearby sea.

When the thin slices of ultimate prosciutto arrived, we savored them for a while in silence until I turned to my companion and said, "This is heaven. This is almost as perfect as a Kentucky country ham."

"Precisely." He grinned in reply.

Southern country ham chauvinists are a fierce lot, given to regional preferences and supporting lore every bit as dramatic as that surrounding hams from Parma. (Smithfield pigs were once fed on a diet of Virginia peanuts, giving those hams their prized flavor. Kentucky and North Carolina tradition holds with putting some tobacco in the smoking fire to ward off insects and give the ham more resonance.) We prize age (a year or more) and complexity of flavor over moistness and accessibility. Salty is the point, although it is possible to have too much of a good thing when the brine overwhelms the interplay of all the other flavors that mark a great country ham. We also know that a very little goes a long way when it comes to country ham, and that makes it an excellent seasoning applied judiciously (and near the finish) in a dish such as Speckled Butter Beans and Country Ham in Lemon Velouté.

But how to get a great country ham has been a dilemma for many years. While hardcore enthusiasts have cultivated a farmer or two who still cure only a dozen or so hams at home each year, the rest of the world must rely on mail order from commercial ham producers—and the quality of country hams from such can vary from great to good to downright citified.

In 1996, however, a two-tiered tasting of country hams for Cook's Illustrated confirmed what I'd suspected for many years: Gatton Farms' Father's Country Ham is among the best commercial country ham you can order. Aged for fifteen months in small batches down in Bremen, Kentucky, the Gatton Farms hams have all the subtlety and distinction of an individual artisan-cured ham. Whole hams ranging from 13 to 16 pounds can be ordered from the company, but, better yet for novices, you can also order a vacuum pack with three slices.

See Things to Order, page 338.

Wylie's Butter Bean and Shoepeg Salad

SERVES 8

King Cotton Produce Company in Montgomery, Alabama, is more than just a produce market. "It's like a Cracker Barrel in a Harry's," says chef Wylie Poundstone—which means it's a terrific down-home restaurant smack dab in the middle of a superb greengrocery. (See Places to Go, page 341.)

There are bins of the freshest fruits and vegetables from the Montgomery region lining the aisles. ("King Cotton's strawberries are the most wonderful thing this side of the Atlantic," says local food fanatic Don Nobles. "They're small and sweet, sweet, sweet. They're worth driving to Alabama for.")

The tables for the restaurant are set in the produce aisles, and the menu items are created from whatever is freshest that day. Wylie, who trained at Johnson and Wales in Providence, Rhode Island, and worked at Emeril's and Commander's Palace in New Orleans before coming back home to Montgomery to ply his trade, says one of his most popular recipes is this simple but delicious salad made with speckled butter beans.

½ cup water
1¼ cups fresh or frozen speckled butter
    beans
½ cup finely chopped red onion
½ cup finely chopped red bell pepper
1 teaspoon minced garlic
¼ teaspoon kosher salt
black pepper
11-ounce can whole shoepeg corn (see
    Note)
¼ cup mayonnaise
2 tablespoons cider or red wine vinegar

In a saucepan with a lid, bring the water to a boil and add the butter beans. Stir very gently with a wooden spoon until the water begins to boil again, then turn the heat to low and cover the pot. Simmer until the beans are al dente (the insides are just tender, and the skins are intact and "pop" a little when you bite them). Fresh butter beans could take from 15 to 25 minutes to cook to this state, depending on how fresh they are. Frozen beans should take 20 to 25 minutes.

If there is more than a teaspoon of water left in the pan when the beans are ready, drain them, or turn up the heat to a brisk boil until only about a teaspoon of water is left, shaking or gently stirring the beans in the pan to keep them from burning.

In a bowl, mix the warm beans with the onion, bell pepper, and garlic. Add the salt and several grinds of fresh black pepper.

Drain the shoepeg corn and add it to the beans, tossing gently.

In a small bowl, whisk together the mayonnaise and vinegar until blended. (Wylie uses cider vinegar, but I like the red wine variety for the appealing pale pink color it gives the dish.) Pour the dressing over the vegetables and toss until they are well coated. Transfer the salad to a non-metal container with a lid. Cover and refrigerate for at least two hours.

ROAD NOTES

FEARRINGTON VILLAGE, NORTH CAROLINA, APRIL 1996

It is just dusk as we arrive at the Fearrington House Restaurant in a beautifully redone old farmhouse outside of Chapel Hill. (See Places to Go, page 341.) My good friend Lee Kaukas has flown down from D.C. to help me uncover the edible treasures of the area, and we are also joined by Dana Felty, the daughter of another good friend and an Antioch College student working as an intern for *Southern Exposure* magazine in Durham.

Lee and I do not know the details yet, but are aware that Dana, barely nineteen, has just suffered the first big crushing heartbreak of her life.

Dana is wearing a brave face, but the melancholy seeps through in involuntary sighs and the occasional mournful stare into space. The little graces of the impeccable service, though—the handsome waiter refolds her napkin and places it in the chair to wait for her when she escapes to the powder room after ordering—seem to be some small balm for her injured spirit.

Before our appetizers arrive, we are each served a single small croustade with an olive-oil-kissed and grilled slice of very fresh tomato atop, and a tiny, demure cup of lemon velouté with the barest whisper of fresh oregano. Its citrus-herb fragrance is crisp and reviving, the veal stock is rich, and the overall effect is delightfully tonic and bracing.

Dana sips thoughtfully. She says, "You know, this is just the kind of thing that you could be dying of pneumonia or some other terrible affliction, but then someone would bring you a demitasse of this and you'd drink it and say, 'Hey, I think I'll live after all.' "

Her eyes begin to twinkle and she grins.

Note: *Fresh corn is sublime, and frozen shoepeg is almost always better in recipes when you can't use fresh; but neither is as tasty in this salad as the canned shoepeg corn recommended. That's because the corn, canned with a touch of sugar, has a specific sweetness that is the perfect complement to the tang of the vinegar. Don't be tempted to use canned butter beans or limas, however, since they will inevitably be overcooked.*

Simple Succotash   SERVES 8 TO 10

From a Narraganset word meaning "boiled whole kernels of corn," succotash might also be translated as "sublime" in the South. There are more elaborate versions of this dish, but my favorite is the simple one here.

1 recipe Classic Southern Butter Beans
   (page 6)
8 ears fresh corn

Prepare the butter beans according to the recipe. Just before they are done, shuck the corn and cut the kernels from the cob according to the directions on page 101, making sure to "milk" the cob. Add the kernels and milk to the pot of beans and bring the mixture to a light boil. Turn the heat down and simmer for another 10 minutes, until the corn is tender.

In addition to shopping at farm markets, some city dwellers can buy fresh produce straight from a community farm cooperative, a contemporary variation on the old-time vegetable-man theme.

Community farm cooperatives are usually operated by small-farm owners living near an urban area. The farmer sells annual shares in his operation, with individuals or families paying a set amount to be supplied with fresh produce all through the growing season. Some farmers offer meat, eggs, and dairy products as well. The farmer benefits by knowing in advance just how much capital he can invest in crop production and by having a market for whatever he can grow. Members help bear the losses of a bad year and share in the blessings of bumper crops in good ones.

The benefits for members are both tangible and subtle. We've belonged to such a co-op operated by Steve Smith of Bedford, Kentucky, off and on for several years. Steve grows produce organically, so we know that the vegetables we get from him have no added chemicals. Our participation in the co-op helps keep at least one small family farm, and the way of life it provides, alive. I love the way it connects our family to the realities of the growing season, and how the vagaries of the yield make us aware of our dependency on nature.

It's also fun. Steve brings the crops to town one day a week and sets up in the parking lot of a nearby church. Members show up to fill their baskets with that week's goodies. Our gatherings have the air of an old-time church social. We sing the praises of the lush tomato crop, lament and grieve when the corn has a bad year. We swap recipes for beets, never having enough for the multitude that seems to spring from Steve's fields every year. We laugh and trade stories with friends we may see only this one time a week. We make new friends over baskets full of okra and greens. Steve met his wife, Karen, the year she joined the co-op.

We develop a relationship with our grower as well. Members are invited out to the farm to weed or relax, or both. We tell Steve about new seeds we've read about or a variety of lettuce we've had at a restaurant, and he follows up by planting to our request as often as it's possible. We can barter. One year our family got vegetables at a bargain price because I helped write flyers and promotional material for the co-op. And when it came time to do the cover photo for this book, the porch of Steve and Karen's house, framed in the purple hyacinth beans and four o'clocks Karen has planted and filled with baskets of goodies from the fields Steve tends, turned out to be the perfect place.

For information on community farm co-operatives in your area, contact your nearby county extension agent.

Virginia Corn Cakes with Butter Bean Ragout   SERVES 8

I had always thought it a peculiar personal quirk that one of my favorite breakfasts was my mother's speckled butter beans, reheated and spread atop a toasted wedge of leftover cornbread from dinner the night before. Then my favorite breakfast spot in Louisville, Lynn's Paradise Café, (see Places to Go, page 341), put this dish on its morning menu. The brainchild of chef Lindsay Roberts, herself a Southern girl with a passion for butter beans, this is a super dish to serve up for Sunday brunch. At Lynn's you can choose to have corn cakes topped with either butter beans or fried apples (page 291), but I suggest you fix both and then have one cake with beans, another with apples, and so on until you are sated.

BUTTER BEAN RAGOUT

4 tablespoons unsalted butter
¼ cup flour
1½ cups hot unsalted chicken stock
¾ cup diced red onion
1½ cups diced ham (not country)
1 teaspoon garlic puree
½ teaspoon coarsely ground pepper
½ teaspoon dried marjoram
2 tablespoons Tabasco sauce
1 tablespoon brown sugar
½ teaspoon kosher salt
3 cups cooked butter beans
1 medium tomato, peeled and diced
½ cup green onions, chopped

In a heavy pot, make a roux: melt the butter over low heat and sprinkle in the flour, stirring all the while. Cook, stirring constantly, for about five minutes, until the roux is golden and piping hot. Slowly add the hot chicken stock, whisking vigorously to keep lumps from forming. Simmer over low heat for a few minutes as the mixture thickens. Add the onion, ham, and garlic puree, stirring to incorporate. Simmer for 15 minutes.

Add the remaining ingredients except for the tomato and green onions. Simmer for 15 minutes more to meld the flavors, then stir in the tomatoes and green onions. Turn the heat very low to just keep the mixture warm while you make the corn cakes.

VIRGINIA CORN CAKES

1 cup yellow cornmeal
1 cup flour
1½ teaspoons baking powder

¼ teaspoon baking soda
½ teaspoon kosher salt
1 tablespoon sugar
1¾ cups buttermilk
2 large eggs
2 tablespoons unsalted butter, melted
oil for frying

sour cream

In a large bowl, blend together the corn-meal, flour, baking powder, baking soda, salt, and sugar.

In a separate bowl, whisk together the buttermilk, eggs, and butter until blended.

Pour the liquid over the dry mixture and whisk together just until everything is combined. (Some lumps are fine.)

Oil a griddle or frying pan so the surface is well coated. Place it over high heat and when it is very hot, but not smoking, ladle on enough batter to make individual cakes about 5 inches wide. Cook until edges begin to brown and bubbles form on top of cake. Turn over and cook on other side until center of cake feels firm, not mushy, when lightly pressed with finger.

Place finished cakes on a rack over a pan in a warm oven as you make more. Make 8 cakes. When all are ready, serve each topped with a cup of ragout and a dollop of sour cream. Or, if you are serving fried apples too, pass the ragout, apples, and sour cream so guests may top as they wish.

ABOUT BUTTER BEANS

In recipes for cooking fresh or dried butter beans and crowder peas, you may notice that salt is never added until after the beans have reached the desired state of doneness. This was a common piece of kitchen wisdom in the South, where such beans were an almost daily staple, and although I have heard it questioned by some modern cooks, it's a precept to which I still firmly subscribe.

In my experience, beans cooked in salted water will reach an edible state, but never turn as creamy inside or have skins that are as tender as those to which the salt is added later. For "proof" that the no-salt rule is correct, I only have to recollect a note I got shortly after my first cookbook was published.

"Thank you for saving my marriage!" the woman wrote. "All these years my husband's been swearing I'll never make soup beans like his mother. When I took your advice about the salt, he swore she'd made the beans that night."

Winter Succotash   SERVES 8

My friend, a transplanted New Yorker, wanted to spread a table of Southern-style delectables for her visiting sister and family. The problems: it was winter and her sister ate no meat. Ellen was doing all right with classic side dishes such as cheese grits and sweet potatoes, but she couldn't find a recipe for a vegetarian dish substantial enough to serve as the main course.

No problem, I thought. Speckled butter beans and field peas make this casserole as satisfying as any meat stew, creating a meal that is distinctively Southern in flavor. Using black-eyed peas which are already cooked means that they disintegrate further during the baking to create a richer broth. But be warned: while unseasoned canned black-eyed peas are fine, don't try to substitute canned speckled butter beans for the frozen. Commercial canning turns this delicious vegetable into a sweet mush. If you can't get frozen speckled butter beans, simply use frozen green limas.

1 cup chopped white onion
1 tablespoon olive oil (see Note)
3 cloves garlic, minced
2 cups canned or cooked black-eyed peas
1½ cups frozen speckled butter beans
1 cup frozen shoepeg corn
¼ cup chopped oil-packed sun-dried tomatoes
2 cups boiling water
salt

Preheat the oven to 400°F.

In a dutch oven or other heavy ovenproof pot with a lid, sauté the onion in the oil until softened. Add the other ingredients, except for salt. Bake, uncovered, for 15 minutes. Lower the temperature to 350°, cover, and bake 30 minutes more, until the butter beans are very tender. Salt to taste. Serve over rice or grits, or with Mizithra Grits Casserole (page 116) or Roasted Garlic Grits (page 117) on the side.

Note: *For a flavorful alternative to olive oil, use a tablespoon of the oil in which the sun-dried tomatoes are packed.*

ROAD NOTES

TEXARKANA, TEXAS, APRIL 1995

I am over the edge of Arkansas, onto the eastern rim of Texas, in search of one of the last great Southern cafeterias. To most, the word "cafeteria" conjures visions of tinned peas and green beans cooked beyond recognition, then smothered in canned mushroom soup, or worse.

For Southerners of a certain age, though, the cafeterias of our hometowns were a veritable smorgasbord of locally grown vegetables cooked dozens of delectable ways. I am at the smack tail end of that certain age.

In my childhood, my family took its dinners out at one of the two Blue Boar cafeterias in downtown Louisville. This was the only place where I would eat spinach, spooned up there in a delicate handmade cream sauce. They fried okra in a light cornmeal batter, had green beans cooked just like my mama cooked them, and served small dishes piled with crisp cucumbers and onion slices in sweet vinegar. Their strawberry shortcake was something to be dreamed about all day before supper, still made with a warm, short biscuit cake, still topped with real whipped cream, still served only "in season."

(I worked in the Blue Boar at Fourth and Broadway the summer after my sophomore year of college, and learned how to carry two overloaded trays at a time—one balanced at head height, the other swaying lightly in front like a rudder—as I negotiated the three dining rooms, one up and one down long flights of stairs. It was that waitress job which gave me confidence for the many others that came after, but already then the food at the cafeteria was on a slow decline.)

But Bryce's Cafeteria in Texarkana, I've been told, has yet to lose its charm— or at least hadn't in 1984, when John Egerton wrote about it in *Southern Food*. I do not leave on a road trip heading south without first consulting his book, and I've not yet been led astray by his recommendations.

Even so, I have apprehensions as I approach Bryce's, more than a decade after reading about it. For one thing, after more than fifty years downtown, the restaurant has moved to a brand-new suburban building off I-30 on the edge of town. I've never known a change such as that to do a restaurant much good.

As soon as I pull into the parking lot, though, my hopes take an upturn. It's still a good fifteen minutes before opening, but already the lot is filling with cars. And no one opts to sit in the car, playing music and running the air conditioning, either. Instead, there's a pack of regulars crammed into the small but pleasant foyer to wait.

While we do, I read the clippings and the laudatory framed letters on the wall. One is from the president of Morrison's, another venerable cafeteria (actually a chain) of the South.

The folks around me pass pleasantries about the weather. "Is this what they call a blackberry winter?" a middle-aged man asks the older gentleman standing next to him, who nods, then grins. "Be a good early crop this year," he says.

Promptly at 11 a.m. the door to the inner sanctum is opened by a smiling young woman, and we begin to wend our way through the serpentine line. I spy big bowls of thick white onion slices and sweet pickles along with the other condiments at the end of the line, and smile.

I choose an interesting tomato aspic and slaw that looks hand-cut, then my heart skips in anticipation when I spy, on the steam table, field peas I've never seen before. "Purple-hull peas" they are called. They look like black-eyed peas, but with a deep lavender hue about them. They're fresh, the line server tells me, then laughs and says, "You never had 'em? Oh, you're gonna love 'em."

She is right. The taste is cleaner, less muddy, and not so brackish as a black-eyed pea. They are buttery and a little sweet, and I soak up every drop of pot likker in the little bowl with a cornstick. I would go back for more, but I also have okra cooked whole in the pod, just to the point of tenderness and with the lightest seasoning of bacon grease, and yellow squash casserole, which also tastes of bacon and onion and which is either the best or second-best squash casserole I have ever eaten in my life. I'm thinking about going back for another bowl, just to see, when I hear a fellow in a gimme cap holding a box-to-go say to the cash register clerk, "Boy it's terrible to have one of them noncooking wives. Beats all I ever seen."

Not so terrible in Texarkana, I think. Not terrible at all when you have Bryce's.

See Places to Go, page 341.

MAiL oRDeR

Sun-dried tomatoes became the ingredient du jour of trendy restaurants a few years ago and are generally thought to be a recently adopted Italian accent. But dried tomatoes were a part of the Southern larder as early as the mid-1800s, showing up in Sarah Rutledge's *Carolina Housewife* of 1847.

Nestled in the Shenandoah Valley of the Blue Ridge Mountains is one of the finest domestic producers of sun-ripened, dried tomatoes today, L'Esprit de Campagne. Owners Joy and Carey Lokey started their business in 1984, intending for it to be a small family operation supplying a few good restaurants and caterers in nearby Washington, D.C. Joy, a San Antonio native and a graduate of the Cordon Bleu in Paris, had worked as a caterer in D.C. for six years, but she and Carey were looking for work with a slower pace.

"We started out drying all the tomatoes in seven little drying units. One summer we took them to the beach with us and dried tomatoes there," she recalls.

But as L'Esprit's reputation grew, so did the company. Today the Lokeys contract with growers throughout the Shenandoah Valley, supplying the seed and overseeing the cultivation of the special Roma variety of tomato they use. Drying takes place in temperature- and velocity-controlled wind tunnels in a warehouse-sized building on the Lokey farm in Berryville, Virginia. Despite the increased size of the operation, the Lokeys still sell out of tomatoes every year.

What makes L'Esprit dried tomatoes so prized? Imported Italian tomatoes are generally salty, while many popular California brands have no salt. L'Esprit uses just a bit for contrast, resulting in a tomato that tastes sweet and very full-bodied. L'Esprit uses no sulphur in its preservation process, and while many other producers hot-pack their tomatoes in oil, L'Esprit doesn't.

"I'm passionate about the texture," Joy says. "I want them to have that bite, not mush out in your mouth."

But Joy adds that the real secret may be the Shenandoah Valley itself: "Heinz used to make its ketchup here because the Shenandoah was so famous for its tomatoes. I believe it's that good old dirt. The Blue Ridge Mountains are the oldest ones in the U.S., and there has to be something in that."

L'Esprit products are distributed nationally at fine food stores, or see Things to Order, page 338.

CROWDER PEAS

Fresh Crowder Peas

Hoppin' John

Limpin' Susan Edisto

Fearrington House Goat Cheese and
Black-Eyed Pea Salad

Pork and Purple-Hull Pea Stew

Bolitos with Sweet Potato Guacamole

Pecan-Crusted Trout with Black-Eyed Pea Relish

Lady Cream Pea Buttermilk Stew

In Carson McCullers's *The Member of the Wedding*, F. Jasmine instructs family and friends to wave a plate of Hoppin' John under her nose should she die, sure that the smell of ham-seasoned black-eyed peas and rice will stir any breath left in her to resurrection.

She is not alone in her devotion to the meaty, brassy flavor of these modest crowder, or field, peas. Wylie Poundstone, chef at the King Cotton Produce Company in Montgomery, says that the company's produce department does its briskest mail-order business when the black-eyed peas come in.

"Crowder peas" is the generic name given to a number of these small legumes, which are actually beans, not peas. The name refers to how closely the edible beans grow in the pod, and technically may be crowder, semicrowder, or noncrowder peas, although those distinctions are usually ignored by folks who are talking about supper and not horticulture.

Black-eyed peas are the most well-known crowders, and are, in some form or another (dried, canned, or frozen), available throughout the United States. They arrived in North America on the slave ships, brought as cheap and familiar food for the slaves, and they thrived in the long, hot summers of the South. As both black and white Southerners moved to other parts of the country, their beloved black-eyed peas followed, along with the tradition of serving them on New Year's Day for good luck.

Although black-eyed peas are the most universally known, they are not the only crowder peas grown and beloved in the South.

The purple-hull, pink-eyed pea of the Deep South is a relative of the black-eyed pea, but, as its name says, has a rosy eye and grows in a long, narrow purple pod. Cooked up fresh, it has a lighter, less earthy taste than the black-eyed pea, but when the two are dried, the black-eyed pea's more intense flavor is superior.

I was so smitten with the fresh purple-hull peas I had at Bryce's that I planted a small patch in my backyard. Even in the more northern climate and shorter growing season of Louisville, the bean thrived, and the dish I made from my small crop, just lightly braised and seasoned, was one of the best summer suppers I've ever had. (For information on ordering seeds, see page 340.)

Another crowder pea prized in the Deep South is the cream pea, lady pea, or lady cream pea—a small, all-white relative of the black-eyed pea. It pairs up perfectly with just a bit of ham or pork seasoning in a classic Southern-style bean soup, and its taste, more delicate than black-eyed peas or pinto beans, works wonderfully in vegetarian combos.

After hearing me wax poetic about dried lady cream peas, a friend, Mary Jane Boyd, brought back a mess of fresh cream peas from the Montgomery Curb Market after a visit to her family's hometown. Like the purple-hull peas, these were delicious quickly cooked and lightly seasoned. Don Nobles (Mary Jane's cousin) notes that these "teeny, tiny pale cousins of the black-eyed pea will pick up the flavor of anything they are cooked with, so just a

---

ROAD NOTES

EDISTO ISLAND, SOUTH CAROLINA, JUNE 1996

It has become fashionable for well-to-do foodies to book a house with a swell kitchen in Provence or Parma and spend a month or so of vacation foraging at local markets and cooking up a storm of regional dishes on site.

Frankly, Scarlett, if I had that kind of time (and a lot less money) I could think of no better place to head than just south of Rhett Butler's hometown of Charleston, to Edisto Island, South Carolina. Okay, so it doesn't have the cachet of a villa in the Dordogne, but it does have a gorgeous stretch of Atlantic Ocean beach where sea turtles come in to nest from May to October; a plethora of affordable vacation rentals, many with excellent kitchens; a spot where you can buy fresh-caught seafood just off the boat; and, best of all, just a few miles up S.C. 174, Pink and George's Produce Stand.

That stand is where I go every morning of a week-long vacation in June of 1996 to discover what we'll be having for dinner that night. Pink Brown and her father, George, lifelong residents of Edisto, live down a dirt road arched by Spanish-moss-draped live oaks. Theirs is a very small house surrounded by dense vegetation, including huge aloe vera plants which set me in a spin of covetous envy. Not far from the house and right off the road is the produce stand, a ramshackle-looking affair from the outside, filled with the best fruits and vegetables I've ever eaten.

Much of the produce is grown by Pink and George in a huge garden behind the house, and virtually all that fills the wooden bins in the small, dark building is locally grown and just-picked. Courtesy of Pink and George, we feast on sugar-dripping South Carolina watermelons, corn still tender from the stalk, a variety of not-always-perfect-looking but perfectly delicious tomatoes, and the finest tiny pods of okra.

When I wax ecstatic over a handful of purple-hull peas still in the pod one afternoon, Pink makes sure the next day that I have a bagful. The first, smaller batch becomes Limpin' Susan Edisto (page 26), while the second makes dinner all by itself, with a skillet of cornbread.

little onion is enough to put in the pan, or a bit of ham or bacon. What's more, they're very textural, even when cooked, and because of that, something I like to do with them fresh is just blanch them and then sprinkle them over fresh mixed greens and toss with a good vinaigrette for a wonderful salad."

There are probably about fifty different names for Southern variations on the basic black-eyed pea, horticulturist Joe Kemble says, such as the Mississippi Purple, with a purple pod and brown seed, the Mississippi Silver, with a silver pod and tan seed, and the Colossus, with a silver-green pod and brown seed. But generally, they are classified as black-eyed, purple-hull, or cream-type peas. And all of them, at least all the ones I've tried, are exquisite fresh, and deeply satisfying dried or frozen. Black-eyed peas and the brown-seeded purple-hull peas, which are sometimes labeled crowder or field peas, seem to hold up canned as well.

Fresh Crowder Peas SERVES 4

This recipe works for purple-hull or lady cream peas popped fresh from the pod, and there is no better way to cook them. Fresh black-eyed peas or fresh crowder peas that were picked some days before cooking may take longer to reach the desired tender stage. These are good with Perfect Fresh Corn Fritters (page 105), which can be made up in about the same time it takes to cook the peas.

1 cup water
2 cups fresh crowder peas
2 tablespoons butter
salt

In a small pan, bring the water to a boil and add the peas. Turn the heat low and simmer for 12 to 15 minutes, until the peas are tender and most of the water has evaporated. (If the water boils away before the peas are done, add small amounts of boiling water to the pan.)

Remove from the heat, add the butter, and cover for 4 minutes, shaking the pan occasionally to mix in the butter. Then salt to taste and serve immediately.

Hoppin' John SERVES 8 TO 10

Serve this dish on New Year's Day—or anytime you're hungry—with Real Cornbread (page 103).

2 cups dried black-eyed peas
6 to 8 cups water
1 smoked ham hock
2 cups long-grain rice
1 medium onion, chopped
1 tablespoon bacon grease or olive oil
salt
pepper
hot sauce or pepper vinegar

Rinse and sort the peas, then cover with water about two inches deeper than the peas, and soak overnight. When you are ready to cook, drain the peas and put them in a pot with 6 to 8 cups of water and the ham hock. Bring to a boil. Boil briskly for 5 minutes, then turn the heat down to maintain an easy boil. Cook, uncovered, for 1½ hours. There should be about 3 cups of liquid left in the pot. If not, add hot water until there is, then add the rice. Stir gently to mix, cover, and simmer over low heat for 20 minutes without lifting the lid.

Remove from the heat and allow the rice to steam, still covered, for 10 minutes. Meanwhile, sauté the onion in bacon grease (or oil) in a separate pan. When the onion is soft and the rice has finished steaming, remove the cover from the pot and with a fork stir in the onion and salt and pepper to taste, being careful not to smash the rice. Serve immediately with hot sauce or pepper vinegar on the side.

Note: *For a meatier and spicier version of the dish, fry up ½ pound of crumbled hot breakfast or Italian sausage with the onion. Leave out the bacon grease or oil.*

Limpin' Susan Edisto   SERVES 4

Though not nearly as well known as Hoppin' John, that dish's close cousin, Limpin' Susan, is referred to in some Southern cookbooks and is usually described as an okra pilau which may include crowder peas and may or may not be made with meat. Actual recipes are few and far between, however, which may be because the dish was made, as this version was, with whatever was freshest from the garden on any given day. On the day that I made it, the crowder peas were the purple-hull variety with brown seeds.

If you live in an area where you can't find fresh crowder peas, then frozen black-eyed peas, butter beans, or limas will work. The okra must also be very fresh, with no black spots or visible withering, and not longer than 3 inches. If the only fresh okra you can find is too old or too large, use frozen instead.

1 cup fresh crowder peas
½ cup chopped sweet white onion
1 tablespoon olive oil or butter
1 garlic clove, minced
1 cup ½-inch-thick okra slices
1 cup peeled and coarsely chopped ripe
    tomato
1 cup long-grain rice
2 cups cold water
¼ teaspoon kosher salt
vinegar-based pepper sauce
salt

In a small pot, cover the crowder peas with water and bring to a boil. Immediately turn the heat to low and simmer for 12 to 15 minutes, until the peas are tender. (If you are using frozen black-eyed peas, the cooking time will be longer.) Set aside.

In a large skillet, sauté the onion in olive oil or butter until softened. Add the garlic, okra, tomato, and crowder peas with any liquid in their pan. Cover and

Montgomery, Alabama's legendary Montgomery Curb Market set up shop with twelve producers in May of 1927, a joint effort of the Junior Chamber of Commerce and the Auburn University Extension Service. By the time the operation moved to its current site at 1004 Madison Avenue in 1943, there were more than 150 sellers. These days, some fifty vendors operate out of the market, and competition is stiff for empty booth space.

The market has served as a model for subsequent projects elsewhere. Since it is a cooperative, each booth owner has stock in the association but operates as an independent businessperson. The by-laws of the organization insist that sellers must produce or make anything they sell, making this a true farmers' market.

And what goodies they offer! The pale, diminutive, buttery lady peas are a marvel, the watermelons are luscious, and the strawberries have no peer. The market is a year-round operation, offering freshly harvested Christmas trees and handmade wreaths in the season, along with homemade cakes and cheese straws, which sell out in minutes.

For decades the market has been open every Tuesday, Thursday, and Saturday.

See Farm Markets, page 343.

simmer over very low heat while you prepare the rice.

In a small, heavy pan with a lid, bring the rice, water, and kosher salt to a boil. Cover the pan and turn the heat down to maintain a low simmer. Cook for 15 minutes. Remove from the heat and allow the rice to steam for 10 minutes without removing the lid.

When the rice is ready, season the vegetables to taste with pepper sauce and salt. Serve immediately over the rice.

Note: *A cup of small fresh shrimp, shelled and deveined, can be mixed into the Limpin' Susan in the last 10 minutes of simmering, for an even more elaborate dish.*

Fearrington House Goat Cheese and Black-Eyed Pea Salad   SERVES 6

The Fearrington House Restaurant outside of Chapel Hill, North Carolina, is a blend of the best of the Old and New South. The restaurant and bed-and-breakfast inn are housed in a structure built around the property's old farmhouse, originally put up

Pepper Patch

Southerners love flavor that bites back. We were putting fresh hot peppers from the garden on the table, or putting them up in vinegar brine, a couple of centuries before the current salsa craze took the American table by storm.

The great-granddaddy of the many hot sauces that now pepper the marketplace is McIlhenny's Tabasco (see Places to Go, page 341). The heat of the cayenne (fermented in a two-syllable "ma-ush," according to our guide at the plant on Avery Island in Louisiana several years ago) is potent even when only a couple of drops are added to the pot. The vinegar, which is the second of only three ingredients (the third is salt), adds a slight but distinctive "whang" to the act, and enhances the flavor of just about any dish it's added to. Tabasco is available virtually everywhere, in both the classic red version and a newer, green jalapeño variety, which may be a little hotter but, for my money, doesn't beat the red's perfect balance of tang and testosterone. Tabasco can be mail-ordered from the company. It's worth calling just to get the Tabasco Country Store catalog, which features cups, hot pads, and other kitchen goodies stamped with the Tabasco logo, plus a line of faux-fine-art Tabasco posters, including a Salvador Dali-esque bottle ribboning apart on an arid surrealist landscape.

Second on my hot-sauce hit parade is another Louisiana product, Cajun Power Original Recipe Garlic Sauce. We first met up at Dupuy's Oyster Shop in Abbeville, Louisiana (see Places to Go, page 341), where Cajun Power was plopped on the table along with ketchup, mayo, horseradish, and lemons for a make-your-own crawfish, shrimp, or oyster dipping sauce. Rich and ruddy, it added just the right complexity to everything it touched, even the french fries. I picked up a bottle of the stuff at the counter where we paid, and have been buying a couple of bottles on every trip to Louisiana since. I don't make gumbo or jambalaya without it, and a dollop can turn any stew or soup into an adventure. You can order the sauce in gift packs or by the caseload.

When we travel, my husband, Ken, and I look for new hot sauces to try. He (referred to by some as Dr. Tabasco) is drawn to the bottles that promise hellfire and brimstone. His current favorite, an ominous green potion called Bat's Brew (Melange de la Chauve-Souris), is made by the Panola Pepper Corporation in Lake Providence, Louisiana, which, the manufacturer swears, is just up the road a piece from Transylvania. This ghoulishly hot sauce is made with both jalapeño and habanero peppers and is so intense that I hardly ever add it to a dish while it's cooking but offer it on the side for hardy souls like Ken.

I am more often attracted by unusual ingredient combinations and, I blush to admit, interesting packaging. The former once led me to bring home from Texas a salsa made with green chile and white chocolate, which was every bit as horrible as it sounds. The latter is why I picked up Holy City Heat at a small gourmet store in Edisto, South Carolina. Made with a hybrid chile called the Charleston Hot, this sauce comes in a charmingly old-fashioned apothecary bottle, the sort Grandma kept her miracle cough medicine in. And although my experience has been teaching me that the more (or odder) the ingredients, the less interesting the sauce, this one's blend—which includes pineapple juice, sweet potatoes, and sesame oil—has a tropical air that seems to work perfectly with the pilaus and gumbos of the Low Country. I don't use it anywhere near as frequently as Tabasco or Cajun Power, but for certain dishes, like Limpin' Susan, it's just what the doctor ordered. Holy City Heat is distributed by Colony South Products.

See Things to Order, page 338, for information on all of these products.

in the early 1800s and rebuilt after a fire in 1926.

At the restaurant, regional products are prepared with techniques of a Continental bent. The result is a perfect fusion of flavor and style, like this delightful salad. Note that you have to slice the cheese 8 hours ahead.

fresh goat cheese in a log about 1½
    inches diameter and 6 inches long
¼ cup olive oil
½ teaspoon dried thyme
½ teaspoon dried tarragon
½ pound dried black-eyed peas
3 cups water
1 small smoked ham hock
1 bay leaf
2 cloves garlic, minced
½ teaspoon kosher salt
1 purple onion, in ¼-inch slices
1 sweet red pepper, in ¼-inch strips
¼ cup dry bread crumbs
leaf lettuce to garnish 6 plates
7 cups mixed salad greens
vinaigrette dressing

Use dental floss to cut the cheese into six 1-inch-thick rounds. Lay the rounds in a small shallow bowl or baking dish. Drizzle them with the oil and sprinkle on the thyme and tarragon. Cover well and chill for at least 8 hours.

Sort and rinse the black-eyed peas. Cook them in the water with the ham hock, bay leaf, and garlic until tender but not mushy, about 45 minutes. Add the salt. Remove the bay leaf and hock, reserving the hock, and drain the peas. Remove the meat from the hock; chop and mix it with the peas. Set aside.

Preheat the oven to 350°F.

While the peas are cooking, roast the onion and pepper pieces under the broiler or on a medium-hot grill, for 10 to 15 minutes, turning once, until browned. Set aside.

Place the bread crumbs in a bowl and dredge the cheese rounds, coating both sides. Place them on a nonstick baking sheet and bake at 350°F for 10 minutes.

While the cheese is baking, cover the six salad plates with the lettuce, then top with mixed greens. Divide the pea mixture, onion, and red pepper evenly among the plates. Drizzle with vinaigrette and top with goat cheese rounds. Serve immediately.

Note: *Goat cheese gives enough resonance to this dish that if you want to make it vegetarian by omitting the ham hock, you can. Just be sure to add a tablespoon of olive oil to the beans in its stead.*

SOUTHERN GOAT CHEESE

Though hardly prevalent, *goats have been a part of the Southern agricultural landscape from early on, particularly in the mountain South and its foothills. Used for meat, milk, and homemade cheeses, the goat was cost-efficient livestock in the narrow mountain ridges, where pastures were small to nonexistent and an animal who could forage among the hills was prized.*

The last two decades have seen a resurgence of goat dairies in the region and a new level of excellence in the artisan cheeses produced at them. For new Southern chefs, goat cheese often provides the tangy, buttery resonance characteristic of Southern foods without the drawbacks of the pork fat traditionally used to achieve it.

Celebrity Goat Dairy outside Siler City, North Carolina, produces more than a dozen varieties of goat cheese, and supplies many of the best restaurants in nearby Durham, Raleigh, and Chapel Hill. Owners Britt and Fleming Pfann produce their cheese with an emphasis on sustainable agricultural techniques.

Fleming, herself a native North Carolinian, is also a big proponent of the produce grown locally. "We get most of our vegetables and fruits right up the road at the Carrboro Farm Market. It's just like the old days; we trade cheese for just about everything we need. I don't think there's any finer produce anywhere than the stuff grown around here."

That produce and Celebrity goat cheeses are featured prominently in the breakfasts served daily at the dairy's seven-room bed and breakfast, opened in 1998. Folks staying at the Inn at Celebrity Dairy get a chance to meet some of the Celebrity goats and see a working dairy in operation.

See Places to Go, page 341.

Pork and Purple-Hull Pea Stew | SERVES 6

The purple-hull peas give this dish a buttery richness. You can also use black-eyed peas, but the overall flavor will be brassier.

This goes well with a hearty multi-grain bread, particularly one with sunflower seeds, and the Peach and Dried Cherry Chutney on page 278.

olive oil

1½ pounds stew pork, cut into 1-inch cubes

1 cup water

½ teaspoon kosher salt

fresh black pepper

2 teaspoons ground cumin

2 teaspoons ground coriander seed

½ cup chopped onion

4 cloves garlic, coarsely chopped

3 medium potatoes

2 cups frozen or canned purple-hull peas

¼ cup port

Preheat the oven to 350°F.

Pour enough olive oil into a Dutch oven (or other ovenproof heavy pan with a lid) to lightly coat the bottom. Over medium-high heat, cook the pork until it starts to turn from pink to white, and browns on the edges. Add the water, and scrape the bottom of the pan lightly to loosen any crust.

Add the salt and three or four grinds of pepper. Add the cumin, coriander, onion, and garlic. Turn the heat down, cover the pot, and simmer while you prepare the potatoes.

Peel the potatoes and dice them into ½-inch cubes. Add them to the pot, cover, and bake for 1 hour. Check after about 40 minutes to make sure the stew is not in danger of cooking dry. Add a little hot water if it is.

When the hour is up, mix in the peas and add the port. Bake another hour. Again, check after about 40 minutes. There should be enough liquid in the pan to keep the ingredients from burning and to hold them together in a sauce. Add a little hot water if it looks as if there is danger of the pot drying. Serve warm.

Bolitos with Sweet Potato Guacamole   SERVES 12 AS APPETIZER

Bean cakes are made throughout the South and were a staple long before hip restaurants started dishing up the black-bean variety. When my mother was a girl in Corbin, Kentucky, kids and workingmen often found a fried patty made of leftover pinto beans seasoned with onion in their lunch sacks.

In south Florida and other areas of the coastal South where a Caribbean influence holds sway, the bean cakes of choice are bolitos—tasty morsels of pureed black-eyed peas.

Bolitos always struck me as the perfect New Year's party appetizer: tasty, hearty, and bestowing a year of good luck on the eater. Guacamole seemed like the perfect condiment, but our annual New Year's bash includes a good friend, Mary Horvath, who is allergic to avocado. From such limits is great invention sprung, and this newfangled guacamole with a Southern drawl is just that. Not only does the sweet potato work as a tasty substitute for avocado but its bright orange color is a delight to the eye. Mary was so pleased with the result that when all the bolitos were eaten, she finished off a small bowl of sweet potato guacamole as dip for tortilla chips.

BOLITOS
1½ cups water
1 pound frozen black-eyed peas
2 cloves garlic, minced
1 teaspoon kosher salt
2 large eggs
½ cup finely ground cornmeal
peanut oil for frying

SWEET POTATO GUACAMOLE
1 large sweet potato
1 tomato, peeled and finely chopped
½ cup finely chopped sweet white onion
1 clove garlic, minced
¼ cup roasted, peeled, and finely
    chopped green chile
salt

Note: *Bolitos are at their very best when eaten hot. If you don't want to spend party time dishing them out to hungry fans straight from the skillet, fry them up ahead of time, drain, and set them out on cookie sheets. When the bolitos are room temperature, cover the cookie sheets snugly with plastic wrap, and refrigerate until party time. When you are ready to serve, reheat them in a 250°F oven for 5 to 8 minutes. Make the guacamole just before you reheat the bolitos, so it will be room temperature when served. Or make and refrigerate it ahead of time, but let it come to room temperature before serving.*

Preheat the oven to 450°F.

In a pot with a lid, bring the water to a boil. Add the black-eyed peas. Turn the heat down to a lively simmer, cover, and cook 30 minutes. Add the garlic and cook, uncovered, for 10 minutes more, until the peas are tender and almost all of the water has evaporated. Remove from the heat and cool to room temperature. Add the salt.

Using a food mill or the fine blade of a food processor, grind the cooked peas to a paste. Roll the paste into 1-inch balls, cover with plastic wrap, and refrigerate 1 hour. Makes 3 dozen.

While the bolitos are chilling, bake the sweet potato for guacamole. Pierce the skin of the potato a couple of times with a fork before placing it in the oven, to keep it from exploding. Bake about 40 minutes, until the flesh is very tender throughout.

When the potato is cool enough to handle, peel it and mash it in a large bowl. Add the tomato, onion, garlic, and chile, and mix well. Salt to taste. Set aside.

When you are ready to fry the bolitos, beat the eggs lightly in a shallow bowl. Spread the cornmeal in a second shallow bowl.

Press a bolito lightly between your palms to flatten it slightly into a disk. (Don't make it so flat that the edges crack.) Dip the bolito in egg to coat, then roll it lightly in cornmeal. Prepare 6 bolitos this way.

Heat about ⅛ inch of peanut oil in a skillet over medium-high heat until very hot but not smoking. (A piece of cornmeal flicked into the pan will skitter.) Place the breaded bolitos in the oil without crowding them. Fry until golden on the first side, flip, and fry until golden on the other. Remove to a rack to drain.

Fry in half-dozen batches, being careful

to clean the oil frequently. (See Note below.) Top each bolito with a dollop of guacamole and serve immediately.

Note: *Clean oil is a must for successful frying. Unfortunately, flecks of cornmeal inevitably end up in the hot oil and need to be removed, or they will blacken and ruin subsequent batches. The cornmeal is really too fine to be skimmed out, so the best solution is to change the oil completely every batch or two. I pour the hot oil into a large metal cup and let the skillet cool just enough so I can safely wipe any solids out with a paper towel, then add fresh oil. I don't throw away the used oil; instead, after it has cooled, I pour it through a coffee filter placed in a small wire strainer. The oil that drips through is clean enough to use another time.*

Pecan-Crusted Trout With Black-Eyed Pea Relish

SERVES 8

My husband thought he'd died and gone to heaven the night he came home to find we were testing this recipe. That seemed only fair, since I was in a heavenly state myself when I first ordered it at the Metropolitain, the terrific New South restaurant in Charlottesville, Virginia, owned by Tim Burgess and Vincent Durquenne (see Places to Go, page 341). I'd had pecan-crusted trout before and liked it, but the Metropolitain's technique of grinding the nuts into a flour created a crust far more delicate and appealing than the usual coating of chunky nut pieces.

Vincent says that cooking the peas just al dente is necessary. "They need to have a little pressure. And you know that little envelope the black-eyed pea has, the skin? If you lose that you simply have no texture." He also insists that using both apple cider and balsamic vinegars is necessary to get a full taste, and after tasting the two blended, I believe he is right.

The trout gets a quick coloring in a skillet but is finished in a very hot oven. Vincent says, "The way we like to work in the restaurant is hot and rest, hot and rest. This seems to keep everything fresh and bring out the flavors." It also makes this a spectacular dish which is not too demanding to prepare for a dinner party. You can divide the recipe by two or four for smaller dinners, although I'd recommend you make the full amount of black-eyed pea relish. It's delicious the next day, warmed up slightly and served with greens or on Grits Cakes (page 113).

RELISH
3 cups fresh or frozen black-eyed peas
2 cups water
4 medium green onions, finely chopped
½ cup chopped red bell pepper (the size of peas)
1 cup chopped green bell pepper (the size of peas)
¼ cup minced red onion
½ teaspoon balsamic vinegar
½ teaspoon apple cider vinegar
1 teaspoon olive oil
1 teaspoon Dijon mustard
salt

TROUT

2 cups pecan pieces

1 cup flour

8 fresh trout, cleaned, boned, and
butterflied

salt

pepper

peanut oil for frying

Preheat the oven to 450°F. Lightly oil enough baking sheets to accommodate the butterflied trout.

To prepare the relish, place the black-eyed peas and water in a saucepan and bring to a boil. Lower the heat and simmer, covered, for 20 to 50 minutes, until the peas are tender inside but still have intact skins.

While the peas are cooking, put the chopped green onions, peppers, and red onion in a large bowl. In a small bowl, whisk together the vinegars, oil, mustard, and salt to taste.

When the peas are cooked, drain, and toss them with the other vegetables. Pour the dressing over them, and toss. Taste and add salt if desired. Set aside, covered, to keep warm while you prepare the trout.

Blend the pecans and flour in a blender on high until the nuts are the consistency of the flour. Place the mixture in a wide, shallow bowl or plate. Salt and pepper both the meat and skin sides of each trout liberally, and dredge them in the pecan flour to coat.

Pour ⅛ inch of peanut oil in a skillet large enough to accommodate a butter-flied trout laid flat. Heat on high until a fleck of pecan flour flicked into the oil dances and turns golden almost immediately. Do not heat the oil to smoking.

Place one trout in the skillet, meat side down, and fry until the edges start to turn golden and the crust begins to color, less than a minute. Gently turn the fish over and repeat on the other side. Transfer the fish to a baking sheet, meat side down.

Fry all of the trout. You will need to replenish the oil every trout or two; make sure it reheats sufficiently before adding the fish. If the skillet gets crumby, wipe it very, very carefully with several crumpled paper towels between trout.

When all the trout have been fried, place the baking sheets in the oven and bake for 5 minutes. Serve the trout as soon as you take them out of the oven, with a large spoonful of relish on the side.

Lady Cream Pea Buttermilk Stew

SERVES 6

The creamy taste and buttery texture of the lady cream pea is the perfect counterpoint to the tang of buttermilk. If you can't get dried lady cream peas, substitute the smallest white navy beans you can find. (Note that cooking may take longer and you may need more water for navy beans. Follow package guidelines.) This dish is perfect with cornbread.

1 pound dried lady cream peas
water
2 tablespoons butter
salt
⅛ teaspoon chopped fresh tarragon
1 cup buttermilk
2 green onions, finely chopped

Rinse and sort the peas, then place them in a heavy pot. Cover with cold water to 1 inch above the peas. Bring to a boil over high heat, add the butter, cover, and reduce the heat to maintain a very slow boil. Cook until the peas are tender, about 1 hour. Remove from the heat and add salt to taste and the tarragon. Stir well, cover, and let steep for at least 15 minutes. Stir in the buttermilk and heat gently until just warmed through. Garnish with chopped green onion and serve immediately.

MAIL ORDER

We had been neighbors only a few months when my new friend Larry Parks took a trip to New Orleans. Even so, he knew enough about me that he was able to find a gift to surprise and delight me: a cellophane-wrapped bag of Camellia-brand dried lady cream peas.

Tiny and milky white, the peas promised an adventure, and he could hardly wait for me to cook them so we could both find out what we'd been missing. It was a taste so buttery and smooth we couldn't imagine how we'd lived so long without it. I tried a couple of different recipes before deciding on the buttermilk-tinged soup on page 34 as the best. When another friend brought fresh cream peas back from the Montgomery Curb Market, we plunged into indulgence again.

I bought several bags of Camellia-brand cream peas on my last trip to the Crescent City, and had decided it would be a treat available only when I, or a friend, traveled. But then I discovered that Gazin's Specialty Foods, which specializes in mail-order food items, will ship Camellia lady cream peas, but only if you order by the caseload.

Now, you may not think that you can eat a whole passel of peas—twenty-four 1-pound bags, to be exact—and you may be right, but I don't think I'll have a problem at all. If you don't want all the bags yourself, they make a super-swell present.

See Things to Order, page 338.

SOUP BEANS, RED BEANS, AND THE HUMBLE PEANUT

Soup Beans

Sheila's Meatless Soup Beans

Winter Navy Bean Soup

Red Beans and Rice

Bean Pie

Boiled Peanuts

Clinch Mountain Peanut Soup

Pickled Peanut Butter Sandwich

Buttermilk Peanut Butter Fudge

Toasted and Spiced Peanuts

Dried beans were a necessity in the pioneer South, but long after established farms and cultivation tempered the need to live on beans through the winter, Southerners held to their satisfying meaty flavor.

You can almost tell what part of the South someone is from by what sort of beans he or she prefers. If you favor soupy pinto beans served up with golden wedges of cornbread, that probably means you come from the mountain South, while folks from the coastal regions are apt to choose highly seasoned red or black beans cooked up with rice. Somewhere in the middle are folks who like both, and are partial to white navy beans and dried butter beans as well. Although the methods of preparation for dried beans are time-consuming, even the busiest two-career families in the South still make time, especially in the damp chill of winter, when nothing says "home" like the steam from a pot of seasoned beans.

Peanuts were home food of another sort. Originating in South America, the peanut traveled to Spain with early explorers returning home and went from there to Africa, becoming a staple in many countries. Africans forced here in slavery brought peanuts with them; the legume served first as a primary food for slaves and as fodder for animals.

In time, though, the peanut's buttery flavor and high nutritional value caused it to show up in many forms in Southern pantries. Eventually, its charm spread across the country. Peanuts can be said to be a universally beloved American, even world, food today, but it's still only in the South, where they are grown, that Americans eat them like a vegetable, fresh picked, salted, and boiled.

Soup Beans	SERVES 8 TO 12

A bowl of soup beans, a wedge of hot cornbread, a slice of fresh onion laid to the side: this is the most fundamental meal of the mountain South, and though it sounds simple, it's hard to beat for satisfaction.

Although soups using other varieties of beans, particularly white or navy, are made throughout the South, it's pinto beans you are talking about when you say "soup beans." And while ham hocks or other meat may be used to season other soups, for this dish you truly need salt pork, also called white bacon, which has a cleaner, sweeter taste, just perfect with the beans.

Traditionally, pintos were soaked overnight before cooking, but the method described here requires a little less advance planning. It still takes a couple of hours for the beans to reach that perfect stage of creaminess, though, so I usually cook my soup beans on the first cold Sunday of the fall. I double this recipe, then pack the extra soup into plastic containers and freeze it, to be taken out and reheated (or turned into refried beans or burrito fillings) as the winter wears on. Cooked dried beans freeze beautifully and can become an instant but substantial supper.

1 pound dried pinto beans
water
½ pound salt pork
salt
1 clove garlic, minced (optional)
1 medium sweet white onion or 12 green
    onions

Rinse the beans and pick through them, discarding any stones or dirt. Place the beans in a large, heavy soup pot and cover with water about 2 inches above the beans. On high heat, bring to a boil and boil, uncovered, for 10 minutes. Turn off the heat and let the beans soak for 1 hour.

Add more water to the pot, if necessary, to bring the level about an inch above the beans. Add the salt pork and stir it down into the middle of the beans. Bring to a boil, cover, and turn the heat to medium-low. Simmer for about 2 hours, or until the beans are soft and creamy inside. (Taste a bean to see.)

Remove the salt pork and set it aside. Remove about ½ cup of beans and mash them to a thick paste. Return them to the pot and stir. Add salt, starting with 1 teaspoon and increasing to your taste. If you like garlic, add it here.

Allow the beans to simmer over very low heat for another 20 minutes, to let the salt seep in. If you like, remove the fat from the salt pork, finely chop the meat, and return it to the pot.

Serve piping hot with Real Cornbread (page 103) and white onion slices or a green onion on the side.

Greens with Pot Likker (page 84) make a mountain feast.

Sheila's Meatless Soup Beans

SERVES 8 TO 12

Sheila Joyce Strunk grew up outside Berea, Kentucky, in a community known as Big Hill. (The natives pronounce it as one word with a definite emphasis on the "big.") Soup beans were standard fare at her family's homeplace, and when Sheila moved to Louisville, she brought along a bean pot and the traditional way of cooking them.

When she and her husband, Ken Pyle, got into the restaurant/club business, first with the Roundtable and later the Storefront Congregation (two spots which featured bluegrass along with beans in the 1970s) and now with the Rudyard Kipling (see Places to Go, page 341), a theater/nightclub/restaurant in Old Louisville, their New Age customers clamored for a meatless version of this country classic. Sheila obliged.

"I find that the trick is using good olive oil or another healthy vegetable oil in the beans to get that full, rich taste," she says. "The seasonings you add after that are up to you. I like to put in some thyme and marjoram, and, of course, garlic gives it a richness."

Sheila's concoction has fooled even the most hide-bound pork fans into believing this soup is made with meat.

1 pound dried pinto beans
water
2 tablespoons olive oil
¼ cup finely chopped onion
½ tablespoon minced garlic
1 teaspoon crushed dried marjoram
1 teaspoon crushed dried thyme
salt

Rinse the beans and pick through them, discarding any stones. Place the beans in a large, heavy soup pot and cover with water about 2 inches above the beans. On high heat, bring to a boil and boil, uncovered, for 10 minutes. Turn off the heat and let the beans soak for 1 hour.

Add more water to the pot, if necessary, to bring the level about an inch above the beans. Add the olive oil. Bring to a boil, cover, and turn the heat to medium-low. Simmer for 1 hour. Add the onion. Continue to simmer for about 1 hour, or until the beans are soft and creamy inside. (Taste a bean to see.)

Remove about ½ cup of beans and mash them to a thick paste. Return them to the pot and stir to incorporate. Add the garlic, marjoram, and thyme. Add salt, starting with 1 teaspoon and increasing to your taste.

Allow the beans to simmer over very low heat for another 20 minutes to let the salt seep in. Serve piping hot with Real Cornbread (page 103) and white onion slices or a green onion on the side.

Winter Navy Bean Soup
SERVES 10 TO 14

While the mountain method of cooking pintos is plain, soups made with the smaller white navy bean are often spiked with vegetables, particularly in the winter, when turnips and carrots or sweet potatoes are added to the pot.

Navy beans also lend themselves well to cooking with smoked ham or a ham hock. The tasso in this recipe adds a little extra bite with its pepper seasoning.

1 pound small navy beans
2½ cups peeled and diced sweet potato
1½ cups peeled and diced turnip
½ cup coarsely chopped onion
½ cup coarsely chopped celery
1 cup diced tasso (see Note on page 42)
salt

Rinse the beans and pick through them, discarding any stones. Place the beans in a large, heavy soup pot and cover with water about 2 inches above the beans. On high heat, bring to a boil and boil, uncovered, for 10 minutes. Turn off the heat and let the beans soak for 1 hour.

Add water to the pot to bring the level to about 3 inches above the beans. Bring to a boil, then add the sweet potato, turnip, onion, and celery. When the mixture begins to boil again, add the tasso. Turn the heat to medium-low, cover, and simmer for 1 to 1½ hours, until the beans are tender. Add salt to taste, beginning with ½ tablespoon. Serve piping hot.

Note: *Tasso is Cajun-style ham, smoked and highly seasoned with cayenne and other peppers. Comeaux's Cajun Corner is one source for it (see page 338 for ordering information). If you can't get tasso, use country or city ham in its place and add a generous dollop of Tabasco or cayenne to the pot with the salt.*

Red Beans and Rice

SERVES 4 TO 6

Over the last decade, I must have had more than a dozen plates of red beans and rice in New Orleans, no two of them the same. Some come with the beans, cooked separately, piled on top of the rice, others with everything cooked together. Some are seasoned with andouille, some with tasso, chorizo, or plain ham. I've also had tasty meatless versions of the dish. Most have been cooked long and hard, the various flavors mingled in a flavorful mush—a throwback to the turn-of-the-century tradition of serving red beans and rice on Mondays, wash day, when the pot could cook all day on the back of the stove with little attention from an otherwise busy cook. Almost all have followed the American trend toward ever-increasing hotness in any pepper-enhanced dish.

For this version, I wanted something lighter, with more subtle distinctions between the elements in both flavor and texture. As my husband, Ken, said, "Red beans usually hit you like a fist. This is more like a friendly slap."

2 cups unseasoned red beans, cooked to tender stage

3 cups liquid (the water the beans cooked in plus plain water, flat beer, or hard cider)

olive oil

½ cup diced onion

½ cup diced green bell pepper

½ cup diced celery

½ cup diced tasso or country ham (see Note)

1 teaspoon minced garlic

½ teaspoon kosher salt

1 cup long-grain white rice

1 teaspoon cider vinegar

Separate the beans from their cooking liquid, reserving both. Add enough other liquid to make three cups.

Coat the bottom of a large saucepan or skillet with olive oil, and heat. Add the onion, green pepper, and celery, and sauté until the vegetables begin to soften. Add the beans and liquid, tasso, garlic, and salt, and bring to a boil. Add the rice, stirring lightly to incorporate it. Turn the heat to the lowest setting and simmer for 20 minutes, covered, until the rice is tender. Stir in the vinegar and serve immediately with cornbread or a crusty white bread. Pass hot sauce on the side.

Note: *If you use country ham instead of tasso (see Note to Winter Navy Bean Soup, above), add cayenne and black pepper, or one of the Louisiana hot sauces recommended on pages 28–29 just before adding the rice. Start with a teaspoon and taste, adding more if you wish.*

LAFAYETTE, LOUISIANA, APRIL 1987

It is 4:30 a.m. and I am in Cajun country, where you are supposed to be looking at the wee hours of the morning after having danced all night to get to them. Not me, though. I've spent the night in fitful sleep, worried I might miss the hotel clock's alarm and be late for this adventure.

I have promised the folks at *Esquire* a piece on making boudin, the signature rice and pork-liver sausage of the region. So tied up is boudin with the local mystique of *les bon ton roulez* that zydeco musicians in the area call the string of bars and nightclubs where they play, from south central Louisiana through eastern Texas, the Boudin Circuit. On the circuit, you buy the sausage while the band is on break, split the steamy links open into a soft bun, and douse liberally with whatever cayenne pepper sauce is sitting on the bar. Downed greedily with icy beer, boudin is bar food divine.

But you don't really have to go to bars to find the best boudin. Several months earlier, on another trip, I discovered some of the region's finest at a little neighborhood grocery/deli in Lafayette called Comeaux's Cajun Corner. When I complimented his wares, owner Ronnie Comeaux (with typical Cajun generosity) said, "You like my boudin? Anytime you want to learn how to make it, you come on back and I'll show you."

Ronnie was just as welcoming when I called him several months later. "Come on down on a Wednesday," he said. "We make the boudin every Wednesday for sure, in the morning."

It wasn't until I was settled in my hotel room on Tuesday afternoon that I found out "morning" meant 4:30 a.m.

Ronnie was actually being gracious. He has been up since three cooking big pots of pork shoulder and pork liver, with plenty of pepper and savories, to make the base for the boudin. When I arrive, he and his wife, Dianne, cheerfully hand me a mug of chicory-rich, fuel-injected coffee and point me in the direction of the stainless-steel sausage-stuffing table, where yards of silvery-white gleaming pig intestines are wound, waiting for the fun to begin.

In truth, it really is fun as we grind the meat with more spices and mix it in vats with perfectly cooked white rice. Then the Comeauxs load the mix in a hopper-like contraption with a narrow neck at the end, and hook on the casing. Boudin stuffing shoots out lightning fast, puffing up the flaccid casing like a giant long balloon blown up at warp speed. It is exhilarating and hilarious.

Since that visit, Comeaux's has been my mail-order source for Cajun meats put up the old-fashioned way. For the andouille and tasso required in these recipes, you simply can't do better.

A few years ago, I met a delightfully prickly restaurateur on the Gaspe Peninsula of Quebec, who wasn't sure she wanted to feed me until we discovered we'd both been to Comeaux's. When I told Ronnie that story, he laughed and said, "Well, next time go to France. I've got a bunch of people over there who order my stuff, and they'll be glad to see you, too."

See Things to Order, page 338, and Places to Go, page 341.

Bean Pie   SERVES 8

The Southern sweet tooth is legendary, and elaborate desserts such as Lane or Red Velvet Cake are often trotted out as proof of how devoted we are to our sugar sops. But even more convincing are the ingredients Southerners have traditionally used in a pinch to make "a little something sweet," particularly pie. Vinegar, jelly, sweet potatoes, green tomatoes, and crumbled Ritz crackers have all ended up in pie pans and on Southern tables, to good effect. And then there is bean pie.

We're talking about unseasoned, cooked red beans or pinto beans here, and the very mention of the ingredient is enough to give most diners pause. But those who hesitate have likely never been at the New Orleans Jazz and Heritage Festival (see page 231) in the late morning or early afternoon, when Omar the Pie Man's truck arrives with its daily delivery of bean pies.

Omar's stand, sitting by itself in the middle of the fairgrounds, does a steady business all day long, vending mini-pies of the more usual varieties: lemon, apple, pecan. But folks will queue up in long lines at the first sign of bean pies.

Earthy as sweet potato, more mysterious than pumpkin, and actually lighter in texture than either one, these spiced bean pastries deliver a punch that is both heavenly sweet and texturally primal. They usually sell out in minutes.

This chess-like version is at its peak within 30 minutes of coming out of the oven. Serve it warm, topped with whipped cream, a small scoop of good vanilla ice cream, or Lemon Buttermilk Sorbet (page 258). You can refrigerate any leftover pie and reheat it the next day, but the texture changes dramatically and to little benefit. Serious bean-pie fans will still like it, but it will not win new converts.

dough for single-crust 9-inch pie

2 cups unseasoned red or pinto beans, cooked until very tender, drained

3 large eggs, room temperature

1 cup brown sugar

½ cup buttermilk

1 teaspoon vanilla extract

½ teaspoon cinnamon

½ teaspoon freshly ground nutmeg

½ teaspoon kosher salt

Preheat the oven to 350°F.

Roll the pie dough into a 10-inch circle, and place it in a 9-inch pan. Fold the overhang underneath the edge, and crimp to make a high, firm rim. Set aside.

Using the fine blade of a food processor or grinder, grind the beans into a paste. Using an electric mixer at medium speed, beat the beans, adding the eggs one at a time. Cream in the brown sugar, then add the buttermilk and vanilla. Add the spices and salt, and beat until well mixed.

Pour the filling into the crust, no higher than the lower edge of the crimped rim. (The filling will rise while baking.) Place the pie on a cookie sheet, and bake on the bottom rack of the oven for 50 minutes, until the custard is firm when jiggled and the top is browned. (If the crust rim begins to brown too quickly, tent aluminum foil over it to protect it.)

Cool the pie on a rack for about 20 minutes. Cut and serve while still warm.

Boiled Peanuts

In the Southern states where peanuts are grown—Georgia, Alabama, Virginia, Florida, and South Carolina—boiled peanuts have long been a nutritious and delicious side dish or snack. But, like the rest of America, I was hardly aware of this delicacy until Jimmy Carter became president. My first boiled peanuts were from a souvenir tin can and were, truthfully, slimy and peculiar. They made me wonder what all the fuss was about.

Fortunately, some years later, on a trip back from the Florida beaches, our family stopped for gas in rural Georgia. As I paid, I noticed a steamy crock pot at the checkout stand. A hand-lettered cardboard sign said BOILED PEANUTS. I decided to try once again.

Unlike their canned cousins, these warm peanuts were delightfully fresh and tender. I popped the nuts from the slightly salty shells as Ken drove, and I could barely keep up. The quart plastic bag that had seemed so large when the checkout guy filled it now seemed but a tease, and we came home to Kentucky with whetted appetites.

Unfortunately, it's hard to satisfy such appetites without going to peanut-growing country. Boiled peanuts are made from green peanuts, freshly dug. (The peanut is a peculiar legume; it flowers above ground but then bends over, so the seeds—the peanuts—grow underground.) Freshly dug peanuts do not transport well. Fortunately, if you go to peanut country in season, roughly July through September, you can find boiled peanuts for sale at roadside stands all over. And at farm markets, you may be able to buy several pounds of raw green peanuts for boiling your own.

6 pounds fresh green peanuts, in the shell
4 tablespoons kosher salt in 4 quarts water

Rinse the peanuts and cook them in the salted water, uncovered, at a lively simmer, for 1½ to 2 hours. (They are done when the shells are tender and the nuts have the firm but creamy consistency of a well-cooked pinto bean.)

Taste. If salty enough, drain and eat immediately, or refrigerate and eat chilled later. If you want your peanuts saltier, leave them in the warm salty water until the desired flavor is reached.

Note: *To eat your peanuts Southern-style, gather everyone around a big bowl of peanuts; pop the shells open with a thumbnail; down the peanuts while guzzling beer, ginger ale, or iced tea; and tell great stories. It's a good idea to cover the table with newspaper, or have plenty of small bowls on hand for the discarded shells. If you want to make a feast of it, serve other finger foods, like deviled eggs and fried chicken. Make sure you have plenty of napkins or paper towels.*

MAIL ORDER

Fresh green peanuts are so perishable that no one will ship them. In fact, they really ought to be boiled in sight of the field from which they've been picked.

But you can get really good boiled peanuts, made from raw peanuts which have been picked and processed immediately (usually in the truck they're going to travel in) to lower the moisture content. These are the kind of peanuts that the Lee Brothers of Charleston, South Carolina, use.

The peanuts come in 5-pound gunny sacks for eating right away or freezing. You can also order special waxed presentation tubs with a Lee Brothers designer label for only $2.50 more, and can get boiled peanuts T-shirts or bumper stickers, if you're feeling downright fanatic. Do-it-yourselfers can order a Boil-Your-Own peanuts kit.

Providing boiled peanuts to the world at large would be quite enough contribution for a couple of guys to make, but Matthew and Ted Lee are not content to stop there. They've taken on the task of ferreting out exceptional Southern products, especially those produced by family farmers or outstanding small companies. Their catalog, hand lettered and sewn up on a sewing machine, grows gradually but gracefully with the addition of a few new products in each biannual edition, and now includes watermelon-rind pickles, Tupelo-gum biscuit bowls, and Wink grapefruit soda.

See Things to Order, page 338.

For the perfect nonalcoholic beverage to quaff with your boiled peanuts, see the note on Blenheim's ginger ale (page 256).

Clinch Mountain Peanut Soup

SERVES 4

Some years ago, a friend invited us to a formal dinner party just so I could meet an elderly friend of hers who was from Virginia and fascinated with Southern cooking.

The gentleman and I settled in cozily on a settee, while hors d'oeuvres made their rounds. After a few quick pleasantries, he leaned toward me on his cane, raised both eyebrows appreciatively, and said, "So you are one of *The Lundys* of Virginia."

I could hear both capital letters and italics clearly in his tone, and I knew we had a case of mistaken pedigree. "Oh no," I said hastily. "My family's not from *that* Virginia."

"And where might they be from?" he asked.

"The western part of the state," I said. "Rose Hill. In the Clinch Mountains."

"Oh my, then you're right. You're not from *that* Virginia at all!"

This peanut soup is also not from *that* Virginia. The classic Virginia peanut soup comes from the proper eastern side, where natives can trace their lineage back across the ocean and through several centuries. Saturated with butter, cream, and smooth peanut butter, the soup served at the King's Arms Tavern in Colonial Williamsburg, for example, is simply too rich for me.

Over in the far western corner of the state, where Daddy's family first hailed from, folks usually don't trace their lineage farther than the next holler, and the cooking is a little plainer. I decided that's how I wanted my version of peanut soup to be. This vegetarian soup, made with freshly ground peanut butter, is a hearty broth of unusual but delicious flavor, perfect for crisp winter evenings.

1 medium onion
2 tablespoons butter
6 to 8 fresh mushrooms
water
½ teaspoon tamari
½ cup hard cider
½ cup freshly ground unsalted peanut
  butter
1 cup nonfat milk
Tabasco
salt

Peel the onion and slice it into four rounds, each about ¼ inch thick. In a cast-iron or other heavy skillet, melt 1 tablespoon of the butter over medium heat. Lay the onion slices in the butter, then flip them over gently to coat both sides. (Be careful not to break the onion rings apart.) Cook over medium heat until the onion is browned and caramelized on one side. Gently turn the slices over and brown the second side. The whole process should take about 30 minutes—20 minutes for the first side and 10 for the second.

FARM MARKETS AND FESTIVALS

BUTTER BEANS TO BLACKBERRIES

George Washington Carver, the Tuskegee Institute botanist who developed more than 300 products from peanuts, encouraged Southern farmers to plant peanuts instead of cotton, particularly since peanuts replace nitrogen in the soil instead of depleting it.

His advice seemed prescient in the 1920s and 1930s, when the dreaded boll weevil made lint out of the cotton fields. Peanuts soon become the primary cash crop of the South, and continue to play a prominent agricultural role today.

Because of this, several peanut festivals take place annually throughout the South. Two worth catching are:

THE GEORGIA PEANUT FESTIVAL, the fourth weekend in October, at Possum Poke in Poulan, Georgia, outside of Sylvester. Once upon a time (in 1987, to be exact) the festival boasted the World's Largest Peanut Butter and Jelly Sandwich, at 12½ square feet. There have been bigger sandwiches built elsewhere since, but in few other places do people celebrate the peanut with the devotion of these Georgians. You can eat peanuts roasted, toasted, and boiled, as well as in pies and candy, including pink divinity. There's also plenty of other good home-style Southern cooking, including black-eyed peas and cornbread. The festival has a parade, clogging, and crafts.

THE PORK, PEANUT, AND PINE FESTIVAL, July, at Chippokes Plantation in Surry, Virginia. The name rolls off the tongue so nicely that the festival ought to have a bluegrass song written about it. The foods served here will tantalize tongues in a different way. Pork chops, sausages, country ham, pork rinds, and barbecue celebrate the first product. Peanut brittle, peanut soup, and a pie made with peanuts and raisins are among the dishes presented by local restaurants and civic organizations. Fortunately, no one tries to cook up the other main cash crop of the region, pine lumber, but you can see ample evidence of it in the craft show and lumberjack demonstrations. Chippokes, established in 1660, is now a demonstration farm. At the Farm and Forestry Museum there, you can see the implements used in each of these industries, including antique peanut shellers.

See Places to Go, page 341.

While the onion is cooking, wipe the mushrooms clean with a damp paper towel, then mince the tops and stems. Melt 1 tablespoon of butter in a large saucepan over medium heat. Add the mushrooms, turn the heat just a bit higher, and sauté for 4 minutes, stirring or shaking the mushrooms in the pan, until they are golden.

Add 1 cup of water to the mushrooms. Add the tamari. When the water begins to bubble, remove from the heat, cover, and let the mushrooms steep while the onions finish caramelizing.

Remove the onion slices to a cutting board. Add ¼ cup of water to the skillet and scrape the bottom gently with a spatula to deglaze. Add this water to the mushrooms.

When the onions are cool enough to handle (it only takes a minute or two), chop them into ¼-inch pieces. Add them to the mushroom pot. Add the cider, and place over medium heat. When the mixture begins to steam, whisk in the peanut butter. When it begins to steam again, add the milk. Heat until it steams again, and add three drops of Tabasco and salt to taste, beginning with about ¼ teaspoon. (If you should use salted peanut butter instead of unsalted, you may not need the additional salt.)

Serve warm and pass Tabasco on the side.

Pickled Peanut Butter Sandwich

Strange peanut butter sandwich combinations could probably fill a book. The fact is that peanut butter straddles the line, able to be the perfect accompaniment for sweet or salty. So we get the classic peanut butter and jelly, or that old hippie variation, peanut butter with bananas and honey on whole wheat bread (sprinkle alfalfa sprouts on top for a surprisingly good contrast), as well as Elvis's favorite feast, peanut butter, mayo, and bacon.

My family's signature sandwich owes a nod to the King's but is much less likely to produce an instant heart attack: peanut butter, mayo, and dill pickle slices on rye bread. Of course, like any good recipe, the proper ingredients and proportions are key.

Begin with a thin, firm, light rye bread, with caraway seeds or without. Next up, a not-too-sweet peanut butter—natural-style or freshly ground is excellent. If you must use a processed spread, go for chunky.

Spread the peanut butter thinly on one slice of bread. On the other, spread mayonnaise—not salad dressing—preferably Hellmann's or Best Foods.

Then lay very thin, very crisp slices of dill pickles on the peanut butter side, one slice thick. When I was young, a local pickle company made excellent hamburger dills. Many today are too flabby. Choose the crispest you can find and slice them superthin.

Bring the two slices of bread together, and savor slowly with a glass of Southern Iced Tea with Lemon (page 264) or an ice-cold Coke in the small bottle.

Buttermilk Peanut Butter Fudge   MAKES ABOUT 1½ POUNDS

My mother's homemade peanut butter fudge was part of every Christmas when I was growing up, and showed up frequently as a last-minute sweet treat, since most of the ingredients were on hand. Southerners

49

tend to be just silly over this candy, which is the very definition of satisfying indulgence.

In my first cookbook, I included a recipe from country singer Dwight Yoakam's family, one his aunt made, which is so rich it's guaranteed to cleave your tongue to the roof of your mouth. That recipe used half a cup of butter and half a cup of half and half, in addition to the peanut butter. While I make no claims for this version's health-food qualities, it is considerably less laden with butterfat. It holds up well for flavor, too, with the buttermilk giving it just a bit of bite.

2 cups sugar
1 cup buttermilk
pinch of salt
½ teaspoon vanilla
½ cup creamy natural peanut butter

Butter a large plate and set it aside.

In a heavy saucepan, bring the sugar, buttermilk, and salt to a boil over medium-high heat. Cook to the soft ball stage, removing from the heat immediately when the candy thermometer reaches 234°F.

Add the vanilla and peanut butter, and stir with a wooden spoon to blend. Then beat energetically with the spoon until the fudge begins to lose its gloss and starts to thicken. Pour quickly onto the plate. Allow to cool to room temperature before cutting.

Note: *If my mother is here when I make homemade peanut butter fudge, she reminds me: "Now, whatever pieces are left after we eat our fill today, put them in a clean coffee can and cover it tight with the plastic lid. Do that and the fudge will get all good and creamy overnight." She's probably right, but we never have any pieces left over to find out.*

Toasted and Spiced Peanuts
MAKES ABOUT 1½ CUPS

Although boiled peanuts are a treat you can experience only while in the region, fresh toasted peanuts, one of the most beloved between-meal snacks of the Deep South, can be easily made anywhere you can find raw peanuts. Use the red-skinned Spanish variety, the fresher the better. And don't be misled into thinking that the oversalted, overroasted peanuts you buy in the can bear any resemblance to this dish. Both the taste and the texture of these peanuts are much more delicate.

½ teaspoon kosher salt
¹⁄₁₆ teaspoon ground cayenne or red chile pepper
1 teaspoon brown sugar
1 tablespoon peanut oil
1½ cups fresh Spanish peanuts, shelled, skin on
1½ tablespoons water

In a cup or small bowl, mix together the salt, cayenne, and brown sugar. Set aside.

In a 9- or 10-inch cast-iron or other heavy skillet, heat the peanut oil over medium-high heat. Add the peanuts, and toast for 8 to 10 minutes, shaking the skillet or gently stirring the peanuts with a metal spatula to keep them from burning.

When the peanuts are golden brown, remove the skillet from the heat and sprinkle on the salt mixture, stirring quickly to distribute it evenly. Drizzle the water over the peanuts. (Don't dump all of the water in at once, and do be careful of sizzling splashes.) Stir or shake very gently until the water is absorbed and the seasonings "set" on the peanuts. Turn the peanuts out into a bowl and serve warm (the best), or let cool and store in a covered container.

Note: *The small amount of seasoning in this recipe merely accentuates the buttery flavor of the fresh peanuts. You may prefer to increase the seasonings, and should feel free to experiment with other favorite spices in the mix.*

GREEN BEANS

Classic Southern-Style Green Beans

Warm Green Bean and Tommy-Toe Salad

Mixed Beans with Coddled Egg Sauce

Deviled Green Beans

Zydeco Beans

Shuck Beans

would not want to discount the heart-red slices of tomato, crunchy disks of cucumber, or ears of corn exuding butter steam; but the very soul and hub of the classic midsummer's Southern supper is a pot of long-simmered, bacon-glistening fresh-picked green beans.

As I've worked on this section, it has occurred to me that there is never anything quick about a genuinely delicious mess of beans. Every step, from the growing to the prep to the cooking, is slow and deliberate—full to the maximum with anticipation of the glories to come.

The pole, or runner, beans preferred in the South generally take a week or more longer to grow than the less-regarded bush beans; and the pods are left on the vine until they reach a maturity that swells them with meaty seeds.

Pole beans must be staked, so Southern gardeners fashioned clever tepees or trellises from sticks and twine.

Harvested beans must be "strung" and snapped by hand—a sweet and leisurely process—then put in a pot to simmer low and long, filling the house, and whetting our appetites, with a fragrance of meaty promise.

Of course, this is not the only way in which Southern cooks prepared fresh green beans. The crop was too plentiful and the possibilities too endless for that. But for most of us, it remains the plu-perfect way we cook our beans.

"One fall day when my father was a boy, the wind turned bitter and cold several weeks early. When the sun set behind the mountains, the air bristled with frost. Granny hadn't picked the green beans hanging on the vines in her garden. The beans she canned each fall were the only green vegetables the family had to eat until the following spring. That year the early frost caught her unprepared, and she simply ran out of time. The sky was clear and purple above the black mountains when the family came in from the fields. Paw-paw brought in an armload of wood and started a fire in the stove. Granny paced around and around the living room. She could not accept losing her beans. She told Paw-paw she had to talk to God. She walked out of the house and down the pasture toward the woods in the twilight. She came home several hours later, stiff and shivering with cold, and announced that God said he would give her one more day.

The next morning Dad watched his breath steam in front of his face as he dressed in his room. Outside, the frozen world sparkled in the new sun, and the grass crunched under his feet as he walked with Granny up the path to the garden. Everything in the garden was dead, had been burned by the frost, except Granny's beans. The bean rows grew vivid, green lines across the white field. Granny picked every bean in the garden that morning and canned them *that afternoon. That night another frost set-tled onto the ridgetop and killed the stripped vines. 'Now let me tell you some-thing,' my father says, 'I saw that.' "*

—Tony Early, "A Worn Path,"
The Oxford American

Classic Southern-Style Green Beans

SERVES 8

I have heard all the arguments and I am tired of them. I know there is an army of nutritionists and nouvelle chefs lined up to swear that if you cook a green bean more than 20, 12, 6, or 2 minutes, you will have robbed it of all its flavor and nutritional value.

Well, until they come by my house some late June, pick up a pot of white half-runners that have simmered for a couple of hours on the back of my stove with white bacon, cart it down to the lab, and run it through every test known to man to determine its content of both vit-amins and minerals, I refuse to believe that old-fashioned, Southern-style green beans aren't as good for you as they taste.

And as for taste, I have yet to put in my mouth a crisp and crunchy, neon-chartreuse, barely blanched green bean prepared by anyone, no matter how famous, and seasoned with anything, no matter how trendy, that can hold a candle to the flavor of green beans cooked the way my mother, and her mother, and her mother before her made them.

To be sure, there are several other recipes in this section which require cook-ing green beans considerably less than the two to three hours called for in this recipe, and they are quite tasty. But I'll wager just about anything that slow-cooked is the only way we'll be asking for them in heaven, with a pan of cornbread, a platter of freshly sliced garden-warm tomatoes, and a chilled bowl of cucumbers and onions on the side.

Shop for green beans at your local farmers' market or a grocery which carries local produce, and look for a variety that has strings. Kentucky Wonder is the best available generally, but if you can get white half-runners where you are, they are sublime. You will need 2 pounds for this recipe, but if you can find more and have the time, you can string and snap any extra, blanch them, and freeze them to cook in the fall.

2 pounds Kentucky Wonder, McCaslan,
    or white half-runner green beans
water
¼ pound salt pork
salt

String the beans (see page 57) and snap them into pieces about 1 inch long. Dis-card any pieces with blemishes or beans that are wilted or withered (but if it's only the green pod which is damaged, save the bean seed inside to cook).

Rinse in very cold water (stirring the beans with your hand to make sure they are rinsed thoroughly) and drain. Put the beans in a large, heavy pot with a lid, and just cover with water. Add the salt pork, using your hand to "bury" it about halfway down in the beans. Bring to a boil over high heat, cover, turn down the heat, and simmer for 1 hour.

After the hour, add salt if needed. (Some salt pork is so briny that you won't need to, but usually some additional salt is required.) Half-cover and simmer for another hour or so, until the beans are very tender and saturated with the seasoning, and the water has boiled down to a bit of rich pot likker. These beans are even better warmed up the second day. (You can also freeze cooked green beans, but the texture will not be as nice when you warm them up later.)

"I can string me some beans," Dwight Yoakam said.

We were standing in the parking lot of a Red Roof Motor Inn outside of Columbus, Ohio, where Dwight had grown up. He had returned the night before, a warm spring evening in 1986, to play to a packed and passionate hometown crowd. I was there as the pop music writer for the Louisville Courier-Journal, working on a story about this eastern-Kentucky-born boy about to be the latest new country sensation.

Though we'd discussed music in some detail, much of that first interview, and others which would follow, was spent talking about our similar backgrounds, growing up

in a very modern, urban culture but still connected, through family and rituals, to a rural Southern past.

Seven years my junior, and therefore technically even more removed by time and distance, Yoakam, like me, had nevertheless grown up with one foot still firmly planted in a life that, for most of our peers, seemed to belong to a time long gone. Much to the surprise (and sometimes disbelief) of our city friends, we'd both made meals of fried squirrel, savored comb honey, and been taken by older relatives on the ritual trip to "smoke the bees." Yoakam had even, at the age of eleven, participated in the butchering of a hog at his grandfather's place in Betsy Layne, Kentucky.

"Those experiences gave me a verbal palette to work with that has hues other people don't have," Yoakam said.

Of those experiences, few were as simple as, and none more compelling and purely Southern than, the summer-long ritual of stringing and snapping beans.

Mountain gardeners have always grown green beans among the corn stalks. The nitrogen of the beans nourishes the ground the corn depletes, while the stalks provide a natural pole for the half-runner beans. White half-runners and greasy beans were the favored varieties because of their pods filled with meaty seeds, all the better for long-simmering with white bacon on the back of the stove.

But along with the flavorful seeds came the bother of the strings. Unlike the stringless (and, to my palate, less flavorful) varieties grown commercially now, these old-timey beans had sturdy strips of fiber running down each side. If you didn't remove them before cooking, you'd end up with a mouthful of something resembling tangled thread.

So the summer ritual of stringing beans was born. When I was growing up, it was always a communal rite, with at least two of my great-aunts, my mother, and cousins sitting on the front porch together to string bushels of beans for canning, as well as cooking and eating right away. For me now, it is usually a solitary task, yielding only enough beans to make a pot for dinner that night. My husband finds the task too annoying—he never seems to get the whole string in one swipe and swears I am too picky about the size of the broken beans. Despite her natural aptitude for both stringing and snapping, my daughter finds the job too tedious for her youthful spirits.

For the women in my family, though, I think the job of stringing beans was actually a respite. They worked hard through those un-air-conditioned hot summer days, especially my great-aunts, who were up at dawn and out back in the big garden behind the house. They tended it and a cranky flock of hens, harvested berries and apples from the bushes and trees that grew around the house, washed clothes in a hand-wringer machine on the back porch, hung them to dry in the yard, and ironed in the so-called "cool" of the evening. They cooked and sewed and cleaned without rest, so to do a job that allowed you—no, required you—to sit still, and in the process to talk and sip iced tea, must have seemed almost a pleasure. At least, that's how it always felt to me.

Learning to snap and string beans was

an initiation of sorts for a child. My great-aunts were like grandmothers to me and, like grandmothers, indulged me to no end. But they were strict when it came to learning how to string beans. Aunt Rae and Aunt Johnnie were big women who wore thin cotton housedresses through the summer. They would sit on the curvy metal swing or chairs painted white, pull the big skirts of their dresses down halfway to the porch floor, then spread their knees wide and dump a big mess of fresh-picked beans into the hammocks their skirts formed. Snap, swoosh, snap, swoosh, pop, pop, pop, pop—with one hand they would toss the ready beans into a big pot set between them, and with the other toss the strings and ends into a newspaper set off to the other side.

I had a tiny rocking chair of my own and got to put it at the knee of one of the aunts, who would fill the skirt of my little sundress with a handful of beans, then watch my stringing-snapping with one eye, while never breaking the rhythm of her own. It takes a measure of practice and a deft but delicate hand to break the tiny, curved and pointed end of the bean just enough, but not break it clean away. You then pull this gently down the length of the bean to cleanly remove the string. Then snap the blunt stem end and pull down the other side the same way. Novices invariably snap too hard, breaking the end completely, or pull awkwardly, leaving part of the string behind. In that case, the first length of bean must then be snapped off delicately to reveal little ends of string, which must be grasped by the fingernails *and tugged gently until the string comes off completely.*

I was shown how to do it, gently and patiently, countless times, and no one ever chastised me for the still-stringy beans I nevertheless produced. But I also didn't get to put them into the big pot. Instead, I had a little pot of my own, and my beans were inspected one by one before being added to the others. Any beans with strings or ends still attached were handed back to me to make right, and bean sections that were broken more than an inch long were rejected with a sigh. I learned quickly how to do them right.

Not to would have placed me outside the charmed circle of that front-porch community. I would not have overheard the bits of gossip or been able to rock in rhythm to the soft lyrical cadences of their mountain voices; I would not have been sustained by the sweet cold swallows of tea, the tinkle of ice in the glasses like a whisper of bells in the background.

I feel connected even now when I sit on my swing in a city far removed from the hills. My daughter, who will string for only just a little while, nevertheless stays longer to keep me company. Sometimes we talk. More often, we just sit and listen to the steady creak of the swing, the counterpoint of ice and glass, and the snap, swoosh, snap, swoosh, pop, pop, pop, pop—plop! of the beans.

Warm Green Bean and Tommy-Toe Salad   SERVES 4

A big pot of green beans was the centerpiece of the traditional midsummer Southern meal that also included cracking-fresh corn boiled on the ear or "fried" in butter in a skillet, cucumbers, slaw, cornbread, and garden-fresh tomatoes. When we had this meal at my great aunts' house in Corbin, the tomatoes alone were a feast for both tongue and eye. Their garden produced a half-dozen varieties. A china plate with flowers around the edge would be layered with slices that ranged from purple-crimson to pimiento-red, from orange-gold to a pale, almost cream-colored yellow. Each had a distinct flavor and all were delicious, but none could tempt me away from my own special bowl of "tommy-toes."

"Tommy-toes" is what my Aunt Johnnie called the tiny crimson cherry and yellow pear-shaped tomatoes she grew by the screened porch door. I thought she grew them only for me, and she indulged me in that idea. I wasn't allowed to so much as touch the full-sized tomatoes she'd bring in and arrange on the porch ledge each afternoon, their perfect domed bottoms turned up to help them finish ripening, but she would always bring in a handful of tommy-toes as well, arranging them among the other tomatoes and letting me know I could stuff as many of those in my mouth as I wanted. I also got a little bowl of tommy-toes with every supper, and could have another for a snack anytime I wanted. It's a wonder my own toes didn't turn tomato-red in the summer weeks I spent with my aunts. I did, however, develop a great affection for the delicious little fruit, especially when its ultra-tomato tang is paired with green beans and onions. This warm salad does that exceptionally nicely.

2 tablespoons olive oil
1 garlic clove
2 cups green bean pieces, strung,
   in 1-inch lengths
water
½ small sweet white onion
1 teaspoon kosher salt
12 cherry tomatoes, halved

Place the olive oil in a cup. Split the garlic clove in half and add it to the olive oil. Set aside.

Put the green beans in a saucepan and add just enough water to cover. Bring to a boil, then turn the heat down and simmer until the beans are just tender, 12 to 20 minutes, depending on the variety and freshness of the beans.

While the beans are cooking, cut the onion half into pieces about ½ inch wide, and separate the layers. (This should make about ½ cup.)

When the beans are tender, drain them, but leave them in the warm pan. Add the onion. Discard the garlic and add the olive oil to the beans. Add the salt and toss gently to coat evenly. Cover and set aside for 5 minutes.

Add the tomato halves, toss gently to mix, and serve immediately with warm French bread and butter.

When my mother decided to move from the family's seven-room house with both attic and basement to a four-room condo with neither, we girded our loins and plunged into preparations for the Yard Sale of a Lifetime.

I was fastidious in my sorting in the basement (which contained one suitcase with a receipt for every single bill my father had paid in his adult life, and another with love letters to my mother, written when she was still single and eighteen by four different fellas, none of them my father). I was also thoughtful about the contents of the attic and bedrooms. But by the time I got around to the first floor, with its many bookshelves and a credenza crammed with odd books, recipes, old cards, and what have you, time was running short and my patience (or curiosity) had about run out.

That's the only way I know to explain just how it was that one of Cissy Gregg's tattered and splattered rotogravure cookbooks ended up in the "Any Book for a Quarter" box. Fortunately for me, my fairy godmother arrived at 7:30 a.m. on the day of the sale, wearing a scarf tied under her chin and cat's-eye glasses. She spotted the Cissy Gregg immediately, pulled it out of the box, snorted with shock, and marched right up to me.

"Do you cook?" she barked.

"Sure," I said.

"Well then why in heaven's name would you let this go?" She shoved the magazine into my hands and pointed square at my nose. "You take this back in the house and don't you sell it for any price. And you'd better thank your lucky stars it was me that found it and not one of these antique dealers."

I do thank my lucky stars every time I flip through the faded newsprint of my treasure—copies of which I occasionally see in antique or old-book stores priced at $25. Cissy Gregg was the food editor of the Louisville Courier-Journal from the late 1940s to the early 1960s, and a more beloved one there's not been since. She published two magazine compilations of recipes, one in 1954 and the other in 1956. Her recipes reveal Southern roots, but are refashioned with a postwar sensibility toward simplicity. Her food invariably tastes good, but the recipes are prized as much for the simple, conversational way she wrote about the food and the process as for any culinary surprises they may reveal.

"Reading Cissy was like standing beside her at the stove," a later Courier food editor wrote. Here are the instructions Cissy gave in 1945 for her Deviled Green Beans recipe, which inspired mine (see page 66):

"Wash and break up the beans and cook in plain salted water until just tender. Taste to find out, and turn off the heat when you think they should cook 'just a little longer'—because they will in the seasonings and no one likes mushy beans. Cream the drippings with the other seasonings. Heat and pour over the beans.

"Now, they were the directions and you can take them or listen to what I did. I mixed the seasonings with the drippings and melted them in my saucepan, if one could call it that in the wildest of imaginations. Then I dumped in the beans which I confess I had cooked in the cool of 'Oh what a beautiful morning' of a day that could be so horrid in the afternoon. Then with two forks, I gently mixed the beans with the seasonings. If you like flavor add a little more of each named seasoning. The original amounts probably would be all right for four cups, but I, same as you, used what amount of beans I had. Allow the beans to simmer long enough to let each ingredient do all that is in its power to do for the good of the beans."

Mixed Beans with Coddled Egg Sauce   SERVES 4

I first tasted beans and eggs together when I moved to New Mexico in the early 1970s. In the mountainous region around Santa Fe, pinto beans were as common as they'd been in the mountain communities of Appalachia, although in New Mexico the beans invariably came seasoned with the region's distinctive chile. Beans were served in bowls of "red" or "green," denoting which kind of pepper they were paired with. They formed the basis of burritos and were mashed, seasoned, and served on every combination plate as "refritos."

They also were served as an essential ingredient in the *huevos rancheros* of the region. I've since discovered that elsewhere—in Arizona, Texas, and California, for instance—authentic *huevos* are generally fried eggs served on a tortilla, topped with salsa and, sometimes, cheese or meat. In Santa Fe, however, the best *huevos* came with a layer of pinto beans between the tortilla and egg. When the egg's runny yolk mingled with the buttery meatiness of the beans, it melded two flavors and textures that are sublimely matched.

So perfect was this culinary marriage that I wondered why I'd never had beans served this way in the South. Probably because I hadn't yet gotten around enough, I would guess. I have since discovered that fresh beans dressed with a soft-boiled egg were a common enough dish in Southern country kitchens, so common that few people ever bothered to set down a recipe for it. Bill Neal's *Southern Cooking* is one of the few sources where such a recipe, Mixed Beans in Egg Sauce, can be found. Bill encouraged cooks to use whatever combination of beans they preferred and noted that the key to this dish is cooking the egg just long enough to set the white, but not so long that it becomes scrambled when added to the beans.

To do this, Bill cooked the beans, then soft-boiled an egg, adding it just as he served. The result is a rich taste with a velvety texture. I found the ritual of boiling the egg, peeling it or scooping it out of the shell, and mixing it in, all just before serving, a bit harrowing for a company supper. So I came up with my own variation, in which the eggs are coddled in the beans in individual serving dishes—a solution as delightful to the eye as to the palate.

Any combination of beans will work in this dish, but I find it especially appealing when the first beans cooked are creamy butter beans and the second are crisp green beans. Because I blanch and freeze fresh green beans in season, and can easily find both baby lima butter beans and speckled butter beans frozen at the grocery, I serve this dish in the fall and winter as well as in the summer, when beans are in season. It's lovely served with buttered toast or warm yeast rolls.

2 cups fresh or frozen butter beans
1½ cups water
2 cups fresh or frozen green bean pieces, strings removed, in 1-inch lengths
2½ tablespoons butter
¼ cup minced onion
salt
4 eggs, room temperature
buttered toast
freshly ground black pepper

In a heavy saucepan, bring the butter beans and water to a boil. Reduce the heat to medium, cover, and cook at a brisk simmer for 20 to 30 minutes, until the beans are tender. Add the green beans and 2 tablespoons of butter. Add more water if the pot looks in danger of boiling dry. Cover, and cook at a low simmer for 10 minutes more. Meanwhile, preheat the oven to 350°F.

When the green beans have cooked for 10 minutes, add the onion and salt to taste. Cook at a low simmer for another 10 minutes.

Meanwhile, warm 4 ovenproof 2-cup-capacity bowls (see Note) by filling them with hot water. Melt the remaining ½ tablespoon of butter.

Check the beans. The butter beans should be intact but very creamy inside; the green beans should be very tender, and there should be about ½ cup of butter sauce left in the pan. If the beans need to cook a little longer, let them, but don't let the pan boil dry.

When the beans are ready, empty the warmed bowls and dry them. Ladle the beans equally into the bowls, then use a large spoon to make a ½-inch-deep well in the center of the beans. Break an egg into each well. Drizzle melted butter over the eggs and place the bowls immediately in the oven. Bake 7 to 10 minutes, until the egg whites are translucent and just barely set.

This is the time to begin making the toast. Butter the slices and keep them warm on a covered plate until ready to serve.

Check the eggs at 7 minutes and, if they're not ready, check again each minute after. Do not overbake them. They will continue to cook in the serving bowls as you bring them to the table, so take them out of the oven when they appear to be just barely set.

Sprinkle pepper over the eggs and serve immediately with the warm toast.

Note: *If you don't have individual oven-proof bowls, you can make this in a 2-quart casserole dish, although the presentation is not as appealing. Simply put the beans in the casserole dish and make an indentation in each of the four quarters. Break an egg into each, and bake according to instructions. Serve immediately.*

JACK'S MAGIC BEANS

The Western North Carolina *Farmers' Market perches on the side of a big hill just west of downtown Asheville. It's a huge operation, with some fifteen metal buildings scattered around the property to house the produce coming in.*

Two of these vast barn-like structures are heated and enclosed, providing a retail outlet for purveyors who sell not only local produce in season but also jams, cider, honey, and home-canned regional delicacies like chowchow and pickled beans. The market is open year-round (all day in peak season; from 8 a.m. until 5 p.m. November to April) and is usually bustling with shoppers, both local folks and travelers who see the signs along the interstate and take advantage of the market's proximity to I-240.

From July through September, there are certain days when the crowd at the market swells to such proportions that long lines form outside the retail barns, sometimes right down the hill into the parking lots. These lines are filled with people waiting patiently to buy a fresh mess of greasy beans.

"They call them that because the skin on them's got a greasy look to it; it's almost slick looking," says Dedrick Cody, the assistant manager at the market and himself a lifelong fan of greasy beans. "They've just got a better flavor, is why," he says in mellow mountain cadences. "More of a bean taste to them."

Dedrick says this variety of green bean, similar to a half-runner, is grown only in the mountains of North Carolina, east Tennessee, and eastern Kentucky. Maybe a little in the westernmost part of Virginia, too, in that nub of state which really ought to belong to Kentucky. And though some people refer to them as "creasy" beans, most locals prefer the descriptive "greasy," with a sharp, not slurred, sibilant. They also go by the name cut-shorts, although most folks will call them creasy cut-shorts or greasy cut-shorts.

"We get local people who know when they're coming in and will line up to buy them, and then we get people who come through Asheville that time of year just because they know they'll be in," Dedrick says. In some years buyers pay up to $45 a bushel, and when the beans are scarce, you'd do best to be at the market at 6 a.m. and prowl around the truckers' sheds as farmers arrive so you can buy your beans on the spot.

My mother grew up eating greasy beans and swears they are delicious. For years now I have stopped at the Asheville market in search of fresh greasy beans, but I've never been there at the right time. In the late spring of 1996, though, I did find a woman selling seed for greasy beans, and bought a plastic pint container full.

"Them's big greasy beans," she told me, "and they've got a different taste than little greasy, but I can't tell you what it is. You want to plant them with Hickory King corn. Now you let that corn come up and hoe once, then you plant the beans, three or four seeds to a stalk, and it'll grow right up the corn stalk, and you won't have to stake them."

I brought the seed home, intending to move the hostas the previous owner had left along our sun-drenched fence in back of the house, and plant the old variety of corn and beans in their place. Instead, I started a new job, and the bean seed and my good intentions gathered dust on a shelf.

Late that summer, though, I got a letter from a woman living near Dayton, Ohio, who'd grown up in Tennessee and had heard from a friend that my first book had a recipe for shuck beans. She wrote to order a book, and in her letter mentioned that she still grew beans from seed her family had in Tennessee, a variety called "creasy" beans.

When I sent her the book, I wrote a note asking her to tell me what she knew about those beans. She did, and along with her letter sent me a small plastic box containing a dozen seeds wrapped in cotton. "These bean seeds are brown striped and grow about three inches. They are supposed to be the true beans. My mother-in-law said they are true and come from back in Tennessee, but now are almost all gone. I hope you enjoy the beans when you plant them. I think you can get you enough from them for your next seeds."

The package was like a fairy-tale gift, akin to Jack's magical beans. And even though I'd planted nothing else that year, I did take half of those seeds out to the fallow raised herb bed, cleared out the weeds that had sprung up there, and nestled them into the rich soil. The Tennessee woman was right. I got just enough beans for seeds to plant the next year.

That next summer, though, was no freer than the previous one, and the only edible thing that thrived in my back yard was the stand of wild poke. My kitchen was full of good produce, however, courtesy of the neighborhood farmers' market, which has been growing by leaps and bounds over the last three years. It was at the market one July Saturday morning that I overheard a conversation about greasy beans.

"There's a farmer up in Berea has got them now and sells them for $3 a pound, and he sells out every one before the morning's hardly over," I heard Mrs. Casey, a Shelbyville grower, tell one of my neighbors.

"Well, I'm heading up to Pike County soon as I get done here," the neighbor said, "and if they aren't sold out already, I aim to get as many as we can haul back."

"If you can bring me some for seed, I'll plant them for next year," Mrs. Casey said.

It took about ten minutes for me to get home, snag the greasy bean seeds, and get back. I took the pint of North Carolina seeds, too, and Mrs. Casey looked them over with a shrug. "These don't seem to be much different than the white half-runners I plant for you every year," she said. But the little plastic box with two dozen brown seeds, now that really caught her attention. She touched them with the tip of her finger and appraised them like jewels. "I'll see if I can get us enough seed for a mess of these next year," she said.

In September she eagerly called me over to her stand to let me know that "enough of them came up to make a small crop for next year."

It's February now, and the region's biggest snow in recorded history still sits on the ground outside. My office is filled with sunlight and promise as I sit here and dream of this summer's coming pot of greasy beans.

Meanwhile, that man up in Berea Mrs. Casey had heard about is Bill Best, a farmer who grows small crops of old-fashioned beans, which he sells at the market. You can't order beans from him, but his son, Michael, is an agricultural business professor at Berea College. Michael and other department members are growing and marketing heirloom bean seeds. To get on a list of prospective buyers, contact Berea's Agricultural Department. See Things to Order, page 338.

"She had been watching the sky for days now, looking for a sign. A change in the weather had come. There was a chill in the wind and it carried moisture with it. The sky was as gray as the feathers of a Mockingbird. There had been forecast of cold weather and the possibility of a first snow. But I knew by her searching that she had chosen to follow signs that had been passed down to her by her heritage, a heritage that came from her beloved Kentucky hill country. A heritage akin to birthright.

"And then one evening, when the wind

had settled silent as a sunset and flakes of snow fell as soft as bird-down, she said to me:

"'I'll put us a mess of Leatherbritches in the kettle to soak tonight. I'll need a piece of smoked side bacon to season and enough cracklings for cornbread. Soft cracklings, mind you, shed of skin.'

"To Mom and most of the hill people of the Big Sandy Country, the first mess of Leatherbritches was a yearly ritual that took place with the coming together of two ingredients: The right green bean and the coming of the first snow."

—Billy C. Clark, *Savory Memories* (University Press of Kentucky, 1998)

Deviled Green Beans   SERVES 4

As Cissy Gregg, former food editor of the Louisville *Courier-Journal*, noted, this recipe is perfect for those summer days with cooler mornings for precooking the beans. You can quickly rewarm them in the sauce later, in the evening. It also makes frozen green beans presentable.

The bacon grease is traditional. The olive oil is healthier. And either is delicious. Eugene's Savory Seeded Corn Pone (page 106) is perfect with this dish.

4 cups green bean pieces, strung,
    in 1-inch lengths
2 cups water
2 tablespoons bacon grease or olive oil
½ cup minced red onion
2 teaspoons Dijon-style mustard
2 teaspoons soy sauce
2 teaspoons brown sugar
salt

Rinse the beans and put them in a pot with the water. Bring to a boil, then lower the heat and simmer, covered, until the beans are just tender, about 15 minutes. (The beans will cook longer in the sauce.) Drain, reserving 3 tablespoons of the cooking liquid. (If the liquid left is less than 3 tablespoons, add water.)

About 15 minutes before serving, melt the bacon grease or warm the olive oil in a wide saucepan with a lid. Add the onion and cook over medium heat until just softened.

While the onion cooks, whisk the water from the beans with the mustard, soy sauce, and brown sugar. Add to the onion and stir. Add the beans and toss to coat. Cover and simmer on low for 10 to 12 minutes, tossing occasionally to make sure all the beans get the benefit of the sauce. Serve immediately.

Zydeco Beans   SERVES 4 AS A SIDE DISH

Zydeco, the percussive, soulful variation of traditional Cajun music played in southwestern Louisiana, supposedly owes its name to an old song about hard times. Its chorus laments, *"Les haricots sont pas salés,"* the beans have no salt. The word "zydeco" is presumed to be a phonetic rendering of *les haricots* and is even occasionally spelled "xariko." These beans are as spicy as the music which gives them their name, and you can salt them to your heart's content.

olive oil
⅓ cup chopped white onion
⅓ cup chopped celery
⅓ cup chopped green bell pepper
2 cups peeled and chopped fresh tomatoes, with juice
2 cups green bean pieces, strung, in 1-inch lengths
1 small clove garlic, minced
½ cup water
¾ cup chopped tasso (see Note, page 42)
salt

Coat the bottom of a saucepan with olive oil, and sauté the onion, celery, and pepper. When the vegetables begin to soften, add the tomatoes, green beans, garlic, and water. When the mixture begins to bubble, add the tasso, cover, and turn the heat to medium. Cook at a lively simmer for 30 minutes, until the beans are tender and well seasoned. Add salt to taste and serve immediately.

Note: *If you want to make this the centerpiece of a meal, serve over long-grain white rice.*

FARM MARKETS AND FESTIVALS

The Western North Carolina Farmers' Market in Asheville has its own exit, number 47, off I-240. If you go, go hungry, because right next to the market is one of the best home-cooking restaurants still operating in the South. Three meals a day are served at The Moose Café, featuring lots of traditional vegetable dishes, cobblers, and pies made from the freshest produce available at the market next door.

Hours at the café are 7 a.m. to 8:30 p.m. (8 p.m. on Sundays), but go early in the dinner or supper hours for the best pick of specialties. Since everything is fresh, popular items like corn on the cob or greasy beans often run out before the customers do. Everything is served with a skillet of cornbread and/or oven-hot biscuits. Jars of sorghum and local honey are passed on the side.

Among the prized items at the market itself is sourwood honey, which gets its pale white color and delicate flavor from the sourwood trees that grow in the region. Sheldon Bateman, who has been "robbing" his own bees for "Oh, Lordy, I don't know, a right good while . . ." and who sells the honey at the market, says, "It's just a different kind of honey, I reckon. I can't exactly tell you what's so special about it, but if you was to taste from a jar of sourwood honey and then another kind, you'd know it for sure."

The honey comes to the market along about August, and sells for $10 to $12 for a quart jar. Black Mountain, a community known for its arts and crafts, about seventeen miles east of Asheville, celebrates with a Sourwood Honey Festival in mid-August every year.

For information on both the café and the festival, see Places to Go, page 341.

MAiL ORDeR

Mark Bassett is a horticulturist working at the University of Florida in Gainesville. I've called him because a colleague of his has suggested that he may be able to give me the definitive word on Southern green beans.

But instead of resolving the conflict of variety advocates I've encountered, all touting the wonders of their specific favorite—white half-runners, pink half-runners, mountain half-runners, greasy or creasy beans, Kentucky Wonders, Romanos—Bassett simply confirms what I've already found: "There are constituencies for individual varieties all over the South."

And then he asks, "Do you know the McCaslan bean?"

Bassett knows the bean because it's prized in southern Florida, around the Dade County area. It's an old-timey pole bean, grown by a family from Georgia named McCasland well before the turn of the century. The McCaslan's demise as a commercial crop was predicted years ago, because it has to be harvested by hand, not machine. Instead, Bassett says, "it has a constituency so devoted to this bean, it's not only survived but thrived. The growers proselytize for it. They cook dinners of it for restaurants or suppliers up on the East Coast to convince them to order the bean, and it works. It's available up and down the East Coast and in lots of places around the country."

The McCaslan has thrived commercially in part because it's fairly identifiable: extra large, long, and lumpy- looking. Break it open and it has a light-green waxy interior and is less watery-looking than a standard green bean.

But looks aren't why folks seek out this bean. "For me," Bassett says, "I think it's the best-tasting snap bean in the world. It has a much stronger aromatic component than other beans. When you cook it, unless you have a tightly sealed pot, the most enticing aroma will fill the house."

I would have taken Bassett's word for it, but didn't have to. A few weeks before I finished this book, a farm couple I'd not seen before showed up at our market. They had perfect cucumbers, about the size of an old vacuum tube and crisp as could be, good squash, and a basket full of long, knobby, full green beans that smelled sweet even raw.

"Lemme tell you about them beans," the gentleman said to me. "I only eat three kinds of green beans in this world: white half-runners, Romas, and them, McCaslans."

I brought a mess home and really enjoyed the stringing, since the largeness of the McCaslans meant I had a potful in no time. The next day, while I cooked them, the house filled up with a sweet, fresh, beany smell like you'd expect in heaven. And heavenly is what those beans were.

No, I won't give up my beloved half-runners; but I'll be glad to cook one or the other right on up to the fall.

If you can't find fresh McCaslan beans in a market near you, you can try growing your own with seed from Southern Exposure Seed Exchange. See Things to Order, page 338.

Shuck Beans

Leatherbritches, shuck, or shucky beans—fresh-picked green beans dried in the pod, kept until winter, soaked in water, and cooked slow with bacon—is the signature dish of the central Southern mountains. To my knowledge—and I've made it a point to try to find out—leatherbritches are cooked nowhere else in the United States. Say shuck or shucky beans to a Southerner from elsewhere, even a town only 50 miles or so removed from the foothills of the Appalachians, and he or she will think you are talking about a type of green bean prized for its seed and prepared by shucking or shelling the bean out and discarding the pod before cooking. But any mountain man, woman, or child will tell you that's not shuck beans at all.

The practice of drying green beans for preservation took hold in early pioneer times. In the southern Appalachian mountains, winters were fierce and food could be scarce—mostly game and whatever had been "put up" from the summer garden. Canning was a modern invention in the region; smoke- and/or salt-curing meats and drying fruits and some vegetables were the preferred methods of preservation.

The local Native Americans, most particularly the Cherokee, are credited with having taught the first white settlers many of these preservation techniques. Smoked or dried game, winter squash, and parched corn all can be found in the Indian diet predating the settlers. Few food writers/scholars have even known about shuck beans, so specific are they to the region, and of those who have, most have suggested they were a dish passed on by the Cherokee. But my theory has been that while the technique of stringing the beans up to dry may have been Indian-influenced, the green beans themselves were brought into the region by these settlers of European origin. Shuck beans, it seemed to me, were in fact an authentic American creation, a blending of cultures in one pot.

Then, in October of 1995, a friend and I visited the Museum of American Frontier Culture in Staunton, Virginia. (See Places to Go, page 341.) This living museum, set in the Shenandoah Valley, features a walking tour of four small working farms. Three represent the primary European cultures which populated the area: German, English, and Irish. These each have a house imported lock, stock, and barrel from the homeland, and are surrounded by a garden, stock areas, and outbuildings typical of a farm in their respective countries in the seventeenth and eighteenth centuries. The fourth farm is typical of American farms of the region in the eighteenth and nineteenth centuries, and at it you can see how the three European traditions plus Native-American and African influences combined to create a new culture in the New World.

Part and parcel of the daily tours are demonstrations of crafts and cooking. At the German homestead, where we began our walking tour, docents dressed in traditional garb were making plum butter in a big copper kettle. One thing led to another, and soon I was talking to Rosa Kesterson, who was born in Rheinland-Pfalz, Germany, actually only a few miles from the farm where the house we stood in was originally located.

We were discussing traditional German ways of preserving fruit, and Rosa told me that it was common to dry apples and peaches in her native country. She even described a cake made with them, something like, but fancier than, the mountain stack cakes I had grown up eating. And then she took me into a small room near the kitchen, where drying apples were hung. The familiar sweet, musty scent made me think of my aunts' house in the fall, when apple pieces were spread on a sheet in a back bedroom when the weather outside was too damp for drying. I was feeling a pleasant wave of nostalgia when I turned around, and there, hung from the rafters by the door, were rows and rows of drying shuck beans.

"I can't believe it!" I whooped.

"You know the leatherbritches?" Rosa asked.

She had learned the mountain name from the handful of visitors with Appalachian roots who'd been just as delighted and surprised as I to discover their favorite food in this unexpected place. In Germany, Rosa told me, the beans are called *getrocken bohne*, literally, dried string beans. Rosa described the traditional German process of preparing them—soaking them overnight, shell and all, then cooking them with smoked meat

for seasoning—nearly identical to the mountain way.

"Do you know *sauer bohne*, too?" she asked me, and I had enough high school German to guess immediately that she meant another familiar dish, which in the mountains we called pickle beans. These are green beans put up in jars in a super-salty brine. They're prepared by rinsing them first, then sautéing them in bacon grease. The smell is pungent, the flavor not unlike sauerkraut but more substantial. And the only differences between the way my mother and hers made the beans were that my mother sometimes added corn cut from the cob to the beans before she canned them, and Rosa's often added dumplings to the pan juices from the beans.

While we were on a roll, I asked Rosa if she'd ever heard of stuffing turkeys with sauerkraut, another mountain tradition I'd come across, though not in my own family. She laughed and said, "We don't do turkeys; but we love to put sauerkraut in the goose."

Going back to the leatherbritches, she said, "It's my understanding that they've been able to document beans dried this way as far back as the fourteenth century in Germany."

For me, part of the mysterious beauty of eating shuck beans had been a sense that I was eating food that stretched back across generations, food that was a direct link to pioneer times. Now that line extends across the ocean and through five centuries. No wonder those of us who grew up eating them think shuck beans are magical.

Drying Shuck Beans

To dry enough for a good mess of shuck beans in the winter, you will need

5 pounds fresh white half-runner beans

Beans gathered late in the season are best. That's when the pods are full of mature white seeds. If you can't find white half-runners, look for green beans with firm pods filled with plump seeds. Don't bother drying varieties of beans which are mostly pod with skinny little anemic seeds. And don't get old beans with well-developed seeds but drying pods. You want full beans in their prime, with crisp, juicy pods.

If you grow the beans yourself, let them run up short poles to keep the beans from lying in the dirt. You don't want to rinse the beans before stringing them up to dry, since any dampness will cause the beans to rot. If the beans you get are dirty, wipe them clean with a barely damp cloth, and then wipe them with a dry one. Discard any beans with blemishes or rust spots. (If the problem area is at one end, you can just break that part off the bean and use the rest.)

Remove the ends and strings from the beans (see page 57) but don't break them.

When all the beans are prepared, thread a large needle with strong thread (some folks use dental floss) 1 to 3 feet long when doubled. I use the shorter length because that makes it easier to find odd drying spaces for the beans around my house. Traditionally, when the beans were hung from the rafters of the porch, longer lengths were used.

Tie a knot at the end of the thread, and push the needle through a bean pod at the midway point of its length, being careful to go between seeds and not through one. (It's much harder to get the thread out of a dried seed than it is to pull it out of the dried pod.) Pull the thread through the bean almost to the end, leaving just enough thread to tie a loop around the bean. The first bean then becomes the "stopper" at the end of the thread.

Thread more beans onto the strand, leaving about 2 inches of thread at the top. Cut the needle off and tie a knot at the end of the extra thread at the top, leaving a loop to hang the strand. Repeat until all the beans are strung.

Hang in a dry, well-ventilated place.

There is some discussion about whether the beans should be hung in direct sunlight or out of the sun. Traditionalists tend to favor the indirect method, saying that the flavor of the dried bean is better. In truth, I have done both and haven't noticed much difference in taste, so I tend to hang my beans wherever convenient, as long as the place is dry and airy. Some folks claim success in drying beans broken and laid on sheets in a commercial dryer, but I have eaten shuck beans prepared that way and found that they don't have as full and concentrated a flavor as beans dried the traditional, slower way.

I've variously dried beans by hanging them from the pegs of a coat rack on an

While the Western North Carolina Farmers' Market in Asheville is so big it's legend, there are plenty of other farm markets throughout the state.

Kathy Purvis, food editor of the *Charlotte Observer*, clocked 350 miles one early spring weekend not long ago checking out close to twenty markets in her North and South Carolina area. She noted that while Charlotte has the official regional market at 1801 Yorkmont Road, making it one of the largest, Columbia, South Carolina's market (in the shade of USC stadium) has a real diversity of goods because it's at a major crossroads in the region. And the Matthews Regional Farmers' Market on South Trade Street in Matthews, North Carolina, offers lots of organic produce, as well as fresh flowers and art.

The Carrboro Farm Market, just outside of Chapel Hill, was immortalized by the late Bill Neal, who shopped there regularly to fill his table and those at his signature restaurant, Crook's Corner (still one of the best places to eat in Chapel Hill, and one of the finest spots to find artful Southern cooking in the United States). Farmers set up on Saturday beside the town hall in the center of Carrboro and offer goodies from greens to gourmet goat cheese. See Places to Go, page 341, and Farm Markets, page 343.

For a more upscale shopping experience, you can try A Southern Season, the big old store and restaurant in Chapel Hill's Eastgate Shopping Center. See Things to Order, page 338.

enclosed sunporch, from indoor window plant hangers whose plants were out on the porch, and from a broomstick laid across the back of two chairs near a sunny window. My aunts, like many folks from the region, had a series of small nails across the upper wood frames of the windows on their screened-in back porch, from which they hung the beans, although the threat of rain or a particularly humid day meant gathering the beans and bringing them inside to wait out the wet spell.

In recent years, some folks in the mountains have taken to drying shuck beans on the ledge under the back window of their car. If you choose to do this, you don't need to thread the beans, but should string and break them as if you were preparing them for cooking. Cover the ledge with a plain white sheet or towel, and spread the beans evenly across it in one layer. (Don't crowd the beans too much or let them overlap.) You will need to "stir" the beans with your hand every day so that they turn and dry evenly on all sides.

Depending on the moisture content of the beans and the general humidity, it can take up to three weeks for beans to dry thoroughly. They are ready when they are crisp, with no pliancy in the pod.

When the beans are dry, remove them

from the thread. Cut the knots at the top or bottom, and you can generally pull the thread right out. If beans break in the process, don't worry. Just gather them all up. Store in an air-tight container away from direct light. These days, lots of folks store their shuck beans in jars or covered coffee cans in the freezer, but it's not necessary.

Cooking Shuck Beans
SERVES 6 TO 8

4 cups dried shuck beans
water
¼ pound white bacon (a ham hock is acceptable)
salt

Rinse the beans three or four times, discarding any that may have turned black. If you see any strings on the beans, remove and discard them. Put the beans in a large bowl and cover them with water 2 inches above the beans. (You may have to lay a plate on top of the beans to keep them under the water.) Soak overnight, for about 12 hours.

Drain the beans and place them in a large pot with fresh water about 2 inches above the beans. Put the white bacon in the pot, and bring the water to a boil. Turn the heat down to a low simmer, and cook for 5 to 6 hours. (Some recipes specify 2 to 6 hours, but I've never had shuck beans cook tender in less than 5 hours.) If the beans begin to cook dry, add boiling water to the pot in moderate amounts.

The beans are ready when the seeds are creamy and the pods tender but not mushy. Add salt to taste, beginning with ½ teaspoon.

Shuck Beans must absolutely be served with a skillet of Real Cornbread (page 103) and a slice of raw onion or a green onion on the side.

Clearly, shuck beans are a good source of fiber, and I've heard folks with mountain roots swear they give the eater uncommon strength. In our family, though, they are also known as something of a love potion.

In the winter of 1972, at the age of twenty-three, I moved to Santa Fe, New Mexico, on my own. It was exhilarating but also terrifying to be in a place where I knew no one. The people I met were friendly and helpful, though, and as the New Year came near, I decided to have a party to thank my new friends.

That was also the very first year I'd spent the holidays away from my home in Kentucky. Worried about how I'd survive in strange surroundings, my mother and aunts had put together a care package for me. Mysteriously, the package actually showed up on my doorstep on Christmas Day, adding an air of magic to the contents inside. Along with the Christmas presents and more conventional comforts, my aunt had sent me a mess of home-dried shuck beans. I decided to cook these special beans for my new friends.

There were other foods at that New Year's feast, but everyone was curious about the strange beans, willing to try at least a small bowl, and, more often than not, eager to return for seconds. One of my generous neighbors, a dark-haired, sparkly-eyed bearded fellow, wouldn't leave the bean pot.

"What did you say these were?"

"How did you say you made them?"

"Where did you learn to do that?"

"What's your family like, anyway?"

He seemed to have a new question each time he came back to fill his bowl and score another golden wedge of cornbread. I didn't mind, since I figured that any man with such an instant and abiding affection for my beloved shuck beans was someone worth getting to know. And that's proved right for all the years Ken and I have been together since.

ABOUT

SALLET GREENS

Poke and Other Spring Greens

Greens with Pot Likker

Collards with Cornmeal Dumplings

Mustard Greens with Crowder Peas

Kentucky Colcannon

Spring Greens Soup

Winter Greens Soup

Gumbo Z'Herbes

But I have never tasted meat,
Nor cabbage, corn nor beans,
Nor fluid food one half as sweet
As that first mess of greens.
—Cotton Noe, *The Loom of Life* (1912)

My mother remembers that as a little girl in Corbin, Kentucky, she would pick wild greens in the spring in the wooded areas around her house. She went with Ma, her maternal grandmother, who had Indian blood and, mother says, was a "doctor woman," someone who knew herbs and poultices and would help ailing neighbors who came to her. Ma knew where in the woods to find the plants for her "cures," as well as stands of poke and creases, all tender in the early spring. She also picked dock and dandelion greens, and gathered watercress along the nearby creek for salads, but she didn't pick fiddlehead ferns or purslane, my mother says, two other wild greens prized in the deeper southern mountains.

"I couldn't tell you now what any of them looked like, except for poke," my mother says. "And I remember once, when your sister was just a baby [the late 1930s], Jessie [Mother's cousin] and I went out and picked a mess of greens, all different kinds. Jessie knew what we were looking for, and I remember that I did, too, but I couldn't tell you now."

What she can tell me now, some 75 years later, is how those spring greens tasted when she was a child.

"I couldn't wait when we'd get home. Ma would clean 'em and cook 'em in water first. I don't know how long they boiled, but you always poured that first water off. And then she'd fry just a little bit of white bacon in a pan, enough to get seasoning grease, and put the greens in, and cook them long enough to get the bacon flavor all over 'em. We ate that with mashed potatoes and cornbread and a good old green onion on the side. I never tasted anything else so good."

Or good for you. Most greens are an excellent source of vitamin A, and also contain vitamin C and some minerals, particularly iron. This last intrigues me most, because when you get a Southerner to talk or write about greens, we seem to revere them not only for their flavor but also as a sort of mystical source of strength.

Blues singer Tony Joe White's "Polk Salad Annie" was "a girl, I swear to the world, made the alligator look tame."

And in *The Ballad of the Sad Café*, Carson McCullers writes: "Each night the hunchback came down the stairs with the air of one who has a grand opinion of himself. He always smelled slightly of turnip greens, as Miss Amelia rubbed him night and morning with pot liquor to give him strength."

As for me, I have the proof of my great-grandmother, who died in her eighties; my mother, still here and potent as the pot likker she loves, at eighty; and my own body's deep, mystical craving for greens.

Sallet, or sallet greens, is how many Southerners refer to any green that is cooked before being eaten. (It's not to be confused with salad, which in the South indicates the usual concoctions of lettuce, fruit, and vegetables—as it does in the rest of the country—and also just about anything which is made with Jell-O, even those dishes others might call dessert.)

The cultivated greens Southerners prefer to eat—collards, kale, mustard, turnip—still loosely define the regions we hail from. John Egerton says there is a Greens Line which runs through the South, much like the Mason-Dixon, and is its equal in dispute. Generally speaking, Egerton says, in the Deep South—lower Louisiana, Mississippi, Alabama, Georgia, South Carolina, and all of Florida—collards are favored. North of that territory, right on to the Ohio and sometimes beyond, turnip greens are the winter green of choice.

Now right there I am ready to both agree and disagree. In my mother's house and those of my southern Kentucky relatives, it was kale that meant greens in the winter, sometimes augmented by a mess of mustard or turnip greens for flavor; but it is always the rich, brackish taste of kale that my mother, and now I, crave when

the air takes a bite and our bones begin to feel brittle. This may be only a family preference, though, since most of the literature I find cites turnip as the preferred greens for mountain folk.

As for collards, they make a strong showing in regions other than those Egerton names, most notably the coastal areas of North Carolina. On the whole, though, John's assessment is right, and the upshot is not only that we tend to prefer the greens we grew up with over all others, but that their bitter, earthy flavor is for most of us a visceral taste of home.

Cooking up a pot of winter greens on the first biting cold day of the season, getting the house steamy (and pleasantly stinky) with slow-simmered fragrance, making the cornbread, mashing the potatoes forever to achieve creamy perfection, then eating the greens, sopping every drop of pot likker with your pone—all this smacks of serious ritual.

The Indians, mountain folk like my great-grandmother, and the slaves of the South knew greens to be medicinal as well as flavorful. Poke was eaten in the spring to cleanse and purify the blood. Kale and collards and their sharper, more bitter relatives were devoured through the winter to keep us strong. They were cheap. They were powerful. We tended to keep our passion for them secret.

Those not from the region seem not to *get* what it is that Southerners feel about greens, and to openly disdain the ways in which we cook them, winter greens especially. In recent years, I have suffered through countless nouveau "Southern" dinners in which turnip greens, collards, or kale have been served up blanched and crunchy "to keep the nutrients in." I have found greens so prepared nearly inedible, and always unsatisfying, and I have come home and cooked my own mess of winter greens for one hour solid.

In *Mountain Country Cooking* (St. Martin's Press, 1996), Mark Sohn writes, "I can't understand why so many chefs serve undercooked, almost raw vegetables. Yes, the vegetables are bright in color, but they are also tough to chew, hard to digest and low in flavor. When it comes to greens, mountain cooks appreciate the importance of long cooking. We take the time to cook our less tender greens for an hour or more. The result is a muddy-green, drab olive or almost brown color, full taste, easy chewing and complete digestion."

And in *Southern Cooking*, Bill Neal advises, "You are not overcooking a vegetable here, but braising it much in a French manner to slowly coax and develop flavors."

In fact, recently there has been a swing of the pendulum, and serious attention paid to the idea that long, slow cooking makes mature greens more easily digestible, and the nutrients in them more accessible to the human body. As for the water-soluble vitamins, such as C, while they do leach out of the vegetable and into the liquid during cooking, only a fool would toss that liquid out instead of savoring every aromatic drop.

This is not to say that all greens are to be cooked for a long time, but that it takes longer to cook more mature greens and winter greens. Wild greens have traditionally been gathered when they are tender, and are traditionally, and tastily, cooked the shortest time. Usually they are parboiled quickly and the liquid drained off. Then the greens are sautéed in oil or bacon seasoning for flavor. Greens found early in the spring, with tender leaves smaller than the hand, are better for recipes with shorter cooking times, while winter greens, like kale, and greens with leaves larger than the hand hold up well in a long, slow simmer. You can generally substitute one variety of green for another in the recipes in this section, as long as you use tender or young greens in the recipes with shorter cooking times, winter or mature greens in those that take longer. As with the recipes for butter beans and fresh field peas, the cooking times will vary depending on the green itself. Your best bet is to simmer and taste and then simmer some more.

As a rule, most greens get not only tougher as they mature but more bitter as well. The long, slow cooking helps to temper that bitterness. Some folks would never serve a pot of greens without vinegar to counteract the bitterness, and others throw a pepper pod in the pot, though neither was the tradition in my home. Edna Lewis, author of *In Pursuit of Flavor* (Alfred A. Knopf, 1988), says, "When I was growing up in Virginia, every house had a round tray on the table holding bottles and jars of oil, vinegar, mustard, salt, pepper and sugar so that everyone could season their own greens."

Poke and Other Spring Greens

SERVES 4

Of all the Southern greens, poke is perhaps the most magical. It's edible only at the very start of its growing season, in the spring; and while it's much prized, it is not cultivated but rather harvested in the wild.

Mr. Peters, father of my junior high and high school friend Pete, became my poke buddy several years ago, hanging plastic grocery bags of the delicacy on my front door every April. Although poke grows wild just about anywhere, even along superhighways and in empty lots, the sudden appearance of this wild green on my urban doorstep seemed like magic to me.

About five years ago, when my family moved to a house in Mr. Peters's neighborhood and adjacent to one of Louisville's large, lush parks, he decided to share his secrets with another food-writer friend and me. That spring, he took each of us for a walk through the park, pointing out the prime poke patches he'd discovered there. He showed us the young plants which were just right for cutting, from a few inches to almost 3 feet tall, all with tender, juicy shoots and young leaves pointing upward. He cautioned us not to wait, but to cut the poke when it first appeared, noting that the stems turn poisonous when they thicken and become hollow, as do the leaves when they mature. The roots and berries are also poisonous.

The tender young shoots and leaves are tonic and delicious, however, and worth the trouble of hunting them out. This I did for a few years, until my mother, standing at my kitchen window one afternoon, said, "Well, Ronni, I don't know why you go digging all through the park for poke when you've got a perfectly good stand right out there." Indeed, she was right, and I now get my spring poke right in my own backyard.

In the South, fresh poke is often sold at farm markets in season. If it's not available where you are, Swiss chard is an acceptable substitute. Actually, any very tender spring green will be tasty prepared this way.

If you are buying greens, get 1 pound. If you are gathering them wild, cook as much as you gather. Measure the wild poke after parboiling. Two cups equals about 1 pound.

1 pound poke or other tender spring
   green
water
1 slab white bacon, ¼ inch thick, or 2
   slices breakfast bacon, or 2
   tablespoons butter
2 green onions, chopped
salt

Rinse the poke very well to rid it of dirt, grass, or twigs. Be sure to cut off any roots on the bottom; they are poisonous. Stems which are thin, green, and pliant may be cooked and eaten, but if they are tough and turning reddish purple, discard. Place the leaves in a large pot and cover with water. Bring to a boil over medium-high heat, and boil 3 minutes. (You may need to use a wooden spoon to push the greens down into the water while boiling.) Drain. If you are cooking poke, repeat the process. Set the greens aside.

In a skillet, fry the bacon to render the drippings, or melt the butter. Remove the meat from the skillet, leaving about 2 tablespoons of drippings. If you are using breakfast bacon, reserve the meat. Sauté the green onions in the drippings over medium heat.

While the onions are cooking, cut the greens into strips about ½ inch wide. Add them to the skillet, and stir to mix and coat them with drippings. Cook 6 to 10 minutes, until the greens are tender and seasoned but not mushy. Add salt to taste. Serve immediately, crumbling breakfast bacon over the top, if you wish.

VARIATION: *Eggs often accompany spring poke; they can be served hard-boiled and sliced on top, with vinegar passed on the side. Another favorite method is to whisk 3 or 4 fresh eggs and pour them over the sautéed poke, then continue cooking, stirring once or twice, until the eggs are set.*

A third way of serving this combo is with deviled eggs on the side. I like to mix mayonnaise, Dijon mustard, minced green onion, minced dill pickle, a dash of white pepper, and a dollop of horseradish with the yolk.

THE "WRENCHING" OF THE GREENS

In certain parts of the rural South you will hear folks say they "wrench" their greens well before cooking, a mispronunciation of "rinse," which is, nevertheless, agonizingly appropriate for the time- and labor-intensive process of cleaning greens fresh from the garden.

Greens love dirt like five-year-olds do. The curlier or more textured the leaf, the more dirt you will find in it. If you buy fresh greens at a farm market or pick them from your own garden, you may have to put them through as many as four separate "wrenchings" to get them clean enough for cooking.

I usually do the first rinse by running each leaf under the faucet individually. Then I immerse the whole mess in a sink full of clear, cold water, swishing through it with my hands several times to shake loose any more dirt. I then transfer the greens to a large colander (or several, depending on how big a mess I'm dealing with), and check the water in the sink. If it has grit visible at the bottom, I drain it, rinse the sink thoroughly, fill it with more cold water, and "wrench" the greens again. I repeat this process as many times as it takes for the sink water to be clear. Even then, I double-check by running my fingers lightly over the surface of several leaves to see if I can feel any grit; and I usually tear a little piece from a leaf and chew it up to make sure it's grit-free. You only need to cook a pot of half-cleaned greens for two hours and then *discover grit between your teeth to realize how important this seemingly obsessive cleaning is.*

Most greens from the supermarket, however, have been rinsed already. Run your fingers over a couple of leaves. If they feel relatively grit-free, just drop the leaves in a sink full of cold water, swish several times, remove to a colander, and check the water. Most of the time, I find the water clear and move on to the next step in preparation. Not all store-bought greens are clean, however, so always do the sink test. And remember that the convenience of store-bought greens is almost always canceled out by the fresher, stronger taste of homegrown or farm-market greens.

Greens with Pot Likker

SERVES 6 TO 8

I am not a fan of phonetically spelled menus, and find it hard to eat in a place, no matter how good, which cutely offers items like "taters, maters 'n' sich." Given that, I guess I should fall into the camp of Southerners who insist that the elixir in which great greens are served is correctly called pot "liquor." But there is something so lip-smackingly forthright about this green and heady broth that it seems to me it is more honestly spelled "likker." Besides, it would seem a breach of manners to dunk or crumble cornbread into something called "liquor," while "likker" just about cries out for such treatment.

Call it what you want, and make it with whatever hearty greens are available. This is a Southern classic. Serve it with cornbread, Mother's Mashed Potatoes (page 171), and Soup Beans (page 39) for the ultimate Dixie dinner.

3 quarts water
¼ pound salt pork, ham hock, or smoked turkey wing
2 pounds fresh greens
2 teaspoons kosher salt
½ teaspoon white pepper, or a dried red pepper pod, rinsed
trimmed green onions or sliced white onion

In a large pot with a lid, bring the water and seasoning meat to a boil. Reduce the heat to medium, cover, and simmer while you prepare the greens for cooking.

Rinse the greens thoroughly and remove any stems. Trim the rough ends from the stems and chop them into ½-inch-long pieces. Set aside.

Tear the leaves into pieces about 2 to 3 inches wide.

Add the salt and pepper to the boiling water. Add the stems and cook, covered, at a lively simmer, for 15 minutes. Add the greens, using a wooden spoon to push them down into the simmering water. You will probably have to add the greens in 2 or 3 batches, letting each batch cook down a bit to make room for the next one. When all the greens are in, cover the pot, and simmer for 1 to 2 hours, until the greens are meltingly tender. Serve hot, with trimmed green onions or sliced white onion passed on the side.

Southerners often refer to a quantity called a "mess," as in "I believe I'll cook me up a mess of greens for dinner." While the word "mess" can be applied to a number of vegetables, particularly beans, it is almost always used when talking about greens. You go to the market to buy a mess of kale, or to the woods to gather a mess of poke. And when you bring it home, you cook up a mess of greens.

In the handy guidebook The Insider's Guide to North Carolina's Crystal Coast and New Bern, *we are told that "a mess is usually about six pounds and that means about two hours cooking time for winter collards and about three hours for summer collards."* In my family, six pounds would have been a few pounds too many for a mess, and those cooking times would have been about an hour too long each.

Though they don't always agree, North Carolinians tend to be remarkably precise about their messes. Kathy Purvis, food editor at the Charlotte Observer, says a mess is "a specific unit of measurement. It equals about a potful and is usually the amount of food—greens or green beans or whatever—that can be eaten by one family, say four or five people, at one meal, with enough left over to heat up for lunch."

But it's John Egerton who defines a mess best when he calls it "an imprecise unit of measure equal to enough."

Collards with Cornmeal Dumplings
SERVES 4

This dish can also be made with kale, but in the coastal regions of North Carolina, and some parts of South Carolina, where cornmeal dumplings with greens is a regional delicacy, collards are preferred.

You will need to make this in a lidded, wide pot (10 inches in diameter is adequate) to give the dumplings enough room. You want enough space between the dumplings for steam to rise and cook them thoroughly. If you must use a narrower pot, cook fewer dumplings. Lay the leftover uncooked dumplings on a cookie sheet, press slightly to flatten, and bake at 450°F for about 5 minutes, until they turn golden. Call them corn pones and serve them hot.

GREENS
¾ pound fresh collard greens
3½ cups ham broth (see page 162)
½ teaspoon kosher salt
¼ cup diced lean country ham, or ½ cup diced ham

DUMPLINGS
⅓ cup all-purpose flour
⅔ cup finely ground white cornmeal
½ teaspoon kosher salt
2 teaspoons baking powder
1 tablespoon bacon grease
¼ cup milk, plus more if needed

Rinse the greens thoroughly. Remove and discard any stems. Slice the leaves into strips about ½ inch wide.

Collard Festival and Bum's

I have not been there, so I am not telling you this as the gospel truth, but for years I have heard that the best collard greens in the South are dished up at Bum's Restaurant in Ayden, North Carolina. When I called the Ayden Chamber of Commerce once to get information on the annual Collard Festival there, I asked B. J. Craft, the executive director, if Bum's greens were indeed the town's best.

"I guess you can't count my mother's," B. J. said with a pleasantly resigned sigh.

I told her not unless her mother had a restaurant.

"Then Bum's is it," she said.

The September festival has cook-offs and a collard-eating contest, and even a collard poetry recitation.

See Places to Go, page 341.

In a wide-mouthed pot with a lid, bring the greens, ham broth, and salt to a boil over high heat. Turn the heat down to medium, cover, and cook the greens at a slow simmer for 35 minutes to 1 hour, until just tender.

While the greens are cooking, prepare the dumplings by mixing together the flour, cornmeal, salt, and baking powder. Using a fork or your fingers, lightly mix in the bacon grease. When well blended, add the milk and stir. The dough should be wet but firm, not runny. If you need more milk, add it a teaspoon at a time, being careful not to make the mixture soupy. When the dough holds together like play-dough or clay, scoop it up by the table-spoonful. Very lightly pat each spoonful into a ball, and lay the balls on a plate. Cover the plate securely with plastic wrap

and refrigerate until the greens are ready.

When the greens are just tender, add the ham to the pot and stir. The broth should come up high enough to cover the greens. If not, add boiling water until it does. Gently drop dumplings into the broth, leaving at least ¼ inch of space around each. Cover, and turn the heat low. Steam the dumplings for 20 minutes. (Don't take the lid off the pot while they cook.) Divide the dumplings among four serving bowls, ladle greens and broth over them, and serve immediately.

Mustard Greens with Crowder Peas   SERVES 4

Pot likker is so prized that most recipes for Southern-style greens assure that you have plenty. This dish, however, has just a bit of liquid and is more like a warm salad. It can be served as such to precede a larger meal, or can stand on its own as a main course with cornbread.

It is tasty made with any sort of greens, including spinach, but mustard greens have a bite that gives the dish an added dimension and are therefore the best choice.

The "knobby onion" in this recipe is an early spring onion which shows up in farm markets; it looks like an extra-large green onion. It is, in fact, a young onion, usually picked to thin out the crop. It is sweeter and a bit milder than a green onion, particularly when it is a Vidalia onion. If you can't find any, substitute a combination of sweet white onion and green onion.

1 cup broth, chicken, vegetable, or ham
2 cups fresh or frozen crowder or other field peas
1 clove garlic, chopped
salt
¾ pound fresh mustard greens
3 tablespoons water
2 tablespoons butter
1 cup chopped knobby onion (or ½ cup chopped sweet white onion and ½ cup green onion, including green part)

In a saucepan, bring the broth and peas to a boil over high heat. Turn the heat to low, cover, and simmer for 30 minutes, until the peas are tender. Remove from the heat. Add the garlic and salt to taste. Cover and set aside to steep while you prepare the greens.

Rinse the greens well; remove and discard the stems. Tear the leaves into pieces about 2 to 3 inches wide. Put the greens in a heavy skillet with a lid, add the water, cover, and set over very low heat. (You may need to add the greens in 2 or 3 batches, allowing the earlier batch to cook down some to make room in the pan.) Cook, covered, until the greens are just tender and have lost some of their brackish flavor, about 20 minutes. Stir occasionally to keep the greens from sticking to the bottom of the pan. If the pan seems to be drying out and the greens are in danger of burning, add another tablespoon or two of water and turn the heat even lower. When the greens are tender, remove them from the skillet and set aside.

Melt the butter in the skillet over medium heat, add the onions and sauté for 2 minutes to soften. Add the greens, and toss to coat them with butter and onion. Salt to taste. Serve immediately with the crowder peas on top.

"Maureen and I cooked as Charlie, Mavis and Martha had taught us—corn dumplings, corn pudding, corn dodgers, cornbread, corn, corn, corn, all that ever-loving corn. We had various types of greens, and we would put on a mess of collards at midnight and take it off the fire at three. That is how we knew when to go to bed—when the greens were tender."

—Kaye Gibbons, *On the Occasion of My Last Afternoon* (G. P. Putnam & Sons, 1998)

Kentucky Colcannon   SERVES 6

In the traditional Irish colcannon, cooked kale or cabbage and onions are mixed with mashed potatoes. My mother had never heard of colcannon until I mentioned it a few years ago, but the memory of its flavor must have been passed to us genetically from Irish forebears, for every pot of kale greens my mother ever served came to the table with a big bowl of mashed potatoes, and fresh green onions or sweet onion slices passed on the side. And we didn't just put the potatoes, greens, and onions on the same plate, but scooped small portions of each together to get the blended flavor in each bite.

This casserole has the same comforting, blended taste that those suppers did.

Colcannon was served in Ireland as a good-luck New Year's dish. The tradition of serving greens for luck on New Year's Day is still a powerful one among Southerners. The colcannon was spiked with trinkets—a wedding ring, a hard plastic baby doll, a coin—and the finder was supposed to get luck of like kind. Trinkets won't hold up well in the long, slow bake this dish requires, but if you want, you can use a pie server to carefully lift up its layers, working around the edges, and slip trinkets in just before serving. You can start your own holiday tradition; just be sure to warn everyone to look before they bite!

2 quarts water
1 pound fresh kale
4 medium-sized Yukon Gold potatoes

2 tablespoons olive oil, plus more for the baking dish
1 teaspoon kosher salt
½ medium-sized sweet white onion
1½ cups hot chicken broth (see Note)

Preheat the oven to 350°F. Liberally oil a 2-quart baking dish that is about 2 inches deep.

Bring the water to a boil in a large pot. While it heats, rinse the kale thoroughly, stripping the leaves off the stems. Trim the stems and put them in the water when it begins to boil. Cover and cook 10 minutes, then add the leaves and cook for another 5. Drain in a colander and set aside until cool enough to handle.

While the greens are cooking, peel the potatoes and slice them in rounds less than ⅛ inch thick. Mix the olive oil and salt in a large bowl, add the potato slices, and toss to coat. Slice the onion half into ¼-inch-wide crescents and set aside.

Make a layer of ¼ of the potato slices in the bottom of the baking dish. Sprinkle ⅓ of the onion crescents over it. Chop the kale stems fine and sprinkle them over the onions.

Make another layer of potato slices, followed by a layer of onion. Cut half the kale leaves into strips about ½ inch wide. (Just grab about half the kale, lay it on the chopping board, and cut through the mound. You don't have to be precise.) Layer the kale over the onion, then add layers of potato, onion, and the rest of the kale, cut the same way. Top with potato slices, drizzling any remaining oil and salt evenly over them.

In **American Cooking: Southern Style**, Eugene Walter tells about visiting Mississippi-born diva Leontyne Price at her apartment in Rome (Italy, not Georgia), where she was preparing a Southern-style supper for friends. He writes:

"When I arrived, she was regally dressed in a Dior hostess gown and seated at the oval table in her dining room overlooking a court with a gently plashing fountain. The coffeepot was beside her, the score of Salome was propped up before her—and she was sorting turnip greens. 'This is how we do it in Laurel, Mississippi,' she said. 'You have to examine each leaf personally, after you've washed it. You must take the yellow part out and you must tear every bit of green leaf off the stalk, in pieces as big as postage stamps. It takes time, but this is how you have to do it. There are as many different ways to cook greens as there are to sing soprano roles. You can put in bacon fat at the beginning, or you can cook bits of fatback with the greens, or you can pour bacon fat over them after they've cooked. You put in just enough water to keep things from sticking. And I'll tell you one thing, buddy,'—she assumed a mock-ferocious expression—'every drop of the pot likker is mine, all mine.' "

Pour the hot chicken broth over all and cover securely. (Use aluminum foil if your baking dish doesn't have a cover.) Bake for 1 hour. Remove the cover and bake 30 minutes more. Serve warm.

Notes: *I use homemade chicken broth which is just barely salted. If you are using a canned broth, or salt your homemade broth heavily, cut back on the amount of salt you mix with the olive oil.*

Spring Greens Soup   SERVES 6

Greens with Pot Likker is usually served in a bowl and is often eaten with a piece of cornbread as a main course, much like a hearty soup. But there are also soups aplenty in the Southern repertoire with greens as their main ingredient. This one is light and lemony, particularly refreshing when made with the young and tender first greens of spring.

1 pound young greens
½ cup water
1 quart chicken broth
salt
2 cups cooked white rice
1 lemon

Rinse the greens thoroughly and remove the stems. Trim any rough ends from the stems and chop them fine (⅛ inch long). Put the stems and water in a large pot. Bring to a boil over high heat. Cover, turn the heat to low, and simmer 10 minutes

While the stems are simmering, cut the greens in very thin ribbons about ⅛ inch wide.

When the stems have simmered 10 minutes, add the chicken broth to the pot. Add salt to taste, and bring to a boil. Add the greens, pushing them down with a wooden spoon. Lower the heat, cover, and simmer 20 to 40 minutes, until the greens are tender. Add the rice, stir, and cook, uncovered, for 5 minutes.

Cut the lemon in wedges and remove the seeds. When the soup is ready, ladle it into individual serving bowls and pass lemon on the side to be squeezed in at the table.

Note: *You may prefer to rinse the lemon well, then slice thin rounds (removing any parts of seeds) to float on each serving of soup. Diners press the lemon with a spoon in the soup to release juice and flavor.*

Winter Greens Soup

SERVES 8 TO 10

My neighbor Johanna Camenisch serves this hearty greens soup every year for a huge pre-Christmas get-together at her house. It is spiked with spicy sausage, and Johanna always makes it with kale, although collards or a mix of greens including mustard and turnip is also wonderful. It's good, as all greens dishes are, served with a skillet of hot cornbread— but it is also delicious with a dark, crusty rye or pumpernickel.

3 pounds fresh greens
2 quarts chicken broth
2 teaspoons kosher salt
6 medium-sized potatoes
½ cup olive oil
2 pounds ground hot Italian sausage
black pepper

Rinse the greens thoroughly. Strip the leaves from the stems and discard. Slice the leaves into thin strips.

In a large pot, heat the broth and salt over medium heat. While the broth is heating, peel the potatoes and slice them into rounds about ¼ inch thick. Add them to the broth. When the broth boils, reduce the heat to medium, and cook at a lively simmer for 15 minutes, until the potatoes are soft enough to be mashed. Remove the potatoes with a slotted spoon, mash them coarsely, and return them to the broth.

Add the olive oil. When the mixture begins to boil again, add the greens. Continue to boil until the greens are just tender, about 20 minutes.

While the greens are cooking, crumble the sausage into a skillet and brown over high heat, stirring to keep it from sticking. Drain the grease from the skillet. When the greens are ready, add the sausage to the soup. Add pepper to taste (lots is good). Keep at a low simmer until ready to serve.

Gumbo Z'Herbes

MAKES 4 QUARTS
SERVES 16

A spicy meatless stew, Gumbo Z'Herbes was a Lenten favorite in south-central Louisiana. Meat was forbidden during Lent, so clever Cajun cooks used the highly flavorful spring greens that were abundant, letting the meaty, mineral tang of collards, mustard, and the like add body to the gumbo. You don't have to wait for

Lent, however. This healthful stew is great year-round and takes on very different personalities depending on which "z'herbes" are added to the pot: spinach and chard are subtle, while mustard and turnip greens sass back at the pepper.

This recipe is written in two sections. The first is a gumbo base, which I make in late summer, when fresh tomatoes and bell peppers of many hues are plentiful. I usually take about a quart of the base and add fresh corn and okra for a summer gumbo to be eaten on the spot. The rest I freeze to use throughout the year.

From fall through the next spring, I combine the gumbo base with the ingredients in the second part, Z'Herbes, to make a spicy stew of greens. Not too spicy, however, since it's always nice to pass an assortment of hot sauces. Any Louisiana-style hot sauce is appropriate with this dish, but a smoky chipotle pepper sauce adds extra meaty resonance.

GUMBO BASE

12 pounds fresh tomatoes

¼ cup olive oil

1 pound white onion, chopped

½ pound celery, chopped

1 pound bell peppers (green, red, and/or yellow), chopped

½ teaspoon kosher salt

¼ teaspoon *each* black, white, and cayenne pepper

Peel the tomatoes and chop them coarsely. Reserve with their juice.

In a stockpot that will hold 6 quarts or more, heat the olive oil over medium heat. Add the onion and sauté until softened. Add the celery and bell pepper, and stir until all is coated with oil. Add the seasonings and stir to mix well. Cover the pot, turn the heat to low, and cook 15 to 20 minutes. (Stir occasionally to make sure the vegetables don't stick. If it looks as if they are browning, turn the heat down.)

Add the tomatoes and juice to the pot, turn the heat up, and stir. When the mixture begins to bubble, cover, and turn the heat down a bit. Cook, covered, for 30 minutes at a lively simmer, stirring occasionally to keep the ingredients from sticking.

This base may be used immediately, or cooled and then frozen in quart or pint containers for up to six months.

Z'HERBES

1 quart gumbo base

1 cup water

1 cup fresh lima beans

1 cup fresh corn kernels (see page 101)

1 cup fresh chopped okra

¼ pound chard, spinach, mustard, or turnip greens

salt

black, white, and cayenne pepper

8 cups cooked white rice

hot sauce

In a 4-quart saucepan, bring the gumbo base and water to a boil. Immediately add the limas, corn, and okra. Cover, turn the heat down, and cook at a lively simmer for 30 minutes.

Meanwhile, rinse the greens thoroughly. Remove the stems and trim any rough ends. Chop the stems into ⅛-inch lengths and add them to the gumbo base in the final 10 minutes of cooking.

Cut the leaves into strips about ½ inch wide. Add them to the pot. Cover and simmer for 20 to 40 minutes, until the greens are tender. Taste and add salt or pepper, if needed. Serve ladled over hot rice. Pass hot sauce on the side.

Note: *Of course you can add garlic! The gumbo will have a clean, green taste without, a more buttery taste with. I like it both ways, as you may, too; so don't put the garlic in the gumbo base. Add it, if the spirit moves you, with Z'Herbes, one chopped clove at a time, to taste.*

ABOUT CORN

Corn on the Cob

Roast Corn in the Shuck

Skillet Corn

Crabby Corn Pudding

Corn and Ajvar Custard

Shariat's Crawfish Corn Cakes with Smoked Tomato Sauce

Real Cornbread

Perfect Fresh Corn Fritters

Eugene's Savory Seeded Corn Pone

Corn may be the lifeblood of the Midwest's agrarian economy, but in the South it is religion.

This grass, cultivated by Central and North American Indians for dozens of centuries before the arrival of the first white settlers, is said by many to be the West's single most significant culinary contribution to the world. It is certainly the staple on which the Southern dinner table is established.

Fresh, or green, corn is consumed all summer long—on the cob, cut from the cob and "fried" in skillets, in fritters, and as the basis of numerous distinctive stews, soups, and casseroles. But it's with grits and cornbread that Southern eaters distinguish themselves as the grain's true acolytes. Although corn in this country is grown overwhelmingly in the Midwest, Martha White Foods of Nashville, the country's leading seller of cornmeal, says its sales indicate that fully 80 percent of all cornbread is made in the South. And as for the other 20 percent, I'm willing to bet that half of those bakers are Southerners now transplanted elsewhere.

As for corn doctrine, that comes in when we get in the kitchen. Although numerous varieties of fresh corn are grown and enjoyed throughout the South, Southerners tend to like white corn—with its small, tender kernel and cornier, less sugary, taste—better than yellow. That preference becomes fierce when the corn is ground into meal or turned into grits. With the exception of Texas and a few pockets, particularly around the coast, Southerners believe both grits and cornbread should come from white corn, for both texture and taste.

As for adding sugar to cornbread, grits, or fresh corn for cooking, don't even think about it—unless, of course, you are making a mash for corn liquor or bourbon, the other corn staples of the South.

Corn on the Cob　　SERVES 4

"Fresh corn on the cob should be cooked *one* minute . . ."

". . . exactly three minutes . . ."

". . . no more than eight . . ."

"The only way to do justice to corn on the cob is to put a big pot of water on high heat, and the second it starts to boil, race to the cornfield, pull a couple of ears off the stalk, and shuck them while running back to the house . . ."

My apologies, dear reader. With our focus on freshness and timing, those of us who write about cooking have turned what should be one of life's simplest culinary pleasures—fresh corn on the cob—into a precision-timed and detail-dictated event worthy of the Olympics. The truth of the matter is, you have to work very hard to ruin an ear of fresh corn. It can be done, of course, as anyone who has been served up a waterlogged and chewy ear that has been warming its heels in a pot of tepid water in a restaurant for a couple of hours will testify. But for cooking and eating at home, nothing could be simpler than summer's best bounty, corn on the cob.

If at all possible, buy farm-market corn and cook it the same day it was picked. The urgency in cooking corn comes from the fact that once it is taken from the stalk, the natural sugar in the ear begins to turn to starch. The longer it is off the stalk, the starchier it becomes, although with so many supersweet varieties available today, most fresh corn has a noticeable sweetness.

Corn expert Betty Fussell wisely recommends that the cook nibble a kernel or two to determine if the corn leans more to the sugary or starchy side of the spectrum, and calculate cooking time based on that, with starchier ears requiring a few more minutes. Although current food fashion touts the 1-minute boiling-water bath as ideal, I have yet to find an ear of corn that tastes "ready" when prepared this way.

I usually boil picked-that-day corn for 3 minutes, supermarket corn for 5 to 8 minutes.

Don't salt the water, and don't add sugar to it.

4 quarts water
8 ears fresh corn
butter
salt

Put the water in a large stock pot over high heat while you remove the shucks from the corn. Rub a damp paper towel over the kernels to remove any stubborn silks.

When the water comes to a vigorous boil, gently lower the ears into it and begin timing. Cook for 3 to 8 minutes, depending on the freshness of the corn and how sweet it is, with fresher, sweeter ears requiring less time than older, starchier ones. Remove the corn from the water, shake to drain, and serve immediately with butter and salt passed on the side. Most people can manage two ears.

VARIATION: *Butter and salt are so perfect with corn that there is little you can do to improve on them. But a brisk alternative is to serve the corn with wedges of lime and pass sea salt mixed with finely ground red chile (1 tablespoon of salt to 1 teaspoon of chile) in a shaker. Yum.*

Corn Picking

Although it is a bit of an oversimplification, from the consumer's standpoint it's safe to say that all corn can be divided into three types: traditional, sugar-enhanced, and supersweet.

Traditional varieties still grown and prized through much of the South include Golden Bantam for yellow ears and Country Gentleman, or Shoepeg, for white. Old-timers (and I include myself among them) like the straight-ahead corny taste of these older varieties when they can be bought and cooked on the day they were picked.

Of the sugar-enhanced varieties, the absolute most popular is the ubiquitous Silver Queen, a tasty white-kernel variety which has an excellent balance between corn and sugar flavors and, if refrigerated, will stay fresh-tasting up to three days from picking.

Supersweet varieties, being bred for the supermarket and long storage, purportedly will stay sweet up to two weeks but will lose moisture and tenderness in the process. I have little interest in these varieties, since the sugar overwhelms the fresh corn flavor.

Silver Queen and supersweet varieties are usually clearly identified as such in the market. To find older varieties, your best bet is to shop farm markets in season.

To pick fresh corn, you need to look at it, and no reputable vendor should mind if you pull back the husks at the tip to inspect an ear. The tassel can be either fresh or just turning brown, but not a brown, soggy mass. Kernels should be well formed and plump, although sometimes the ones at the end of the ear may still be small while the rest are fine and tasty—pull the husk down to be sure.

Don't take an ear that has visible signs of rot or insects. If you get home with an ear that has an isolated "bad place," you can cut it out with a sharp knife before cooking and still have an edible ear.

If I have to do other errands, I take a cooler to the farm market and store fresh corn and other produce in it, since even a short time in the heat of the car in July or August will damage corn.

Growing your own is the best way to experience the just-picked splendor of corn on the cob. The catalog for Southern Exposure Seed Exchange offers not only a full variety of heirloom and more recent hybrid seeds but good information on the qualities of each and how to grow them.

See Things to Order, page 338.

See Things to Order, page 338.

Roast Corn in the Shuck
SERVES 4

Corn roasted this way is the perfect side dish for a summer's supper of grilled burgers and hot dogs, and you don't have to steam up the kitchen with a pot of boiling water.

8 ears fresh corn in shucks
4 tablespoons butter
salt

Light the coals in the grill and let them heat up while you prepare the corn.

Gently pull the shucks back from the ears, without breaking them off. Remove the silk, rubbing the corn with a damp paper towel to get any stubborn pieces. Rub ½ tablespoon of butter over each ear. Pull the shucks back up to cover the corn and tie them with a small piece of twine, or make a small cap out of aluminum foil to close the top.

When the coals are glowing red hot, place the rack about 4 inches above them, and lay the corn across the rack. Grill for 25 minutes, turning every 5 minutes. Keep a spray bottle of water handy in case any of the shucks catch fire.

Set the corn aside while you grill burgers or other meats. The shucks will keep the ears warm. Pass salt on the side.

Note: *Some folks prefer to remove the silks, pull the shucks back up, and soak the ears in cold water for 20 minutes or so before grilling, then add the butter when the ears are cooked. This method is good and minimizes the possibility that any shucks will catch fire, but I think the flavor of the butter-roasted corn is superior. I also think unsoaked corn has a stronger grill taste.*

Removing the shucks altogether and wrapping the corn in aluminum foil is another technique for grill roasting, but the flavor is not nearly as intense as the grassier, smokier taste of ears roasted in the shuck.

Skillet Corn

SERVES 4

Called either fried or creamed corn, this dish was a summer staple and is actually preferred by many Southerners—myself included—over classic corn on the cob. That's because the natural creaminess of the corn is intensified in the cooking. I find it so rich that I can make a meal of this corn and sliced tomatoes alone, although I am happiest when supper also includes a pot of Classic Southern-Style Green Beans (page 56) and a platter of

fresh cucumbers and onion slices. I also think it is perfect for breakfast.

I am calling the dish Skillet Corn because both of its common names have now become associated with other dishes of poor repute. Some restaurants have started serving an abomination called fried corn, which consists of perfectly delicious fresh corn on the cob desecrated by dunking it in a deep-fat fryer full of hot oil. The result is chewy and flavorless, except for its fundamental fried-food taste. Creamed corn has come to mean the canned, super-sweet, viscous concoction available in groceries. This delectable dish holds no relation to either. It may, in fact, be the finest dish ever to come out of Southern country kitchens.

6 ears fresh corn
4 tablespoons butter or bacon grease
4 tablespoons half and half
salt
pepper

Cut the kernels from the ears and milk the cob according to the description on page 101. Melt the butter or bacon grease in a heavy skillet over medium-high heat. Add the corn and its milk, and stir to coat. Add the half and half. Cook, stirring frequently. If the corn begins to dry out, add milk or water, a tablespoon at a time. Don't add too much; the mixture should be thick, not soupy. If the corn is in danger of sticking or burning, turn the heat down.

Cook 8 to 10 minutes, until the kernels are tender but still fresh-tasting. Add salt and pepper to taste, and serve immediately.

Crabby Corn Pudding   SERVES 4

Charleston's John Taylor has a recipe in *The New Southern Cook* (Bantam Books, 1995) for a corn and crab pudding that is barely more than its two main ingredients held together by cream and a pinch of seasoning. It's heavenly, but the first time I made it, my husband, born and bred into Chesapeake Bay steamed-crab culture, smacked his lips and said, "Don't you think this needs a little Old Bay seasoning?"

A little Old Bay, some Tabasco, and a few other alterations later, we ended up with this spicier, cornier variation on a pairing that's classic throughout the South.

4 ears fresh corn
½ cup fresh crabmeat
2 tablespoons white cornmeal
¼ cup minced onion
½ tablespoon Old Bay seasoning, plus a
    dash for garnish
¼ teaspoon kosher salt
6 drops Tabasco
1 cup half and half

Preheat the oven to 350°F. Grease a 1-quart or slightly larger casserole dish.

Cut the corn from the cob and milk it (see below). Pick over the crabmeat, dis-carding any bits of shell. Mix all the ingredients together lightly, then pour them into the casserole. Sprinkle Old Bay lightly over the top. Bake for 35 minutes, until the pudding is firm. Serve warm.

"Milking" the Corn

Corn graters, which show up often in catalogs devoted to old-timey implements, were a godsend to the farm housewife faced with a massive harvest of corn that needed to be removed from the cob and put up in Mason jars for the coming winter. But my mother—and most Southern cooks getting a dozen or so ears of corn ready for frying or making into succotash—had nothing but scorn for this tool.

"It cuts too deep and makes the kernels too big," she'd say contemptuously. "Corn cut with that's not fit to eat."

Her way of cutting corn off the cob is now mine, and I'm convinced it's the best. She would hold each ear, point down, in a large bowl, then cut down with a very sharp paring knife, removing only the tips from each kernel. Then she would take a spoon and scrape it up the cob, using the edge to "milk" the rest of the corn and its juice from the kernels. If the cob was especially fresh and moist, she might then run her thumb down the cob again to squeeze out more juice.

The only change I've made in her technique came about when my daughter, Meghan, watched me getting splattered with corn milk one afternoon and said, "Why don't you turn the spoon over and scrape down the cob away from you so everything flies in the bowl instead of onto your apron?"

Progress!

Corn and Ajvar Custard
SERVES 4 AS A SIDE DISH

Corn is the perfect companion for many elements of Southern cooking: seafood, okra, and, of course, sweet bell peppers. Pimientos are not only delicious paired with corn, they are gorgeous—their deep orange an accent to the kernels' pale yellow. I've discovered that if you swirl a teaspoon of pimiento paste on top of a bowl of the simplest corn chowder, guests will "ooooh" and "ahhh" over your culinary skill.

It's simple to make your own pimiento paste, but recently I've started using ajvar, the Middle-Eastern spread of roasted red peppers, garlic, and eggplant that has lately become ubiquitous in gourmet stores that specialize in foods of the Middle East. Either will enhance this dish.

4 ears fresh corn
2 tablespoons butter
1 egg
½ cup milk
1 tablespoon all-purpose flour
1 teaspoon kosher salt
½ cup ajvar or pimiento paste (see Note)

Preheat the oven to 350°F.

Cut the corn from the cob and milk it (see page 101).

Put the butter in a 1-quart casserole and place it in the warming oven to melt.

Lightly beat together the egg, milk, flour, and salt. Add the ajvar, and stir to combine. Add the corn and stir.

Remove the casserole from the oven, and swirl the melted butter around carefully to coat the inside of the dish. Pour the extra butter into the corn mixture, and stir to blend. Pour the mixture into the casserole, and bake for 30 minutes, until the custard is firm. Serve warm.

Note: *To make your own pimiento paste, drain 4 ounces of jarred pimientoes or pimiento pieces. Add a teaspoon of minced fresh garlic and pulse in a blender until pureed.*

Shariat's Crawfish Corn Cakes with Smoked Tomato Sauce
SERVES 4

Chef Anoosh Shariat grew up as a vegetarian in Iran. For all of his professional life, he's worked in the Southern United States, first in Texas, and now as owner of one of Louisville, Kentucky's most innovative restaurants, Shariat's. (See Places to Go, page 341.) The South, he says, is where a chef who relies on fresh produce should be: "The vegetables you can get here, the fruits that are grown in the region, are so remarkable. The flavors are better than anywhere else, and there are so many regional styles of cooking you can draw from to prepare them."

This signature dish combines traditional Deep South corn cakes with Louisiana's sacred crawfish and a dash of spice from Texas. If you can't get fresh crawfish, substitute fresh crabmeat, picked over to remove any pieces of shell.

SAUCE
4 ripe tomatoes
3 cloves garlic, peeled
1 tablespoon olive oil
salt

CRAWFISH CORN CAKES
1 tablespoon finely ground white
    cornmeal
1 tablespoon all-purpose flour
1 teaspoon baking powder
¼ teaspoon ground red chile
¼ teaspoon ground coriander seeds
¼ teaspoon ground cumin
¼ teaspoon paprika
pinch of cayenne
2 cups fresh corn kernels
½ cup chopped crawfish tail meat
¼ cup finely chopped celery
¼ cup finely chopped red onion
¼ cup finely chopped green onion
¼ cup finely chopped fresh cilantro

2 eggs
olive oil for frying

Roast the tomatoes and garlic on a grill or under the broiler until the skin on the tomatoes bursts and the garlic is lightly browned and softened. Remove the skin from the tomatoes. Puree the tomatoes, garlic, and olive oil in a blender until smooth. Add salt to taste, and set aside.

Combine the cornmeal, flour, baking powder, and dry spices, and set aside.

In a mixing bowl, combine the corn, crawfish, celery, onions, and cilantro. Whisk the eggs lightly and add them to the bowl, mixing well. Add the flour mixture and combine. Set aside for 10 minutes before cooking.

When you are ready to cook, heat the olive oil in a wide nonstick or cast-iron skillet. Spoon the crawfish mixture into the hot skillet in portions about the size of golf balls. Flatten the balls slightly with a spatula, and fry on both sides until golden brown. (Don't crowd the skillet. Fry in batches, adding more oil if necessary.) Serve hot with the tomato sauce.

Real Cornbread   SERVES 8

This is the recipe for real cornbread the way my mother made it, and her mother and her mother before her. Accept no substitutes. Drippings are bacon grease or butter. If you are concerned about limiting saturated fats in your diet, you can flavor three parts canola oil with one part butter or bacon grease. You can also cut the amount of drippings in half without seriously damaging the cornbread, although the flavor will obviously not be so rich. But please note that in my family we do not serve additional butter with cornbread, the bread being rich enough already.

4 tablespoons drippings
2 cups finely ground white cornmeal
1 teaspoon kosher salt
½ teaspoon baking soda
½ teaspoon baking powder
1 large egg
1½ cups buttermilk

Turn the oven to 450°F. Put the drippings in a 9-inch cast-iron skillet. (Use an equivalent-size baking pan if you must, but if there ever was a reason to go out and buy a cast-iron skillet, Real Cornbread is it.) Place the skillet in the oven and let the drippings heat while you prepare the batter.

In a big bowl, mix the cornmeal, salt, soda, and baking powder. Add the egg and buttermilk, and stir until just blended.

The drippings should be good and hot, but not smoking, by now. Carefully remove the skillet from the oven and swirl gently to coat it with drippings. Pour the rest of the drippings into the batter. It should crackle and pop. (If it doesn't, don't worry; just leave the drippings a little longer the next time you make cornbread.)

Mix quickly and lightly, just to blend, then pour the batter into the hot skillet and put it back in the oven. Bake 20 to 25 minutes, until the bread is set in the middle, the edges are browned, and the top crust is golden. Serve hot, cut in wedges and lifted straight out of the skillet. If you prefer, turn the skillet upside down and let the cornbread slip out on a big plate—if your cast-iron is seasoned well, it will.

"If God had meant for cornbread to have sugar in it, he'd have called it cake."

That line began an essay I wrote for Esquire almost two decades ago, and later became the opening for the last segment of a play some friends and I did called "Kinfolks, Cornbread and Hillbilly Women." Called "The Tao of Cornbread," the piece compared the humble graces of great cornbread to those of growing up in Southern mountain culture. The piece also included the recipe for Real Cornbread (page 103), and when it was over, we never failed to have a half dozen or so audience members come up to tell us that was exactly the way they remembered their mother, or grandmother, or great-grandmother making cornbread.

One night a woman came up and said, "Now that is exactly how my mother made cornbread for us every night; only we didn't cut the cornbread into wedges at my house. No ma'am! My mother said, 'Breaking bread was good enough for the Lord Jesus, so it's good enough for us.' And she turned that pone out on a plate and passed it, and we just broke off a piece."

We were moved almost to tears by this

beautiful story. Then this lovely gray-haired woman leaned in conspiratorially and said, "Of course, I always held my hand like this (she held her hand up with fingers spread and curved in a wide claw) so I could get as much of that good crust as possible."

Perfect Fresh Corn Fritters

MAKES 2

Corn fritters have lately become the base du jour for a number of restaurant dishes, particularly tapas-like appetizers. They are a terrific concept, providing not only ballast for accompanying sauces and toppings but a wonderful sweet flavor of their own. Unfortunately, in execution I've often found restaurant fritters lacking—sweetened for no good reason, too floury, too spicy, or filled with old and therefore unpleasantly chewy corn. To find the perfect fritter, I've experimented with a number of combinations of fresh corn, meal, flour, and liquid, and finally decided that the formula here provides a cake which is pure corn in flavor, tasty enough to stand on its own, and subtle enough to combine well with other recipes.

You can increase the ingredients proportionately for up to four ears of corn. For more than that, make extra batches.

3 tablespoons finely ground white corn meal
1 tablespoon all-purpose flour
$\frac{1}{16}$ teaspoon baking powder
$\frac{1}{16}$ teaspoon baking soda
$\frac{1}{8}$ teaspoon kosher salt
$\frac{1}{2}$ cup buttermilk
kernels from 1 ear fresh corn
1 teaspoon bacon grease, peanut oil, or canola oil (see Note)

Blend the dry ingredients together. Add the buttermilk and stir just until mixed. Add the corn.

Heat the grease or oil in a wide, heavy skillet over medium-high heat, until very hot but not smoking. Swirl or use a spatula to spread the oil, evenly coating the skillet. Pour any extra into the batter, and stir.

Pour enough batter into the hot skillet to make cakes about 3 inches wide. Don't crowd the pan. Cook the cakes until the edges are solid and turning golden. Flip with a spatula, and cook on the other side until lightly browned. Transfer to a rack set over a pan in a warm oven until all the cakes are done. Serve hot.

Note: *I use either a well-seasoned cast-iron skillet or (when I am making more than one batch) a well-seasoned griddle to make these. Because of the seasoning, not much oil is needed to create a nonstick surface. If you are using a skillet that has not been seasoned, you may need to use more oil, but don't add more than a tablespoon of the heated oil to the batter.*

If you are unsure of your cooking surface, mix a little batter without the corn first, and fry a single cake to see if you will need extra oil.

Eugene's Savory Seeded Corn Pone

SERVES 4

While extolling the virtues of mustard seed as a seasoning in *Hints and Pinches*, Eugene Walter suggests you sprinkle some along with benne (sesame) seeds onto a thin batch of cornbread. I've been doing this off and on for some years now, trying several variations on the cornbread theme, and have decided that this one—with a very thin pone akin to mush—is absolutely the best.

You really must have a seasoned 9-inch cast-iron skillet to make this. (You really must have a seasoned 9-inch cast-iron skillet to live, so get one!) And you will need to have all your ingredients and gear ready when you start, since the recipe, while simple, must be prepared quickly.

The finished pone is a little rough around the edges, and that's part of its charm. Lift the triangular wedges out of the skillet with a pie server, serve it piping hot, and eat it with a fork. It does not need any additional butter at the table.

2 cups water

⅛ cup sesame seeds

1 teaspoon whole black or brown
mustard seeds

2 tablespoons butter

1 cup finely ground white cornmeal

½ teaspoon kosher salt

Preheat the oven to 450°F.

Put the water on to boil in a covered pot.

In a 9-inch cast-iron skillet over high heat, toast the sesame seeds, stirring or shaking the skillet constantly so they don't burn. When they just start to turn golden brown (after a minute or so), remove the pan from the heat and toss in the mustard seeds. (Stand back a little; the mustard seeds may pop.) Stir for 30 seconds, then transfer the seeds to a small, sturdy bowl, making sure they are all out of the pan.

Put the butter into the hot skillet and the hot skillet into the oven. Mix the cornmeal and salt in a heavy bowl. Slowly pour in all of the boiling water, mixing with a wooden spoon as you do. The mixture will clump together more like pie dough than a bread batter. Mix with a stirring and pressing motion of the spoon until all the meal is uniformly moistened.

Remove the skillet from the oven and carefully swirl the melted butter around to coat the inside. Pour about half the butter into the cornmeal and mix, leaving a good tablespoon's worth in the skillet.

Turn the meal mixture out into the skillet and, using the back of the wooden spoon or a metal spatula, pat and press the pone to fit the pan. The top and edges will be a little rough. That's fine.

Using the back of a clean wooden spoon, press the seed mixture against the sides of the bowl to crack some of the seeds, releasing more flavor. Then sprinkle the seeds as evenly as you can over the top of the pone, leaving about a half-inch margin around the rim. (This will keep the seeds from hitting the edge of the pan and burning during baking.) Use the clean wooden spoon or a spatula (or your fingers, if they aren't too sensitive and you are careful not to touch the hot edge of the pan) to lightly press the seeds into the batter to secure them.

Put the skillet in the oven and bake 18 to 20 minutes, until the pone is set and golden brown around the edge. Slice in 6 pie-shaped wedges and serve immediately. This is an excellent bread to serve with soups or salad, or to use with any recipe which calls for cornbread as an accompaniment.

MAIL ORDER

Fresh white cornmeal is hard to come by outside of the South, but there are those of us who will insist it is essential for making real cornbread.

One of the best-known and most beloved commercial distributors of flour and cornmeal in the region is the White Lily Foods Company of Knoxville, Tennessee. Their soft-wheat flour has no peer for making biscuits, and their cornmeal mixes—one with buttermilk, one without—are excellent. White Lily used to be available only south of the Mason-Dixon, and there are legendary stories of Southern chefs working in the North who would drive trunkloads of the products back after a trip home. These days, though, you can find the flour through many gourmet food sources, including the Williams Sonoma catalog; or you can order directly from the company. See Things to Order, page 338.

(Please note that White Lily's cornmeal products are self-rising, so when using them, eliminate the baking powder, baking soda, and salt listed in any recipe.)

There are also a number of small mills and granaries in the South which have excellent cornmeal and great grits available by mail order. You'll find some listed in Things to Order, which begins on page 338. One worth making a road trip for is the Nora Mills Granary in Sautee, Georgia, near Unicoi State Park in the Chattahoochee National Forest. The granary has been producing stone-ground products from its water-powered mill since 1876, and visitors can see the original equipment and get a quick lesson in the history of milling. There's an adjacent gift shop which also sells fresh-baked goods made with the mill's products.

Nearby Helen is a regional tourist attraction, a make-believe Bavarian village in the Appalachians. Visitors find the experience either truly charming or a little odd, but nestled among the faux-Alpine attractions in the town are some places where Appalachian mountain culture still holds sway. Betty's Country Store carries fresh produce out front, fresh baked goods in the back, and a century's worth of products—from jawbreakers to Moon Pies, pickled pig's feet to the *Farmer's Almanac*—in between. Mountain Valley Kitchen features country cooking, north Georgia style, including Nora Mills grits served daily. At Unicoi State Park, there is an annual Appalachian crafts show in February, and a standing display of quilts made by regional artisans, one of the largest in the country.

The mill is open year-round.

See Things to Order, page 338, for information on Nora Mills, and Places to Go, page 341, for interesting stops in Helen.

ABOUT

GRITS

True Grits

Grits Cakes

Mizithra Grits Casserole

Roasted Garlic Grits

"A ceremonial offering" is what John Egerton calls grits. He goes on to say, "Grits are an all-purpose symbol for practically anything of importance to Southerners. They stand for hard times and happy times, for poverty and populism, for the blessings and curses of a righteous God. They stand for custom and tradition, for health and humor, for high-spirited hospitality. They also stand for boiling, baking and frying."

I would be less than honest if I did not acknowledge that I, like many modern-day Southerners, did not come to a true appreciation of grits until later in life.

Although grits are assumed to be essential to the very definition of Southern cooking, the Grits Line actually cuts a course different from that of the Mason-Dixon. Up until quite recently, in most of Kentucky, east Tennessee, the westernmost parts of North Carolina, and Virginia, grits, while familiar, were not a common course at any meal, not even breakfast. Cornmeal mush, sliced and fried, was more likely to appear on your plate alongside eggs and country ham.

During the brief period in the 1970s when grits went global with the presidency of Jimmy Carter, it became de rigueur for the dish to appear at any Southern diner worth its biscuits and gravy. Unfortunately, the grits that were served—usually a quick-cooking variety still watery enough to ooze across the plate—were rarely palatable and certainly not inspiring.

In the last few years, true grits—stone-ground, slow-cooked, and judiciously seasoned—have become the American answer to polenta. Hardly memorable when served alone, grits are the perfect harmony singer, adding substance and a subtle taste of corn to numerous pairings, from fried eggs to robust roasted garlic. True grits now show up in great American restaurants from coast to coast, from Canada to Mexico. Versatile in application and a comfort to the soul, they should be a part of every good home cook's pantry.

True Grits   SERVES 4 TO 6

The recipe I used when I first began cooking grits required constant stirring over direct heat for ten minutes, then continued cooking, with occasional stirring, in the top of a double boiler for another thirty. This does produce foolproof, creamy grits, but I found the first ten minutes of attention often tempted me to forgo grits for something a little more carefree. Over time, however, I got a bit more daring, and soon discovered that it's possible to make an equally good pot of grits, with only occasional stirring, in a double boiler.

If you don't have a double boiler, you don't need to go out and buy one. You can improvise with a metal bowl or saucepan which nests securely on top of another pan without touching the boiling water in the pan below.

Grits can accompany any meal, in the place of mashed potatoes, and they are delicious topped by any sauce you would normally put on pasta. (Serve them warm, in a mound, with a nest in the top filled with freshly made pesto!) Plain grits are at their ultimate best served with an egg fried over easy, country ham, and red-eye gravy. Douse the grits with the gravy, then cut the egg up, and mix it into the grits. Take a small bite of ham with each bite of grits and egg. Oh, and don't forget the biscuits!

Leftover grits can be spread ½-inch thick on a lightly buttered baking sheet or pie pan, refrigerated, then prepared as Grits Cakes (page 113).

MAIL ORDER

In the process of trying to get them to cook more quickly and appear less, well, gritty, most commercial processors remove the germ and most of the gumption from grits. The end result is a bland, mealy mess on the plate. To make truly great grits, and find out what this Southern obsession is about, you need to start with an excellent product, and that means a bag of old-fashioned stone-ground white corn grits.

Several small mills around the South still process grits the way they ought to, but few commercial groceries stock such a specialty item. Some health food stores do carry grits (Arrowhead Mills is a reputable brand), but most often they stock the yellow-corn variety. Fortunately, stone-ground, white corn grits is an item you can mail-order easily, and there are several sources to choose from.

My favorite, and one which has proved most reliable through the years, is Hoppin' John's. Established in Charleston by cookbook author John Martin Taylor, this bookstore and Low Country specialty food shop is still operated by John's sister, Sue Highfield, who will cheerfully fill your order for a 2-pound bag of first-rate grits and also sell you some excellent cornmeal or a country ham, if you wish. Hoppin' John's also carries a line of delicious Low Country condiments and is a wonderful source for quality cookbooks. See Places to Go, page 341.

Another source for great grits is the Falls Mill and Country Store in Belvidere, Tennessee. In addition to grinding some of the best grits and cornmeal in the South, Falls Mill also has a museum, which showcases not only the traditional milling trade but also a collection of antique machinery, including nineteenth-century power looms and carding machines. There is an 1895 log cabin available for overnight guests. See Places to Go, page 341.

Adams Milling Company of Alabama produces "old-fashioned whole heart grits," which have won the hearts of many a Southern cook with their nutty flavor.

See Things to Order, page 338.

1 teaspoon kosher salt
4 cups water
1 cup coarsely ground grits

Bring the salt and water to a boil in the top of a double boiler over direct heat. At the same time, put water in the bottom of the double boiler and bring it almost to the boiling point.

When the salted water is boiling, pour the grits slowly into it, stirring as you do, to prevent lumping. Place the top of the double boiler over the bottom, and turn the heat up, so the water in the bottom is gently boiling. Cook the grits 30 to 40 minutes, stirring occasionally to keep them from sticking to the bottom of the pan. If the grits begin to thicken too much, add more boiling water, a bit at a time. When the grits are done, they should be creamy and thick enough that they won't run when placed on a plate, but not so thick that they "set up."

Serve warm with butter or gravy for additional seasoning.

Grits Cakes
SERVES 8

Pan-fried grits cakes were the perfect way to use leftover grits in traditional Southern kitchens; but in the restaurants of the New South, they have become what toast points were in the club cuisine of the 1920s. Smothered with wild mushroom ragout, garden-fresh ratatouille, sautéed shrimp and ham, tasso cream gravy, or another choice from what seems to be a limitless selection of inventions, grits sometimes lose their pure glory in the hoopla over what goes on top.

Not at the Metropolitain in Charlottesville, Virginia, which has one of the cleverest and most delicious menus in the New South (see Places to Go, page 341). There West Virginian Tim Burgess and his partner, French-born, Virginia-smitten chef Vincent Durquenne, prepare traditional regional products with a subtle attention to detail which enhances even the plainest dish. Their fried grits were the best I had anywhere in my travels through the South. When I asked Vincent for his secret, he was generous.

His best tip was his method of chilling the grits after they've cooked. Every recipe I'd ever encountered said to pour the grits into a loaf pan, regrigerate, and then cut into slabs for breading and frying. Alas, no matter how long I chilled them or what knife I chose for the cutting, the process never worked easily. The slabs would break into pieces and have to be patted back together, or would compress from the pressure of the knife and have to be patted into flatness for frying. The process was mildly frustrating and the end result, while tasty, would never have the ethereal texture I had hoped for, and finally savored at the Metropolitain.

The restaurant gets that texture by chilling the grits on a baking sheet or in a shallow pan, spread only about ½ inch thick. Voilà! The knife moves through the shallow grits, neither compressing nor breaking the slab. And it's a piece of cake to lift the slabs with a spatula into the dredging flour. What's more, you can cut the grits cakes in a variety of playful shapes, such as triangles; or even use straight-edged biscuit or deep cookie cutters to create whimsical patterns. As Vincent says, "Once you've got the recipe down, that's when the fun begins."

I've left many of Vincent's instructions in the recipe which follows, since they are often more clearly descriptive than traditional recipe prose.

5 cups water
1 cup stone-ground white grits
dash of white pepper
4 ounces butter, plus more for the pan
4 ounces white cheddar cheese, grated
salt
flour
peanut oil

Grease a shallow-sided baking sheet with butter.

Bring the water to a boil. Slowly pour in the grits, whisking as you do. Lower the heat immediately "or you redecorate your kitchen in grits," Vincent cautions. Stir in the pepper, and simmer over very low heat, stirring frequently, for about 30 minutes. (You can use the double boiler method described on page 111 if you don't want to stand constant watch over the grits.) The grits are ready, Vincent says, "when things start being pretty unctuous."

Add the butter and cheese, and stir until melted.

Add salt to taste, beginning with ½ teaspoon. ("There is nothing worse in the world than grits without salt," he says. "My cooks once forgot to salt the grits,

and I made them eat the whole panful that night, so they would never forget again. They never have.")

Pour the grits onto the baking sheet, and spread them out evenly, about ½ inch thick. Let them sit 10 minutes to cool. Cover tightly with plastic wrap, and refrigerate for 5 to 6 hours, until thoroughly chilled.

When you are ready to serve, cut the grits into rectangles, about 2 by 3 inches. Dredge each piece in flour, coating both sides and the edges.

If you are frying the grits in batches, turn the oven on, at very low heat, and arrange a rack over a pan to keep the first grits cakes warm and crisp while you fry the rest.

At the Metropolitain, they deep-fry grits cakes, but it is easier to pan-fry at home, and the results are equally delicious. In a heavy skillet, heat ¼ inch of peanut oil until very hot but not smoking. Use a spatula to gently lay the grits cakes, one at a time, in the oil, being careful not to overcrowd the skillet. Fry until you see the bottom edges turning golden, about 3 to 4 minutes. Turn them over, and fry the other side for 3 to 4 minutes, until golden also. Transfer to the warming rack in the oven until ready to serve.

Be sure to skim the oil after each batch, removing any grits or batter left behind. Add more peanut oil when necessary, to keep the level deep enough to come halfway up each grits cake, and be sure the oil reheats sufficiently after each addition. When all the grits are fried, serve immediately, since they do not keep or reheat well.

A few years ago, I met a woman in California who told me that once, when she found herself with a ridiculous surfeit of persimmon pulp, she and a lover filled an old bathtub with it and took what she described as "a highly sensuous double dip." I thought this might be the strangest food indulgence I'd ever heard—until I discovered the St. George, South Carolina, Rolling in the Grits Contest.

St. George calls itself the "Grits Capital of the World," and, as if serving grits with eggs, bacon, ham, and country-fried steak, topped with butter, catsup, peanut butter, or Cheez Whiz one weekend in April each year isn't enough to claim that title, locals revel—literally—in this singular, gritty competition.

About 400 pounds of instant grits are poured into a plastic swimming pool and soaked with water (really about the only truly *good* thing to do with instant grits). Each preweighed contestant gets ten seconds to hop in the grits, wearing a swim suit (knit is preferred for its excellent absorbency), and roll around, soaking up the atmosphere, as it were. When the contestants hop out, they are weighed again, and the one with the most grits adhering wins.

There are more conventional sights to be seen at the event, which is part of the town's annual World Grits Festival, including a parade and displays of grits grinding, and, of course, plenty of Southern specialties to go with the grits. The festival usually takes place during the third weekend in April, although the date fluctuates, depending on Easter. See Places to Go, page 341.

Note: *Vincent says, "Once you've mastered this recipe, you can do anything you want with it. You can add herbs at the end with the cheese, or you can cook the grits in country ham broth instead of water. If you want to do an influence, say Asian spices in the grits, that's the fun part. You can even put squid ink in, and make them black."*

Vincent told me that his most French interpretation of fried grits is when he mixes in foie gras. I told him that there is a classic Southern breakfast dish made not with grits, but with its kissing cousin, corn mush, and cooked chicken liver, ground to a paste-like consistency. "There you go," he said. "All great tastes end up being Southern."

"Thomas Jefferson came home from France so Frenchified that he abjured his native victuals."

Thus said Patrick Henry, who was Jefferson's political rival, and therefore not bound to stick to the truth when slinging mud, even of the garden variety. The truth is that Jefferson had a passion for the finer aspects of French cooking, but it was not one whit greater than his enthusiasm for the extraordinary products of his home. Virginia ham, turnip greens, black-eyed peas, crab, sweet potatoes, and juicy corn on the cob were but a few to grace his table. Jefferson combined the best aspects of each culture to set *a table with no peer in the new republic.*

It should be no surprise, then, that today in Charlottesville, just a few miles up the highway from the beautifully restored gardens and buildings of Jefferson's Monticello, one of the best young chefs plying his trade in Southern style is Vincent Durquenne, born in Paris and reared in Brittany.

"People ask me, 'What's a French guy doing in Charlottesville?' I say, 'I came here for a woman; I stayed for fried chicken.' "

Chicken isn't his only Southern passion. "The vegetables and fruits you can find here make me think of the best in Europe—often better. I love the black-eyed peas. I eat a plate of them and say, 'This is better than cannellini.' "

Durquenne's black-eyed pea relish tops delicate pecan-crusted and pan-fried trout to create one of the signature dishes (page 116) at the Metropolitain, the Charlottesville restaurant he owns and cooks at with his West Virginia–born partner, Tim Burgess. He sometimes seasons his exquisite fried grits cakes (page 113) with foie gras, or serves them as a gateau, layered with portobellos.

See Places to Go, page 341.

Mizithra Grits Casserole

SERVES 6 TO 8

It's impossible to imagine a Derby brunch or Mobile Mardi Gras buffet without a casserole of golden savory cheese grits at the center of the table. Classically, this dish is laden with grated cheddar cheese (up to a pound for 6 to 8 servings), butter, and cream. But as more and more distinctively flavored cheeses have become available throughout the South, clever cooks have used them to cut back on the quantity of cheese without sacrificing the quality of flavor. My favorite is hard mizithra, a tangy Greek whey-based cheese that is also naturally low in fat. If you can't find mizithra, substitute a good parmesan or romano, freshly grated.

6 cups water
½ teaspoon kosher salt
1½ cups stone-ground grits
¼ cup butter
2 cups freshly grated mizithra
3 cloves garlic, minced
3 large eggs
½ cup milk

Preheat the oven to 350°F, and lightly grease a 2½-quart baking dish.

In a heavy pan, bring the water and salt to a boil. Pour the grits slowly into the water, stirring as you do, to prevent lumping. Turn the heat down, so the mixture is at a slow simmer, and cook for 10 minutes, stirring frequently to prevent sticking. Remove from the heat, and add the butter, cheese, and garlic. Mix until the cheese and butter melt.

In a bowl, beat the eggs lightly with the milk. Slowly add about ½ cup of the hot grits to the egg mixture, whisking as you do. When the eggs are warmed, pour them into the pan of grits and stir well. Pour into the baking dish and bake for 50 minutes, until the grits are set and golden. Serve warm.

Roasted Garlic Grits

SERVES 4 TO 6

This recipe is just a little more trouble to make than standard cheese grits, but, oh my, is it ever a delicious side dish. And it's lowfat as well. Use it anytime you would normally serve mashed potatoes.

1 large head garlic
olive oil
4 cups water
1 teaspoon kosher salt
1 cup stone-ground grits
2 eggs
½ cup milk

Preheat the oven to 350°F.

Remove the loose outer skin from the garlic, then rub the head lightly with olive oil. Place it on a baking sheet, and bake for 30 to 35 minutes, until soft. Set aside to cool.

Generously grease a 1½-quart casserole. In a heavy saucepan, bring the water and salt to a boil. Slowly pour in the grits, stirring all the while to prevent lumping. Turn the heat down, so the grits cook at a simmer. Cook, stirring frequently, for 12 to 15 minutes, until the water is absorbed and the grits have softened some. Remove from the heat.

Remove the pulp from the garlic by lightly squeezing each clove. The roasted pulp will pop right out. Place it in a blender with the eggs and milk, and pulse until well blended. (Some of the garlic will be pulverized, and some will be in small chunks.)

Add the egg mixture to the grits, stirring constantly as you do. (The grits should be warm, but not so hot that they cook the eggs as they are added. If you suspect the grits are too hot, add about ½ cup to the egg mixture first, to warm it up, then add the eggs to the grits.)

Pour the grits into the casserole and bake for 50 minutes, until they are set and golden. Serve warm. Any leftovers may be chilled and fried the next day according to the recipe on page 113.

ABOUT GRITS

THE SPRING GARDEN

Benne-Coated Asparagus

Green and Gold

English Pea Shortcake

Spring Peas 'n' Lettuce

Sweet Peas and New Potatoes

While my memories of the plenty of summer vegetables and the harvest of the fall are vivid and rooted in my childhood, my appreciation of the delicious early offerings of spring came about when I was older. In part, I think this is because I grew up in the city in a time when the first and fleeting rewards of the garden hardly ever made it farther than the gardener's kitchen. We never got baskets of asparagus and fresh peas from our country relatives the way we received cucumbers, tomatoes, and green beans; and in the 1950s and early 1960s, neither made much of an appearance on the grocer's shelf. My formative experience with the canned variety of asparagus made a negative impression which wasn't eradicated until I was nearly grown.

I didn't have my first taste of fresh asparagus until I was in my early twenties, but I remember the moment well. A friend and I were clearing a long-unused garden plot at another friend's house in New Mexico, preparing to plant that spring. It was Polla Clare who came upon the wistful stand of new asparagus sprouting amid weeds, and she cried out in pure pleasure. It was nearly lunchtime anyway, so we squatted there in the sun and dirt, snapping stalks, then swishing them clean in the watering can and eating until we nearly foundered. It was one of the sweetest, purest tastes I'd ever encountered, and I've been a fool for fresh asparagus since.

So were the gardeners of the South, my early experiences notwithstanding. The early stands of asparagus and first crop of peas were prized for their unpredictability as much as their sweetness. Summers come on quickly and mercilessly in much of the Deep South, and spring crops are often abbreviated, even lost to heat and humidity.

Perhaps because of their rarity, little is done to either asparagus or peas in the kitchen, except for some simple techniques to enhance their natural flavor.

Benne-Coated Asparagus SERVES 4 AS A SIDE DISH

Benne, or sesame, seeds are used to season many fresh vegetables along the eastern shore of the South, but none pairs up so exquisitely as fresh asparagus.

1 pound fresh asparagus
salted water
1 tablespoon butter
3 drops green Tabasco, or other hot
   green pepper sauce
⅓ cup sesame seeds
salt
4 fresh lemon wedges, seeds removed

Rinse the asparagus well, and break off the tough ends by lightly bending each spear until it naturally snaps. Discard the ends and set the rest aside.

In a wide skillet, bring ½ inch of lightly salted water to a boil. Lay the asparagus in the water, let it return to a boil, and turn the heat down to a slow simmer. Cook for 8 minutes, then drain the asparagus in a colander.

Carefully wipe the hot skillet to remove any water, then add the butter. Melt it over medium-high heat. Add the Tabasco, and mix to blend, then toss in the sesame seeds and toast them, shaking the skillet gently but constantly, until the seeds start to turn golden.

Add the asparagus, sprinkle lightly with salt, and gently toss with a spatula to coat the spears with sesame seeds. Serve immediately, spooning on any seeds which didn't stick to the spears. Pass lemon wedges on the side, so guests can squeeze juice to accent to taste.

STeAMiNg ASPARAgUS

The first thing you need to know about fresh asparagus is that it must be washed, washed, washed before you cook it. The tightly wound petals at the top just love to clutch dirt. It takes an immersion or two in a sink of cold water, with plenty of swishing, plus a final rinse under running cold tap water before you can be confident the spears are grit-free. (It's a wise—and yummy—idea to nibble one raw, just to test.)

The lower part of the asparagus stem is tough and stringy, so you don't want to cook or serve that part. Cleverly, asparagus has a natural breaking point, just where the tough stem begins. To find it, hold the top half of a stem lightly with the fingers of one hand and use the palm of your other hand to gently bend the bottom. The stem will snap at the correct breaking point. Do this carefully a couple of times and it will become second nature, so you can snap through a couple of pounds of asparagus in nothing flat.

Some people are intimidated by the classic ritual of cooking asparagus standing on end, presumably so the stem tenderizes in the water while the petals steam to doneness without turning to mush. Pictures in magazines show orderly rows of stalks, gathered in military bunches and bound by that kitchen twine everyone else seems to have in their cupboard but I never do. Catalogs offer pricey metal contraptions for holding the stems in place, and even cunningly decorated tall and narrow pots to be used for nothing except steaming asparagus.

Here's a secret: It really doesn't make *that* much difference if the tops and bottoms cook in the same water for the same amount of time, as long as you don't overcook. Okay, so the culinary police are probably sending out a SWAT team right now to slap my hands and revoke my spatula, but I've been—shudder—cooking asparagus the wrong way for several years now, and enjoying every bite.

My favorite method is to cook spears lying on their sides in a skillet with a lid. This way I can use just enough water to immerse the asparagus, which can cook one or two layers deep. I salt the water lightly, bring it to a boil, lay the spears in, cover with the lid, and turn the heat as low as it will go. The asparagus simmers for about 8 minutes (a minute or two less for thin stems, a minute or two more for plump ones). Try it.

SPRING FLING

It was one of those gorgeous early April spring days which has you out and about, from dawn to dark, to absorb all the sunshine available. That's why I wasn't in to get my friend Cia White's call.

"I've got a cook's question," said the message she left on my machine. "Can you think of any reason on earth not to use lime juice instead of lemon when making hollandaise? Are you there? Okay, I guess I'll just find out."

"It was one of the most delicious things I've ever put in my mouth," she said when I called back the next day. "I can't tell you why it should make such a difference, but the lime added a whole undercurrent to the flavor, made it all the more complex. We ate it on everything."

Everything, in that instance, included steamed spears of the first crop of spring asparagus and tiny new creamer potatoes, cooked until just tender; but it could also mean peas, poke greens, or artichokes. Simply make your preferred hollandaise recipe, substituting an equal amount of freshly squeezed lime juice for the lemon.

Green and Gold — SERVES 4

This once-popular ladies' lunch item got its name from the pale green of asparagus spears sandwiched between the contrasting golds of toasted cornbread squares and creamy cheese sauce. You can make it, as many frugal cooks did, using leftover cornbread wedges spilt open, buttered, and toasted, but I think the graininess of basic cornbread somewhat overwhelms the delicate flavor of the asparagus. Instead, I prefer a very thin, very light corn pone, and a mild cheese sauce with a whisper of fresh nutmeg.

This recipe will serve four for a light lunch, along with a salad and fresh fruit, but I confess that my husband and I have no trouble at all polishing off the whole thing in one sitting as an early spring feast.

¾ pound fresh asparagus
2 tablespoons salted butter
½ cup finely ground white cornmeal
¼ teaspoon kosher salt
1 cup boiling water

SAUCE
2 tablespoons salted butter
3 tablespoons all-purpose flour
1 cup nonfat milk
1 cup grated mild white cheese
fresh nutmeg

Preheat oven to 450°F.

Rinse the asparagus well, and break off the tough bottom stems by lightly bending each spear until it snaps. Set aside.

MAIL ORDER

My editor swears to me she has seen genuine mountain ramps as far north (and citified) as her produce market in New York City. Well I'll be.

In the southern Appalachians and the Ozarks, ramps are the most celebrated vegetable in the spring harvest.

Used to be you had to go to the source to get this mountain delicacy, and if you didn't have kin to forage and fry for you, your best bet was to show up for one of the annual ramp festivals, such as the Ramp Convention the first Sunday in May in Waynesville, North Carolina. There you could sample this wild onion (a member of the lily family, though you wouldn't know it by smelling it) in meatloaf, scrambled eggs, and casseroles, or take it straight, sautéed, boiled, or deep-fried.

Ramp fanatics swear they are good for curing colds, and keeping your HMO happy by staving off a bunch of other ills. But it's as a culinary marvel that the ramp is most prized. Ramp lovers adore the flavor, although they don't necessarily agree on what that flavor is, or how strong.

"In truth, the pungent odor of ramps can peel bark off a tree," a 1973 editorial in the *Charlotte Observer* declared. Other writers have found it similar to the fragrance wafting from an occupied goat pen.

In 1978, Mimi Sheraton noted in *The New York Times* that ramps taste like a combination of garlic, leeks, and green onion, "without the sting but with a strong perfume that lingers on the breath." She also called them "those mellow, tender bulbs," which really stirred up the dander down in North Carolina. The *Charlotte News* columnist Bob Colver fired back a salvo in print saying, "Ramps, Ms. Sheraton, taste like a combination of goat sweat, sour milk and battery acid. If that's your idea of perfume, remind me not to get on an elevator with you. And ramps don't 'linger on the breath' either. They pitch a tent, build a cookfire and settle in for a week or two." It's worth noting that most ramp enthusiasts consider Colver's words a spirited defense of their beloved plant.

Take my word for it, or that of the thousand or so folks who flock to Waynesville each year: ramps taste real good.

To find out for yourself, you can go to Waynesville, or you can order from some of the folks who specialize in ramps.

Glen Facemire, Jr., and his wife, Norene, sell fresh ramps, in season, from their business called Ramps, From the Seed to the Weed, in Richwood, West Virginia, which we must tell you, after all this North Carolina talking, is the self-proclaimed Ramp Capital of the World. The rest of the year, the Facemires sell products such as ramp jelly and ramp salt, dried and pickled ramps, and ramp bulbs, seeds, and postcards.

From January until the ramps run out, usually by the end of May, Cherry River Food Land in Richwood, West Virginia, sells ramps at the store, ships them throughout the continental U.S., and serves them up in April at the annual Richwood Ramp Feed.

Meanwhile, back in North Carolina, Brevard, to be exact, Art Magraf has developed a line of gourmet ramp products including salad dressing, barbecue sauce, and a ramp-flavored vinegar.

For information on these products, see Things to Order, page 338; and on the festivals, see Places to Go, page 341.

Put the butter in a 9-inch cast-iron skillet or a baking pan and set it in the oven to melt.

In a heavy crockery or metal bowl, mix the cornmeal and salt, then add the boiling water, and mix to form a creamy batter. (You may need to add more water, a little at a time. The batter should be soft and spreadable, but not soupy.)

Remove the skillet from the oven and carefully swirl the melted butter to coat the pan. Pour the extra butter into the batter, stir just enough to mix, then turn the batter out into the skillet, using the back of a spoon to smooth it evenly to the edges. Put the skillet in the oven, and bake 12 to 15 minutes, until the edges are crisp and golden brown and the top is beginning to turn golden.

While the bread is baking, cook the asparagus by whatever method you prefer (see page 122) for 8 minutes, or until tender. Drain and leave the asparagus in the colander.

While the asparagus is simmering, make the sauce. Melt the butter in a heavy saucepan over medium heat. Sprinkle the flour over the melted butter and cook, stirring with a wooden spoon to keep it from burning, for 2 minutes. Slowly stir in the milk, whisking to keep lumps from forming. (If it seems as if lumps are forming anyway, remove the pan from the heat and whisk until everything is smooth, then put the pan back over the heat.) Stir constantly until the mixture begins to thicken somewhat, usually just a couple of minutes. Add the cheese, and stir until it melts. Remove from the heat and cover to keep warm.

When the cornbread is ready, turn it out of the pan onto a plate and cut it in quarters. Lay each piece on a plate, and cover it with asparagus spears. Top with cheese sauce and grated fresh nutmeg. Serve immediately.

English Pea Shortcake
SERVES 6

Thomas Jefferson had dozens of varieties of peas in his garden, and while historians suspect that some of them were, in fact, crowder peas, that's still a lot of English peas, as they are called in the South. While the variety of peas may be plentiful, there is really but one great way to cook them fresh out of the garden, and that is the method below. Peas cooked this way can stand on their own for a full meal, as far as I'm concerned, though most folks like to make them a side dish. One of the most delightful suggestions for serving them I've found came from Cissy Gregg, who'd read about pea shortcake in a cookbook by Haydn C. Pearson. While Mr. Pearson's pedigree was New England, your biscuits should be the Southern kind—made with soft-wheat flour (such as that sold by White Lily—see Things to Order, page 338) and rolled thin—for this recipe.

PEAS

3 pounds unshelled fresh peas
4 tablespoons butter
¼ cup water
salt
pepper

SHORTCAKE

2 cups soft-wheat flour
½ teaspoon kosher salt
1 tablespoon baking powder
¼ cup unsalted butter
½ cup milk

Preheat the oven to 400°F.

Shell the peas and set them aside.

Prepare the biscuits by sifting the flour, salt, and baking powder together in a large mixing bowl. Rub the butter in lightly with your fingers until it's evenly distributed. Add the milk and stir, or use your hands to mix it with the flour, until the dough sticks together easily and can be patted into a smooth ball. You may need a little more milk, or a little more flour, to get the right consistency. Be careful to use a light touch and handle the dough only enough to get it to stick together.

Turn the dough onto a floured surface and roll it quickly and lightly with a rolling pin to about ½ inch thick. Use a straight-sided biscuit cutter to cut it into 12 rounds. (After you've cut the dough once, you can lightly pat the scraps together and roll it out again for more biscuits.) Place the biscuits about ½ inch apart on a cookie sheet, and bake 12 to 15 minutes, until the tops begin to brown.

While the biscuits are baking, prepare the peas. Melt the butter in a skillet or saucepan with a snug-fitting lid. Add the water and, just as it comes to a boil, add the peas. Toss lightly with a spoon until the peas are coated. Cover and cook over medium-low heat for 5 minutes, shaking occasionally. Check the peas. If it looks as if the pot might boil dry, add a tablespoon or two of water. Cover and cook another 3 to 5 minutes, until the peas are tender. Add salt and pepper to taste.

As soon as the biscuits are ready, remove them from the oven and use a fork to break 6 open. For each serving, lay 2 biscuit halves in a wide soup bowl, and ladle hot peas over them. Serve immediately, with a warm whole biscuit on the side.

Spring Peas 'n' Lettuce
SERVES 4 AS A SIDE DISH

Marion Flexner's classic *Out of Kentucky Kitchens*, originally printed in 1949 and reprinted by the University Press of Kentucky in 1989, is a treasure, as much for its curiosities and lore as for its many delicious recipes. One which piqued my interest early on was a charmingly English-sounding technique for steaming peas with a lettuce cap.

Although the peas are steamed much longer than I thought prudent, and I couldn't quite imagine the point, I nevertheless had to try it, just for curiosity's sake. Mrs. Flexner advises that when peas, onions, butter, and seasoning are in place in a saucepan with water, the cook should then cover the whole with a small head's worth of lettuce leaves "sealing them in" to cook. I found that the fresh peas I prepared this way were, in fact, pretty tasty, and the fragrance as they, and the lettuce, steamed was simply delicious.

But it seemed a waste to cook all that lovely lettuce into total limpness and then discard it, as the instructions said. It seemed a double waste when I noticed later that the cooled leaves were stiff and saturated with the butter they'd absorbed during the cooking. So I adapted the concept to the recipe below, which still might charm Peter Rabbit, and will please contemporary eaters as well.

Because of the long cooking time, this recipe is better with peas from the grocer than with superfresh ones straight from the garden. Frozen peas are also good.

2 cups shelled fresh green peas
8 pearl onions
1 cup water
2 tablespoons salted butter
1 teaspoon sugar
½ teaspoon kosher salt
6 large leaves romaine or curly leaf lettuce
freshly ground black pepper

Rinse the peas and set them aside. Trim the ends from the onions and remove the outer paper skin.

In a saucepan with a lid, heat the water and butter over medium heat until the butter melts. Add the sugar, salt, peas, and onions. Turn the heat very low, cover, and simmer for 20 minutes.

Near the end of the cooking time, rinse the lettuce leaves well and slice them into pieces about 2 inches long and ½ inch wide. When the 20 minutes are up, stir the lettuce into the peas. Cover, and cook for an additional 10 minutes. Add pepper to taste, and serve immediately.

Note: *It was a lazy spring evening when I tested the final version of this recipe, and I really wanted to make a meal out of it and not much more. So I cooked up a half recipe of True Grits (page 111), adding a little half and half to the grits toward the end of the cooking time for some extra oomph. I filled a soup bowl about halfway with hot grits (a little over half a cup), then poured a cup of the hot peas and lettuce over that. It was* *heavenly, and my husband and I finished off the pot by ourselves.*

Sweet Peas and New Potatoes

SERVES 4 TO 6 AS A SIDE DISH

Every April of my childhood, after the first run of three or four warm days, there would appear on the corner of the block where I lived a young man selling daffodils from a galvanized tin bucket. He would be there in the afternoon when I came walking home from school, one bunch held out in his hand, thrust just into the lane of oncoming traffic, the rest clumped merrily at his feet.

The young man changed from year to year. My ritual didn't. "How much a bunch?" I'd ask, too shy to look at anything but his shoes and the yellow blossoms next to them.

"Quarter," he'd answer, bored as always.

"Stay right here. I'll be back in ten minutes."

I'd run home, afraid he'd be gone the moment my back was turned. I'd breathlessly burst into the kitchen, spinning some story to my mother about a special tablet I had to have for school the next day, or some such. I'm sure she knew better from the start, but after the first year, she knew the ritual, too, so would hand over a quarter with a smile just barely playing about her lips. I'd promise to look both ways before crossing the street to the drugstore, and burst out the door, on the run again.

The man was still there, of course, destined to his station until all his flowers were gone or rush hour ended, the latter inevitably coming first. Some years the sweeter boys would let me pick out my own flowers, and I could spend a good five minutes contemplating the identical blooms. One year, the soft-hearted vendor must have caught my look of disappointment when the bunch he pulled out for me looked sparser than usual. "Here," he said, pulling a second bunch, then a third from the bucket. "But don't tell any of your friends where you got 'em."

When I came home and pulled the flowers out from behind my back, my mother always feigned surprise. I know, though, that the thanks and love she expressed over my gift were genuine; and the delight we both took in this annual ritual, which marked the beginning of spring, is one of the sweetest recollections of my childhood.

When I was about ten years old, my mother began to give me a ritual gift back each spring. I had been to a friend's over the spring break and had been particularly taken with a dish her mother had served: chunks of ham with fresh peas and new potatoes in a thick, sweet cream sauce. I came home still moony over it, and my mother (who hardly ever used a written recipe herself, so didn't think to ask others for theirs) sat me down at the white porcelain table in the kitchen and had me reconstruct the dish for her from memory—quite possibly the beginning of my career as a cookbook writer.

I'm guessing now, some nearly forty

years later, that Evelyn's sauce was a béchamel made with the juices of the simmered ham and vegetables. What evolved in my mother's kitchen was a somewhat simpler dish, but one equally delicious.

To keep it light for spring, she eliminated the ham from the pot, and the flour from the sauce. Instead, she served this as a side dish with the first spring ham dinner, often for Easter. We used the butter rolls that came with the dinner to sop up every drop of the creamy broth. In time, we realized that the ham was superfluous, and this simple pea-and-potato dish became the centerpiece of a meal that my mother prepared for me every spring, even after I'd moved into a home of my own.

It's comfort food by taste and texture, for sure, but for me, the comfort it gives runs even deeper. If you serve it with butter rolls on the side, that will make it even better. If you have a clump of daffodils on the table, that will make it perfect.

1 pound shelled fresh green peas
12 new potatoes, no bigger than golf balls
6 to 8 pearl onions
water
¼ teaspoon kosher salt
2 tablespoons salted butter
2 tablespoons half and half
fresh black pepper

Put the peas and potatoes in a heavy saucepan. Trim the onions, remove their papery skin, and add them to the pot. Add water, just to cover, and the salt. Place over medium heat and cook, covered, at a lively simmer (do not boil) for 25 minutes, or until the potatoes are tender when tested with a cake tester or fork.

Add the butter. When it is melted, add the half and half, stir, and remove from the heat. Grind on pepper to taste, and serve immediately.

PLANT A RADISH, GET A RADISH

Those radishes bagged in plastic and sold in groceries year-round aren't good for much more than adding visual or textural interest to a tossed salad. Some, grown limp with age, aren't even very good at that. Never do they have the bite and brisk fragrance of fresh radishes pulled straight from the garden, and never do they seem to herald, as locally grown spring radishes do, a season just around the corner, full of crisp and succulent pleasure.

Good, crisp radishes were prized enough in my family to be eaten out of hand as a between-meal snack. My mother also sliced them thin and passed them around the table as a condiment, the perfect spark for beans or greens or roast beef. When she was a child, she told me, she and her cousin Cleta Mae would take cold biscuits out in the garden and pull spring radishes out of the ground to eat with them.

You can serve a more elegant variation on this tasty theme by making radish butter. Once common on Southern tables, this spread seems to have been forgotten; but surely it deserves a revival, especially now that there seems also to be movement back to late-afternoon English teas. Cooled biscuits, or sandwiches on white bread with the crusts trimmed off, are the perfect foil for this mildly spicy butter.

To make it, simply rinse, trim, and mince a radish fine. Mix with softened, unsalted butter—about a tablespoon of butter to each medium-sized radish—and spread. One tablespoon of radish butter will top six crackers generously. If you want to be even fancier, you can add a teaspoon of minced chives and a few drops of fresh lemon or lime juice.

ABOUT TOMATOES

Dothan, Alabama, Tomato Sandwiches

Blue Moon of Kentucky Tomato Sandwiches

Tomatoes Stuffed with Garden Egg Salad

Pepper Cheese Biscuits

Golden Gazpacho

Fresh Tomato Gravy

Meatless Tomato Gravy and Soup

Fried Green Tomatoes with Cream Gravy

Macaroni and Crowder Pea Salad with Charred Green-Tomato Dressing

Green Tomato Mincemeat Pie

Guy Clark sings, "Only two things that money can't buy. That's true love and homegrown tomatoes." Both are prized beyond reason in the South, and in the old days, when they were still referred to sometimes as "love-apples," it was suspected that the right tomatoes just might be able to fetch a person some of that true love.

These days, money actually can buy you "homegrown" tomatoes at roadside stands and farm markets, where the fabulously flavored and variously colored old varieties are coming back into fashion. These are tomatoes with descriptive or evocative names like Radiator Charlie's Mortgage Lifter, Mule Team, Dad's Sunset, Arkansas Traveler, Yellow Brandywine, Cherokee Purple, and Georgia Streak.

Summer garden tomatoes, grown locally, are often from heirloom seeds, passed down through generations because the fruits they produce have outstanding and highly distinctive flavors, ranging from a low-acid, rose-like sweetness to a lemony-tart tang. The colors can range from pale buttercup-yellow to a red so deep and dark it is almost purple.

Along with their pedigrees, some of the tomatoes have wonderful stories. Golden Ponderosa is a West Virginia heirloom whose seeds were traded by employees of the C&O Railroad, beginning at the turn of the century; Old German was a Mennonite heirloom passed from family to family in the Shenandoah Valley of Virginia, and Radiator Charlie really did pay off his mortgage in Logan, West Virginia, by selling his specially bred tomato plants at $1 each.

Tomatoes have even inspired a collection of poetry, assembled by Charlottesville, Virginia, writer/editor Mariflo Stephens. More than five dozen paeans to the plant are included in *Some Say Tomato,* by authors ranging from Pablo Neruda to Emily Morris, who wrote "A Tomato I Once Knew" when she was in the fourth grade in Knoxville, Tennessee. See Things to Order, page 338.

"One summer evening when I was pregnant and hot, I made myself a promise (to compile a book of tomato poems)," Stephens writes. "It was after a small dinner party at my friend Judy Longley's stone house in the country and I sat in her living room wishing for the glass of wine my pregnancy denied me. Judy asked if she could share a recent poem and began reading 'Cash Crop.' Listening to it, I was lulled into a state of transformation more complete than any glass of wine can manage. I was a child again, rummaging among tomato vines for some magic."

Magic is how I remember the tomatoes of my childhood. First the tiny tommy-toes my Aunt Johnnie let me eat still warm from the garden, each globe a perfect fit in my mouth, one bite of acrid-sweet love just for me. A few years later, in the city, I would sit on the back-porch concrete steps with my next-door neighbor's daughters. We would talk about our someday dreams and, as we talked, reach behind us to a washtub filled with tomatoes just picked "up in the country" and brought home. We'd rub them like apples on the edges of our seersucker shorts to loosen the flecks of earth that still clung to them. The first bite was all sweetness and secret pleasure at the cracking of the skin between the teeth. Then we would salt the juicy dent we'd made, using the glass shaker released from its duty in the kitchen for this summer night's tomato party. Bite and salt, bite and salt, until all that was left was the stem, to be tossed in the yard. More dreams. Then another tomato.

There is nothing better you can do with a homegrown tomato than to eat it out of hand, sitting on the porch and spinning dreams into a Southern night. The next best thing is to take a mess of tomatoes, all different colors and flavors, slice them thick, and arrange them gaily around a plate to be passed at a supper full of garden vegetables. After that, try the recipes which follow.

Summer Tomato Sandwiches, Now and Later

The absolutely best summer lunch is a fresh tomato sandwich, but its definition is a matter of personal preference. A few years ago, when *Southern Living* staff members were polled on what makes the best tomato sandwich, go-withs ranged from the classic (cucumbers) to the strange-until-you've-tried-it (peanut butter or potato chips).

The most descriptive "recipe" for a tomato sandwich in that issue called for "white bread, a very ripe tomato, mayo, salt, pepper and a *sink*."

But truly the most flavorful was the following recipe, handed down through generations of a Dothan, Alabama, family. The tomatoes are permeated with the aura of onion, but not its bite. They are so delicious that, although the recipe makes five sandwiches, the first time I made them, my husband and I polished off the batch in a sitting.

The only problem with Dothan, Alabama, Tomato Sandwiches is that they take more than eight hours from tomato picking to sandwich eating. Sometimes that is just too long to wait. For those days, I've gotten hooked on the second recipe, Blue Moon of Kentucky Tomato Sandwiches, which we traditionally have right after coming home from the local farm market on the first day really ripe tomatoes show. The market also features buttery mild garlic, grown on the Blue Moon farm outside of Winchester, and a really tangy, crusty sourdough bread. Combine these ingredients with a first-rate olive oil and you've got a great sandwich to eat *now*, standing over the sink, right before you slice the tomatoes and onions to make the Alabama sandwiches for later.

Tomato Party

White Beauty, Yellow Oxheart, Green Zebra, Eva Purple Ball, Pink Brimmer, Scarlet Topper: the flavors are as distinctive as the colors and names of the heirloom and specialty tomatoes becoming more commonly available at farm markets. Curious cooks want to try them all, but it can be a daunting task in a single season, even for the serious tomato lover.

One clever idea for getting a taste of plenty without letting any tomatoes go to waste is to host a midsummer Tomato Tasting Party. As with a wine tasting, the host invests in several varieties, then invites friends over to sample. Place slices of each tomato on a separate plate with a name tag, and take tasting notes so you can remember what you liked best next time you're at the market. Set out bread and the makings for tomato sandwiches so you can eat up the excess.

Sometimes when you find a tomato you truly love, you can't get enough of it at the market. No problem. Tomatoes are one vegetable which even the garden-thwarted seem able to grow. A splendid source for seeds for the old and flavorful varieties is Southern Exposure Seed Exchange, whose catalog not only contains full planting information and descriptions of fruits, vegetables, and flowers, but also often has stories about where the seeds originated and how they have been passed on.

See Things to Order, page 338.

Dothan, Alabama, Tomato Sandwiches　MAKES 5 SANDWICHES

1 large ripe tomato, peeled
1 large sweet white onion, peeled
10 slices white sandwich bread
3 tablespoons mayonnaise
1 tablespoon Dijon-style mustard
salt
pepper

Slice the tomato into 5 rounds and the onion into 6, all about ¼ inch thick. Layer them in a glass or ceramic dish, beginning and ending with onion. Cover tightly with plastic wrap, and refrigerate for at least 8 hours.

When you are ready to serve, trim the crusts off the bread, cutting the slices into circles equal to or just a little larger than a tomato slice. Combine the mayonnaise and mustard and spread it on each slice of bread. Discard the onion. Lay a slice of tomato on a slice of bread, add salt and pepper, and top with another slice of bread. Eat immediately.

Blue Moon of Kentucky Tomato Sandwiches　MAKES 3 SANDWICHES

1 small garlic clove
2 tablespoons olive oil
1 ripe tomato
6 slices crusty sourdough bread,
　　¼-inch thick
salt
pepper

Mince the garlic and whisk it with the olive oil. Set aside.

Peel the tomato and cut it into ¼-inch-thick slices. Spread each piece of bread with olive oil, including flecks of garlic. For each sandwich, cover one slice of bread with tomato. Salt and pepper to taste, then top with another bread slice. Eat immediately.

Tomatoes Stuffed with Garden Egg Salad   SERVES 4

Stuffed tomatoes were once a scrumptious Southern ladies' luncheon dish. Filled with salads of chicken, ham, or seafood, they were made with tomatoes so drop-dead ripe, you could eat them gracefully with a spoon. With the proliferation of apple-hard all-season tomatoes, however, this dish lost much of its charm. I think it's an entree well worth reviving when tomatoes are in season. This recipe features an egg salad which is more veggie-chunky, and therefore both crisper and healthier, than the kind we usually make for sandwiches. Served with Pepper Cheese Biscuits still steaming from the oven (page 139), this savory meal for four makes me want to play bridge again.

6 eggs
3 green onions
3 to 4 small inner stalks of celery, with leaves
1 small cucumber
4 tablespoons mayonnaise

2 teaspoons Dijon-style mustard
¼ to ½ teaspoon minced fresh dill weed
1 teaspoon fresh lemon juice
salt
freshly ground pepper
4 medium-large ripe tomatoes
lettuce leaves
parsley, for garnish

In a saucepan, cover the eggs with cold water and bring to a boil over high heat. Cover the pan snugly, remove from the heat, and let the eggs steep for 15 minutes, then drain and plunge them in cold water.

While the eggs are steeping, mince the green onion, using both green and white parts. Mince enough of the celery and leaves to make ½ cup. Peel the cucumber and halve it lengthwise. Remove the seeds with a spoon, then mince. Set aside.

Peel the eggs, slice them in half, and remove the yolks to a bowl. Mash the yolks lightly with a fork. Add the mayonnaise, mustard, dill, and lemon juice, and mix well. Chop the egg whites into small pieces, and add them and the vegetables to the yolk dressing. Mix together, and add salt and pepper to taste.

Rinse and dry the tomatoes; cut out the stems, but don't peel. Use a sharp knife to *almost* quarter each tomato vertically, but don't cut through all the way, so the sections still hold together.

When you are ready to serve, lay lettuce leaves on four plates. Place a tomato on each, and fan the sections open to make a cup. Spoon in egg salad. Garnish with parsley, and serve with hot biscuits.

Pepper Cheese Biscuits

MAKES 12

The red pepper in these biscuits doesn't really stand out but acts more as an undercurrent to the cheese flavor.

1 cup soft white flour, plus some for rolling the biscuits
½ teaspoon baking powder
¼ teaspoon baking soda
¼ teaspoon kosher salt
¼ teaspoon ground cayenne or red chile pepper
2 tablespoons cold, unsalted butter
½ cup grated sharp cheddar cheese
½ cup buttermilk

Preheat the oven to 425°F.

In a large bowl, blend the flour, baking powder, soda, salt, and pepper. Cut the butter into small chunks. Using your fingers, lightly rub the flour and butter together until the mixture is meal-like. Add the cheese, and mix. Pour the buttermilk into the center, and with your hand quickly fold it in until the flour mixture is just moistened and the dough can be patted into a ball.

Turn the dough out onto a lightly floured flat surface and, using quick, light motions, roll it to a little less than ¼ inch thick. Use a 2½-inch biscuit or cookie cutter with straight sides to cut out rounds. Pat together the excess dough, roll it out, and cut again until all the dough is used.

Place the biscuits on an ungreased cookie sheet and bake 15 minutes, until the bottoms are lightly crusted and the tops are just turning golden. Serve warm.

Tomatoes with cucumbers. Tomatoes with okra. Tomatoes with corn, on grits, in Creole sauce. In the South, tomatoes go with just about everything. Why, heck, there's even a recipe for tomato chocolate cake. But one place tomatoes do not go is into any recipe for eastern North Carolina barbecue sauce. Swabbing hickory-smoked pork in vinegar seasoned liberally with pepper (and possibly even a few nontomato secret ingredients) is a religious ritual in that part of the state, where folks will not tolerate apostasy. Writer Tom Wicker calls "the iron law of barbecue" these words posted on the wall of a Maryland barbecue place owned by a transplanted east Carolinian: "We don't hold with tomatoes."

Golden Gazpacho

SERVES 6 AS AN APPETIZER SOUP OR SALAD

Gazpacho has been a Southern staple since at least the beginning of the 19th century. Somewhere between a cold soup and a salad, this dish has many regional interpretations, including a classic Pensacola rendition which uses soaked hardtack and includes mayonnaise.

One recent and delectable trend among

restaurateurs is to use grill-roasted tomatoes and peppers in the dish, adding another dimension of smoky flavor. The low acid of the yellow tomatoes and the sweetness of yellow peppers in this version make for a subtle difference in taste, as well as a dramatic one in color. You can also roast the tomatoes in a hot oven, and grill the pepper under the broiler, but the flavor is not quite so memorable.

Because the tomatoes roast at the edge of the grill, you can grill them and the pepper a day ahead, while cooking that day's meal on the rest of the grill.

4 ripe yellow tomatoes
¼ cup extra-virgin olive oil
1 small clove garlic, minced
1 large yellow bell pepper
1 small sweet white onion, chopped
1 medium cucumber, peeled and
   chopped
salt
black, lemon, or cayenne pepper
1 cup white bread crumbs
1 lime

Choose tomatoes with wide, somewhat flat bottoms, so they will sit upright on the grill. Remove the stems and use a knife to dig a small well, about as big around as your thumb, ¾ of the way down inside each tomato. Mix the olive oil and garlic, and spoon it equally into the wells. Set aside.

Light some coals in a small grill with a cover, and let them burn until the flames have died down and they are covered with light ash, usually 30 to 40 minutes. Set the tomatoes around the edges of the grill, and cover. Roast for 10 minutes. Uncover and turn the tomatoes with tongs, so the part which has been nearest the rim of the grill is now toward the center. Grill uncovered for 10 minutes more.

While the tomatoes are roasting uncovered, lay the whole pepper over the hottest coals and roast, turning it several times, until the skin is blistered and blackened all over. Place it in a paper bag and set aside.

Remove the tomatoes from the grill and let them come to room temperature. When they can be handled, turn each tomato upside down over a bowl and allow any juices to run out. Rub off the skin, chop the tomatoes coarsely, and add them to the bowl.

Remove the pepper from the bag, rub off the skin, and discard the stem, seeds, and white membrane inside. Chop the pepper and mix it with the tomatoes, onion, and cucumber. Add salt to taste. Add whichever pepper you prefer (lemon pepper will give the dish a brighter, more citrusy tang, while cayenne will make it hot).

Cover well and refrigerate for 2 hours, or overnight. When you are ready to serve, add the breadcrumbs and a generous squeeze of fresh lime juice. Toss lightly to mix.

Fresh Tomato Gravy
MAKES ABOUT 2½ CUPS

This country-kitchen staple is ridiculously simple to prepare, and so delicious it could have been the inspiration for that old saying "Tastes good enough to make your tongue so happy it'll slap you senseless."

Folks used fresh tomato gravy just like they would regular gravy—as a sauce on meats, poured over biscuits or a slice of cornbread, on grits, and with mashed potatoes. Add about two cups of cooked rice to it and you have red rice, or Spanish rice, a popular side dish. It's also wonderful as a sauce for many fresh vegetables that have been steamed or roasted; and it's quick and sublime on pasta.

4 pieces thick-sliced bacon (about ¼ pound)
½ cup chopped sweet white onion
2 cups peeled and chopped ripe tomatoes, with juice
salt
pepper

In a wide skillet, fry the bacon over medium heat until crisp. Remove to a paper towel to drain. Pour off the bacon grease, leaving about 1 tablespoon in the pan.

Sauté the onion in the bacon grease over medium heat for 1 minute. Add the tomatoes and juice. Cook, stirring frequently to keep the mixture from sticking. When the tomatoes begin to bubble and the gravy thickens, remove from the heat.

Salt and pepper to taste. Serve over biscuits, meat, or vegetables with the bacon crumbled on top.

VARIATION: *For a meatless variation on this theme, and instructions on how to turn either gravy into a delicious fresh tomato soup, see the next recipe.*

Meatless Tomato Gravy and Soup
MAKES ABOUT 2½ CUPS

The tang of bacon in classic tomato gravy is replaced in this meatless version by flavorful dried porcini mushrooms, reconstituted then cooked in butter. Look over the porcinis after soaking to make sure you're not getting any twigs or bits of earth. If the soaking water is gritty, strain it before adding it to the gravy.

¼ cup dried porcini mushrooms
¼ cup very hot water
2 tablespoons butter
½ cup finely chopped onion
2 cups fresh or canned peeled tomatoes, with juice
salt
pepper

Cover the mushrooms with the hot water and let them steep for 10 minutes. Lift the mushrooms from the water, squeeze them very lightly, and chop both stems and caps fine. Set both water and mushrooms aside.

ABOUT TOMATOES

In a skillet over medium heat, melt the butter and sauté the onion for 2 minutes. Add the mushrooms and sauté for 2 minutes more. Add the tomatoes and the mushroom-soaking water and heat until the mixture begins to bubble. Stir and cook for a minute or two more, until the mixture has thickened to the consistency of gravy. Add salt and lots of freshly ground pepper. Serve immediately.

VARIATION: *Fresh tomato gravy is also the base for a quick homemade tomato soup, created simply by adding ¾ cup milk and ¼ cup half and half to this or the previous recipe. Make sure you heat the milk and half and half before adding them to the tomato mixture. If you heat them all together, you risk curdling the milk. That won't affect the taste, but it is less appetizing in appearance.*

Fried Green Tomatoes with Cream Gravy   SERVES 4

Many years ago, at his first summer supper with us, my sister's brand-new husband startled the rest of the family when he poured cream gravy over bright red slices of ripe tomato. We found it odd enough to tease him good-naturedly, until we noticed that he hardly seemed to care about our jibes at all, and had a smile of serene satisfaction on his face as he ate. So, slowly, one after another, we each slid a bite of tomato over into the gravy on our plates and tried it. Delicious! It became a sometimes treat I still savor—especially at summer breakfast.

Thinking back, I wonder why we thought the combination of gravy and fresh tomato was odd, since we ate our fried green tomatoes smothered with gravy anytime they were served—and that was just about anytime my mother could get them in the market or from a generous gardening neighbor. It occurs to me that we simply didn't think of those crisply golden discs of green tomato as a vegetable. No, they were the centerpiece, the entree, as meaty and satisfying as the pork or beef or chicken they replaced.

These days, I sometimes serve green tomatoes as a side dish, and when I do, I usually dredge them in buttermilk and seasoned corn flour, then fry them in peanut or canola oil, for a treat that is somewhat healthier than the way my mother made it. But my mother's method is what I use when the green tomatoes are the centerpiece (sometimes the only piece) of an evening's meal, and when good gravy, seasoned with bacon grease, is part of the object of the game.

Fried green tomatoes can anchor a meal. They go with any number of other vegetable dishes, and are especially good with fresh butter beans. Feel free to serve sliced red tomatoes also, and if a little of the gravy gets on a slice, well, give your thanks to my brother-in-law, Dave.

Pick green tomatoes that are full-sized and feel a little moist inside, not rock-hard. Very firm tomatoes just starting to turn pink in places are good as well.

3 large green tomatoes
1 cup all-purpose flour

1 teaspoon kosher salt

¼ teaspoon freshly ground black pepper

1 large egg or ½ cup buttermilk

approximately 8 tablespoons bacon grease

1 cup milk, room temperature

Rinse the tomatoes, cut out the stems, and slice them a little more than ¼-inch thick. In a shallow bowl, mix the flour, salt, and pepper. Put the egg, whisked until lightly beaten, or the buttermilk in another shallow bowl.

Put a skillet over medium heat and add 3 to 4 tablespoons of bacon grease, enough to be about ⅛ inch deep when melted.

Dip each tomato slice in the egg or buttermilk, turning it to coat both sides, then dredge both sides in the flour. Handle the slices gingerly so that your fingers don't remove the coating.

When the bacon grease is hot but not smoking, carefully place the coated tomato slices in it (use a spatula to protect your fingers), and fry over medium heat until golden on both sides, turning only once. Don't crowd the slices in the pan. Fry in batches, adding bacon grease, to keep it at the same level, after each batch, and making sure the grease is very hot, but not smoking, before you put the slices in.

Drain the slices briefly on paper towels, then transfer them to a rack over a pan in a warm oven until all the slices are fried and the gravy made.

To make the gravy, after the last batch of tomatoes is fried, turn the heat to low and scrape the bottom of the pan with a metal spatula to loosen any crust. Sprinkle 1 tablespoon of the seasoned flour into the warm drippings and cook on low, stirring, for about 1 minute, until the flour is nicely browned.

Slowly pour in the milk, stirring all the while to prevent lumping. (It is sometimes necessary to use a wire whisk to stir away persistent lumps. Remove the pan from the heat while you do.) When the gravy is smooth, turn the heat up to medium-high and cook, stirring constantly, as it bubbles and thickens. It will take a minute or two to come to the desired thickness. As soon as it does, transfer it to a warm pitcher or bowl and serve immediately with the warm green tomatoes.

Macaroni and Crowder Pea Salad with Charred Green-Tomato Dressing

SERVES 4 AS A MAIN DISH, 6 TO 8 AS A SIDE DISH

In the summertime, black-eyed and other crowder peas show up in a variety of cold salads or relishes, the most popular being a vinegar-dressed, pepper-speckled melange known, among other names, as Texas, Louisiana, or Alabama Caviar. This salad, though, is made with a tangy, creamy dressing based on charred and blended green tomatoes. It's substantial and satisfying enough to serve as a summer supper on its own, with a pan of Eugene's Savory Seeded Corn Pone (page 106) and Southern Iced Tea with Lemon (page 264) or, if you want to do this truly Southern-style, cold butter-milk.

Any crowder peas may be used, fresh, frozen, or dried, just so long as they are cooked to the very tender stage.

DRESSING
1 large green tomato (or 2 small)
1 garlic clove, minced
¼ cup olive oil
½ cup nonfat plain yogurt
¼ teaspoon kosher salt

SALAD
2 cups cooked crowder peas
1 celery rib, chopped fine
1 large green onion, chopped fine
4 cups macaroni, cooked al dente, still
    warm

Prepare the dressing first. To char the tomato skin, insert a fork in the green tomato at the stem end and hold it over an open flame, turning it as if you were roasting a marshmallow. When the skin has charred and blistered all around, it will rub off. (If little bits of skin are left on, don't worry; it will just add to the flavor.)

Remove any hard core at the stem end, quarter the tomato, and place it in a blender with the other dressing ingredients. Puree until smooth.

In a large bowl, combine the peas, celery, onion, and macaroni. Add the dressing and mix well. Cover tightly and refrigerate for 2 hours.

peeling tomatoes

One late September afternoon, I drove over to the neighborhood fruit market to pick up a single red ripe tomato for BLT sandwiches for supper that night. Just inside the door sat a bushel basket, brimming over with the last harvest from the owner's tomato plants.

"I'll give you the whole thing for ten dollars," he said as he saw me kneel down and start to pick through the variously sized, oddly shaped bounty, looking for that one tomato that was mine. I had a ton of other things to do and, although it was a bargain, looked his gift horse right in the mouth and said, "No, thanks."

"Okay," he said as I headed to the back, where he keeps the lettuce, "I'll give it to you for five dollars." He must have seen me waver, because he jumped right in with what he thought was the kill. "Two bushels. Two bushels for five bucks. I've got another one just like it right in the back."

Now this almost scotched it, because even though I'd begun to think I was a fool not to give up an hour to deal with a bargain bushel of tomatoes, the thought of double that nearly overwhelmed me. So we proceeded to haggle, him insisting I must take the second basket for my five, me equally insistent that I'd buy only the one. I left triumphant, five dollars shorter and toting only one basketful of tomatoes to the car.

Back in my kitchen, I set up a quick assembly line: on the stove, my big stainless-steel stockpot full of water. In one of the double sinks, a half foot of water and all the ice cubes from the freezer. When the water in the stockpot started a lively boil, I tumbled ten or so tomatoes into a wide, long-handled metal colander and immersed it in the pot. I counted to ten slowly, lifted the colander and tomatoes out of the pot, dumped the tomatoes in the ice water, then did another batch.

I moved each ice-water batch to the empty sink next to it as I added another. The hot/cold bath shocked the tomato skins so they slipped right off in my hands. I cut out the stems and any bad spots, and popped the whole tomatoes into heavy-duty freezer bags. Tightly sealed, each filled bag went straight into the freezer.

I was done in what my mother would have called "no time," actually just under an hour. For that hour's work and $5, we had fresh tomatoes for making pasta sauce, soups, stews, and casseroles straight through February. Midway through February, when I pulled the last tomatoes from the freezer to make a batch of Fresh Tomato Gravy (page 141) to spoon over stone-ground grits, I sighed. Sure wished I'd taken that second bushel.

Green Tomato Mincemeat Pie

SERVES 8

Green tomato pies, with a taste as tart as green apples but a creamier texture, were favorites in the South. They can be made simply by substituting sliced green tomatoes for sliced apples in your favorite apple pie recipe.

My friend and fellow food writer Sarah Fritschner discovered that green tomatoes are also the perfect foil for apples in a meatless mincemeat concoction. This is her recipe; it makes 4 to 5 quarts of the savory stuff, enough for several pies. The mincemeat alone is also quite marvelous served as a compote alongside meats, soup beans, or several of the butter bean or crowder pea recipes in this book.

GREEN TOMATO MINCEMEAT
2 quarts cored green tomatoes
1 tablespoon kosher salt
1 orange
1 lemon
2 quarts peeled and chopped apples (or apples and firm pears)
1 pound raisins
½ cup butter, melted
3½ cups brown sugar
¼ cup apple cider vinegar
2 teaspoons ground cinnamon
1 teaspoon ground nutmeg
1 teaspoon ground cloves
1 teaspoon ground ginger
1 teaspoon ground allspice

Chop the tomatoes into pieces about the size of raisins—use a food processor, if you wish. Combine them with the salt in a colander, and place it in the sink to drain for an hour.

Meanwhile, rinse the orange and lemon, cut them open and remove the seeds, but leave the peel. Mince, again using a processor if you wish. Combine the citrus in a large, nonreactive pot with the apples, raisins, butter, sugar, vinegar, and spices.

When the tomatoes are finished draining, rinse them and press them firmly, then add them to the pot. Bring the mixture to a boil over high heat, stirring, then turn the heat to low and simmer—usually an hour or more—until as thick as commercial mincemeat. You will need to stir often, more frequently at the end, to keep it from sticking. (The cooking time varies, depending on how moist the ingredients are at the outset.)

When the mixture is appropriately thickened, cool and use it to make pies, or put it up in glass jars and refrigerate until ready to use. Makes 4 to 5 quarts.

PIE
pastry for double-crust 9-inch pie
4 to 5 cups mincemeat
½ cup bourbon or other spirits (optional)
½ cup chopped pecans

Preheat the oven to 425°F.

Line a 9-inch pie pan with half the pastry. Mix the mincemeat, spirits, and pecans, and fill the crust. Cover the pie with a top crust, and slash air vents in it. Bake for 15 minutes, then reduce the heat to 350° and bake for 30 minutes more, until the crust is nicely browned. Allow to cool some before cutting, but serve warm. A scoop of vanilla ice cream is delicious on top.

CUCUMBERS AND MELONS

Gregg's Freezer Pickles

Cucumber Mousse

Zippity Honeydew

Watermelon Salsa

In the colonial South, cucumbers were planted in the watermelon patch, their shared preference for well-drained soil and long, hot summers making this a perfect pairing. The tradition continues in some contemporary Southern gardens, but I have paired cucumbers and melons here because that is how I best remember them coming to our summer supper table.

The fresh green, viny scent of both filled the kitchen with the heady assurance that summer had really, truly arrived. Cucumbers showed up first, I'm sure, their time to maturity being so much quicker, particularly the short, crunchy cukes my family favored for growing, pickling, and eating.

It would not be long after, however, that the first ripe cantaloupe or super-sweet honeydew would be ready as well. My mother did nothing except slice these garden treasures and pass them around on plates, refreshers between bites of the slow-simmered summer vegetables that filled the other bowls on the table.

When tomatoes were perfectly ripe, she would cut a juicy red one into chunks, then peel a cucumber and do the same. These she would toss with smaller chunks of sweet white onion and add only salt to dress it. It's still my—and my daughter Meghan's—favorite salad.

Melons were eaten as either vegetable or dessert. I come from a long line of melon salters. It's a technique I subscribed to myself for an early year or two, but stopped once I got a bite of unadulterated, sugary watermelon. Nevertheless, the taste for something both sweet and briny persists, and the recipe for watermelon salsa here satisfies it well.

Although I will buy, on occasion, long and waxy supermarket cucumbers in the dead of winter, longing for the taste and crunch in salad, they cannot compare to the "pickling" cucumbers we get in season. Never more than six inches long, not much more than an inch around, and nubby-skinned, they are not waxed and almost never require peeling. I like to eat them dipped in salt as a midday snack. We can never seem to get enough, no matter how late the summer lasts. Gregg Swem's freezer pickle recipe (page 152) assures that we can have their brisk bite all winter.

There is little you can do to improve on the perfect flavor of melon, but it is important to know how to pick a good one. Melons which are heavy for their size are riper than those which feel hollow or light. Always scan the surface of any melon, rejecting those with bruises, soft spots, or cuts. There should be a clean break at the stem end; a cut stem indicates the fruit was cut from the vine before full ripeness. And melons, such as cantaloupe, that have an indentation at one end must pass the sniff test. Smell the indentation. If you get a sweet, clean melon scent, you're set. If the spot smells green and grassy, the melon isn't ripe yet. If it's winey, or musky, it's probably too ripe. If it's a honeydew and the skin feels tacky, that's an indication of sweetness.

Gregg's Freezer Pickles

MAKES ABOUT 1 QUART

My friends Gregg Swem and Wade Hall have a backyard garden just up the street, which I admire all summer long as I walk the dog past. When I took them fried pies last March, little did I guess I'd get the blessings of that garden in return. Come August, Gregg handed me a plastic container filled with the most delectable slivered pickles I've ever eaten. Sweet as bread-and-butters, but twice as fresh and crunchy, these freezer pickles are as simple to make as they are scrumptious.

Use homegrown or farm-market cucumbers which have not been waxed, since the peels are essential both for looks and taste. Eight cucumbers about 6 inches long should be enough.

4 cups cucumber slices, paper-thin
water
2 tablespoons kosher salt
1½ cups sugar
½ cup white vinegar

The thinner you can slice the cucumbers, the better. Don't peel them; don't remove the seeds.

Arrange the slices in a large crockery mixing bowl (don't use metal or plastic).

Measure out enough water to cover them, combine it with the salt, and add it to the bowl. Soak at room temperature for 2 hours. Drain, but don't rinse.

Dissolve the sugar in the vinegar. Pour it over the cucumbers and lightly mix. Put the cucumbers and brine in a clean freezer container. (If you use two or more small containers, divide the brine evenly.) Cover tightly and freeze. (This is how they become crisp.)

The pickles will thaw in a couple of hours at room temperature, or overnight in the refrigerator. Refrigerate any leftovers.

Cucumber Mousse

SERVES 10

Although it takes a lot of effort to improve on the basic goodness of cucumber sliced and chilled, Southern cooks have been willing to go the distance to try. One of the most delectable creations to appear at afternoon luncheons is the cucumber mousse, a pale and shimmering chilled concoction of fresh grated cukes, gelatin, and something white and very creamy to bring it all together.

1½ cups nonfat plain yogurt
2 cups water
2 envelopes unflavored gelatin
minced zest and juice of 1 lime
2 cups peeled and grated cucumber (6 small)
1 tablespoon minced fresh dill weed
½ teaspoon kosher salt
½ cup mayonnaise

Drain the yogurt for 1 hour in a cheese-cloth-lined colander or through a paper coffee filter in a cone or strainer.

Very lightly oil the inside of a 1½-quart gelatin mold.

When the yogurt is ready, put 1 cup of cold water in a large bowl and sprinkle the gelatin over it. While it's softening, bring another cup of water to a boil. Pour the boiling water over the gelatin and stir until it is all dissolved. Add the lime zest (but not the juice).

Mix the cucumber, dill, salt, and lime juice into the gelatin. Fold in the yogurt and mayonnaise, and stir to blend. Pour into the mold, cover tightly with plastic wrap, and chill until firm, at least 1 hour.

About 15 minutes before you are ready to serve, turn the mold upside down over a plate and tap gently on the bottom to release the mousse. If it doesn't come out easily, place the mold in warm water in the sink for 10 seconds (no more), then try again. Cover the mousse tightly with plastic wrap and return it to the refrigerator for 10 minutes to firm up. Serve immediately.

Recipes for aspic are common in old-time cookbooks. Such gelatin suspensions of fruit, vegetables, and meat were especially beloved in the South, where their cool, silky texture seemed the perfect antidote to unrelenting heat.

Traditionally, gelatin was mixed with fresh fruit or vegetable juice, chicken or beef broth, and an appropriate medley of comestibles was chopped fine or minced to be folded into it. Cooks were playful. Gelatin was molded in Bundt pans to turn out as voluptuously rippled rings; special pans in the shape of fish, chicken, vegetables, or fruit were part of any fine old-fashioned kitchen. And clever cooks added herbs and spices, creams or cheese, and/or secret ingredients whose mystery diners would ponder while gobbling up each chilly bite.

"Congealed salad" was the technical name for these dishes, but if you flip through old community cookbooks, you'll discover a charming misspelling. Inspired by the hidden ingredients, or perhaps just looking for a prettier term, many cooks called them "concealed" salads.

With the invention of commercially flavored and colored gelatin products, these salads became the ultimate convenience food. Stir up a box of Jell-O, pour in a can of fruit cocktail, chill, and you have an easy salad for supper. Most Southerners insist on calling any dish with Jell-O, no matter how sweet, salad. This even includes a concoction, popular in recent years, that features crushed pretzels and sweetened whipped nondairy creamer.

Unfortunately, commercial gelatin mixes are inevitably sweetened and almost always fruit-based, so the more savory aspects of aspics were lost in the modern translation. There are two recipes in this book which hark back to the older tradition, however, Cucumber Mousse (page 152) and Ginger

Grapefruit Gelatin Surprise (page 256). I was a little intimidated the first time I worked with unflavored gelatin some ten years ago, but have found it a wonderfully easy and creative ingredient. I like experimenting with my own blends of flavors, and I appreciate the control it gives the cook when balancing sweet flavors with tart.

Zippity Honeydew   SERVES 6 TO 8

Eugene Walter considered this "one of the most delightful summer desserts imaginable." He was right.

1 ripe honeydew melon, 4 to 5 pounds
juice of 2 limes
⅛ cup crystallized ginger, cut in slivers
⅛ cup candied citron, cut in slivers

Cut the melon in half and remove the seeds. Cut it in slices, and peel. Cut the slices into pieces about 1 inch square and ½ inch thick. Put them in a bowl and pour the lime juice on them. Sprinkle in the ginger and citron, and toss lightly to coat the melon with juice and distribute the citron and ginger throughout. Cover tightly and refrigerate for 1 hour. Serve chilled in individual bowls, making sure to spoon ginger and citron over each serving.

*In **The Untidy Pilgrim,** Eugene Walter's rambunctious novel of Mobile life and manners, the characters discuss grief, and one offers her "receipt" for recovering from her beloved father's death:*

"In two days I was ready to either enter a nunnery, or close all the shutters of this house and become grief's recluse. Then I had two signs from heaven that all was well: one was that I found Papa's pornographic library where he hid it (there's part of the masculine nature I'll never understand) and the other was that I received a box of sugared ginger from a lovely friend. Between the two things I was saved: those awful satyrs and fauns seemed to say of Papa 'Not an angel and not yet to be,' while Miss D'Ete's ginger said sharply, 'Be gingery, be caustic, breathe fire in grief's face.' So there you are: that's how it was."

Watermelon Salsa   SERVES 4 TO 6

This crisp, cool salsa is delicious on any number of dishes, including Shariat's Crawfish Corn Cakes (page 102), Okra Corn Fritters (page 105), and Hoppin' John (page 25). But it also works exceptionally well as a refreshing salad on its own. It was created by Fisherville, Kentucky, chef Sara Gibbs when she was working at a Middletown restaurant called the Cottage Café, where country cooking is prepared with flair. (See Places to Go, page 341.) "I made it for the Ohio

BUTTER BEANS TO BLACKBERRIES

Valley Harvest Festival [see page 219], and it was supposed to go on top of something else we were serving, but I don't even remember what now," Sara recalls. "People were just coming up for cups of the salsa and eating that alone."

I was one of those people, and the notation I scribbled in my notebook is splashed with pale pink watermelon juice and enthusiastic exclamation points. Make this for a midsummer cookout and watch everyone's eyes light up.

Look for a 3- to 4-pound supersweet variety of melon.

4 cups watermelon flesh, seeded and diced small
⅓ cup minced red onion
⅓ cup minced cilantro
1 tablespoon minced fresh green jalapeño
1 tablespoon minced fresh red jalapeño (or other mild fresh pepper)
½ teaspoon kosher salt
2 cloves minced garlic
2 tablespoons fresh lime juice

Toss all of the ingredients together in a glass or pottery bowl to mix. Let stand at room temperature for 30 minutes, then serve immediately.

WATERMELON SUNDAY

Mark Twain may have been the first to discover the biblical implications of watermelon. "It was not a southern watermelon that Eve took; we know it because she repented," he observed. It took a South Carolinian, John White, to link the two in ritual.

White was the owner of Greenville's legendary Beacon Drive-In for more than fifty years. The Beacon is the home of the famous "a plenty" (a sandwich platter served with french fries and onion rings mounded in such proportions on top, you can't even see the sandwich underneath), not to mention delicious homemade beef hash, outstanding barbecue, and iced tea so good it sells at the rate of 1,200 to 1,500 gallons a week.

For more than a decade, the Beacon was also home of the Easter Sunday sunrise watermelon service—a drive-up community congregation which featured a sermon from the high front steps of the restaurant, delivered to patrons in the parking lot. The service was followed by a purely Southern communion of free ice-cold watermelon slices and tea.

Alas, the service grew so large that Mr. White had to discontinue it a few years ago. In May of 1998, he sold the Beacon to three partners, Sam Maw, Steve McManus, and Kenny Church. McManus says all three were longtime fans of the Beacon, and while they probably won't bring the watermelon service back, everything else is slated to remain the same.

That means you can order your site-made onion rings regular (in nearly inch-wide slices) or in "knots"—a golden, crispy pile of the chunky centers. It also means you'd better order fast or risk getting barked at by J.C. ("Come on, come on, come on down the line. Next, next, next.")

J.C. Strobel is the man who's been taking customer orders at the Beacon in rapid-fire fashion for the last 47 years. He stores up to twenty orders in his head at a time, and sorts them by categories before he spits them out ("Three outsides, two slices, five cheese, two with slaw . . .") to Fred and A.J., who've been turning over the burgers and piling rings and fries on the plates for nearly as many years themselves. And they aren't even the longest-term employees at the Beacon.

J.C. is undoubtedly the most quoted, however, with plenty of his proclamations canonized in hand-lettered signs scattered around the place. *J.C. says: It's fine to pass in line.* Or, my personal favorite, *J.C. says: Let's don't boogie jive, let's merchandise.*

You'd do well to peruse the menu with its sixty-plus sandwiches and twenty-plus side dishes and thirty-plus combination plates before you face J.C. The Beacon is open six days a week. See Places to Go, page 341.

OKRA

Braised Fresh Okra

Okra and Tomatoes

Okra Grits with Winter Tomato Gravy

Okra Corn Fritters with Sorghum Pepper Relish

Lemon Okra Soup

Bibb Lettuce Salad with Okra Croutons and
Buttermilk Dressing

Okra was plentiful on the table when I was a child, but I never saw it growing until I planted my own small crop a few years ago. All I wanted was to be able to pick the unripe pods at their tenderest state—about 1½ to 3 inches long—but I got a breathtaking tropical garden first. The plants grow tall and the flowers are crepe-paper delicate, but showy, like those of hibiscus, to which okra is related.

The marvelous flowers were soon followed by tiny, succulent pods, which, lightly braised in ham-seasoned water, became a summer staple. We had okra fritters and melanges made with other fresh vegetables from the farm market, okra providing the silken base. As the season went into fall, and the plant continued to produce, I should have picked and frozen pods—okra freezes excellently. But that fact made me lazy, since I knew I could continue to get good okra from the grocery's freezer for winter gumbo. Instead, I let the pods get ridiculously long, some as much as nine inches before they began to dry on the plant, which now had an eerie but equally striking appearance. If you have the long, hot growing season necessary, I suggest you plant okra as much for the visual delight it provides in the garden as the edible delight on the table.

Braised Fresh Okra SERVES 4 TO 6

"Ladies' fingers" was a term used for okra in the Old South, and it's useful to remember as you shop for this vegetable. Ideally okra pods should be small, like those romanticized digits—no more than 3 inches long. That said, I confess I have used longer pods of okra (sliced and fried, or simmered in a stew) when I have found them truly fresh-picked, with flesh that is still juicy and tender. But if you lightly pinch a pod between your fingers and can feel the fibers, or any suggestion around the stem end that the okra has begun to turn woody and tough, don't bother.

The velvety juice is the very essence of okra, and any recipe that promises to deliver the vegetable without it has missed the point. The texture is silken, not slimy, and an elegantly simple delight in this dish, served with any cornbread and sliced garden tomatoes.

While frozen okra works well in other recipes, this particular one should be made only with fresh okra.

2 to 4 dozen fresh okra pods,
   1½ to 3 inches long (use the lesser
   number of pods if the pods are larger)
½ cup ham broth (see page 162)
salt

Rinse the okra, and trim any tough stems, but leave the caps on. In a wide skillet with a lid, bring the ham broth to a boil. As it warms, taste, and add salt if necessary.

When the broth begins to boil, add the okra, cover, and turn the heat to low. Simmer for 7 minutes, or until the okra is just tender. Remove the okra to a warm plate, bring the broth to a boil, and cook for 3 more minutes. Pour about 2 tablespoons of broth over the okra, and serve immediately.

VARIATION: *In* Cross Creek Cookery, *(Simon & Schuster, 1942), Marjorie Kinnan Rawlings prepared a meatless version of this dish, cooking the okra in an open pot full of boiling salted water for "exactly seven minutes from the time the water resumes its boiling." She served the whole pods on warmed individual plates arranged like spokes around small bowls of hollandaise sauce. If you don't feel like making hollandaise, substitute melted butter, laced with fresh-squeezed lemon juice.*

HAM BROTH

The preferred Southern *seasoning for cooked vegetables is cured pork, a culinary choice first made for convenience (pigs were plentiful throughout the South and their cured meat products available year-round, but still popular because of its extraordinary complementary flavor.*

Throughout this book you will find suggestions for getting the characteristic volup- *tuous, salty resonance of Southern cooking without using ham or bacon. Any substitution I recommend for traditional pork seasoning is here because it is delicious in its own right. I will tell you truthfully, however, that I use those substitutions primarily when my vegetarian (or "chicken and fish, only") friends are coming to dinner. When it's just me I'm cooking for, I prefer ham or bacon, although often in smaller amounts than were traditional.*

To that end, I like to have homemade ham broth on hand, just as I do turkey and chicken broth. I make it in much the same way, using the bone and any leftover meat from a whole holiday ham. This is simmered for an hour or more in a stockpot filled with water to cover the bone, augmented by celery and onion. Then I remove the solids from the broth (pressing both vegetables and meat to extract flavorful juice) and refrigerate it overnight. The next day, it's easy to skim the fat, which has solidified on the top, and discard it. I then transfer the broth to individual plastic containers (1- and 2-cup sizes) and freeze until needed.

I add no salt to the broth, since the ham will have some. (When I use country ham scraps and bone, I make sure to label the broth clearly as such, since it will be highly salted from the meat, too much so for cooking delicate vegetables, but just right for dried beans or bold soups and stews.)

Of course, whole hams appear with less frequency on our dinner table than chicken or turkey, so my stash of frozen ham broth often runs out. It's easy to make more using ham hocks, and it's also possible to make a quick broth for a recipe (Braised Fresh Okra, page 161, for instance) on the spot, by simmering a small chunk of salt pork or white bacon for 30 minutes in the amount of water called for in the recipe plus ¼ cup (which is about what tends to evaporate).

Okra and Tomatoes   SERVES 4

There are precious few fresh vegetables that don't cozy up nicely to simmered tomatoes, but okra is simply sublime in this role. Its velvety juice and nutty flavor are set off perfectly by the natural acidity of the tomatoes.

This is probably the most popular way of preparing okra as a supper side. It's also the basis for a number of more elaborate dishes. You can add fresh corn, small shrimp, and/or crowder peas to the pan, and serve over a mound of long-grain rice for a typical Southern main dish.

Mix red and yellow tomatoes for a vibrant look. You can serve this with any of the cornbread recipes here, but it is especially good with Eugene's Savory Seeded Corn Pone (page 106).

½ cup finely chopped sweet white onion
2 tablespoons olive oil or bacon grease
2 cups chopped fresh okra
3 medium fresh tomatoes, peeled and
    chopped
salt
freshly ground black pepper

Sauté the onion in the oil over medium heat until softened. Add the okra and the tomatoes with all their juice. Cover and simmer over low heat for 15 minutes. Add salt to taste, and simmer, covered, for 5 minutes more. Top with a dash of pepper just before serving.

"I ate so much okra when I was a kid, I couldn't keep my danged socks up."

Okra Grits with Winter Tomato Gravy   SERVES 4

This is a dish I would describe as a curious comfort. You may find the porridge-like grits odd at first, but each successive spoonful becomes more delicious. It is most soothing in the first chill of winter, and so the recipe here uses frozen okra and canned tomatoes.

If you have grits left over, lightly grease a pie pan, spread the mixture in about 1 inch deep, cover snugly with plastic wrap, and chill. Use the next day to make Grits Cakes (page 113). These may be eaten as is, but are also excellent topped with left-over tomato gravy.

Winter Tomato Gravy also makes a scrumptious bacon-and-tomato sandwich, when fresh tomatoes at the grocery are as appetizing as golf balls. Make the gravy as described here, then spread it on thick slices of sourdough bread and top with crumbled bacon. Yummm.

OKRA GRITS

1½ cups frozen okra slices
¾ teaspoon kosher salt
3½ cups water
⅔ cup stone-ground white grits

Rinse the okra with cold water to break up clumps. Shake it in a colander to dry, chop it coarsely, and set aside.

In a heavy saucepan, combine the salt and water, and bring to a brisk boil. Slowly pour in the grits, stirring all the while to keep the mixture from lumping. Add the okra and stir. Turn the heat to low, and cook at a slow simmer for 20 minutes, stirring very often to prevent sticking.

While the grits are cooking, make the gravy.

WINTER TOMATO GRAVY

4 pieces thick-sliced bacon (about ¼ pound)
½ cup chopped sweet white onion
14½-ounce can of whole tomatoes
crushed pepper

In a wide skillet, fry the bacon over medium heat until crisp. Remove it to a paper towel to drain. Pour off all but 1 tablespoon of the bacon grease.

Sauté the onion in bacon grease over medium heat for 1 minute. Add the crushed tomatoes and juice. Cook for 6 to 8 minutes, stirring frequently to keep the mixture from sticking. When the tomatoes begin to bubble and the gravy thickens just a bit, remove from the heat. Add pepper to taste. Serve in individual bowls over hot okra grits, with the bacon crumbled on top.

Okra Corn Fritters with Sorghum Pepper Relish MAKES 12 TO 15 CAKES

Very tender young okra and farm-fresh white-kernel corn are essential for these delicate fritters. And while a fresh tomato sauce might be the expected accompaniment, this slightly sweet pepper relish actually provides a better complement, without overpowering either the okra or the corn taste.

SORGHUM PEPPER RELISH

1 large red bell pepper
½ cup finely chopped sweet white onion
1 tablespoon sorghum syrup
salt
3 drops Tabasco

Roast the pepper over an open flame or under the broiler until the skin blisters and pops. Allow to cool until you can rub the skin off. Remove the stem and seeds, and chop fine. Put the pepper in a bowl, and mix in the onion and sorghum. Add salt to taste and the Tabasco. Toss to mix, and set aside while you make fritters.

OKRA CORN FRITTERS

2 dozen pods fresh okra, 1½ to 2 inches long
2 cups water
3 ears of fresh corn

½ cup finely ground white cornmeal
½ teaspoon kosher salt
1 egg, beaten
½ cup buttermilk
canola oil

Slice the stems from the okra, but leave the caps on. In a wide saucepan or skillet with a lid, bring the water to a boil. Add the okra, cover, and cook at a lively simmer for 3 minutes. Drain, and pour cold water over the okra. Pat it dry and slice it into rounds ½ inch thick. Set aside.

Cut the corn from the cobs and milk the cobs (see page 101). Set aside.

In a bowl, mix the cornmeal and salt. Add the egg and buttermilk, and mix until just blended. Add the okra and corn with its milk, kneading gently with the back of a wooden spoon to incorporate them into the cornmeal mixture.

Lightly oil a griddle or cast-iron skillet and place it over medium-high heat. When it is very hot but not smoking, drop batter onto the surface to make cakes about 2 inches wide. Fry them until golden on both sides. Serve hot, topped with Sorghum Pepper Relish.

Lemon Okra Soup SERVES 4

The viscous juice of okra makes it a natural thickener for soups, from the varied gumbos of the coast to hearty beef and vegetable combos. Okra's interesting, ribbed texture and its nutty flavor hold up well in any stew pot. Try adding it to your favorite multivegetable soup. This particular soup, however, is quite delicate, and makes for a quick evening repast.

4 cups chicken or vegetable broth
salt
¼ cup minced sweet white onion
2 cups sliced okra, in ⅛-inch-thick rounds
2 cups cooked long-grain rice
1 lemon
black pepper

In a medium pot, heat the broth until it's steaming. While it's heating, taste, and add salt if necessary. Add the onion and the okra, and cook at a lively simmer for 5 minutes. Add the rice, and heat thoroughly.

While the rice is heating, scrub the lemon in clear water and cut it in half through the middle. Remove any visible seeds, and cut four very thin, round slices from the inside center, for garnish. Extract juice from the rest of the lemon, discarding any seeds.

Remove the soup from the heat and add the lemon juice. Ladle the soup into four bowls, and float a lemon slice on top of each. Pass the peppermill at the table.

On his journey through the South, gathering material for American Cooking: Southern Style *(Time-Life Books, 1971),* Eugene Walter stopped in Savannah for a meal featuring the region's classic okra soup, prepared by a Mrs. Henrietta Waring, widow of Dr. Antonio Waring, a prominent pediatrician. Noting the delicate balance of the okra and acid tomato against the clean flavors of celery and parsley, Walter asked for her secret.

"It's my own variation," Mrs. Waring said. "I think one should be flexible with recipes. Naturally I have a secret with this soup, but I'll tell you, it's classic Savannah okra soup but I use V-8 juice instead of water and tomato paste. One has to be adventurous."

For even more adventure when you're serving your own variation of okra soup, try the Savannah trick of crushing a brilliant red bird's-eye pepper in each soup bowl, then tossing it out before pouring in the soup. You won't get the bite in the flavor, but the lovely aroma will be enticing.

Bibb Lettuce Salad with Okra Croutons and Buttermilk Dressing   SERVES 6

Fried okra makes a quick and surprisingly delicious crouton for a tender green salad, and buttermilk dressing provides a satiny, pungent contrast.

Fresh okra is sublime here, if you can find small, unblemished pods. If you can't, don't despair, since sliced frozen okra works perfectly. That makes this an especially nice salad year-round.

SALAD
1 cup sliced okra, ¼-inch thick
1 head Bibb or Boston lettuce
½ cucumber
12 cherry tomatoes

½ cup corn flour (see Note)
½ teaspoon kosher salt
canola or peanut oil for frying

BUTTERMILK DRESSING
1 tablespoon cider vinegar
1 teaspoon brown sugar
¼ teaspoon kosher salt
¼ teaspoon minced celery leaves
2 drops Tabasco
½ cup buttermilk
1 tablespoon finely minced green onion

If you are using fresh okra, chill it for at least 20 minutes before dredging and frying. If you are using frozen okra, defrost it in a colander at room temperature for 20 minutes.

While the okra is coming to the proper temperature, make the dressing by whisking together the vinegar, sugar, and salt. When the sugar and salt are dissolved, add the other ingredients and whisk to blend. Set aside.

Prepare the salads on six individual plates. Rinse and pat dry the lettuce leaves and divide them evenly among the plates. Peel the cucumber, and dice it into ¼-inch pieces. Divide them evenly, arranging them over the lettuce. Stem, rinse, and halve the tomatoes and arrange them on the sides of the plates.

When you are ready to serve, place the corn flour in a wide-mouthed bowl and mix it with the salt. Pour about ½ inch of oil into a skillet, and heat it over high heat. Crumple some paper towels and place them in a wide colander near the stove.

Dredge the okra pieces in the corn

flour until thoroughly coated. Shake to remove excess flour (see Note). When the oil is very hot but not smoking, add the okra in small batches, being careful not to crowd the skillet. Fry until browned on the first side (30 seconds to 1 minute) then flip the pieces over with a spatula and fry for a few seconds more on the other side, until browned. Transfer the okra with a slotted spatula to the crumpled paper towels. Continue frying until all the okra is done.

When the okra is ready, pour the buttermilk dressing over the salads, then top each with several pieces of fried okra, dividing it evenly among the plates. Serve immediately.

Note: *To expedite the frying, I use a curved, slotted metal spatula to remove the okra from the dredging flour, shake the excess off, and then drop the okra in the pan. I use a flat, slotted metal spatula to turn the okra in the pan and remove it to the paper towels for draining.*

If your skillet is small and it will take more than 3 batches to fry the okra, preheat the oven to 200°F before you begin frying. After each batch drains, place the fried okra on a plate in the oven to keep warm.

Note: *If you can't find corn flour in the store, simply process cornmeal in the blender until it's a powdery consistency.*

ABOUT OKRA

iRiSH pOTAToeS

Mother's Mashed Potatoes

Mountain German Potato Salad

Frogmore Soup

At my great-aunts' house in Corbin, certain foods were given specific names to distinguish them. Milk became "sweet milk," in deference to the buttermilk that was equally apt to be used in cooking or sipped ice cold with dinner. And when I was sent to Brewer's store for a loaf of bread for sandwiches, I was told to get "light bread," in contrast to the cornbread we would have for supper. Potatoes came in two varieties, too, either sweet or Irish potatoes.

My mother still uses the term "Irish potato," and now that I think of it, she intends it to be more specific than simply a designation for all white potatoes. It doesn't mean those tiny potatoes with red or pale gold skins, which are "new potatoes," and which she likes especially to add to a pot of green beans in the last 30 minutes of cooking, or to simmer in water until just tender, drain, and toss with plenty of salt and butter. No, an Irish potato is a good-sized, mature spud, what someone else might call an Idaho or a baker, and this is what she uses exclusively to make her fabulous mashed potatoes (no waxy varieties, please) and potato salad.

Technically, the term should be Peruvian potato, for the tuber originated in that country, arriving in Europe sometime after Columbus first returned from the New World. It was cultivated in Spain as food for sailors; but it was in Ireland that the potato first took hold as a primary food crop, hence the appellation. The white potato didn't appear on this country's tables as a fundamental food until the late 1800s, and only became established as a staple during the Depression.

Potatoes were more prevalent in the cooking of the mountain South, where they were easily grown and were hence more readily available than the rice of the Deep South. They seemed to fit perfectly into mountain menus, which owed much to Irish roots. I've already mentioned my mother's custom of eating mashed potatoes with greens and onions, taking small bites of each together, which, in essence, echoes the flavor of colcannon. My mother's use of the term "Irish potato" seems poetic, as much a reference to the context in which she served them as to any horticultural origins.

And if her language is lyrical, her mashed potatoes are a pure symphony.

Mother's Mashed Potatoes SERVES 6 TO 8

Since I wrote my first cookbook in 1991, the sorry state of mashed potatoes in restaurants—where instant flakes whipped into a tasteless blob once reigned—has improved immensely. Now any restaurant worth its salt and grind-at-the-table pepper proudly serves up real potatoes. Alas, they are apt to be served with lumps still in them, to prove their authenticity. And too many restaurants dress them up with the likes of roasted garlic, chipotle peppers, pesto, or whatever else may be the seasoning of the moment. Now, I am glad to get these real potatoes in any guise, but I still believe there is nothing so fine as the simple, exquisite potatoes my mother made with just potato, salt, butter, and milk. Potatoes mashed to a velvety smoothness, as she did them, are perfect with any number of dishes, from butter beans to field peas, greens to succotash. Served alone, they become the ultimate comfort food for a solitary supper on a chilly night. To me, my mother's mashed potatoes are among the most essential foods for survival—of the spirit as much as of the body. That is why her recipe is here.

To make mashed potatoes correctly, you must mash, not whip, the potatoes by hand. To do this, you'll need a potato masher. You'll also need mature Idaho potatoes, the sort you'd use for baking, although smaller. New potatoes, red potatoes, or waxy potatoes of any kind will not give you the proper cloud-like texture. And while trendy Yukon Gold potatoes are tasty in other recipes, I find their slight sweetness annoying in pure mashed potatoes.

6 medium baking potatoes
1 to 2 quarts boiling water
8 tablespoons salted butter
¾ tablespoon kosher salt
1 cup (approximately) whole milk, room temperature

Peel the potatoes, and cut them into quarters. Put them in a heavy pot with a lid and a sturdy handle. Pour in enough boiling water to cover them, and add a pinch of salt. Cook, uncovered, at a low boil for 20 to 30 minutes, until the potato quarters break apart when pierced with a fork.

When the potatoes are ready, remove the pot from the heat. Put the lid on, then slide it back just a bit, and drain the water off, being careful not to burn yourself.

Using a potato masher, mash the potatoes until no lumps are visible. Add the butter in clumps, and continue mashing until it is melted and thoroughly incorporated. Sprinkle on the remaining salt, and mash to incorporate. Take a little taste of the potatoes. If you detect tiny lumps, mash a few times more.

Rap the masher against the edge of the pot a time or two to dislodge any potato, then use a big spoon or fork to continuously whip the potatoes while you gradually pour in the milk. You may not need it all. When the consistency is light and fluffy, neither runny nor stiff, stop adding milk, and beat the potatoes a little more. "The more you beat 'em, the better they are," my mother says.

Taste, and add more salt, if desired. Serve immediately—and I do mean immediately. Mashed potatoes which have to cool their heels even for a few minutes are not as divine as those straight from the pan.

WARM SPRINGS, VIRGINIA, OCTOBER 1995

Most bed and breakfasts or little inns are mom-and-pop establishments with small staffs, sometimes no more than Mom and Pop themselves. Consequently, few are able to accommodate walk-in guests.

My friend Lynn Winter and I know this as we wind our way along the red-and-gold-splattered Allegheny Mountains to Warm Springs, Virginia. But we are so taken by the town's quiet beauty, and the promisingly hospitable look of the Inn at Grist Mill Square, that we decide to try our luck.

And lucky we are. Innkeeper Janice McWilliams greets us as warmly as if she's been waiting for us all day, offering to put us up in a room in the renovated blacksmith's shop, if we don't mind sharing a king-sized bed. Who could complain with a view like the one from the private deck of that room? There are gorgeous hills off in the distance, and the deck itself seems to float like a tree house amid limbs full of crisply changing leaves.

Lynn takes a brisk jog in the fading afternoon light, while I opt for a more leisurely stroll through the town's ups and downs. When we come back, rejuvenated, we find a table set for us in the Simon Kenton pub. With candles on the table, dark wood walls, and tankards of ale, it feels just like it might have back in 1771, when pioneer Kenton took a job here to earn the supplies to sustain him on his trek into Kentucky territory.

It is such a refreshing respite that we don't even mind missing a seasonal dip in the restorative springs for which the town is named. Instead, I mark the inn down as a place to come back to and, as a token of thanks for her Southern welcome, give Janice a copy of *Shuck Beans* . . . She, in turn, sends me a note a few weeks later, noting the many shared traditions of our upbringing, particularly the way our families turned mashed potatoes into a rite: "I mean, my father mashed the potatoes with a ricer and a *silver* fork while mother stood by adding warm butter and hot milk. It is the *only* way."

The inn and restaurant are in five restored buildings surrounding the old mill; accommodations include seventeen rooms ranging from guest rooms to full apartments.

See Places to Go, page 341.

Mountain German Potato Salad

SERVES 8

No family reunion, funeral supper, or summer picnic was ever complete without a big bowl of cold potato salad with mayonnaise dressing, such as the one on page 195. But particularly in the mountain South, where German cooking traditions could be found, good cooks also made a hot potato salad.

This recipe is based on one used by my friend Mary Horvath's mother, Catherine Kraft. Mary says she compares all German-style potato salads to this one, and all come up lacking. I agree. The secret isn't in any fancy ingredient, but in the technique, particularly the overnight steep in the refrigerator, which allows the dressing to ripen and the potatoes to absorb all of its flavor.

Mary thought the recipe probably was handed on from one of her German grandmothers, but a conversation with her mom revealed that the original was actually in the Betty Crocker Picture Cookbook of 1950. Catherine made some changes in that recipe, and I, in turn, have made a few of my own, including the use of red onion, strictly for color, and the option of reducing the bacon grease considerably.

You can reheat this dish a second and even a third time, and the flavor will be just as good, although the texture will change somewhat. What you cannot do, however, is eat the salad without refrigerating overnight and reheating. The dressing will taste raw, and the flavors will not have had a chance to blend and mingle.

Note: *My mother loves the taste of celery, and always had celery seed on hand for those times when she ran out of crisp stalks. It was one of the few spices she used liberally, and so it was always quite fresh in her kitchen. It's a seasoning which has fallen out of favor in recent years, however; if you have some on your shelf, chances are good it has been around for several years. Don't use it. Buy a new stash, and indulge yourself with pinches in salad dressings, stews, and casseroles. You'll be glad you did. If you can't get celery seed, chop the leaves from a stalk of fresh celery very fine, at least one brimming teaspoonful, and use that instead.*

6 medium white potatoes
boiling water
6 slices bacon
¾ cup finely chopped red onion
¾ cup water
2 tablespoons flour
½ cup cider vinegar
1½ teaspoons sugar
1½ teaspoons kosher salt
½ teaspoon celery seed
black pepper

Scrub the potatoes, cutting out any eyes and blemishes. Place them in a pot with boiling water to cover. Cook at a lively simmer for 20 to 30 minutes, until a cake tester pierces through the middle easily.

While the potatoes are cooking, begin the dressing. Fry the bacon crisp, being careful not to burn it or let the grease get hot enough to smoke. (I fry it in two batches, draining but reserving the grease after the first, to keep everything under control.) Set the bacon aside on paper towels; reserve the grease in the skillet.

When the potatoes are cooked, drain, and plunge them in cold water. The peels should slide off easily; if not, use a knife to pull them away. Cut the potatoes into ½-inch cubes, and lay them in a shallow pan—a roasting pan is what Mary's mother uses.

Fry the onions in the reserved bacon grease, over medium-high heat, until they begin to soften.

While the onions are frying, combine the water and the flour in a small jar with a lid. Screw on the lid, and shake until they are completely blended. Set aside.

Whisk together the vinegar, sugar, salt, and celery seed. Turn the flame to low, add the vinegar mixture to the softened onions, and stir. Add the flour water, and simmer until the mixture thickens, which happens quite rapidly. Pour the hot dressing over the warm potato cubes. Add several grinds of pepper, and crumble the bacon on top. Toss everything lightly with a spatula to coat the potatoes well, but don't overmix; it will make the potatoes mushy. (The salad is still tasty if the potatoes get mushy, but not as attractive.)

Allow the salad to cool to room temperature, then cover it securely with plastic wrap, and refrigerate overnight.

When you are ready to serve, reheat the salad over boiling water. If you don't have a double boiler large enough to accommodate it, rig one up by setting a good-sized saucepan into a larger one with water in the bottom. Stir the potatoes lightly a few times so they are heated thoroughly. Serve warm.

Note: *Mary's mother, following the original recipe, uses all of the bacon grease in the dressing. I decided to try the recipe with only 3 tablespoons of the grease, with an ample amount of brown bacon flecks in it. The result was delicious, although Mary says it's even more velvety and intense with the full complement. Catherine says she always chooses breakfast bacon that is very lean in the first place for this dish. Sometimes, when she spies a particularly lean batch of bacon at the grocery, she buys it and freezes it specifically to use in this salad later.*

Frogmore Soup

SERVES 6 GENEROUSLY

Frogmore stew, the tasty antecedent to this sustaining soup, gets its charming name from a tiny town once on St. Helena Island, near Hilton Head, South Carolina. The "stew" is actually a seafood boil, usually consisting of shrimp, spicy sausage, new potatoes, and corn on the cob, all cooked in seasoned water and devoured from paper plates on picnic tables covered in newspaper.

I wanted to have the same medley of flavors, but served up in a fashion more compatible with eating in the dining room. From that desire came this luscious soup. It appears in the potato section because it's the addition of creamy tubers that seems to bring the whole into harmony.

1½ pounds fresh medium-sized shrimp, in shells
2 quarts water
1 tablespoon Old Bay (or other seafood boil) seasoning
1 teaspoon kosher salt
14 new potatoes, in skins
2 cups corn, cut from the cob (see page 101)
1 pound andouille (or other spicy hard sausage), in ½-inch-thick rounds
1 cup buttermilk
½ cup minced green onion

Rinse the shrimp in cold water. In a large stockpot, bring the 2 quarts of water, Old Bay seasoning, and salt to a rolling boil. Add the shrimp, and cook until they are just done (pink and white), about 3 minutes. Using a large strainer, remove them from the pot and plunge them into ice-cold water.

Immediately add the potatoes to the pot, and boil until tender, about 15 minutes.

While the potatoes are cooking, remove the shrimp from the chilled water, and peel them.

When the potatoes are done, remove them from the water and set them aside. Strain the cooking liquid through cheesecloth or a coffee filter in a strainer. Wipe the stockpot clean with a paper towel, and return all but ½ cup of the liquid to it.

Add the corn and andouille, turn the heat to low, cover, and simmer for about 10 to 15 minutes.

While the corn and sausage are simmering, finish peeling the shrimp, and halve 12 of the potatoes. In a blender, or using a masher, blend the remaining 2 potatoes and the half-cup of cooking liquid into a thick slurry.

When the corn is tender, add the slurry and the buttermilk to the pot. Keeping the heat low so the milk doesn't curdle, heat until steamy. Add the shrimp, and heat for 1 to 2 minutes, until the shrimp are warm. Serve, garnished with green onion, in big bowls.

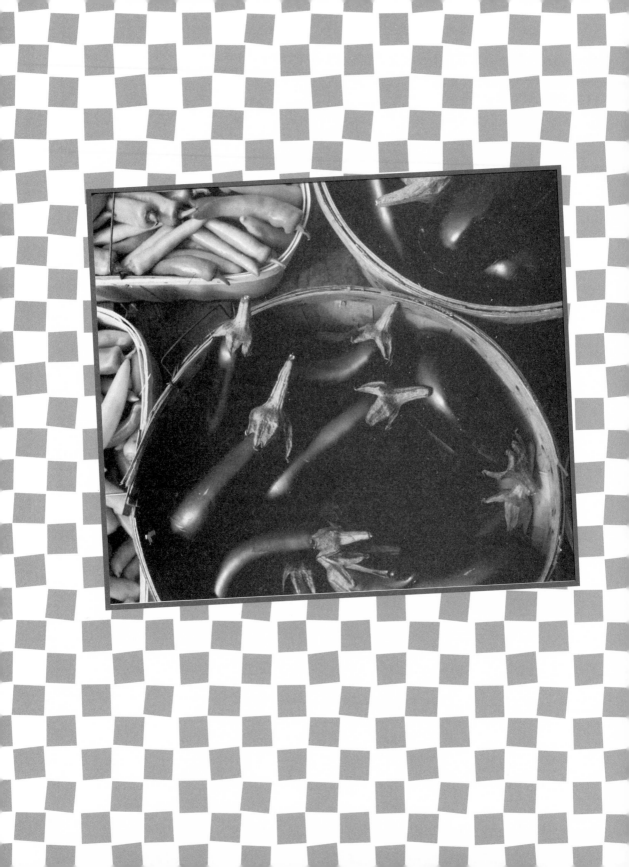

eggplant

High Holy Grilled Eggplant and
Green Tomato Sandwich

Kentucky Creole Eggplant Dip and Pudding

New South Moussaka

Although James Beard suggested it was Spanish, Portuguese, or Italian immigrants who introduced eggplant into the United States, other sources say it most likely arrived from North Africa with the slaves. This would seem to be borne out by its popularity in the Southern coastal areas and cotton belt, where black cooks plied their art. Eggplant shows up in soups, casseroles, and garden ratatouilles. Like peppers, it is stuffed with savory fillings. (In the Cajun part of Louisiana, this takes on a certain whimsical charm, since the hollowed-out shells, filled with seasoned meat, oysters, shrimp, and crawfish, are sometimes called pirogues after the region's typical hollowed-out bayou boat.)

Thomas Jefferson grew white and purple varieties in visually pleasing alternating rows, as he also did with purple, white, and green sprouting broccoli. Most Southerners, however, grew up with the familiar deep-purple, large-globe vegetable found in virtually any produce department. Farm markets increasingly offer more eggplant varieties, in an array of colors and sizes, with flavor which is more delicate and less bitter. Any of them will work in the recipes here.

To salt or not to salt? Aye, that is the question. In the olden days, cooks religiously soaked the sliced flesh of eggplant in cold salted water for up to an hour before cooking, to lessen the "bitterness."

Modern cooking science swears there is no proof that this accomplishes anything. I believe the science; truly, I do. It's just that it doesn't work in my kitchen. I have sadly discovered again and again that, while the newer varieties don't seem to require it, purple globe eggplant which has not been presalted cooks up with a bitter whang to it, while that which I salt first is pleasantly sweet and nutty.

I lightly sprinkle the slices with salt on either side and leave them to "sweat" for 20 minutes. Then I quickly rinse and pat them dry with paper towels. The recipes here include this step, but you may use your own discretion.

While the salt question is speculative, freshness is essential. Eggplants should have shiny skin that is taut, taut, taut. There should be no cuts, and definitely no brown soft spots on the eggplant, since they will make the flesh bitter throughout.

High Holy Grilled Eggplant and Green Tomato Sandwich
MAKES 6 SANDWICHES

Virtually anything that can be cut into a disk will ultimately end up breaded and fried in the Southern kitchen, from okra to onions to green tomatoes to dill pickles. These are actually pretty tasty, but I have never thought the same about fried eggplant. If the crust is properly quick-fried, the vegetable itself is still tough and tasteless; if it's cooked long enough to make the eggplant creamy, the breading is too saturated with fat. I prefer eggplant grilled and dressed in this Southern-style sandwich.

Although *aioli* has only recently become a restaurant byword around the country, the French trick of adding fresh minced garlic to creamy mayonnaise was popular decades ago along the Alabama, Mississippi, and Louisiana Gulf Coast. Eugene Walter says that Mobile cooks heard the word as "high holy," however, and that's what it became in Southern kitchens—an appropriate moniker for a condiment so celestial. I use Hellmann's mayonnaise as my base, because it is a delicious commercial product, but you may use homemade mayonnaise or a brand of your preference. Do *not* use "salad dressing."

These vegetables are best grilled outside over a charcoal fire, but you can also use a broiler.

2 large globe eggplants, about ¾ pound each

salt

olive oil

½ cup mayonnaise

2 cloves garlic, minced

3 large green tomatoes, with no red visible

2 foot-long baguettes (or 6 long, crusty rolls)

6 romaine lettuce leaves

pepper

Light the coals in the grill and let them burn until the flames die down and they are covered with a light ash, usually 30 to 40 minutes. Lightly grease or oil the rack, and place it 5 to 6 inches above the coals. Begin preparing the ingredients just after you light the coals.

Peel the eggplants, and slice each into 6 rounds about ½ inch thick. Salt lightly on each side, and lay the rounds out on paper towels to sweat for 20 minutes. When the time is up, rinse each slice quickly and blot it dry with a clean paper towel. Liberally brush the slices with olive oil on both sides, and set them aside.

In a small bowl, whisk together the mayonnaise and garlic to make *aioli*.

Discarding the stem end, slice each tomato into 4 rounds a little less than ½ inch thick. Liberally brush the slices with olive oil on both sides, and set them aside.

Slice the ends off the baguettes. Cut each bread into 3 equal lengths, and split them open lengthwise to make sub-style sandwich buns.

Rinse the lettuce leaves and pat them dry.

When the coals are ready, arrange the eggplant slices over the center, and grill for 5 minutes on each side. Turn and grill for 5 more minutes. Turn again, and grill for 2 to 3 minutes more.

When you have turned the eggplant the second time, arrange the green tomato slices around the edges, and grill for 2 minutes. Move the eggplant slices to the edges of the grill, turning them as you do, and move the tomato slices to the center, also turning. Grill the tomatoes for 1 minute more. They should be lightly browned, warm, and softened. Remove them and set them aside.

Cook the eggplant for 2 to 3 more minutes at the edges of the grill, until darkly browned outside and creamy within. Remove.

Slather the *aioli* on the bottom slice of each baguette. Arrange 2 eggplant slices over the *aioli*, and 2 tomato slices over the eggplant. Salt and pepper liberally, and finish with a lettuce leaf and the top of the baguette, dressed with the remaining *aioli*. Eat immediately.

Kentucky Creole Eggplant Dip and Pudding

SERVES 2 AS A MAIN COURSE OR 4 AS A SIDE DISH

Here I've combined elements of two very different classic eggplant recipes—one for stuffed eggplant, from Marion Flexner's *Out of Kentucky Kitchens* (The University Press of Kentucky, 1949 and 1989), and the other for *Aubergines à la Creole* from *The Picayune's Creole Cook Book* (Random House, 1989)—to create two other recipes, neither quite like either of the first. And so it goes in the home cook's kitchen.

The mashed eggplant and tomato sauce dip is delicious with crackers or on slices of firm French bread. Or you can go on to

make the pudding, for an unusual and very tasty entree or side dish.

EGGPLANT
1 eggplant, about ¾ pound
salt
1 teaspoon olive oil

TOMATO SAUCE
1 cup fresh chopped tomatoes
1 tablespoon chopped sun-dried tomatoes in oil
¼ cup minced sweet white onion
1 tablespoon chopped fresh celery leaves
1 tablespoon brown sugar
½ tablespoon Worcestershire sauce

PUDDING
2 eggs
½ cup buttermilk
1 tablespoon unbleached all-purpose flour
½ cup pecans

Preheat the oven to 350°F.

Peel the eggplant and slice it into rounds ½ inch thick. Sprinkle each side with salt, and lay the rounds on paper towels to sweat for 20 minutes. Liberally oil a baking sheet with the olive oil.

While the eggplant is sweating, combine all of the tomato sauce ingredients in the top of a double boiler, and begin slow-cooking them over boiling water. Stir occasionally.

When 20 minutes are up, quickly rinse the eggplant slices and pat them dry with a paper towel. Lay the slices on the baking sheet, and turn them so that both sides are lightly oiled. Bake for 20 minutes. Remove from the oven, turn the slices over with a spatula, and bake 10 more minutes. The eggplant should be toasty brown outside and very soft inside.

In a large bowl, coarsely mash the eggplant with a potato masher or fork. Add the tomato sauce (which should be thick and a deep burgundy red), and combine well. Salt to taste. If you are going to use this as a dip or spread, cool a bit and serve.

If you are making the pudding, whisk together the eggs, buttermilk, and flour. Mix thoroughly with the eggplant and sauce. Fold in the pecans. Pour into an oiled 1½-quart casserole and bake at 375°F for 20 minutes, until the custard is set and the top is browned. Serve warm as a side dish, or as a main course with green salad and bread.

VARIATION: *For a more substantial main course, you can substitute ¾ cup small fresh shrimp for the pecans.*

New South Moussaka SERVES 4

Most Greek immigration to the American South occurred after the Civil War and was concentrated along the Gulf Coast and in cities. Former fishermen, boat and net makers were able to continue in their trades along the Gulf. Tarpon Springs, Florida, a tiny tourist town crammed with good Greek restaurants, still celebrates its Greek heritage and sponge industry. (See Places to Go, page 341.)

In the cities, those Greek immigrants with a penchant for cooking and hospitality often found work in restaurants, and some eventually established places of their own, which were among the best-loved dining establishments of the twentieth-century South. The Bright Star in Bessemer, Alabama, and John's in Birmingham are two prime examples. The menus at these places struck a good balance among seafood, Southern-style, and Greek-influenced cooking. And they introduced a generation of Southerners to delicious dishes that could be easily made from the plentiful produce of the region.

Although Jean Anderson's *The American Century Cookbook* (Random House, 1997) dates the general popularization of moussaka (outside of Greek American communities) as the mid-1960s, Southern cooks had been preparing variations on this theme—usually called simply eggplant casserole—at least since the 1950s. In *Cissy Gregg's Cookbook*, a 1954 supplement to the Louisville *Courier-Journal*, there is one such recipe with a decidedly Southern twist—the eggplant slices are breaded and fried before being placed in the casserole. The dish is made with ground lamb (some Southern cooks substituted the more generally available ground beef), but has little seasoning.

I've gone a few steps further with this adaptation, eliminating the usual béchamel topping (or its contemporary adaptation, a self-bake custard of eggs and cheese) and cutting back considerably on fat by grilling the vegetables prior to baking. The result is an absolutely sensational meal that is both filling and good for you.

olive oil
1 eggplant, about ¾ pound
salt
1 red bell pepper
1 medium-sized baking potato
water
¾ pound ground lamb
½ cup chopped onion
3 cloves garlic, minced
½ teaspoon dried, or 1 teaspoon freshly minced, rosemary
14½-ounce can tomatoes
¼ cup red wine or cooking sherry
¼ cup raisins
freshly ground black pepper

Preheat the broiler. Preheat the oven to 350°F. (If your broiler and oven are combined, preheat broiler first; then, after broiling eggplant slices, bring oven to 350°F.) Use olive oil to lightly grease a 1½-quart casserole or baking dish.

Peel the eggplant and slice it into rounds ⅛ inch thick. Salt each side, and lay the rounds on a paper towel to sweat for 20 minutes.

While the eggplant is sweating, cut the pepper in half lengthwise, remove the stem, seeds, and white membrane, and lay the halves cut-side down on the broiler pan. Broil until the skin blackens and blisters. Remove the pepper, but leave the broiler on. Peel the pepper, and cut it into ⅛-inch strips.

Peel the potato and cut it into thin rounds. In a large skillet with a cover, bring ½ inch of salted water to a boil. Add the potato slices, using a spatula to spread them evenly across the pan. Cover, turn down the heat, and simmer for 3 minutes, until the potatoes are tender. Remove from the heat and drain. Wipe the skillet with a paper towel. Line the oiled casserole with the potatoes.

In the skillet, over medium heat, cook the lamb, onion, garlic, and rosemary until the lamb is just browned. Add the tomatoes and wine, cover, and simmer on low while you do the next step.

Quickly rinse the eggplant slices and pat them dry. Lay the slices on the broiler pan and broil until the eggplant begins to soften and the top begins to brown. Don't crowd the pieces; broil in batches until all are done. Turn the slices over and brown the second side.

Remove the meat sauce from the heat, add the raisins, and stir. Add salt and pepper to taste.

Layer half of the eggplant slices over the potatoes and top with half the sauce. Layer the rest of the eggplant, then top with the peppers, and cover with sauce. Cover the casserole with a snug lid or aluminum foil, and bake for 1 hour. Serve warm.

Earlier in the twentieth century, Kentucky lamb was a prized gourmet item—in cities to the north. Although the state raised a substantial quantity of the commercially available lamb in the United States, virtually all of it was shipped out of state, primarily to Chicago. With the exception of the barbecued mutton tradition around Owensboro, in the western part of the state, sheep just weren't eaten in these parts. Eventually commercial lamb production fell off.

But the mystique of tender, delicate Kentucky lamb remains. And with good reason. Maybe it's the same limestone-filtered water that makes for great bourbon and strong thoroughbreds, but lamb from Kentucky does seem to taste a little finer. And in the last decade, there's been a slow resurgence of interest in eating it, even in the bluegrass.

I buy Kentucky lamb from Kurz Meat Shoppe in Louisville, a place I first went to because it was convenient, but which I now patronize steadily because owner Willie Mitchell is a man who cares about quality. That's demonstrated not only in the prime cuts of meat and farm-raised poultry he sells, but also in the array of sausages he makes. Ranging from apple-cinnamon pork patties for breakfast, to a special Cajun venison blend, to a surprising Hungarian rope sausage, flavored with paprika and fresh lemon rind, Willie's recipes deliver on flavor, without a lot of fat.

No great sausage can be fat-free, of course, but Willie has experimented with blends to cut the fat level back as much as possible and still produce a juicy, flavorful link. My favorite? Rosemary Lamb, with lean, fresh Kentucky lamb and rosemary in an almost delicate combo. I like to have some frozen for those last-minute supper crises: added to cooked butter beans and potatoes it's an instant cassoulet. And I confess I generally use it in my New South Moussaka recipe instead of the ground lamb, rosemary, and garlic combination.

Now you can, too. Kurz Meat Shoppe is willing to ship frozen home-style sausages (no MSG, no preservatives) to anywhere they can be delivered overnight. See Things to Order, page 338.

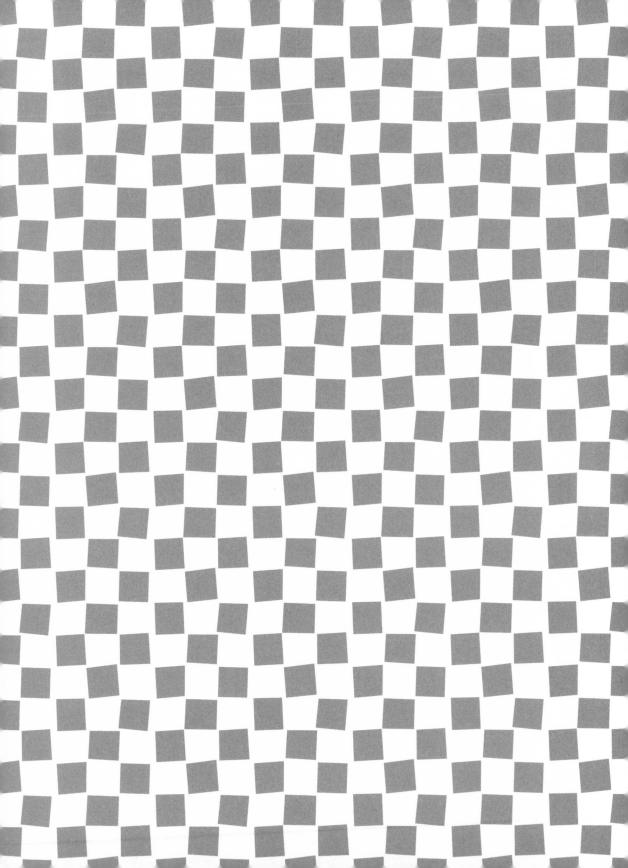

BELL PEPPERS

Lamb and Rice Stuffed Peppers

Maque Choux Stuffed Peppers

José's Hush Puppies Stuffed with Shrimp Provençal

Creamy Red Pepper Soup

Stewart's Potato Salad with Bell Peppers

White Cheddar and Roasted Red Pepper Cheese

Sweet peppers showed up on the Southern dinner table all summer long. My mother served them raw, with stems and seeds removed, and sliced—the dark green bell peppers in long, narrow strips, the pale banana peppers in little rounds. We ate them as a relish, like trimmed green onions or cucumber wedges, taking little bites to fill out the flavor of the beans or meat or vegetable on our plate. For a between-meal snack, I liked to pour some salt in the palm of my hand and dip the bittersweet bell pepper strips in it.

Sweet peppers were also cooked in the Southern kitchen. They are part of the holy Cajun Trinity—along with onion and celery—that defines gumbo, jambalaya, and étouffée. Black cooks tossed hot pepper pods into pots of greens or beans, giving them a distinctive "soul food" difference.

Pimiento cheese was de rigueur not only on every Southern picnic table but stuffed into tender celery stalks at Christmas and Thanksgiving. And peppers popped up in salads, from classic potato salad to a strange lime-green Jell-O concoction my mother used to serve, which had cabbage and carrots as well.

Hot peppers came to the table sliced very thin and passed on small saucers decorated with delicate flowers around the edge, belying the peppers' powerful punch. Hot pepper jelly of translucent gold, flecked with pieces of red and/or green, or dyed bright ruby-red or emerald, was a traditional Christmas gift. A popular Southern appetizer consists of this jelly simply spooned out over a softened slab of cream cheese and served with corn chips or crackers.

The prevailing pepper of my youth was the dark-green bell, with cameo appearances by its long, lighter cousin called either the Hungarian pepper or (more commonly) banana pepper. In groceries today, bell peppers of red, yellow, and sometimes even purple hue are offered—often for a king's ransom. I see no agricultural reason why red peppers should cost up to five times as much as their green kin, but as long as customers are ready to pay the difference, I'm sure it will exist. This makes the farm market an even more attractive place to buy peppers in season. Not only are the prices more reasonable but a greater variety of pepper shades and shapes is available. My favorite in recent years is the lipstick pepper—plump, triangular, about as long as my thumb, and colored a bright red reminiscent of the pucker of 1940s film stars. Its flavor is even sweeter than the standard red bell pepper, and I like especially to use it in quick table condiments, such as the Sorghum Pepper Relish served with Okra Corn Fritters (page 164).

Stuffed Peppers

Filling hollowed-out vegetables with savory stuffings is a favorite cooking trick, and bell peppers look as if they were designed for the job. It's curious, then, that so little creativity seems to have been applied to the basic premise. Say "stuffed pepper" to anyone who's eaten one in the last fifty years, and he or she will inevitably think of a filling of hamburger, rice or breadcrumbs, onions, and maybe tomato sauce. Modern Southern cooks were sometimes a little more daring, and used pork sausage or added corn to the mix.

Even in earlier versions, stuffed peppers were primarily a way to use leftover meat. In *Cross Creek Cookery* (Scribner, 1971), Marjorie Kinnan Rawlings advises filling the pepper with leftover bits of beef, ham, or lamb mixed with a cream sauce. The first stuffed-pepper recipe here is a snazzier variation on the lamb theme. The Cajun-style Maque Choux (pronounced "mock shoe" and meaning a savory smothered corn dish) makes use of the bell pepper's natural affinity for corn in any form.

Pick peppers which have thick, rather than thin, flesh, and make sure they have no blemishes, since you don't want to have to cut out any plugs which stuffing might run out of.

You may use bell peppers of any color for these recipes. I prefer the sweeter flavor of red peppers, and love the look of yellow and red peppers mixed on a platter. Don't invest in the high-priced purple peppers, however, since they turn a drab khaki when heated.

If you find large peppers, you can split them in half lengthwise to stuff them. (If removing the stem makes a gap through which the stuffing will leak, fold a 4-inch square of aluminum foil to make a strip about 1 inch wide, and curve it around the top to make a collar.)

If you find small peppers, they can be stuffed whole. They will need to stand on end in the baking pan, however, so select ones with even bottoms. If you nevertheless get a tipsy one, make a thick aluminum foil strip, as described above, and curl it around the bottom of the pepper to help support it while baking.

Lamb and Rice Stuffed Peppers
SERVES 6

3 large, or 6 small, bell peppers
¾ pound ground lamb
¼ cup minced onion
1 clove minced garlic
½ teaspoon dried, or 1 teaspoon freshly minced, rosemary
2 cups cooked white rice
¾ cup finely chopped almonds
¾ cup raisins
¼ teaspoon kosher salt
white wine or water

Preheat the oven to 350°F.

Rinse the peppers. If you are using large peppers, cut out the stems, leaving as much of the fleshy tops intact as possible.

Split the peppers in half and carefully remove the seeds and white membrane. Lay the peppers, with the cavity up, in a baking pan. If you are using small peppers, trim the tops off evenly, and carefully remove any seeds and white membrane from inside. Stand on end in the baking pan.

In a bowl, toss the lamb, onion, garlic, and rosemary with a fork until well blended. Add the rice, almonds, raisins, and salt. Mix with a wooden spoon to blend, patting the mixture together so it makes a cohesive mass, though not as firm as a meat loaf. Add a tablespoon or so of wine or water, if needed, to moisten and make it stick together.

Spoon the mixture equally into the peppers, patting gently with the back of the spoon and mounding it up. When the peppers are filled, pour wine or water into the baking pan, no more than ⅛ inch deep. Bake for 50 minutes, until the mixture is golden brown on top and the peppers are tender. Serve warm with a side dish and salad.

Maque Choux Stuffed Peppers
SERVES 6

3 large, or 6 small, bell peppers
6 ears corn
½ cup minced onion
2 garlic cloves, minced
½ cup diced tasso (see page 42)
1 cup peeled and diced fresh tomato
½ teaspoon kosher salt
1 cup buttermilk

4 tablespoons corn flour (see Note on page 107)
water

Preheat the oven to 350°F. Prepare the peppers for stuffing as in the previous recipe.

Cut the corn from the ears according to the description on page 101. Mix the corn and its milk with the onion, garlic, tasso, tomato, and salt. In a small bowl, whisk together the buttermilk and corn flour until blended. Add to the corn mixture and mix thoroughly.

Spoon the mixture equally into the peppers, patting gently with the back of the spoon and mounding it up. When the peppers are filled, pour water into the baking pan, no more than ⅛ inch deep. Bake for 50 minutes, until the mixture is golden brown on top and the peppers are tender. Serve warm with a side dish and salad.

Note: *If you prefer, you can eliminate the tasso, making this a meatless dish. If you do, use plenty of ground black pepper and ground red chile or cayenne to season the filling. Peppers can also serve as a hearty side dish.*

José's Hush Puppies Stuffed with Shrimp Provençal
MAKES 20 TO 24

French-born and trained, José Gutierrez melds Continental flair with an appreciation for the superb products of the South in his position as executive chef at Memphis's Peabody Hotel. (See Places to Go, page 341.) He also adds a dash of humor. He tells me that one of his tricks is to substitute moonshine for cognac to give traditional French recipes a Southern twang. When I ask how he gets the moonshine, his answer is "Very, very, carefully."

Here he pulls a switch on the traditional idea of stuffed peppers, choosing instead to stuff hush puppies with Shrimp Provençal, which has been jazzed up for both eye and palate with minced red bell pepper.

As to how he ended up in Memphis, he explains, "I was in Houston and they told me Elvis was still alive. What could I do but come to Memphis?"

HUSH PUPPIES
4 leaves fresh basil (optional)
1 cup yellow cornmeal
1 large egg
¼ cup diced onion
1 teaspoon flour
dash of salt
dash of pepper
1½ quarts peanut oil

Cut basil into very thin ribbons and mix with remaining ingredients except peanut oil. Set aside for 30 minutes while you prepare the Shrimp Provençal. When you are ready to fry, heat the peanut oil to 300°F in a heavy pan deep enough to accommodate all the oil with 4 inches of space at the top.

Scoop about 2 tablespoons' worth of batter into the heated oil. Fry several hush puppies at a time, but make sure not to crowd the pan. Fry until they turn an appetizing brown—it doesn't take long. Remove from oil and let drain on rack set over paper towels. When they are cool enough to handle, scoop out the center, leaving only the thinnest yellow cornbread layer on the inside. Remove nearly all the center. Fill with Shrimp Provençal.

SHRIMP PROVENÇAL
12 medium uncooked shrimp
2 tablespoons unsalted butter
½ cup peeled and diced carrot
½ cup diced celery
½ medium red bell pepper, minced
3 shallots, minced (about ½ cup)
1 clove garlic, chopped
1 tablespoon dry vermouth
1 cup cream
½ teaspoon kosher salt
½ teaspoon pepper
½ cup minced fresh parsley

Peel and devein the shrimp and roughly chop them. Melt the butter in a wide, deep skillet, and add the vegetables and garlic, cooking over medium heat until soft but not brown, about 5 minutes. Add the shrimp and cook for 1 minute, or until they become just opaque. Add the vermouth and cream, and cook for 3 minutes, stirring often. The cream will thicken somewhat as it cooks. Add salt and pepper to taste.

These may be served three to a plate on a bed of lettuce lightly dressed with vinaigrette, or passed as an appetizer. (They're a perfect finger food.) They may also be prepared up to an hour in advance and kept in a warm oven.

Creamy Red Pepper Soup

SERVES 6

This soup simmers for less than 30 minutes, and so makes a wonderful summer supper dish, served with bread and butter and a plate of sliced cucumbers. Or it's perfect to complete a feast of fresh ears of corn. The soup is at its best served immediately, but you can also refrigerate it and serve it cold.

3 tablespoons butter
1 large white onion, chopped
8 large red bell peppers, coarsely
　chopped
5 cups defatted chicken stock
1 teaspoon minced fresh thyme
salt
freshly ground pepper
1 cup half and half

In a large pot, melt the butter over medium heat, and cook the onion until it begins to soften. Add the peppers, and toss until all the pieces are coated with butter. Add the stock, turn the heat up, and bring to a boil. When the mixture begins to boil, turn the heat down, cover, and simmer for 20 to 25 minutes, until the peppers are tender but not mushy.

Remove from the heat and allow to cool for a few minutes. Processing no more than 2 cups at a time, pulse the peppers and broth in a blender on low speed until the mixture is a blend of puree and chunks. (Hot mixtures sometimes "explode" through the cap of the blender, so the safest way to do this is to cover the top of the blender with a kitchen towel, folded a couple of thicknesses, and use a hot pad to hold the top on as you process. You must also not overfill the blender, hence only 2 cups at a time.)

When all the soup is pureed, add the thyme and salt and pepper to taste. Stir in the half and half and serve immediately.

Stewart's Potato Salad with Bell Peppers

SERVES 10

From the post–World War II era right through the turbulent sixties and seventies, Fourth Street in downtown Louisville, Kentucky, was a sea of Southern womanhood every Saturday and on Monday nights. That's when mothers and their daughters, with an occasional reluctant little brother in tow, would trek from store to store for hours of shopping. You'd find most of the Louisville matrons shopping—even in the summer—wearing flowery hats and crisp white gloves. And while their daughters might forgo the haberdashery, you can bet they were still clad in stockings and sported a purse with shoes to match.

There were plenty of restaurants in downtown Louisville, but only one place where these mother/daughter teams really *loved* to dine, Stewart's Dry Goods. Upstairs in the venerable department store was a tony tearoom, painted in pastels and set with cloths on the tables, but what my mother preferred was the more relaxed luncheonette in the basement, where a hard-shopping gal could lean back and relax.

The menu offered lovely ladies' lunch items like date-nut bread with cream cheese, or cream cheese, olive, and nut sandwiches. My mom and dozens like her more often than not preferred to make a meal of nothing more than Stewart's signature potato salad. The salad was revered in its heyday, but grew to near mythic proportions in memory when Stewart's shut its downtown doors for good in the early 1980s. Old-timers swore that the potato salad served at the store's suburban location simply wasn't the same.

The secrets to Stewart's great salad were two: homemade mayonnaise and slivers of green bell pepper. I confess I have never had the patience to make my own mayo. I like Hellmann's mayonnaise. Spiked here with a little fresh lemon, it replicates the Stewart's flavor superbly.

As for the pepper, it must be cut in small pieces, no wider than ⅛ inch, no thicker than 1/16.

Except for the slight change in mayonnaise, this recipe is like the one popularly known as the authentic Stewart's potato salad.

5 large Idaho potatoes
1 small onion, finely chopped
½ cup finely chopped celery
1 small green bell pepper, seeded, stemmed, and finely chopped
2 ounces chopped pimiento
3 hard-boiled eggs, chopped
1 cup mayonnaise
⅓ cup juice from pickle relish or sweet pickles
1 teaspoon fresh lemon juice
salt
freshly ground black pepper

Boil the potatoes until tender. Let them cool, then peel and dice them into cubes about the size of a bouillon cube. Put them in a large mixing bowl and add the onion, celery, bell pepper, pimiento, and eggs. Toss lightly to distribute evenly.

Mix the mayonnaise, relish juice, and lemon juice until blended, then add it to the bowl and mix well. Add salt and pepper to taste.

For the full Stewart's experience, serve on chilled individual salad plates covered with leaves of iceberg lettuce and garnished with a lemon wedge. Pass crisp saltine crackers on the side. And while you eat it, put your feet up and relax.

White Cheddar and Roasted Red Pepper Cheese   MAKES ABOUT 2 CUPS

Pimiento cheese earned its welcome not only by being tasty but also by being convenient. Unfortunately, the commercially produced spreads that are now available in groceries throughout the South usually emphasize the latter trait, sacrificing the first to goopy, too-sweet dressings used to bind the more savory elements of the spread together.

This recipe is a snap to pull together and adds a snappy flavor to any luncheon or buffet. Make sandwiches on thin-sliced crusty French bread with buttery Bibb lettuce, or on a light wheat bread with very, very thin slices of tart apple. You can also serve it spread on savory sesame crackers or mounded into celery sticks. I like to spread it thick on a piece of bread, pop the whole thing in the toaster oven or under the broiler, and let it grill until the cheese starts to turn brown and golden.

You can use plain pimientos in jars, of course, but for flavor's sake I like to use the faintly smoky roasted red peppers (put up in just a bit of olive oil) that are easily found in fine-food stores and ethnic markets. If you use the plain pimientoes (or choose to roast your own peppers), mix a dash of good olive oil with the juice from the peppers before adding it to the dressing.

MAIL ORDER

Pepper Jelly

Probably because of its jewel-like colors—red, green, or amber flecked with red and green—ribbon-festooned, half-pint jars of pepper jelly are popular Christmas gifts around the South. But like that other popular edible holiday tradition—fruitcake—pepper jelly has as many foes as friends, and jars sometimes end up being passed from one unappreciative family to another until they find that happy home where someone likes to slather the hot, sweet condiment on ham, dollop it into soup beans, or pour it over softened cream cheese to make an instant dip.

If you have never tried pepper jelly, you can order a sampling of the South's finest from the A. M. Braswell Food Company of Statesboro, Georgia, which has been commercially producing distinctive and delightful Southern-style preserves, jellies, and relishes since before World War II.

Braswell's makes both red pepper and green pepper jelly, and, in a bow to contemporary tastes, has added jalapeño jelly in recent years. The company is also a great source for fantastic fig and pear preserves, and produces a savory artichoke relish extrapolated from a recipe handed down by Albert M. Braswell's grandmother. See Things to Order, page 338.

The Lee Brothers, of boiled peanut fame, also sell Mrs. Sassard's Hot Pepper Jelly through their mail-order business (see page 338). And one of the more unusual pepper jellies offered is the Serendipity of the Valley Jalapeño Orange Jelly made from wild oranges that grow in the Rio Grande Valley. The jelly, along with a tart Wild Orange and delicate Ruby Red Grapefruit, is made in small batches which they sell by mail. See Things to Order, page 338.

8 ounces white cheddar cheese

4 ounces roasted red bell peppers in olive oil

⅓ cup mayonnaise

2 teaspoons oil and juice from the peppers

1 teaspoon freshly squeezed lemon juice

Coarsely grate the cheese into a large bowl. Chop the peppers into ¼-inch dice and add them. Toss with a fork to mix.

In a smaller bowl, whisk together the mayonnaise, pepper juices and oil, and lemon juice until smooth. Pour over the cheese and lightly mix together until well blended. Cover tightly and chill until ready to use.

SQUASH

Pattypan and Leek Buttermilk Soup

Stuffed Mirliton

Lime Chayote

Dudley's Spaghetti Squash with
Spicy Peanut Sauce

Middle Eastern Ratty-too

Crookneck Squash Casserole

Winter Squash and Hominy Soup

Pumpkin Grits Pudding

Odd as it may seem, I was in my twenties before I cooked my first zucchini—part of the recipe for minestrone I made weekly as a cook at Santa Fe's Jefferson Street Soup Company. It's not that I wasn't familiar with summer squash. Oh no, we'd had plenty when I was growing up, but with a choice of flavorful varieties in an amusing array of colors and shapes, the bland zucchini had never held much fascination. Even its somewhat playful-sounding name (our daughter's first teddy bear was called Zucchini) didn't compare to the descriptive, melodious names of squash I grew up with: yellow crookneck, pattypan or cymling, and the lilting mirliton rolled off the tongue with a Creole trill of "r" and "l."

These days, I like zucchini as well as the next cook (but perhaps a little less than most gardeners, remembering well the summer we grew the Zucchini That Ate the Whole Garden). It is dependable, nearly indestructible, and always available at the grocery. Nevertheless, if it's flavor I'm looking for in a squash recipe—and the simple ones here require just that—yellow crookneck or pattypan simply can't be beat. And as for winter squash, there is nothing like the honeyed, orange-fleshed sweet potato squash, so tasty you need do nothing but bake it and serve it up drenched in butter.

Pattypan and Leek Buttermilk Soup

SERVES 4 AS A MAIN COURSE, 8 AS AN APPETIZER

Such a dilemma! Pattypans are also called cymlings, a name so pretty it's hard to pass it up when titling a recipe. But pattypan seems best to describe the down-home charm of this tangy soup. You can make it with other summer squashes, such as yellow crookneck or even zucchini, but pattypans, with their firmer skin and pale color, are the most attractive both visually and texturally.

This is a light and pleasant soup to serve warm, but the flavor is most sensational after it's been chilled, making it a fine choice for supper on a hot summer night. It matches up very well with a dark rye bread. We also like to serve a creamy local goat cheese seasoned with dill on the side.

3 medium-sized leeks (about ½ pound total)
1 tablespoon butter
2 medium-sized pattypan squash (about 1 pound)
1½ cups defatted chicken stock
¼ teaspoon kosher salt
3 cups nonfat buttermilk
fresh herbs (optional)

Clean the leeks thoroughly (see Note), and chop both whites and undamaged greens into ½-inch pieces. Melt the butter in a medium-sized pot, then sauté the leeks over medium heat until tender, 7 to 10 minutes, stirring occasionally to keep them from sticking.

While the leeks are cooking, trim the squash (but don't peel) and cut them into ½-inch cubes. When the leeks are softened, add the squash, stock, and salt to the pot. Bring to a boil, then turn the heat down to a lively simmer, and cook, covered, until the skin of the squash can be easily pierced by a fork (about 15 minutes).

If you are going to serve the soup warm, remove the pot from the heat, quickly stir in the buttermilk, taste, and add more salt, if needed. Serve immediately.

If you are going to serve the soup chilled, transfer the contents of the pot to another container, and chill for at least an hour. When you are ready to serve, stir in the buttermilk; taste and add more salt, if needed, then serve.

In either case, you may wish to garnish with snippets of fresh dill, basil, savory, cilantro, or another herb (although I like the soup's simple, tonic brace without additions).

Note: *Leeks love to collect grit between their many layers. To clean, first chop off the root end and any dark tough ends of the green leaves. Rinse well to remove surface dirt. Cut the leek in two lengthwise to expose interior. Hold under cold running water, fanning the* *layers a little with your thumbs so the water can rinse between them. Also rinse the cutting board and knife before chopping the cleaned leeks. Should any grit appear during chopping, put chopped leeks into a colander and rinse again before adding to recipe.*

Stuffed Mirliton
SERVES 4 AS A SIDE DISH

Unless you live in southwest Louisiana or the Alabama or Mississippi areas of the Gulf, chances are you see this squash in your grocery identified as chayote. That's what it's called in Florida and the Southwest as well. But here we'll use the Creole name, since the delicacy of the mirliton shines in this recipe done in a simple, French-influenced style.

2 medium mirlitons
½ tablespoon butter
⅛ cup minced onion
1 cup soft white bread crumbs
3 tablespoons fresh grated parmesan
freshly grated nutmeg

Preheat the oven to 350°F.

Split each squash lengthwise to make two wide halves. Remove the seed and discard. Steam the halves, face down, over water, but not in it, for 25 minutes, until the flesh is very tender. (If you do not have a vegetable steamer that will accommodate the 4 halves, you can improvise by placing a cake rack in a skillet, with water below it.)

Use a small spoon to carefully scrape the flesh from the squash, leaving the skin intact. Puree the flesh in a food processor or blender.

Heat the butter in a small pan and sauté the onion until it begins to soften. Add the bread crumbs, and toss until just golden. Add the squash puree, and stir until everything is heated well. Remove from the heat, and stir in the parmesan.

Place the squash shells in a lightly oiled shallow baking pan. Fill each with squash puree, mounding it slightly. Bake 15 to 20 minutes, until browned and bubbly. Serve immediately.

Lime Chayote — SERVES 4

For this recipe I use the name "chayote" rather than "mirliton," since it has more of a tropical, south-of-the-border flavor. By either name, the pale green, avocado-shaped, ribbed squash you buy should be firm to the touch and unblemished. Some folks insist on peeling the skin. It's a simple task if you have a smooth-skinned variety (just use a potato peeler), but more difficult if the chayote is deeply ribbed. Then you will need to cut it into sections and use a sharp knife. But truthfully, I find the skin flavorful and never too tough, so I just leave it.

Don't pass over this recipe because of its apparent simpleness. It's a wonderful way to make friends with this slightly sweet, delicate squash.

2 medium chayotes
1 teaspoon butter
juice of ¼ lime
ground red chile
salt

Peel the chayotes and split them in half, discarding the seeds. Slice them very thin.

In a sauté pan or small skillet, melt the butter over very low heat. Add the squash, and toss to coat. Cook the squash over very low heat for 15 to 20 minutes, turning occasionally, until it is just turning tender. Remove it to a warm plate and drizzle lime juice over it. Sprinkle *very* lightly with ground red chile and salt. Serve immediately.

Dudley's Spaghetti Squash with Spicy Peanut Sauce — SERVES 4

This may seem an odd recipe to come across in a cookbook about Southern food. After all, isn't the spaghetti squash a purely California invention? And doesn't this particular sauce smack of eastern Indian cuisine?

The fact is, smart Southern cooks and gardeners have always appropriated new tricks to their tables, and spaghetti squash certainly fills the bill.

No one knows for sure where the squash originated, although it appears to be a New World crop. Everyone pretty much agrees that it was Los Angeles–based produce distributor Frieda Caplan who got it on the market with a splash in the 1970s. Southern cooks, already big fans of squash, embraced it with a passion, enchanted by the pasta-bilities of its thin vegetable strands and the fact of its lower calories compared to the pasta it replaced in most recipes. A large part of the commercial crop now comes from Georgia, and the squash graces Southern tables in the fall and winter.

The threads that are pulled from the inside of cooked spaghetti squash are perfect for saucing, and the first generation of dishes were inevitably tossed in marinara. But the kitchen at Dudley's Restaurant in Lexington, Kentucky (see Places to Go, page 341), decided to take a different tack when asked to use locally grown spaghetti squash for their presentation at the first Ohio Valley Harvest Festival (see page 219). They came up with the spicy peanut topping featured here, which is quite at home among more traditional Southern dishes.

Although common lore has encouraged us to believe that the South has had only two populations through its history— white Southerners descended from English immigrants and black Southerners descended from African slaves—the truth is much more diverse. In colonial times, the South had the most polyglot population in the English colonies, including, most notably, those of Spanish, French, German, and, later, Italian descent. Greek immigrants in the South had an impact on the restaurants established there; and the cooking of India and other Middle Eastern cultures was an influence as far back as the earliest days of coastal trading, preceding the arrival in recent years of a large population of Indian immigrants, many of whom now have restaurants.

Curries, chutneys, and the spices of the East are all elements of traditional Southern cooking, going back to the early trade days of the coastal South. Their hot, sweet flavors nicely complement the chicken or pork, beans and greens most of us expect on the Southern table.

Try this as a side dish with field peas, greens, and cornbread.

1 cup hoisin sauce
1 cup crushed roasted peanuts
1 teaspoon minced fresh ginger
½ teaspoon minced garlic
6 ounces pineapple juice
1 teaspoon sambal (see Note)
salt
2-pound spaghetti squash
olive oil
½ cup chopped green onion

Preheat the oven to 375°F.

To make the sauce, puree the hoisin, peanuts, ginger, garlic, pineapple juice, and sambal until smooth. Taste, and add salt, if necessary. Set aside.

Slice the squash end to end. Scoop out the seeds and discard. Brush the cut surface with olive oil, and lay the halves face down on an oiled baking sheet. Bake for approximately 30 minutes, until the surface of the squash is soft and does not spring back when touched.

Remove the squash from the oven, and let it cool only until it can be handled. Use a fork to "comb" from end to end, lifting out the interior meat of the squash in strands, like spaghetti.

Place the warm squash strands in a large bowl, and toss with the spicy peanut sauce until thoroughly coated. Chill. Serve topped with chopped green onion.

Note: *Sambal is an Indonesian condiment consisting of a paste of hot chiles seasoned with various spices and lime juice. It's available at specialty food stores and many Chinese markets.*

Note: *The squash is also quite yummy dressed with strips of grilled chicken or pork and slivers of cucumber. Serve as a main course.*

"Eveline looked up and sniffed the air. Out in the kitchen Moddy was cooking a succulent ratty-too of the first vegetables, the primeurs. Or 'preemers' as she said.

"'Much better the second day, iffen I can keep your greedy paws outen it,' Moddy had told her as she chopped the onions."

—Eugene Walter, *The Likes of Which*
(Decatur House Press, 1980)

| Middle Eastern Ratty-Too | SERVES 6 |

Ratatouille, the popular dish from Provence that makes the most of the summer garden by combining squash, tomatoes, onions, garlic, and herbs in olive oil, was a natural for Southern cooks. It takes only some subtle changes in the spices to convert this classic summer dish to a new sensation, one with a Middle Eastern flair. This has been my family's favorite version of "ratty-too" for two decades now, delicious when it's first made and even better frozen, then thawed out and simmered to provide a taste and vision of summer in December.

Use whatever summer squash are available, but be sure to include some bright yellow crookneck for the best color. Serve with cornbread or over grits or rice.

1 tablespoon olive oil
1½ cups chopped onion
3 teaspoons cumin seed
3 teaspoons coriander seed
6 cloves
1 clove garlic, sliced
6 summer squash, 5 to 7 inches long
4 medium-sized fresh tomatoes
¼ teaspoon ground turmeric
1 teaspoon kosher salt

In a heavy 4-quart saucepan with a lid, heat the olive oil over medium-low heat. Add the onion, and cook until it is transparent.

While the onion is cooking, grind the

cumin, coriander, and cloves together until fine. Sprinkle the ground spices over the onion. Add the garlic. Cover, and cook 3 minutes, while you prepare the squash.

Wash the squash, remove the stems, and cut it into ½-inch-thick pieces. Add them to the pot, stir, cover, and turn the heat to low. Simmer while you peel the tomatoes and chop them into 1-inch cubes. Add them and their juice to the pot.

Add the turmeric and salt, and stir. Cover, and turn the heat up to medium. Cook, covered, for 30 minutes, or until the squash is meltingly tender. Taste and adjust the salt. You can also add more of the spices, if you like.

Crookneck Squash Casserole   SERVES 4

The squash casserole I ate so greedily at Bryce's Cafeteria in Texarkana (page 17) seemed to me very similar to one I used to have at the Lone Oak Restaurant outside Scottsville, Kentucky. The chief difference was that Bryce's tasted as if it had been seasoned with bacon grease instead of the butter of the Lone Oak's.

I called Bryce Lawrence, Jr., who, with his brother Richard, still runs the family restaurant, and he was very gracious and apologetic, but said he just simply could not tell me how they made that casserole. "It's an old family recipe, like most of ours," he explained. "But our recipes are

our livelihood, and we never give any of them out, even to our most faithful customers."

Such reluctance isn't unusual from longtime restaurateurs in the South. In fact, when I asked Mrs. Forest Stice, owner of the Lone Oak, for her recipe for Meal Pie for my first book several years ago, she demurred, but gave me her squash casserole recipe for consolation. I've adapted it here, with bacon added to give it a Texarkana twist. I won't suggest that this is the same casserole you'll have if you stop by Bryce's, but I'll guarantee that if you make it, you won't have any leftovers.

4 cups sliced fresh yellow summer
    squash
4 slices bacon
⅛ teaspoon kosher salt
4 tablespoons sugar
¼ cup minced white onion

Preheat the oven to 350°F. Meanwhile, steam the squash for about 12 minutes, or until very tender. While the squash is steaming, fry the bacon until crisp, and set it aside. When the squash is tender, mash it together with the bacon grease, salt, and sugar, then add the onion, and stir until the mixture is thoroughly blended. (If you have steamed the squash in a steamer that holds the juices with the vegetable, the mixture will be juicy. If you haven't, you may want to add a few tablespoons of the steaming liquid left in the pan to make it soupy.)

Pour the mixture into a buttered casserole dish, and bake until it has firmed up and begins to brown (35 to 45 minutes, usually). Crumble the bacon on top, and serve immediately.

Note: *In some squash recipes, zucchini and yellow summer squash are interchangeable. Not this one. Zucchini is too watery and not flavorful enough for this casserole. Pattypan squash works well, however, although it may take you a little longer to steam its somewhat tougher skin to the tender stage.*

Winter Squash and Hominy Soup
SERVES 4

Winter stews of squash and hominy (dried corn kernels with hull and germ removed) were made by the first Southerners, the Indian tribes that lived throughout the region. New settlers enthusiastically took the nourishing dish as their own. This recipe can be made even more quickly by substituting a can of unseasoned pumpkin puree, but the baked squash gives it a better flavor. This soup does not reheat well.

1 small (1- to 2-pound) sweet potato
    squash, or other winter squash, or
    pumpkin
1 tablespoon butter
1 cup finely chopped onion
2 cups chicken or vegetable broth
15½-ounce can white hominy, drained
⅛ teaspoon ground red chile
salt

Preheat the oven to 425°F. Lightly grease a baking sheet. Pierce the flesh of the squash a few times with a fork or, if the skin is too tough, cut small gashes with a knife. Place it on the baking sheet, and bake until tender when pressed with a finger, about 40 minutes.

Remove the squash and let it cool enough to be handled. Cut it in half, and discard the seeds and stem. Scoop the flesh out; discard the skin. Puree using a blender, food processor, or potato masher.

Melt the butter in a pot over medium heat, then add the onion and sauté 1 minute. Add the broth and hominy, and stir. Add the squash puree, stir, and bring to the point just before boiling, when the mixture is very steamy but not yet bubbling. Remove from the heat, and stir in the ground chile. Add salt to taste. Serve immediately.

Pumpkin Grits Pudding
SERVES 6

The pumpkin was one of the first native foods European settlers adopted, and one that served them well as they moved west. Early Southern colonials and pioneers dried the flesh to eat while traveling, cooked slabs of the squash next to the hearth to be served with butter (when it was available), and mixed it with that other New World food find, corn, which had been dried. This recipe harks back to that early pairing but is hardly the rough fare of that era. In fact, it's quite creamy and delectable—and makes an excellent savory side dish for Thanksgiving dinner.

4 cups water
1 teaspoon kosher salt
1 cup stone-ground white grits
1 cup milk
2 tablespoons butter
1 cup canned pumpkin puree
1 tablespoon minced fresh ginger
1 teaspoon ground cardamom
nutmeg

Bring the water and salt to a boil, and slowly pour in the grits, stirring as you do. Cook at a low simmer, stirring frequently, for 25 minutes, until the water is absorbed and the grits are becoming creamy. Continue to cook for another 5 minutes, stirring and adding the milk, a little at a time. Taste the grits. If they are softened and creamy, proceed to the next step. If they are still a little gritty, continue to simmer on low until they reach tenderness.

When the grits are ready, stir in the butter until it is melted. Stir in the pumpkin puree, ginger, and cardamom. When the mixture is blended and steaming, remove it from the heat and cover it. Allow it to sit for 15 minutes, then serve immediately with fresh nutmeg grated over the top.

Sweet potatoes

Sweet Potato Hash

Subtle Sugar and Spice Sweet Potatoes with Peanuts

Sweet Potato and Corn Chowder

Ginger Sorghum Sweet Potato Pie

Sorghum and Sweet Potato Ice Cream

Lord, how we love them. Red as the clay of north Georgia, orange as a sunset on the Gulf shore. There is something in the honeyed, earthy flavor of the sweet potato that evokes the very Southern dirt they are pulled from.

You will hear Southerners assert that there is a difference between a common sweet potato and something they call a yam. In fact, the real yam is another vegetable altogether, the very soul of much African cuisine. When black slaves first tasted the somewhat similar sweet potato in the land of bondage, they called it after the food of home.

In the 1930s, savvy sweet potato producers in Louisiana christened their product "yams" to distinguish them from paler—and many think less flavorful— sweet potatoes from the North, particularly New Jersey. Southerners, myself included, still look for the potatoes with dark red or deep orange flesh, for their richer flavor and sweetness. And Louisianans still celebrate the yam with an annual festival in Opelousas. It's called the Yambilee and is held in the local "Yamatorium."

To understand what the Southern passion for this potato is about, you need to buy the reddest unblemished sweet potato you can find on the first really cold, crisp day in the fall. Take it home and preheat the oven to 425°F. Rinse the potato and dry it. Pierce it three or four times with the tines of a fork, and rub it all over with a little bit of butter or oil.

When the oven is good and hot, put the potato on the rack (put a cookie sheet under it if you don't want to wipe out caramelized juices from the bottom of the oven later) and bake for 45 to 75 minutes (depending on the size of the potato) until a fork moves easily through the middle.

Pop that potato in a bowl or on a plate and use the fork to make a slash through the top, then press the sides together to plump up the sweet flesh inside. Place a big dollop of the best butter you can buy on top, and watch while it oozes inside. Get yourself a tall glass of really cold milk. Eat the potato as soon as it is cooled enough to pop a bite in your mouth without burning. Now you see.

In addition to their exquisite taste, sweet potatoes are jam-packed with vitamins and minerals. They are better than carrots in most cooked recipes, having a more distinctive flavor and maintaining their color through long cooking. I use them regularly in soups and stews, and it was one of the latter—a beef stew which also had butter beans in it—that prompted my friend and fellow writer Shirley Williams to tell about the potatoes her father grew in Dwarf, Kentucky.

"We had sandy soil down by Troublesome Creek, and that's where he'd plant his sweet potatoes. He'd plow those rows perfectly straight, then cross over them, also straight, to make these perfect squares. In each square, he'd plant the potatoes in a mound that he'd build up just like a pyramid. Each mound was shaped just so, exactly in a pyramid. And don't you know, he grew the most amazing sweet potatoes.

"One time up at Berea College, my cousin, Bob, was bragging on those potatoes, and the professor told him he was lying. Said you couldn't grow good sweet potatoes up there in the mountains. So Bob hitchhiked home that night, got a potato, and brought it back to put it on that professor's desk the very next day.

"That professor apologized. And he took it home, and cooked it up, and fed a family of four on it. Said it was the best sweet potato he'd ever had."

Sweet Potato Hash SERVES 4

This was an idea born from necessity one evening, when I discovered the Irish potatoes I'd intended to use for hash had instead sprouted. Fortunately, I had good sweet potatoes on hand, and the result was a dish so delicious I'll make it intentionally again and again. It's great for either brunch or a cool winter supper. I like it served with hot biscuits, or with hot, buttered whole-grain or sunflower-seed toast.

6-ounce slice country ham
1 cup warm water
1 tablespoon sorghum syrup
4 to 5 drops Tabasco
4 cups peeled and diced sweet potato (2 medium-sized)
1 cup finely chopped onion
4 fresh eggs (optional)
butter, to fry the eggs

To render drippings for the hash, fry the ham in a hot skillet on both sides until some browning occurs. Remove the ham to a plate and trim the fat. Return the fat to the skillet, and fry it for 2 to 3 minutes, pressing with the back of a metal spatula to extract as much grease as possible. Remove the fat.

Turn the heat to medium. Pour the warm water into the skillet, and use the spatula to deglaze. Add the sorghum syrup, and stir to dissolve. Add the Tabasco and diced sweet potatoes. Cover, and simmer for 5 minutes.

Chop the ham into ½-inch dice while the potatoes are simmering. When 5 minutes are up, add the ham and onion. Simmer, covered, for 5 more minutes. The hash can be served immediately as is, or you can remove it from the heat and leave it covered while you fry the eggs over easy. Serve an egg on top of each serving of hash.

Subtle Sugar and Spice Sweet Potatoes with Peanuts SERVES 4

Many post–World War II recipes load sweet potatoes with added sugar and flavorings. This recipe presents the potato with only enough sugar and spice to bring out its natural sweetness. The crushed peanuts on top re-emphasize that subtle taste, but be sure to toast and spice your own peanuts, since the kind you will find commercially will be too salty and spicy, and will overwhelm the potatoes.

MAIL ORDER

Route 11

I was testing recipes from the finalists in a national cookbook competition, so I can assure you that the food I put on the table the night my husband's colleagues came to dinner was both interesting and delicious. Still it was the mail-order tin of Route 11 sweet potato chips from the Shenandoah Valley that took the prize.

I'd heard about Route 11 on a food foray which led me through Middletown, Virginia, where the chips—including Route 11's flagship (Irish) potato chips in regular, barbecue, lightly salted, salt and vinegar, and dill varieties—are made at the Old Feed Store. Alas, the Spud Master fries only on Fridays and Saturdays, and we couldn't find the chips for sale anywhere else in town.

Fortunately, Route 11 will gladly mail-order, and so, many months later, I had a couple of 3-pound tins gleaming in my kitchen. I thought the regular chips were outstanding— lightly salted and perfectly crisped on the outside, with just enough thickness to give them resilience and a fine potato taste, but not enough to make them chewy.

But it was the sweet potato chips with cinnamon and sugar—a perfectly lovely blend of sugar, spice, and salt— that captivated everyone who came to our house, especially Pat Wasley, dean of the Graduate School of Education at Bank Street College in New York, and a woman who knows great food.

I'd put out small glass bowls of the chips for our guests to munch on with drinks before the meal, and was delighted when Pat brought one right to the table. We found they were excellent with green salad and a perfect accompaniment for the fruit-enhanced lentil soup I served.

I refilled all the remaining bowls and brought them to the table, where we polished them off with coffee, but Pat really won my heart when I caught her eyeing the bowl of brown-sugar-flavored whipped cream I'd served with dessert. We grabbed chips simulta- neously and dipped. I was smitten right away with the taste, which managed to be both homey and exotic. Pat went back and forth, finally deciding that while the whipped cream was a good addition, nothing could beat the straight sweet potato.

Her devotion continued. Less than two months later, she reported back that she had already made her way through four tins. If you want to know what the excitement is about, see Things to Order, page 338.

water

2 large sweet potatoes

1 tablespoon butter

2 tablespoons brown sugar

⅛ teaspoon ground cayenne or red chile

½ teaspoon kosher salt

¼ cup coarsely crushed Toasted and
　　Spiced Peanuts (page 50)

¾ pound sweet potato (1 medium-sized)

water

1 tablespoon butter

1 cup finely chopped sweet white onion

2 cups chicken broth

1½ cups frozen shoepeg corn

salt

fresh nutmeg (optional)

Half-fill a large saucepan with water, and bring it to a boil. While you are waiting for the water to boil, peel the sweet potatoes and cut them into 2-inch chunks. When the water boils, add the potatoes to the pot. Cook at a lively simmer until the potatoes are soft when pierced by a fork or cake tester (about 12 minutes). Remove from the heat, and drain.

Add the butter to the pot and sprinkle the sugar, pepper, and salt over the potatoes. Use a potato masher or fork to mash the potatoes to a creamy consistency. Mound them on four individual plates, and use a serving spoon to make an indentation in the top of each mound. Place 1 tablespoon of peanuts in each indentation, and serve immediately.

Peel and dice the potato. Place it in a small saucepan and add enough water to just cover. Bring to a boil over high heat, cover, and turn the heat to medium. Simmer for 15 minutes, until the potato is quite tender.

While the potato is cooking, melt the butter in a 2-quart or larger pot, over medium heat. Add the onion, and cook until transparent. Add the chicken broth, turn the heat up, and bring to a boil. Add the frozen corn, and bring to a boil again, then turn the heat low and simmer, covered.

When the potatoes are ready, puree them in their cooking water with a fork or potato masher. Add them to the simmering corn mixture. Add salt to taste. Cook on low for 20 to 25 minutes, until the corn is tender. Serve immediately, grating fresh nutmeg into each bowl, if you wish.

Sweet Potato and Corn Chowder　　SERVES 4

The pureed potatoes add a velvety creaminess to this recipe, which is sheer heaven. You can substitute pumpkin or winter squash, but the sweet potato is best.

Ginger Sorghum Sweet Potato Pie

SERVES 8

The best-known sweet potato pie of the South is one made with cooked sweet potatoes, mashed and seasoned, much as you would make a pumpkin pie. This pie, however, with grated sweet potatoes in a pecan-pie-like filling, has been around for decades and is much preferred by many, myself included, for its unusual texture and distinctively fresh quality. I've added minced ginger to emphasize the latter, while the sorghum accentuates the earthy richness of the sweet potato. This is a pie to make when company is coming, since it is best served warm out of the oven (it should be refrigerated if you're not going to eat it right up) and a very small slice will suffice even the most eager sweets eaters.

pastry for single-crust 9-inch pie
½ cup chopped pecans
2 cups peeled and grated raw sweet potato
1 tablespoon minced fresh ginger
2 eggs, beaten
1 cup sorghum syrup
1 tablespoon salted butter, melted
1 cup half and half

Preheat the oven to 350°F.

Place the pastry in a 9-inch pie pan and

FARM MARKETS AND FESTIVALS

The Ohio Valley Harvest Festival happens in early September, usually the second weekend, in downtown Louisville, Kentucky. On the belvedere overlooking the Ohio River, more than sixty regional farmers and producers set up stands offering the best of the harvest. Meanwhile, some forty Louisville, Lexington, and southern Indiana restaurants operate booths where, for a buck or three, you can sample original dishes created from produce grown locally. Watermelon Salsa (page 154), Shariat's Crawfish Corncakes with Smoked Tomato Sauce (page 102), Dudley's Spaghetti Squash with Spicy Peanut Sauce (page 205), and Sorghum and Sweet Potato Ice Cream (page 221) are all inventions from the harvest festival.

In addition to great food, the event often features live bluegrass music, craft demonstrations, and a raffle for a handmade quilt. Carol Cassedy (whose Red Plum Jam recipe is on page 308) owns Whitestone Farms, an organic producer in Bagdad, Kentucky, with her husband, Linn. In addition to raising fruits, vegetables, and kids, Carol is a quilter; she made the first quilt to be raffled at the event.

"You know, in the past, farm wives would make quilts and sell them for seed money the next year," Cassedy says. "Any money we make from the raffle goes to next year's harvest festival, so the way I see it, I'm continuing the tradition."

See Places to Go, page 341.

MAIL ORDER

There's molasses and then there's sorghum, and if you're interested in good eating, sorghum is what you want. Unfortunately, this can be a bit of a confusing proposition, particularly since up until a few years ago the term "sorghum molasses" was used regularly to describe the syrup from sorghum grain. Now pure sorghum producers call their product sorghum or sorghum syrup, to distinguish it from molasses.

Regular molasses is made from the juice of sugarcane (or sometimes beets), boiled to refine it. Light molasses comes from the first boiling, dark from the second, and blackstrap from the third. All of the sugar molasses are somewhat bitter, with blackstrap being downright medicinal, and none of them has the buttery complexity of the syrup produced from sorghum, a cereal grain.

Sorghum is just about the elixir of the gods. Richer than even the best honey, it's the preferred topping for hot biscuits (mixed with butter in a 3 sorghum to 2 butter ratio) and the character-giving sweetener in such distinctively Southern desserts as pecan pie and stack cake. It pairs up perfectly with sweet potatoes, much the way that brothers and sisters sing in surer harmony than those who aren't kin.

For many years, real sorghum was hard to get, but recently there's been a revival in its production and marketing. In the mountain South, particularly, you can find numerous fall festivals dedicated to the art of old-fashioned sorghum making, with mules pulling the wheels to grind the cane, and big black kettles of the syrup boiling out in the crisp open autumn air. One of my favorites is the Morgan County Annual Sorghum Festival in West Liberty, Kentucky, the last full weekend every September. One of the largest is held in Blairsville, Georgia, over three weekends, beginning in mid-October.

You can find sorghum at farm markets throughout the South and Midwest, and in specialty stores, particularly those carrying down-home foods. But make sure that what you are getting is 100 percent pure sorghum and not cane syrup colored and flavored to look like sorghum, or molasses masquerading under the sorghum name.

It helps to know your source, or to mail-order from a reputable seller. The folks at the Knox County Co-operative Extension near my birthplace of Corbin, Kentucky, sell pure sorghum put up in attractive gift packages. As would be expected, you can get great-tasting real sorghum from the president of the Kentucky Sweet Sorghum Producers Association, Danny Ray Townsend, at Townsend's Sorghum Mill.

If you can't get to Blairsville, Georgia, for the Sorghum Festival, the chamber of commerce will be glad to put you in touch with a local producer who will sell you sorghum by mail order.

The sorghum produced by Alan Overholzer in eastern Kentucky also comes highly recommended, but since Mr. Overholzer is Amish and doesn't have a telephone, you'll need to write to him.

Sorghum is a seasonal product, so its availability can vary, depending on the time of year and also on how well the sorghum crop fared.

For sorghum sources, see Things to Order, page 338.

For festival information, see Places to Go, page 341.

crimp the edges to form a rim about ½ inch high. Lightly press the pecan pieces into the bottom of the crust, being careful not to pierce the crust as you do.

Combine the sweet potato and ginger. Blend the eggs with the sorghum syrup, melted butter, and half and half. When thoroughly blended, fold in the sweet potatoes and ginger, then pour the mixture into the pie shell.

Set the pan on a cookie sheet to guard against possible drips and bake in the center of the oven for 50 to 55 minutes, until the top of the filling is set and there is no liquid in the center. The filling should still be soft enough that it quivers when you nudge the pan. Let the pie cool 30 minutes before slicing. (The filling will continue to cook out of the oven, and will firm up even more as it cools.) Slice and serve warm.

Sorghum and Sweet Potato Ice Cream   MAKES ABOUT 1¼ QUARTS

The concept may sound a little peculiar at first, but one bite of this velvety, delicious ice cream and you will be convinced. The recipe was devised by Rick Doering, when he was chef at 211 Clover Lane in Louisville, for the Ohio Valley Harvest Festival. Sweet potatoes were plentiful, and Rick's supplier had provided him with plenty of beautiful bronze sorghum. Rick decided to experiment. The result is fabu-lous—a dish you may well want to serve for your next holiday dinner in lieu of that same old pumpkin pie.

This is best made the day before you want to serve it.

1 pound sweet potatoes
½ cup sorghum syrup
¼ to ½ cup sugar
5 egg yolks
1 quart half and half
½ teaspoon ground cinnamon
¼ teaspoon ground cloves
¼ teaspoon ground allspice

Preheat the oven to 425°F. Bake the potatoes for 40 minutes, until soft, or microwave on high for 5 minutes. When the potatoes have cooled, peel, and puree them with the sorghum syrup in a blender or food processor.

Taste the puree and set it aside. Depending on the sweetness of the puree, mix ¼ to ½ cup of sugar with the egg yolks in a medium saucepan until blended. Add the half and half, and stir. Scrape the bottom of the pan to incorporate all the egg mixture into the half and half. When blended, cook over medium heat, stirring often, until the temperature is 170°F, or until custard coats the back of a metal spoon.

Mix together the custard, pureed potatoes, and spices. Refrigerate until completely cooled. Freeze according to your ice cream maker's directions. Chill the ice cream in the freezer for 6 to 8 hours before serving.

MAIL ORDER

Joni Miller's *True Grits* (Workman Publishing, 1990) is an opinionated and conversational compendium of great goods you can mail-order from Southern food sources. Since Miller is "president for life" of the New York chapter of the Moon Pie Cultural Club (world headquarters at 11706 Musket Lane, Charlotte, North Carolina 28217), I tend to listen up when she says something tastes real good. What she says about Garber Farms Cajun Yams is that they are "outrageously delicious."

These deep-red Jewel-variety sweet yams are grown on land just outside of Lafayette, Louisiana, by the Garber family. They hand-select the best of the crop for filling mail orders from mid-October through mid-January, just in time for the winter holidays. Once you order, you get on the mailing list and will be notified about the coming harvest in subsequent years.

See Things to Order, page 338.

Roots

Turnip Custard

Ginger Beets

Nutmeg Carrot Grits

Joe Castro's Corn Risotto with Fresh Carrot Broth

It's a turnip that Scarlett O'Hara finds hidden in the red clay of Tara and lifts to the sky as she declares, "As God is my witness, I'm never going to be hungry again." While turnips are hardly the first vegetable one thinks of when contemplating the harvest of the South, such roots, including beets and carrots, and winter crops like Brussels sprouts, are indeed what kept many of us from feeling hunger pangs in the scant months of winter.

Carrots were usually sliced and simmered in a bit of water, butter, and brown sugar. The favorite Southern way of cooking turnips—and also a delectable way to prepare beets—is to dice the root and add it to a pot of the plant's greens in the last 30 minutes or so of simmering. They mate up just as nicely in the pan as they do in the garden. Turnips, and the occasional rutabaga, were also often mashed with butter and milk and served just like potatoes. As a child, I liked turnips raw and eaten like an apple from my right hand, each bite dipped in a little mound of salt I held cupped in my left.

ter? But while the lusciousness of those three ingredients might outshine a lesser partner, the turnips in this recipe hold their own. If you are a lifelong turnip hater, put your disdain on hold. Cooking the roots with just a bit of sugar in the water neutralizes the brackish aftertaste and turns the turnip's characteristic flavor both buttery and mellow. In fact, this dish is so delicious, if Scarlett could have cooked her salvaged turnip this way, she might have been content to marry Rhett and the two of them open a little restaurant in Reconstruction Atlanta, preceding the current Southern cuisine craze by a century and a quarter.

2 cups water

1 pound turnips

1 teaspoon sugar

1 cup chopped sweet white onion

1 tablespoon salted butter

½ teaspoon kosher salt

2 eggs

1 cup half and half

nutmeg

Turnip Custard

SERVES 4 AS A SIDE DISH

As my friend Sarah Fritschner often observes: What's not to like in a recipe with fresh eggs, rich cream, and sweet but-

Preheat the oven to 350°F. Butter the inside of a 1-quart baking dish.

Set the water to boil in a medium saucepan over high heat. While you're waiting for it to boil, peel the turnips and cut them into 2-inch pieces. When the water comes to a boil, add the sugar and turnips. Cover, return to a slow boil, and cook for 5 minutes. Add the onion and cook 15 minutes more, until the turnips are tender when pierced with a cake tester. Drain, and add the butter and salt. Mash with a potato masher to make a slightly chunky puree.

Whisk the eggs and blend in the half and half. Add the turnip puree, and stir to blend. Pour into the prepared casserole, and grate nutmeg lightly over the top.

Bake for 23 minutes, until the edges are just firm and the center is set on top although still a little wiggly when you jostle the casserole. Remove, and let sit for a minute or two before serving.

Ginger Beets SERVES 4 AS A SIDE DISH

My first dinner at the Horseradish Grill in Atlanta was a pure sybaritic delight. (See Places to Go, page 341.) Then-chef Scott Peacock knew perfectly how to balance classic Southern traditions and the best of new tricks of the trade—a tradition that continues even now that Scott is no longer there. I remember delicate crabcakes from that meal, delicious black-eyed peas with greens and real cornbread, but nothing impressed me more than the ginger beets. At the Horseradish Grill, they knew just what to do to bring everything together. When I called to see if they'd share their knowledge, they sent along this wonderful recipe from Executive Chef Dave Berry, who had been Scott's sous chef (and beet master).

The version here has been downscaled from Dave's, which came in restaurant pro-

portions. In addition, I remember the beets there being cooked quite tender, but I liked this crunchier version even more. If you want to try it with softer beets, leave them in the oven for an additional 15 to 20 minutes.

1 pound beets (4 medium)
½ cup apple cider vinegar
⅓ cup sugar
¼ teaspoon kosher salt
1 clove
1 ounce fresh ginger, sliced thinly

Preheat the oven to 350°F.

Trim the beets, leaving a stub of stem at the top and a bit of root at the bottom, so you don't cut into the beet itself and cause it to bleed. Rinse the beets thoroughly to remove any dirt, and place them in a shallow baking pan. Bake for 30 minutes, until the outer edges are tender when pierced by a fork but the centers still have some resistance.

While the beets are baking, prepare the ginger syrup by bringing the remaining ingredients to a boil in a noncorrosive saucepan, stirring at first until the sugar and salt are dissolved. When the mixture boils, turn the heat down and cook at a lively simmer for 12 minutes, until the mixture thickens to a light syrup. Remove from the heat.

When the beets are baked, remove them from the oven and plunge them into cold tap water. Use a sharp knife to cut off the ends and pull the skins off. (The skins should come away easily, but if they don't, peel them with the knife or a vegetable peeler.) Cut the beets into bite-size pieces and toss them with the ginger syrup to coat. You may serve immediately, or refrigerate, tightly covered, for several days.

Nutmeg Carrot Grits

SERVES 6 TO 8

Another combination of carrot and corn flavors, quite easy to make and very delicate. Freshly grated nutmeg is really essential here (see margin).

6 cups water
1 teaspoon kosher salt
1½ cups stone-ground white grits
½ pound gruyere cheese, grated
3 large eggs, beaten
½ teaspoon freshly grated nutmeg
1 pound carrots, peeled and grated

Preheat the oven to 350°F. Lightly grease a 2½-quart baking dish.

In a large, heavy saucepan, bring the water and salt to a boil. Slowly pour in the grits, stirring all the while to prevent lumping. Turn the heat down so the grits cook at a simmer. Cook 12 to 15 minutes, until the water is absorbed and the grits are softened. Remove from the heat.

Add the cheese to the grits, and stir until melted. Slowly add about ½ cup of the hot grits mixture to the beaten eggs, whisking as you do. When the eggs are warmed, add them to the remaining grits, and mix well. Add the nutmeg and carrots and mix well. Pour into the greased baking dish and bake for 50 minutes, until the grits are set and golden. Serve warm.

In eighteenth-century England, lords and ladies often carried personal pocket nutmeg graters of ivory or silver so that they could add the freshly grated spice to a dish at the moment it was presented. Fresh nutmeg was equally prized in the antebellum South, supplied by Yankee peddlers who thus earned Connecticut the appellation of the Nutmeg State. Eugene Walter tells us that some of the more unscrupulous of these peddlers would use long winter evenings by the fireside at home to carve imitation nutmegs from a pine knot with a fragrance which led innocent buyers to believe they were actually getting the rare spice.

I'm afraid that my early experience with nutmeg, ground and packed in bottles which sat on the grocer's shelf, and then my mother's, for months, could have led me to believe that it actually was wood.

But my opinion of the spice changed dramatically for the better once I bought my own nutmeg grater (white plastic and stainless steel, not ivory and silver, and looking like a tiny mandolin). What an exquisite flavor freshly grated nutmeg imparts to the simplest dish, underscoring the subtle delicacy of foods such as grits or eggs, without overpowering them.

Fresh whole nutmegs will keep well in a tightly covered container (my grater has one built in!) for a couple of months. You can also grate nutmeg on a small general-purpose grater, but you're apt to add some knuckle to the dish in the process.

Joe Castro's Corn Risotto with Fresh Carrot Broth

SERVES 4

Joe Castro has made his reputation as executive chef at the English Grill in Louisville's legendary Brown Hotel with a menu that jazzes up the region's best recipes and products with exotic touches from the regional cooking ranging from Mediterranean to Caribbean.

I asked Joe for something rooted in the classic Southern flavor system, with an emphasis on the taste of fresh produce. His response was this recipe for creamy, corn-enhanced risotto set off by a sparkling carrot broth.

I went to the basement and dug out my old juice extractor just to make this recipe, and it was worth the trouble. Cooks without a juice extractor needn't worry, however. Most natural food stores sell fresh carrot juice, which they make on the spot or which has been quick-frozen. Just get the absolute freshest juice you can. Joe says, "The key to this dish is not overworking the carrots, to maintain all of their flavor fresh from the field."

The cooking of the risotto, which requires the paced adding of liquid and slow, almost constant stirring, reminded me of making grits, and, indeed, with the fresh corn added, there was a resemblance in flavor, as well.

CORN PUREE

1 shallot, finely chopped
1 tablespoon olive oil
1 garlic clove, minced
1 cup corn, cut from the cob (about 2 ears)
1 teaspoon finely chopped fresh thyme
salt
pepper

In a small, heavy skillet over medium-high heat, sauté the shallot in the olive oil until transparent. Add the garlic, corn, and thyme, and cook, stirring to keep the mixture from sticking, for about 5 minutes, until the corn is tender. (You may need to turn down the heat, or add a teaspoon or two of water, to keep the corn from sticking.) Add salt and pepper to taste, and set aside.

CARROT BROTH

1½ cups fresh carrot juice (about 12 carrots, peeled)
1 tablespoon chopped red onion
1 tablespoon chopped celery
salt
pepper

If you are juicing the carrots yourself, add the onion and celery during the process. If you have bought the carrot juice, mince both onion and celery as fine as you possibly can before them adding to the juice. Add salt and pepper to taste, and set aside.

RISOTTO

1 tablespoon olive oil
2 cloves garlic, minced
1½ cups Arborio rice
4 cups hot chicken stock
salt
pepper

In a heavy saucepan, heat the olive oil, then sauté the garlic for 20 seconds. Add the rice, and toast it in the oil, stirring frequently to keep it from burning, for 5 minutes. When the rice turns golden brown, add a cup of chicken stock. Adjust the heat so the stock is cooking at a lively simmer, and cook, stirring gently, until the stock is absorbed. Add another cup of stock, and continue stirring and cooking, adding the remaining 2 cups of stock, one at a time, until all is absorbed and the rice is tender and creamy.

When the rice is ready, gently fold in the corn puree. Taste, and add salt or pepper, if needed.

Heat the carrot broth until just steaming ("like a good tea," Joe describes it), then ladle it equally into four pasta bowls. Place the risotto in the center. Serve immediately.

Note: *Joe uses 2 cups of sautéed asparagus julienne as a garnish for this dish, but I liked it just fine without. If you wish to add the asparagus, sauté it quickly in a skillet with a little olive oil as soon as the rice is finished.*

ROAD NOTES

NEW ORLEANS, END OF APRIL, 1996

The New Orleans Jazz and Heritage Festival, held from the last weekend in April to the first in May every year, is the best and most bodacious celebration of the diversity of American music and Southern cooking in the world. At the fairgrounds on Thursday through Sunday, some dozen stages are filled nonstop from morning to evening with music ranging from pure commercial pop to West African kora melodies. There's hot jazz, cool jazz, Dixieland and bebop, zydeco, chanky-chank, bluegrass, and enough blues to turn the Mississippi River indigo. Every afternoon you have a chance to join a handkerchief-swishing, umbrella-jouncing parade behind a second-line band. And when all of this gets to be a bit much, you can retreat to the shelter of the gospel tent and have goosebumps raised right up your back with the power of the Holy Ghost and rolling riffs from a big, loud, cheesy organ.

The music tents are set up around the perimeter of the infield, while in the center, some 200 food booths, manned by restaurants, churches, community centers, and social groups, dish out some of the best food this side of your grandma's. Like the music, it's a lesson in roots and branches, as well as the pure traditions of Southern cooking. Steamed crawfish, shrimp étouffée, and fried chicken compete with Caribbean-spiced jama-jama (spinach), doro wot from Africa, and Cuban treats like masa tamal wrapped in banana leaves.

We begin eating just inside the infield, making a ritual stop at the Plum Street "sno ball" booth. New Orleans sno balls are unlike any other I've ever had. The ice is neither as fine as shaved ice nor as chunky as the snow cones I had as a child. Instead, it's just the right consistency to form a cool, satiny base for the flavoring. You can pick from an array of neon-colored fruit flavors, all with the option of "cream," which, as near as I can tell, is a combo of sweetened condensed and regular milk, but we always order coffee, a mahogany-colored rich espresso, which fortifies us for the afternoon's eating of jambalaya, Cuban sandwiches, oyster po' boys, spicy chicken, and one of Omar's famous bean pies.

Eight hours of this is as exhausting as a full day at any job, but New Orleans is not a town to let you let down, so we return to our hotel long enough to shower and catch a quick nap, then it's down to the French Quarter or over to Tipitina's or the Maple Leaf for dancing until you drop. And then you sleep and do it all over again.

This much *bon temps* is more than we can handle annually, so my husband and I and our good friends can usually make the trip only two years in a row, and then we have to take a break for a festival or two. This year we are here with two teenagers in tow, Meghan and her best friend, Amy. Maybe it's the added stress of balancing the parent act with the party animal, but Ken and I find that on our last night the idea of a quiet dinner in a sit-down restaurant sounds more appealing than a final Cajun two-step around town.

So we find ourselves on Frenchman Street, just east of the French Quarter, a block away from the great jazz spot Snug Harbor, standing in line at the Praline Connection. It's nine o'clock, early for a New Orleans supper during Jazz Fest, but already there's a crowd waiting outside the Praline Connection, staring longingly at the clipboard in the hands of the dapper young man in bow tie and black bowler sitting on a stool outside the door.

We decide to at least beg a menu from the doorman, to dream about sustenance. The Praline Connection offers a bit of everything New Orleans is known for, some with interesting variations. The gumbo is called Gumbo Zaire, and I'm not sure if this is a reference to African origins or a vernacular pronunciation of the traditional Gumbo Z'Herbes, since, like that dish, it's made with greens and okra, plus crab. I find my eyes drawn away from the more exotic entrees, though, to a couple of real Mom dishes: Chicken Livers with Hot Pepper Jelly, and Beet and Onion Salad. When I tell Ken my choices, he raises an eyebrow quizzically: "Feeling a little iron poor, are you?"

Maybe the earnest young charm of Amy and Meghan has won the doorman's heart, for he suddenly calls our name before he calls a couple of folks I'm almost certain were ahead of us. It's a joy to sit down at the simple, white-clothed table and watch the servers dance through the crowded room with a stunning combination of alacrity and grace. Our server solicitously brings us sweetened tea in big tumblers and warm bread from the oven. When my food arrives, it's more comfort.

The chicken livers are good, though deep fried instead of pan-sautéed as I had hoped. But it's the salad that truly wins my heart. Piled in a bowl big enough to pass around the table for everyone to share, it's about as straightforward as such salads get: sliced beets and rings of onion on a bed of chopped lettuce and slivered cabbage, swimming in nothing but the beet juices. But what juices! Tart and a little hot, the beets provide the zing while the onions—probably Vidalias since the season is right—are the sweet accent. I eat every bite of the enormous serving, and sop the juice with my cornbread. Now when I'm feeling a little poor in spirit at home, I make my own, using the Ginger Beets on page 228. When I feel the need to dress things up, Buttermilk Dressing (page 166) provides just the right creamy contrast.

Meanwhile, the night in New Orleans goes on. But we indulge ourselves with pralines bought at the restaurant's adjacent candy store and head off to a good night's sleep, fortified with vitamins, iron, and a bit of bayou spice.

ABOUT

MOUNTAIN MUSHROOMS

Morels Fixed the Only Way

Morels Fixed Another Way

Morels Fixed a Third Way

Miles's Wild Mushroom and Potato Hash

I grew up thinking mushrooms were a relatively recent addition to the cooking of the South. It took a trip to Arkansas to awaken me to the mushroom-foraging traditions of the mountain South, and to show me the region's delicious, time-honored ways of serving morels and other mushrooms.

Morels Fixed the Only Way
SERVES 1

Jim Long says there's only one way to fix fresh morel mushrooms: very lightly breaded and crisply fried. As you'll discover on the next pages, there actually are some other ways to prepare this prize, but Jim's way is how Southern mountain folk in both the Ozarks and the Appalachians have cooked morels (also called "dry land fish" or "hickory chicken" in those parts) for years.

You'll need half a dozen good-sized morels, more if they're smaller than your thumb, to make a serving for one. Serve this with a wilted salad of fresh greens, a pan of cornbread, and a big glass of buttermilk, and you're home.

6 large morels
½ cup corn flour (see Note on page 107)
¼ teaspoon kosher salt
1 egg, beaten
oil for frying

Rinse the mushrooms well and quickly to remove any dirt, if necessary. (Most commercially available morels have already been cleaned and require only a light rub with a damp paper towel.) Split the morels in half lengthwise.

Mix the corn flour with the salt in a bowl. Put the beaten egg in a separate bowl. Pour ⅛ inch of oil into a skillet. Heat on high until very hot but not smoking.

While the oil is heating, dip each mushroom half into the egg to coat it completely, then dredge it in corn flour. Fry in the hot oil until golden on each side. (Don't crowd the pan; fry in batches, if necessary. Skim the oil after each batch and add more oil if needed, bringing it back to the proper temperature before adding the mushrooms.) Drain on a wire rack set above paper towels, and serve hot.

Morels Fixed Another Way
SERVES 1

My omelet at Dairy Hollow House arrived piping hot despite the trek from the main kitchen to the little cabin where I was staying. One of the great qualities of an omelet is its resiliency, despite its apparent delicacy. But while I'll be the first to give omelets their due, there is really no way to prepare eggs so lovely as the way my mother always did it, in a very soft, buttery scramble.

This method works beautifully for the sorts of eggs and wild greens dishes Southerners prepared in the spring, and it lends itself perfectly to serving fresh morels. The other ingredient in this recipe is green garlic, available often now from gourmet greengrocers and from farm markets in the spring. Green garlic is the first tender bulbs of garlic pulled from the ground, while still no larger than a good shooter marble. Its powerful smell but delicate taste reminds me of the ramps prized in the Southern mountains. If you can't get green garlic or ramps, substitute fresh green onions, greens and whites mixed, with just a pinch of minced fresh garlic. It won't be the same, but it will be good.

This is a dish ideally made for one or two persons and eaten on the spot. The recipe serves one, but you can double it. If you try to increase it any more and make it in a large pan, you'll lose control over the eggs. I make it in an 8-inch sauté pan when I am cooking for myself, or a 9-inch skillet when Ken joins me. You will need a heat-resistant spatula or spoon with a wide, flat edge for moving the eggs.

4 small or 2 medium morels
1 tablespoon minced green garlic
2 eggs
1 tablespoon butter
1 slice good toasting bread
salt
pepper

Rinse the mushrooms well and quickly to remove any dirt, if necessary. (Most commercially available morels have already been cleaned and require only a light rub with a damp paper towel.) Remove the stems and chop them fine. Slice the heads into rounds and set them aside with the green garlic, handy to the stove.

Break the eggs into a cup or bowl. With a whisk or fork, break the yolks and drag them through the whites enough to striate but not to blend. Set them near the stove.

Melt the butter over medium-high heat. While the butter is melting, place the bread in the toaster, but don't begin toasting. When the butter just begins to bubble, add the morels and garlic and begin slowly counting to 45 as you shake them in the pan. (The butter should be hot enough to make the mushrooms and garlic hop, but nothing should be browning.)

When you have counted to 45, pour in the eggs. (This is when you should start the toaster.) When the eggs just begin to set around the edges and on the bottom (less than a minute), use the spatula to gently lift and move them, allowing the liquid egg on top to pour onto the hot surface. Repeat. Remove the pan from the heat immediately. Count to 10 and use the spatula to lift and move the eggs a third time. The eggs should be very soft, but the whites should be cooked and not translucent. Serve immediately with salt and pepper to taste, and toast on the side.

EUREKA SPRINGS, ARKANSAS, APRIL 1995

The Ozarks remind me of the mountains of eastern Kentucky, except their elbows aren't as sharp and angular. I've encountered a similar generosity and warmth in the people I have met, not to mention the familiar lilting cadences of their accents. They share an enterprising spirit, too, I think, as the road begins to curve and rise, and I notice a number of shingles on the fences of small holler farms touting homegrown mushrooms for sale, shiitakes and morels particularly. I make a note to ask herbalist and Ozark wild-food specialist Jim Long if either is indigenous.

Long is on my list of people to meet while I'm in Eureka Springs. First, however, is a woman who I've suspected has been living an alternate version of my life for some years, Crescent Dragonwagon.

CD, as she likes to be called, first came to my attention a decade and a half ago, when I fell in love with a picture and description of the Eureka Springs bed and breakfast she owns and operates, Dairy Hollow House. Just two rooms in an old house perched on the side of a hill back then, the "inn" offered an enticing mix of creature comforts (hot tub and thick quilts), mountain assets (hikes in the hills behind the inn), and counterculture tone (gourmet vegetarian food).

Through lots of hard work and attention to detail, CD and her husband, Ned Shank, have expanded Dairy Hollow House to its current three-structure, six-suite size and have established a reputation as award-winning innkeepers. CD has also garnered a reputation in the cooking world with a series of cookbooks about the foods served at Dairy Hollow House, based on her self-christened "Nouveau'zarks" cuisine. Built around the products and traditions of her adopted Ozark home; adapted with an old hippie's attention to organic produce, low fat, natural sugars, and little meat; and seasoned with a flair that can only be attributed to her New York City background, CD's books offer killer New Age variations on old-time themes.

My favorite of her collected tomes is *Soup & Bread: A Country Inn Cookbook* (Workman Publishing, 1992), my favorite meal at Dairy Hollow House the daily breakfast in a covered, warmed basket—delivered right to your door! (What blessed respite to have all the homey comfort of a bed and breakfast without the requisite morning chatter among the guests at a common table.)

My first morning at DHH, the willow basket, covered with a blue-and-white-checked cloth, holds a huge cup of fresh fruit and edible flowers from the garden; a piping-hot chive omelet filled with local shiitakes, morels, and organic spinach, seasoned with a bit of garlic and parmesan; four oven-baked strips of bacon; a couple of corn muffins spiked with kernels of fresh corn; an assortment of inn-made jams; and a bottle of fresh apple juice. The next morning I eat heartily again (shirred eggs in a ramekin and homemade apple-chicken sausage) and pack the remaining fresh fruit, bottle of juice, and homemade ginger and fruit muffins for the road. Generosity is the creed at Dairy Hollow House. (See Places to Go, page 341.)

CD is equally generous with the names and numbers of producers in the region, which is how Jim Long and I end up chatting for almost two hours in rocking chairs on the farmhouse porch.

Lean and lanky, with a full brown mustache, twinkling eyes, and perpetual gimme cap perched on his head, Jim, just approaching fifty, tells me how he ended up in the Ozarks, a national expert on wild mountain food.

He was born in west-central Missouri "in the furthermost foothills. I remember as a child standing on the plains and looking to the Ozarks, already with longing. I've been most comfortable in the hills."

His home now is in Oak Grove, so close to the Missouri border that his zip code is an Arkansas one but his area code is from Missouri. There he runs Long Creek Herb Farm. Its gardens contain some 350 herbs for the seasonings and teas he produces and sells. (See Things to Order, page 338, and Places to Go, page 341.) Jim grows a vegetable garden for himself and sometimes landscapes in the area. He also writes columns for *The Herb Companion* and *The Ozark Mountaineer*, as well as articles and books on regional foodways. I have been through *Recipes, Cooking Practices and Foods from the Era of the Civil War* (Long Creek Herbs, 1992), making notes to remind myself to find out what a "walking onion" and a "spice bush" are. But first and foremost, I want to know from Jim if one commonly held wisdom—that traditional cooks of the mountain South almost never used herbs and spices—is based in fact.

"What I've found in older recipes, and I've been collecting them all my life, is that there's lots of herbs but a different attitude about what they are. My mother and grandmother (from eastern Tennessee) were good cooks, but if you'd asked them, they didn't consider that they used herbs. Still, they had sage and chives. And they didn't just season with salt and pepper. They picked things from the wild—greens and things that grew around where they lived.

"For instance, there were lots of old varieties of wild garlic, and you can tell where an old house has been long after the foundation and chimney are gone just by the stand of garlic next to it.

"Fennel and dill were prevalent in the area. Wild ginger grew in shady, moist places across the Ozarks, Tennessee, Kentucky, and the Carolinas, and folks made a nonalcoholic ginger beer from it. Things got even richer as you moved further south and the growing season got warmer. I mean, lemon verbena is a tropical plant, but there it is in *Gone With the Wind*."

I ask Jim about the mushroom farms I've seen in the area. Are they something new? He says the commercial production of mushrooms locally is, as are the shiitakes, but "wild mushrooms have always been a really big thing in this part of the country. And morels, we've got five different varieties around here. In the spring, they're the main course for dinner and there's only one way to fix 'em, my way [see page 237]. That, a spring green salad, and a glass of iced tea is the best meal you'll ever eat."

We get started then on the roll of all the other "best meals you'll ever eat" and make our way through a variety of beans and peas. ("Best right out of the garden to boil 'em till they're just tender, then season them with a little butter," Jim says, then adds, "Of course, I've got a friend whose mom seasons them with a little bit of bacon grease and that's pretty wonderful, too.") Then we move on to cornbread.

"I grew up eating corncakes, cooked on the stove in a skillet when my mother didn't want to fool with making cornbread," Jim says. "Now about the best meal you'll ever have is hot corncakes, boiled eggs, and fresh spinach. You put vinegar on the spinach, mustard on the eggs, and butter on the corncakes, and you're set."

Jim remembers that cornbread was looked down on by some folks, including one grandmother who made a version she called "dog bread" and fed only to the pets. "It was thick cornbread with lots of cracklings and bacon grease, and I remember getting scolded when I was a little child because I was caught hiding in the pantry, eating dog bread."

Back to my list of questions. Jim tells me that the botanical name for the spice bush is *Lindera benzoin*, and that it tastes similar to allspice and was a primary seasoning in stews, particularly those made with venison. The "walking onion" was an Egyptian, or winter, onion that got its descriptive name because, like most bulbs, it had a tendency to advance across its territory from year to year.

Awed by his wide-ranging knowledge, and ever hopeful of finding one item that has eluded me for years, I ask Jim if he knows anyone in the region who makes real "hickory syrup." (My father remembered it from his boyhood, and swore no other syrup was its better—not even Vermont's finest maple.)

"Not around here, but I found it in Pigeon Forge, Tennessee," Jim says. "This was a while back, and it was being made and sold at the place that's now Dollywood. They were boiling down the hickory bark, and I don't know if they were adding corn syrup to it, or what. But it was the most wonderful, hickory, smoky syrup . . . about one of the best things you'll ever eat."

Back in the 1940s, just before the war factories lured my parents to Detroit, Mother and Daddy lived for a while on a little piece of land on the far side of the Laurel River. You had to take a boat across the river to get to the house from the nearest road, and Mother said the house itself wasn't much, just a one-story frame with four rooms. But like all old Kentucky farmhouses, it had a good porch for sitting on. The solitude must have been sustaining, because I never heard either one of them talk about "the old place on the river" without a twinge of regret about the hard times that took them from it.

A couple of years ago, when the local newspaper ran an article about the couple who run Blue Moon Garlic outside of Richmond, that twinge turned to a full-blown sigh from my mother. "Now you know, that's just what I wanted to do down at the old place on the river," she told me.

Turns out that my mom, who can't even grow a houseplant without the intervention of kindly, green-thumbed friends and relatives, decided that she and Daddy should grow garlic there and sell it in local groceries.

She got some garlic sets and started her own crop out behind the house. "You can't believe how wonderful it was," she told me. "So much better than the dried-up bulbs you could buy in the store then. So much better than the dried-up bulbs you can buy in the store now, for that matter. But Pap and I couldn't figure out a way to distribute it. And I thought that was a real shame, because right after the war it seemed like everybody was cooking spaghetti and eggplant Italian-style, and I bet there would have been plenty of people to buy our garlic then. So I guess that field just kept on growing wild. I bet it's still there today, and I'm telling you, that was the best garlic I've ever eaten."

To me, Blue Moon Farm, perched high on a bend in the Kentucky River in Madison County, produces the finest garlic I have ever eaten, bar none. Perhaps it's because Leo and Jean Pitches Keene, spouses, friends, and sole laborers on the farm, give every aspect of the garlic business—from planting to cleaning to packaging and mailing—focused, personal attention. Perhaps it's because all of their crop is raised organically; or perhaps it's because, over the last decade, they've experimented with dozens and dozens of varieties to determine which ones are best suited to the farm's soil and growing conditions and are most desirable to discriminating palates. Or maybe it's just the magic name of the farm itself, which refers to the celestial phenomenon of two full moons in one month, called a blue moon around these parts.

Whatever the cause, the garlic I buy from Blue Moon Farm at our local farm market is unfailingly juicily fresh and blessed with subtly complex flavors. I like being able to choose from ten or so varieties each year, picking up German White for all-purpose use in the kitchen, the large-cloved, spicy Siberian for roasting, and Machashi for its complicated interplay of butter and bite.

Best of all, this is a treasure I can share, since the Keenes also operate a small mail-order business for garlic aficionados around the country. Their self-produced catalog offers a wealth of information about garlic and their operation. A great way to learn about the many varieties of garlic they offer is the Chef's Delight, an eight-variety sampler. They also offer braids, their own garlic powder, and a guide to planting and growing garlic, plus other products they think are worthwhile, including Ecologic Bulb Booster 4-1-1, an organic crab/shrimp-meal fertilizer produced in Bayou La Batre, Alabama.

Because they are a mom-and-pop venture and have to keep costs down, they ask that you send $2 for the annual catalog, a fee that is refunded with your first order. The catalogs come out in June, and shipping begins in August. The Keenes prefer that you correspond by mail. See Things to Order, page 338.

Morels Fixed a Third Way

SERVES 4 AS AN APPETIZER, 2 AS A LIGHT ENTREE

This recipe was inspired by the elaborate dish I had at James at the Mill. I use arugula instead of chard, because I like its slightly brassy attitude, because it's easily available in most groceries now, and because rocket, as the green was called in the South, was a frequent spring green, picked wild in the woods and fields, lightly sautéed, and served up with cornbread or mush.

If you can't find green garlic, use green onions, both white and green parts, with a pinch of fresh garlic, minced.

You can serve this on grilled mush, as it's prepared here, but you will need to prepare the mush at least four hours before you want to serve it. You can also serve this on Grits Cakes (page 113), which also require several hours of advance preparation. If you want instant gratification, serve it over Mother's Mashed Potatoes (page 171) or with Eugene's Savory Seeded Corn Pone (page 106).

CORNMEAL MUSH

1 cup finely ground white cornmeal

1 teaspoon kosher salt

4 cups water

1 tablespoon butter

Mix the cornmeal with the salt. Bring the water to a boil in the top of a double boiler. As you do, heat enough water in the bottom of the boiler to just bubble underneath, but not touch the top pan when inserted.

When the water is boiling, slowly pour in the cornmeal in a very thin, steady

243

trickle, stirring all the while with a whisk. (To control the pour, I hold the cornmeal in my hand instead of pouring it from a cup.) Continue whisking until the mixture begins to bubble. Remove from the direct heat and place over the water in the bottom of the double boiler.

Add the butter. Use a wooden spoon to stir until the butter melts, scraping the bottom of the pan to make sure there is no crust forming. Cover, and cook for 20 minutes, stirring occasionally to prevent sticking.

Pour the mush into a well-buttered pie tin and allow it to cool at room temperature for 10 minutes. Cover well with plastic wrap and refrigerate for at least 4 hours. (The mush can be made the day before and refrigerated until ready to use.)

MORELS AND GREENS
2 tablespoons butter
1 dozen small morels
2 tablespoons green garlic, minced
2 cups arugula

When you are ready to prepare the morels and greens, preheat the broiler on high. Remove the mush from the refrigerator, cut it into 4 wedges, and use a flexible pie server to carefully lift each wedge from the pie tin and place it on the broiler pan. (If the first piece should break, simply pat it back into place.)

Melt the butter in a skillet or sauté pan. Drizzle about half over the top of the wedges, using the back of the spoon to spread it evenly. (Reserve the remaining butter in the pan for preparing the morels and greens.) Place the wedges under the broiler. Broil for 8 to 12 minutes, until lightly golden on top, while you prepare the mushrooms and greens.

Rinse the mushrooms well and quickly to remove any dirt, if necessary. (Most commercially available morels have already been cleaned and require only a light rub with a damp paper towel.) Split them in half lengthwise. Set aside with the garlic.

Rinse the arugula to remove any dirt or grit. Shake to remove excess water, but don't pat dry. Slice to make ribbons about ¼ inch long. Set aside.

Place the pan with butter back over medium-high heat, and add the garlic and mushrooms. Sauté for 1 minute, then add the arugula, stirring it down to wilt it and coat it with butter. It takes about 2 minutes to heat the arugula through. Remove from the heat.

Remove the mush wedges from the broiler and place them on individual plates. Top with the mushrooms and greens, and eat immediately.

Note: *It's not quite so subtle, but you can prepare the same dish using half a cup of broken walnut pieces in place of the morels.*

JOHNSON, ARKANSAS, APRIL 1995

James at the Mill is the restaurant at the Inn at the Mill, a hotel and conference center built around an 1830s gristmill in Johnson, just south of Fayetteville. (See Places to Go, page 341.) The restaurant is in its own building next to the lodge, a dramatic gray-shingled structure, sharp and angular, which reminds me of a stylish mountain ski lodge in, say, Telluride—an impression underscored by the smell of woodsmoke in the air.

Inside, huge windows look out on a glorious view of the crest of the surrounding hills. The two-level dining room is dramatically decorated by the branches of a sycamore, which rises through its center. Dark-green leather and deep-purple-plush upholstery cover the banquettes; Swedish modern wood-and-metal chairs flank tables draped in thick white cloth. It's a striking dining room, but not one that inspires me to expect anything particularly "Southern-style" from the kitchen. The staff is friendly, though, and my server graciously accommodating as I mix and match entrees and sides to create a sampler plate from the menu selections. The service feels distinctly Southern, even homey.

Later, when we talk by telephone, chef/owner Miles James will tell me that the impact he wants from his restaurant is just this: "When you walk in, you feel like you're someplace else. When you get your food, you feel like you've come home."

Surprisingly light potato-rye bread and pumpernickel with a rich, moist tunnel of prune puree through the middle (like homemade bread and apple butter rolled into one) are just what the weary traveler needs. But when the pièce de résistance arrives—locally grown chard that is wilted and served with a wood-seared slab of corn mush—I am apprehensive. It is served in a most Charlie Trotterish presentation, the slab of mush and other ingredients all cut in perfect rounds and stacked, floating in a pool of pale green onion coulis with a grill-charred green onion stuck jauntily in the top. I am not opposed to dramatic presentation per se, but experience has taught me that too much emphasis on the visual often equals a neglect of flavor.

One bite of Miles James's creation, though, and I am convinced. The wilted chard has a perfect blend of tart and bacony seasoning that complements but doesn't overwhelm the greens' naturally nutty flavor, a flavor underscored by chunks of meaty morels throughout. It is topped by a slightly sweet layer of spaghetti squash, which is itself topped by grilled fresh plum tomatoes. All of it is capped by the mush, enhanced with just a hint of grated cheese, bursting with the flavor of freshly ground cornmeal underscored by a hint of hickory smoke. The coulis is just an upscale presentation of the jelly glass of freshly picked and trimmed green onions my aunts put on the table at every summer meal. Best of all, the "stacked" presentation gives the diner a little bit of everything in each bite, which would satisfy my mother's strictest sense of how things are supposed to be eaten.

It is hard for me to imagine that anything will compare with this dish, which has captured the distinctive flavor system of the tradition I grew up in, but presented it in a new and thoroughly pleasing way. In the interest of research, however, I order banana cake, and am presented with another brilliant concoction. The moist, fragrant cake has been individually baked, is covered with a caramel glaze encasing fresh banana slices and pecans, and is served with a scoop of lightly malted, homemade vanilla ice cream on top. It looks like the centerpiece from a glossy magazine spread on uptown down-home desserts (and, indeed, will be featured in just such a magazine a few months later), but it tastes like a memory straight from someone's grandmother's kitchen.

Indeed, Miles tells me later that the banana cake recipe is his Texas grandmother's. "The only thing I changed is to use Tahitian vanilla beans, and I add malt to the ice cream to make it taste like a milk shake."

Miles and his wife, Courtney, own and operate the restaurant at the lodge, which was designed by Courtney's architect father. When I am there it has been open only four months, but the *Arkansas Times* has already given it the paper's first five-star rating. (Since then Miles has established a growing national reputation as one of the best young chefs working in the Southern vernacular.)

Miles, who grew up in Fayetteville and has a boyish voice sweetened by a Southern accent, tells me he attended the New England Culinary Institute, worked with Mark Miller at the Coyote Café, and at Tribeca and Park Avenue cafés in New York and the River Café in London.

"The Coyote definitely influenced me. That's where I got the notion to do things in very spectacular style, but using local foods at their freshest. When I went abroad, my style changed in another way. I was most influenced by Tuscan food. I liked the simplicity in ingredients and procedures."

But the foundation of Miles's culinary art is definitely regional. He says, "I spent a lot of time in my formative years in the kitchen with my mother and grandmother. I had no dad, so I was around cooks a lot when I was growing up. When I went to school, I studied architecture, but I was going to my job as a cook more often than I was going to class, and I eventually realized that was what I really wanted to do."

Miles says that his goal for the restaurant is to "definitely define the food of this region." He calls his style of cooking "Ozark Plateau Cuisine" and identifies its two major components as an adherence to the flavor system he grew up with and a reliance on locally grown products. I ask him if the morel mushrooms in the cornmeal-chard dish aren't a bit of an affectation and he laughs. "We've got morel mushrooms sprouting wild on the ridge right behind the restaurant—mushrooms just like the ones you'd order from the Northwest and pay a fortune for a pound, except maybe ours are even better. And they're just there for the picking! I love this land, love it."

Miles's Wild Mushroom and Potato Hash

SERVES 4 AS AN ENTREE, 6 TO 8 AS A SIDE DISH

Miles James shared this wonderful recipe, which makes use of the meaty flavors of the many mushrooms which grow in the Ozarks Plateau. At James at the Mill, they serve this as a side dish, and Miles notes that it is great with game, like venison, or hearty meats, such as lamb. When I made it at home, however, we ate the hash as a main course with a simple salad of greens, apple, and onion in vinaigrette. It's nice to have a little sourdough bread on the side to sop up the very last of the juices.

1½ pounds Irish potatoes
2 tablespoons canola oil
½ pound mixed "wild" mushrooms
    (shiitake, portobello, oyster, crimini)
⅛ cup fresh chopped thyme
1 cup heavy cream
1 white onion, finely diced
1 red bell pepper, finely diced
salt
pepper

Peel the potatoes and dice them about ½ inch square. In a large, deep-sided skillet or sauté pan, heat the canola oil over medium-high heat. When hot but not smoking, add the potatoes. Cook until they begin to turn golden on the bottom. Use a spatula to gently turn them, and brown the other side, scraping any crust up from the bottom of the pan as you do.

While the potatoes are cooking, wipe the mushrooms clean of any grit and remove the stems. Place the stems, thyme, and cream in a heavy saucepan, and heat slowly on low.

Chop the mushroom caps coarsely. When the potatoes begin to brown on the second side, add the mushrooms, onion, and bell pepper. Stir to mix, again scraping any potato crust from the bottom of the skillet to prevent burning. Cook until the potatoes, onion, and pepper are tender, about 4 minutes. If you need to turn the heat lower to prevent sticking, do, and take a little longer to cook, if necessary.

When the vegetables are tender, strain the cream, removing the thyme and stems, and add it to the hash. Add salt and pepper to taste. Bring to a boil, stirring just enough to keep the mixture from sticking. When the cream boils, remove from the heat. Serve warm.

ROAD NOTES

THE OZARKS, APRIL 1995

All of my experiences in Arkansas were marked by the wit, warmth, and hospitality of the folks who made me feel so welcome there, and make me long to go back soon. All but one.

It is in a mountain town I'd rather not name, where I stop for the night. I've driven long and hard all day, and am looking forward to the "curving front porch with handmade rockers" that made me choose this inn out of the half dozen others I'd seen advertised. I want to do nothing so much as to rock back and forth in the growing stillness, as the perfect sunny afternoon turns into a sweet crisp evening. But my host, the owner, has other plans.

Although the light is fading quickly between the ridges, he is in a great hurry to move some shrubbery from one side of the porch to the other—the other being directly in front of the chair that I, the only guest that night, have chosen. Chopping at the ground furiously with a hand-hoe, he starts, unbidden, to tell me why such an excellent man as he is in such an unlikely place as this.

He is not from the Ozarks, of course. He and his wife have come here from someplace much farther north and much more civilized. He chose this location only because the inn was a bargain price. Saving money has been of the utmost importance to this man ever since his life was changed by a TV wise man who preached about the coming financial Armageddon and the clever investments one could make to avoid it.

My host made all the right investments, of course, then, based on more sage TV advice, moved himself and his wife to this spot, which, despite the obvious beauty that soars behind, above, and around him, he finds almost abhorrent.

"It's the people," he tells me. "They're peculiar. I mean, they're nice enough, but not too bright. And they don't know how to take care of themselves. Take that fellow there," he says, pointing with his little hand-hoe across a field, where a rough-looking old pickup truck moves easily down the road, guided by a guy, who looks to be about my age, in a faded work shirt and gimme cap.

"Now that fellow's quite the green thumb," my host says. "He's got a big old garden he's always fooling around with at home. And I've offered him a job countless times to come over here and do the landscaping and repair jobs for me. I'd pay him well. More than minimum wage. But he's just too no-count and lazy. Would rather work in his garden and fiddle around with a bunch of old trucks he's got out in his yard."

When I ask, my host owns up that the fellow does do quite a bit of work for his neighbors, fixing their tractors and motors and all. Has even saved the inn some pretty expensive repair costs on the furnace and generator. "You wouldn't believe how little he charged me," my host says with a laugh. "Anybody that foolish about money can't have saved a penny in the bank. I don't know what he'll do once the economy crashes."

I, of course, know quite well, or at least hope I do, that if the banks fold and the stocks crash and the job market goes flying out the window, a fellow who can grow a field of food for his family, and keep the motors running for himself and his friends, will fare better than the smartest investor on Wall Street.

But here's the funny thing: I am sure that even if things play out my way, my hosts will have their skin saved. No doubt, their generator will keep right on running, the heater will roar, and the toilets flush, whether they have cash to pay their handy neighbors or not. And if things get real hard, well, some morning they will probably find a box on the big curving porch, filled with squash and canned beans, put-up corn and cabbage, apples from the orchard, maybe even a jam cake; just like generations of folks who've had hard times in the mountains have found before him. One piece of wisdom the guy in the pickup truck has that my host seems to have missed: You can't eat a certificate of deposit, no matter how secure.

HONEYBELLS, RUBY REDS, CALAMONDINS, & OTHER CITRUS

Lime-Butter Fish

Ginger Grapefruit Gelatin Surprise

Lemon Buttermilk Sorbet

Kentucky Lime Pie

Orange Blossom Special Cake

Kathy Cary's Lemon Pound Cake Pudding with Hot Toddy Sauce

Southern Iced Tea with Lemon

Citrus Julep

Calamondin Marmalade

A couple of times during my college years, a friend and I impulsively piled into whatever car was available and took off for Florida. These were not typical Spring Break trips, trolling for fun and sun on the beaches of Fort Lauderdale or Daytona, but were more spontaneous quests, searching for something inspirational and exotic to spark up a life that seemed far too predictable. Twice I experienced just that.

Once was on a very early morning, camped next to a saltwater lagoon on one of the tiny middle keys on the way to Key West (which we deemed, even in the early seventies, way too touristy). This key was too small to be marketed, though, and we'd spent a good night sleeping on sand, lulled by the sound of waves. Shortly after daybreak, I crawled out of our lopsided and mosquito-ridden tent into brilliant sunlight playing on crystal water. At just that moment, a silver-coated, glistening dolphin broke the lagoon's surface, arched gracefully toward the sky, and seemed to grin in my direction. She re-entered the water with barely a splash.

The second moment came on another trip, in the dead of night (or, more accurately, deep dark morning) when it seemed as if we'd been driving forever on a straight, bleak stretch of flat central-Florida highway, going nowhere. Suddenly that highway became an alley between orange groves, glowing in the moonlight with delicate white blossoms. We rolled down the windows and gulped in great draughts of perfumed air, laughing giddily. The alley stretched for miles through the quivering blooms, and I felt as if I were in some festive procession, a bridesmaid in a wedding for celestials. I was transported to another time and world altogether—one full of strange excitement and discovery.

Our daily glass of orange juice, the lemons and limes sold by the dozen at the market, which we squeeze over everything from fish to iced tea to Mexican beer, the pink-hued grapefruit juice lined in glass jar after glass jar in the supermarket aisle are all so common now, we forget how exotic and magical the citrus grown in Florida once seemed. There was a time when a single orange served after dinner was a delicacy as rare as the most elaborately prepared torte.

Citrus fruits were introduced to Florida in the sixteenth century by the Spaniards, and became an integral part of the food culture there shortly after. The fruits took hold throughout the rest of the South during the Civil War, and have permeated the larder with their tart bite and pungent fragrance since—enhancing everything from iced tea (which is never served without the offer of a lemon wedge, unless you're getting fancy and using an orange or lime) to scrumptious orange cakes.

Each citrus fruit has a distinct flavor,

but the various varieties of oranges and tangerines can be used interchangeably in some of the recipes here. If you have a chance to use Satsumas, HoneyBells, or Valencias in lieu of the standard juice orange, do. I prefer Florida citrus fruits over their California kin, for their deeper flavor and more abundant juice—and I am not alone in this preference, Florida providing the lion's share of oranges marketed nationally. Like many Southerners, I'm partial to Indian River oranges and grapefruits, but also have a soft spot for the Ruby Red grapefruit from Texas. When I'm shopping, I look for thin skins and a full, moist-feeling pulp when the fruit is ever so gently squeezed. Color is immaterial, since ripe oranges and lemons, especially, can come to market green around the edges.

Frozen juice concentrate can't hold a candle to the real thing, squeezed fresh early in the morning, and bottled lemon and lime juices are not worth the money. You'll find it an excellent investment to buy either a hand-levered or electric juice extractor. And a simple zester is worth its weight in gold for all the intriguing flavors a teaspoonful of minced lemon, lime, or orange rind will add to most recipes.

Lime-Butter Fish   SERVES 4

Butter is not the ideal fat for pan-frying, since it burns at a very low temperature, but it fills out the edgy flavor of the lime and onion marinade so perfectly in this dish that it's worth the trouble. Clarify-

ing the butter first helps, and using plenty of it is necessary. The end result is sublime.

Most skillets aren't large enough to fry all of the fish at once, but it's easy to fry in batches. Just warm a plate in the oven at its lowest setting before you begin frying. Turn the oven off, and lay the first batch on the warmed plate in the oven while you fry the second. If you can, it is even better to fry the fish in two skillets at once.

4 limes
2 pounds fresh cod or other firm white
    fish, in palm-sized filets
kosher salt
1 small sweet white onion, sliced thin
½ cup butter
1 cup white corn flour
freshly ground black pepper

Juice the limes. Pour half the juice into the bottom of a wide, shallow, nonmetal baking dish or container which will hold the filets in a single layer. Lay the filets in the juice and salt them liberally on both sides. Lay the onion slices over the filets, then pour the rest of the lime juice over that. Cover the dish tightly, and marinate in the refrigerator for 30 minutes.

While the fish is marinating, clarify the butter by melting it over low heat until it foams. Remove from the heat. Skim the foam from the top and discard it. Pour off the yellow liquid and set it aside. Discard the white milk solids remaining.

When the fish is marinated, sauté the onion slices in 1 tablespoon of the clarified butter until softened and turning transparent. Set aside.

Mix the corn flour with ½ teaspoon of kosher salt and plenty of pepper. Dredge the filets in the flour, coating both sides.

Put half the remaining butter in a skillet wide enough to accommodate half the filets, uncrowded. Set it over medium heat until the butter begins to get bubbly. Lay half the filets in the butter, and fry until just turning golden on the first side. Turn and fry on the second side, until just golden as well. Remove to a warm plate in the oven. Fry the second batch as you did the first. Spread the onions over the fish and serve.

VARIATION: *You can also serve the filets in open-face sandwiches with lime-onion mayonnaise. To do this, zest one of the limes before juicing and mince the zest finely. Also mince 2 teaspoons of onion. Mix these with ¼ cup of mayonnaise and ¼ teaspoon Tabasco or other hot pepper sauce.*

While the fish is frying, toast 1 slice of thin white bread for each person. Spread with the mayonnaise and top with the finished filets and onions.

FARM MARKETS AND FESTIVALS

In Winter Haven, Florida, they throw a Florida Citrus Showcase the last week of January through the first of February every year, in conjunction with the Polk County Fair. Cook-offs and fruit display competitions, foods made with lemons, limes, grapefruits, and, of course, oranges, and tours of citrus groves all celebrate the fact that Florida produces the most grapefruit in the world and 75 percent of all the oranges consumed in the United States.

But they don't produce it all. Over in Mission, Texas, they are proud as only a bunch of Texans can be of their homegrown Ruby Red grapefruit, produced there since 1929. The Texas Citrus Festival, held the first or second weekend in February since 1932, trots out a bunch of citrus-infused foods, features a parade with King and Queen and a passel of princesses, and, of course, has a cook-off. But most exciting of all is the annual Friday-night fashion show, with local folks wearing handmade creations from regional produce, ranging from seed buttons to clothes of material elaborately decorated with pulverized tangerine skins.

If that's not enough for you, then you won't want to miss the Plaquemines Parish Fair and Orange Festival on the Gulf of Mexico in the southernmost point of Louisiana, where it's rumored that the first mandarin orange was grown back in the 1850s. Like most Louisiana food fests, this one is heavy on the seafood and gumbo, but it also features lots of citrus fruit, including the locally grown Satsumas. It's held the first full weekend of December.

See Places to Go, page 341.

Ginger Grapefruit Gelatin Surprise

SERVES 8

Cool gelatin dishes such as this one and Cucumber Mousse (page 152) used to be the very definition of refreshing during the scorching Southern summer. The surprise here is the brisk snap of Blenheim's ginger ale (see below), which gives this otherwise cool salad pizzazz. If you can't get Blenheim's, spike a standard ginger ale with ⅛ teaspoon finely minced fresh ginger and a dash of cayenne.

Any juicy grapefruit will do, but a red-fleshed variety provides more visual interest.

1 cup nonfat yogurt
12-ounce bottle Blenheim's ginger ale, Extra Pale
¾ ounce unflavored gelatin
2 grapefruits
water
1 cup white grape juice
1 tablespoon honey
1 tablespoon fresh lime juice
lettuce leaves

Use cheesecloth to line a strainer which can hold at least 1 cup, or put a paper filter in a clean coffee filter holder. Fill with the yogurt, and leave it to drain over a bowl or other receptacle while you prepare the gelatin. The yogurt should drain for at least 4 hours.

Pour the ginger ale into a bowl and sprinkle the gelatin over it to soften. (It will look weird. Don't worry.)

Peel the grapefruits over another bowl to catch the juice. Remove the pith, seeds, and white membranes, leaving only chunks of fruit. Lay these in the bottom of a shallow 1-quart dish or gelatin mold. Add cold water to the reserved grapefruit juice to make 1 cup.

Bring some water to a boil, and pour 1 cupful into the gelatin and ginger ale. Stir to dissolve the gelatin. Add the grapefruit juice and the white grape juice, then pour the mixture over the grapefruit pieces. Allow it to come to room temperature, then cover securely with plastic wrap and refrigerate for 4 hours, until the gelatin is set.

When you are ready to serve, mix the drained yogurt with the honey and lime juice to blend. Cut the gelatin into individual slices and serve it on lettuce leaves, topped with a spoonful of the yogurt.

MAIL ORDER

The Spaniards brought ginger to the Americas in the sixteenth century, and it quickly became popular through the South, not only for flavoring dishes but also for preserving food.

It was also in the South, in 1903, that Blenheim's ginger ale, the pluperfect, hoo-hah, yeah buddy, most outrageous ginger ale, was born.

The elixir marketed by Dr. C. R. May and Mr. A. J. Matheson, the original owners of the Blenheim Bottling Company of Blenheim, South Carolina, had (and has) as its source an artesian mineral spring discovered in 1782 by James Spears. Legend has it that Mr. Spears, a Whig, was fleeing Tory troops when he literally stumbled on the spring, dropping a shoe into it in the process. He could not pause at that moment, but returned several days later to retrieve his shoe, and at that point also tasted the water.

The taste was potent and sharply mineral. Why this did not simply convince Mr. Spears to wash his feet with more regularity, I cannot tell you, but I am glad it didn't. Instead, he became convinced of the water's curative properties and spread the word. Soon wealthy plantation owners were building homes nearby, and over the years local doctors began advising patients with stomach problems to drink from the spring. One of these was Dr. May, who seems to have had some particularly whiny malingerers in his practice. Several of his patients complained about the strong taste of the plain mineral water, so Dr. May doctored it with Jamaican ginger to make it more palatable, and—voilà!—a soft drink was born.

"Soft" drink may be a misnomer when it comes to Blenheim's ginger ale, however. For starters, the water from the spring contains traces of some twenty-two minerals. Then there is the ginger, added in emphatic amounts. In addition, the scorched back of my throat tells me (and some old recipes for ginger ale would seem to concur) that there's surely some cayenne in there somewhere. This makes for a drink that is bubbly, smooth, sweet, creamy, and absolutely hot as hell. And that's just the original Extra Pale. For those of us with a real spirit of adventure (or streak of masochism), Blenheim also makes "Old #3," a version that is extra, extra hot.

Blenheim's ginger ale is an acquired taste that some do not care to acquire. I heard about it the first time we visited Pawley's Island ten years ago, and spent a good part of my one-week vacation tracking down some. Perhaps my expectations were too intense, for when I finally did get my hands on a bottle and poured the pale, golden liquid over ice, none of us was entranced. My daughter wouldn't even approach the glass, which was spewing little pepper bubbles. My husband turned his nose up at the first taste, and there it stayed for many years. I finished off the drink reluctantly, loathe to give up on a genuine local food find, but not really charmed by the initial sting in my eyes or the burn it left in the back of my throat.

You know how sneaky those burns can be, though. Something about it lingered in my memory, and when we were in South Carolina again, I had to have more, first out of curiosity, but increasingly in delight.

In South Carolina, I discovered that Blenheim's is perfect to quaff while picking through a peck of fresh boiled peanuts. Back home, I started to order Blenheim's by the caseload. With those golden bottles sitting around in the fridge, I began wondering what else one could do with such a clever drink.

Leave it to Low Country magician John Taylor to come up with a perfect spell in *The*

New Southern Cook (Bantam, 1995): carrots glazed in orange marmalade and Blenheim's ginger ale. (Peel the carrot. Quarter it lengthwise and cut it into 2-inch pieces, John says. Put the pieces in a saucepan, pour ½ cup of Blenheim's ginger ale over them, and add ½ tablespoon of orange marmalade. Boil over high heat until the carrots are cooked, but firm, and the liquids have become a glaze. Serve immediately. Makes enough for one.)

Inspired by John, I tried cooking a sweet potato, peeled and sliced about ¼ inch thick, in Blenheim's ginger ale to cover and a tablespoon of butter. I covered the pot and simmered until the potato was fork-tender (15 to 20 minutes), then let it boil vigorously, uncovered, for a few more minutes, until the liquid thickened to a glaze. The result was sweet with heat, a perfect quick fix for any holiday supper.

I also marinated a small pork roast in a couple of bottles of Old #3. Steeped in the fridge for two days, the pork absorbed enough to be both peppy and fragrant when browned and then roasted in a Dutch oven on top of the stove. And Blenheim's ginger ale is the secret, snappy ingredient in Ginger Grapefruit Gelatin Surprise (page 256).

But the best discovery I've made so far was pure serendipity. All of the recipes I tried ended up leaving partially filled bottles of Blenheim's ginger ale. I tried mixing some with iced tea (pretty good if the tea is sweetened) and orange juice (not as tasty as one would hope) before I remembered a dab of bourbon in the cupboard.

Folks, this is the combination that both were born for. Either strength of Blenheim's cozies right up to the whiskey with ease. Pour both over ice in whatever proportion pleases you most, although I like mine heavy on the ginger ale. Make it with a rich, mellow bourbon and its yin will meld with the Blenheim's yang in a perfect marriage. Stuff a stem of fresh mint in the top of the glass and you've got a ginger julep. See Things to Order, page 338.

Lemon Buttermilk Sorbet

SERVES 4 TO 6

1 large lemon
3½ cups buttermilk

This is an inspired combination, and so easy to make. It will stand alone, served in small portions, after a harvest feast, but is at its best when paired with a fruity tart dessert such as the Peach Cobbler on page 276.

This recipe is perfect for a Donvier or other quart-size hand ice cream maker.

½ cup white sugar
½ cup brown sugar

Mix the sugars together. Zest the lemon and mince the zest finely, then juice the lemon. Mix the juice and sugar in a nonreactive saucepan to dissolve the sugar. Add the zest and simmer over very low heat for 5 minutes.

In a bowl, combine the buttermilk and lemon syrup. Cover securely and refrigerate overnight. Prepare the sorbet according to your ice cream maker's directions.

GINGER SNAP CRUST

ginger snaps to make 1½ cups crumbs
    (about 24, but the number may vary
    according to size)
¼ cup sugar
¼ cup melted salted butter

Preheat the oven to 350°F.

In a blender, using the pulser, process the ginger snaps on high to make fine crumbs. Transfer them to a bowl and mix in the sugar. Drizzle the melted butter over the crumbs and mix with a wooden spoon until all the crumbs are moistened.

Put the mixture in a 9-inch pie plate, and use the palm of your hand to smooth it into an even disk on the bottom of the pan. Begin gently pressing the crumbs from the center, working outward evenly. The crumb mixture will compress and become smoother under your palm, and crumbs will move up the inside edges of the pan. When the bottom is just smooth and a relatively even edge of crumbs lines the sides of the pan, use your fingertips to lightly press around the inside edge of the pan, compressing and smoothing those crumbs just to the rim of the pan (but not over it). Lightly press any loose crumbs into the crust. Bake for 6 minutes to set the crust. Remove and cool completely before filling.

FILLING

3 egg yolks
14 ounces sweetened condensed milk
½ cup fresh lime juice (about 2 limes)

Texas Ruby Red grapefruits show up in Southern groceries along about November, but folks who have been ordering theirs from Frank Lewis Alamo Fruits swear there is no comparison. Frank Lewis Royal Ruby Red Grapefruits sport flesh of a deep, deep red and oodles and oodles of juice. Each one weighs a pound or more, and you won't even consider dousing them with sugar, they're so naturally sweet. Lots of folks opt to send them at Christmas, but they are usually available November through December. And when grapefruits aren't in season, peaches, plums, and other fruits are. You can even order supersweet, just-picked Royal Starr cantaloupe—a southwest Texas specialty—for a few brief weeks in the middle of July.

See Things to Order, page 338.

Kentucky Lime Pie   SERVES 8

Key lime pie is one of the most distinctive regional recipes of the South, correct only when made with fresh Florida key limes. But fresh key limes are difficult to get outside of Florida, and the season is short. This version of the classic is made with regular (Persian) limes, and uses a ginger snap crust and bourbon-laced whipped cream to give it a little extra zing.

Beat the yolks with an electric mixer until they are thick and lemon-colored. Add the condensed milk and blend. Slowly pour in the lime juice, beating as you do, and continue to beat until the mixture is very thick. Pour into the pie crust. Cover tightly with plastic wrap and refrigerate overnight (or for at least 6 hours). Serve topped with bourbon whipped cream.

BOURBON WHIPPED CREAM
1 cup whipping cream
2 tablespoons sugar
1 tablespoon bourbon

Whip all the ingredients in a chilled mixing bowl until the cream is fluffy and stiff enough to hold its shape when mounded. Put a generous dollop on each piece of pie before you serve it.

Orange Blossom Special Cake
SERVES 12

"If I'd known you were coming, I'd have baked a cake . . ." This could have been the sound track for my childhood. Although I was born in Corbin, Kentucky, my parents moved to Louisville because of a job for Daddy when I was a year old. I grew up in the city, then, but was closely connected to my family and the traditions of rural southeastern Kentucky through trips back "home" and the welcome visits of friends and kin.

My mother has always lived in a house that has more beds in it than there are people living there. When I was growing up, those extra beds were filled with aunts and uncles and cousins—some passing through on their way farther north in search of jobs; some staying for the while it took for some crisis to settle out in their lives; and some simply there for a day or two of sitting around the big oak table in our dining room, filling up on my mother's fried chicken, shuck beans, and cornbread and my father's wonderful stories.

I thought it was a charmed way to grow up, because whenever a knock came at the door, I didn't know what fun and what fascinating person might be there. One of my best memories is throwing open the door, when I was about six years old, and finding my vibrant blond-haired cousin, Betty Jean Rookard, holding a Betty Crocker bake set just for me. It was a perk from her husband Jack's new job at General Mills. And I guess it was the start of a lifetime of cooking for me.

I would bake a little cake, no bigger around than a compact disc, and frost it ever so carefully with the bright fuchsia icing that came in the box. Then my mom would put it smack in the center of the table, so everyone could admire it all through dinner. When the dishes had been cleared, my daddy would get out a big, long knife and, just as solemnly as if he were dividing up our inheritance, split that cake into four equal parts for my mother, my sister, himself, and me. Those times when Pat was out on a date and there were only three of us at the table,

Daddy would look at that extra piece for a slow, solemn minute and then say, "Well, I believe if nobody else will, I have to have that last piece of cake. I believe that's about the best cake I ever had."

No wonder I grew up thinking that I could cook, despite several early years when all the evidence looked to prove the contrary. But while my *cooking* skills measurably improved over time, I'm not sure I'd claim that my *baking* skills did. Oh, I could make cakes that were tasty, but usually they came out lopsided or fallen in the middle. It wasn't until I started writing cookbooks and studying other people's research into the science of cakes that my efforts began to live up to my father's praise.

While the stack cakes, jam cakes, pound cakes, and red velvet cakes I loved in my youth were somewhat forgiving in the kitchen, it took me a long time—and the assistance of an article by Stephen Schmidt—to master the essential white layer cake which forms the basis of this typically Southern citrus-charged dessert.

Schmidt is the author of *Master Recipes* (Ballantine, 1987), and his recipe for this cake appeared in *Cook's Illustrated* in 1995. The secret to perfection is in the order of preparation as much as in the ingredients, and once I learned to do things Schmidt's way, it was simple to adapt the cake for the zingy citrus-grove flavor of the recipe here. While pure orange extract may be a little difficult to find, it's worth the look. Try a specialty food store if you have no luck at the supermarket.

Don't use butter instead of shortening for preparing the pans, or your layers will stick.

ORANGE CAKE

vegetable shortening and flour, for preparing pans
1 cup milk, room temperature
¾ cup egg whites (5 to 6 eggs), room temperature
1 teaspoon orange extract
1 teaspoon almond extract
1 teaspoon vanilla extract
2¼ cups cake flour
1¾ cups sugar
4 teaspoons baking powder
1 teaspoon salt
12 tablespoons unsalted butter, softened

Preheat the oven to 350°F. Set an oven rack in the middle position. (If your oven is small, use two racks as close to the middle as possible.) Coat the inside bottoms and sides of two 9-inch cake pans liberally with shortening and then flour. (It takes about a tablespoon of each for each pan.) Be sure to roll the pans so the flour coats everywhere, then turn them over and rap once sharply to remove excess flour.

Pour the milk, egg whites, and extracts into a bowl, and whisk until blended.

Use an electric mixer at slow speed to blend the cake flour, sugar, baking powder, and salt. Add the butter and continue beating at slow speed until the mixture resembles moist crumbs. There should be no dry flour in the bowl.

Reserve ½ cup of the milk mixture. Add the rest to the flour mixture and turn the mixer up to medium speed. Beat for 1½ minutes. (If it's a handheld mixer, make it 2 minutes.) Add the rest of the milk and beat 30 seconds more. Stop the mixer and scrape down the sides of the bowl. Beat again at medium (or high) speed for 20 seconds.

Pour the batter into the cake pans, dividing it evenly and using a rubber spatula to spread the batter to the pan walls and to smooth out the top. Place them in the oven with at least 3 inches of space between pans and from the oven walls. (If the oven is too small to do this, use two racks and stagger the pans.)

Bake for 23 to 25 minutes, until a cake tester inserted in the middle comes out clean. Remove from the oven and let rest for 3 minutes. Use a knife to loosen the sides from the pans if necessary. Carefully invert the pans onto cooling racks. Remove the pans, then carefully turn the layers over onto other racks to keep the tops from indenting. Cool completely (about 1½ hours) before icing. Completely cooled cake layers may be wrapped securely in plastic wrap and kept overnight to frost the next day, if necessary.

ORANGE BUTTER FROSTING

6 cups confectioner's sugar
¾ cup unsalted butter, softened
5 to 8 tablespoons orange juice, freshly squeezed
1 tablespoon orange zest, minced

Using an electric mixer at low speed, beat the sugar, butter, and 5 tablespoons of orange juice until just blended. If very stiff, add more orange juice, a tablespoon

at a time. Sprinkle the zest over the frosting. Increase the mixer speed to medium (high for a handheld mixer), and beat 1½ minutes, until light and fluffy. Stop and scrape down the sides of the bowl twice during the process.

To frost, place one layer on a serving plate and use a small spatula or knife to spread the frosting a little more than ¼ inch thick over the top. Carefully lay the second layer on top, and spread frosting generously over the sides and top.

Note: *Any extra frosting may be refrigerated and can provide a quick, yummy treat, spread on graham crackers, butter cookies, vanilla wafers, or (this one's the best) ginger snaps.*

Kathy Cary's Lemon Pound Cake Pudding with Hot Toddy Sauce   SERVES 12

Kathy Cary has been spreading the gospel of new Southern cooking for several years, from the kitchen of her Louisville restaurant, Lilly's (see Places to Go, page 341), through national magazines, and in her appearances at the James Beard House in New York. It's a passion rooted in memories of the kitchens she grew up in, and her best dishes are always those that stick close to home. This cream-and-butter-rich citrus dessert with a robust bourbon kick is just such a one. Cary prefers to use Woodford Reserve, a single-barrel premium bourbon from her home state.

POUND CAKE

½ pound unsalted butter, room temperature

1½ cups sugar

6 large eggs

3 cups all-purpose flour

½ teaspoon baking powder

1 cup buttermilk

1 tablespoon minced lemon zest

Preheat the oven to 350°F. Grease a large loaf pan.

With an electric mixer, cream the butter until light and fluffy. Add the sugar slowly until combined well. Add the eggs one at a time, beating well after each.

Sift and resift the flour with the baking powder. Add the flour to the butter mixture a cup at a time, alternating with half cups of buttermilk and mixing well after each addition.

Stir in the lemon zest.

Pour into the prepared loaf pan and bake for 75 to 90 minutes, until the top is firm and golden and a cake tester comes out clean. Allow to cool in the pan for a few minutes, then turn out on a rack and leave to cool. You may make the cake the day before and, after it has completely cooled, wrap it well in plastic wrap to store.

LEMON CURD

6 egg yolks

zest of one lemon, minced

⅓ cup fresh lemon juice

¾ cup sugar

6 tablespoons unsalted butter, cut in ¼-inch chunks

In a metal bowl or the top of a double boiler, beat the yolks well, then whisk in the lemon zest, juice, and sugar. Place over a pan of barely simmering water and stir in the butter, a piece at a time. Cook until the curd thickens and coats the back of a metal spoon. Remove from the heat, cover the surface directly with plastic wrap, and chill. The curd may be made a day in advance and refrigerated.

CUSTARD

2 cups half and half

1 cup heavy cream

¾ cup sugar

3 large eggs

2 egg yolks

In a heavy skillet over medium heat, heat the half and half, cream, and sugar until the sugar is dissolved. While they are heating, whisk together the eggs and yolks until fully blended. Very slowly add the hot cream mixture to the eggs, whisking constantly. Strain through a fine sieve and reserve. The custard mixture may be made ahead and refrigerated.

When you are ready to prepare the pudding, remove the curd and custard from the refrigerator. Preheat the oven to 350°F. Butter the inside of a 9-by-11-inch baking pan.

Slice the pound cake ¼ inch thick. Place slices in a single layer to cover the bottom of the pan. Spread half the lemon curd over this. Cover with another layer of cake, then the rest of the lemon curd. Pour the custard over all.

Place the baking pan in a larger pan containing 2 inches of water. Bake 30 to 40 minutes, until the custard is set.

HOT TODDY SAUCE
12 tablespoons unsalted butter
2⅔ cups brown sugar, packed
½ cup fresh lemon juice
1¼ cups bourbon

While the pudding is baking, prepare the hot toddy sauce.

In a heavy skillet over medium heat, melt the butter. Add the brown sugar and lemon juice, and cook, stirring occasionally, until the mixture boils. Add the bourbon and return to a boil. Remove from the heat.

When the pudding is ready, remove it from the oven and allow it to cool for a few minutes. Dish it up into bowls and serve with warm hot toddy sauce passed on the side.

Southern Iced Tea with Lemon   MAKES 1½ QUARTS

The most bewildering concept I've encountered on a menu was a parenthetical note I saw at a restaurant in Michigan when I was in my teens. It came right after the listing for iced tea and it said, "(in season)." In season? I grew up in a place where frost could come as early as October and snow has been known to fall in double digits, but never had I dreamed that iced tea could have a season. Iced tea appeared at all special meals, including Thanksgiving and Christmas, and would no more have been left off the bill of fare than the turkey. From spring through late fall there was a pitcher always ready in my mother's kitchen for anytime sipping, and the same is true now in mine. Even in the very dead of winter, when cups of hot tea become the mid-day beverage of choice, I still make iced tea, as my mother did, for any company dinner. What's more, my guests— including my mother—tell me (and I blushingly agree) that mine is the best.

What are the secrets? Tea is one of those rituals about which there are fiercely held rules and long-standing traditions. Here are the things I think are essential, and a few that are not.

First, your tea should be orange pekoe. For hot tea, I like darjeeling on a daily basis, lapsang souchong when it snows, jasmine and Earl Grey for occasional excitement. But plain orange pekoe seems to make the crispest, cleanest draught for icing. Luzianne is my brand of choice, but Lipton's does just fine and is often cheaper, not a small consideration when you brew a quart-and-a-half pitcher almost every day.

I used loose tea for several years, tolerating the fuss and bother of stainless-steel tea balls until the final one broke in my hands, spewing wet tea leaves all across the kitchen. I switched to tea bags, discovered I could tell no difference in the flavor—nor could my regular guests—and haven't gone back. I use five bags of Lipton's or six of Luzianne for a quart-and-a-half pitcher.

That pitcher is either heavy-duty glass or thick stoneware. My favorite is a lemony-yellow Hall pitcher my long-lost friend Cindy gave me years ago. The pitcher must be tempered and sturdy enough that you can pour boiling water right into it without fear of it shattering. It cannot be plastic and, if metal, must not be aluminum, for both absorb and give off strange background odors and flavors.

You must make the tea by pouring boiling water over the tea bags in the pitcher. I've read directions for iced tea which call for putting the bags into a saucepan of hot water, but to have the proper briskness, it's best for the water to hit the leaves, not nestle them.

The water should be actually boiling, but not for long. Grab it just when the bubbles start to burst through the surface. You need a quart of water. If your tap water isn't clear and clean-tasting, use bottled spring water. Pour the boiling water straight on the tea bags, soaking them through, then leave the whole thing to steep for at least an hour, preferably until the tea has come to room temperature.

Here is an interesting thing I've discovered. Letting the tea steep longer doesn't make it stronger. I've forgotten the bags in the pitcher overnight and still had perfect tea the next day. Nevertheless, it's good to take the bags out after an hour or two.

Although you should never do this with tea bags when making hot tea, I always squeeze mine gently with a wooden spoon or my fingers when I remove them, to get all the flavor.

Now here comes the part I've discovered many folks (particularly Northerners) find difficult to believe—although not to swallow: To the brewed tea, add 1 cup of granulated sugar.

Yes, that's a lot of sugar. Yes, you can cut that in half, if you must; leave it out altogether, if you want. You'll still have a pleasant drink. But if you want truly great iced tea, put in the whole cup of sugar.

Don't decide you'll let everyone add sugar to taste later, since it won't dissolve, and they'll make an unholy racket clanking spoons in ice-filled glasses, trying to get it to. If you suspect that some of your guests won't drink tea with sugar, make two pitchers, one with and one without. (But take my word for it, here's what will happen: Everyone will pretend they are thinking about having unsweetened tea when you give them the option, but then will say "Oh, let me have just one glass with sugar in it." That is all they will drink thereafter, and you'll be putting sugar in the unsweetened pitcher of tea for refills before the night is over.)

Stir the sugar until it's dissolved and then add cold water from the tap, about a cup or cup and a half, to fill the pitcher.

DO NOT serve the tea until it is completely room temperature. If it's the least bit warm, it will melt the ice in the glass, diluting the tea and making the drink tepid—not what you want at all. When the tea is ready, fill a tall glass with ice cubes to the brim. (Crushed ice will melt, again diluting the tea.) Pour the tea over it.

Now, cut a lemon into eight wedges. DO NOT cut it into circles. Squeeze a wedge into the tea, dropping the spent wedge into the glass so the oils in the bruised rind will also add flavor. Stir it quickly to disperse the lemon, sit back, and sip. Ah, that's real tea.

If you do not consume the full pitcher in one day, you may want to put it in the refrigerator overnight. Cover it securely with plastic wrap, or it will pick up refrigerator flavors. I have never had tea turn cloudy in the refrigerator, although I've been told this can happen and that a quick splash of boiling water added to the tea will clear it.

Citrus Julep MAKES 12

It may help you accept what I am about to say if you know that I grew up one block away from Churchill Downs, which is, on the first Saturday in May of each year, the largest mint julep factory in the world. I have had mint juleps at the track, at the bar, at Derby parties, and in my home. I hold one in my hand almost every year at my dear friends Dick and Gail Kaukas's Derby party, as an assembled hundred or so of us watch the horses come out on the track, sing "My Old Kentucky Home," and, yep, shed some real tears. Maybe it's that little dab of salt water, but when I subsequently bury my nose in the de

rigueur sprig of mint to reach the necessarily shortened straw through which I pull that first frosty, breathtakingly bourboned draft, it tastes absolutely delicious. If I taste a mint julep at any other time in any other place, it tastes like skunk water.

People don't like mint juleps, honey, and don't let anybody tell you they do. People drink them out of curiosity or for tradition's sake, but nobody drinks them for taste. People who don't like bourbon can't abide them, since the added water, sugar, and mint don't do a darn thing to hide the bourbon's taste. And people who do like bourbon are even more contemptuous.

If you absolutely must make a mint julep, here is what you do: First, get yourself some real fine crushed ice. Not so soft as the "snow" they use now to make fruit-flavored ices commercially, but ice that has been crushed to almost slivers, like the ice that is perfect for making ice cream in an old-fashioned hand-crank freezer. You may have to buy commercially crushed ice, bring it home, wrap a big handful in a clean dish towel, and whale on it with a small hammer or the handle of a heavy table knife to get the right consistency, but it's essential that you do.

Now, take a julep cup or good water glass and in the bottom put a heaping teaspoon of superfine sugar (regular won't dissolve as well) and a tablespoon of clean-flavored water. (If your tap water's not good, use bottled spring water.) Add several leaves of fresh mint, preferably just picked, then take a wooden spoon and mash and muddle the mint into the sugar water to make a syrup. Bruising is the point, to release the volatile oils of the mint.

Pack the glass to the brim with the finely crushed ice and then pour some *good* bourbon over that until it saturates the ice. (If your bourbon is too good— one of those boutique bottles of single-barrel premium bourbon—for heaven's sake, don't make it into a julep—just sip it.)

Push a gorgeous, leafy stem of mint into the ice to garnish the top, and push a plastic or paper straw in next to it. Cut the straw just below the mint so that when you sip, you bury your nose in it.

Now, if you don't have to make a genuine julep, but just want a good, sweet fruit-and-bourbon drink for the summer, here's the ticket.

1 lime
1 orange
1 lemon
1 cup sugar
1 cup water
1 cup fresh mint leaves
finely crushed ice
good bourbon
sprigs of mint

Zest the lime, orange, and lemon, and set the fruit aside. Combine the sugar and water in a saucepan, and bring it to a quick boil. Add the zest, turn the heat to low, and simmer for 2 minutes. Remove from the heat and allow to cool.

Put the mint leaves in a quart jar or a crock, and use the back of a wooden spoon to bruise them, to release the oil. Pour the syrup, including the zest, over the leaves and let them steep for 1 hour. When the steeping is completed, juice the lime, orange, and lemon, and strain them into a pitcher. Strain the mint syrup into the pitcher, using the back of a spoon to press the mint leaves and zest against the strainer to extract any remaining juices. You can refrigerate the syrup for up to a day, or use it immediately.

For each citrus julep, fill an 8-ounce glass or julep cup with finely crushed ice. Pour 3 ounces of bourbon over the ice, then top off the glass with the syrup. Garnish with mint sprigs and short straws.

VARIATION: *Omit the mint and add 1 ounce of thinly sliced ginger to the sugar and water along with the zest just after the mixture comes to a boil. Either of these syrups makes a delicious nonalcoholic citrus-ade. Just mix equal amounts of syrup and plain or sparkling water, and serve over ice.*

MAIL ORDER

HoneyBells and Other Gems by Mail

The Cushman Fruit Company in West Palm Beach, Florida, is still owned and operated by the family of Ed Cushman. In 1945, Ed happened upon an interesting hybrid in a shipment of grapefruits and oranges to his retail fruit store. Bell-shaped and fiery orange in color, the fruit was supremely juicy with an outrageously sweet taste. In fact, it was Ed's wife who said it tasted sweet as honey, and Cushman HoneyBells were born.

The name was trademarked by Ed, and he marketed this cross between a Dancy tangerine and a Duncan grapefruit with savvy: each order of superjuicy HoneyBells comes with its own plastic bib, printed with the Cushman story. Soon the mail-order business was booming, even though HoneyBells are available only in January. (Don't wait until January to order, though, or you may end up ordering for next year. Early November is not too soon to place an order.)

Through the rest of the year, Cushman's mail-orders navel oranges, Valencias, tangerines, Crown Ruby Red Grapefruits, huge blueberries, cherries, mangoes, and more, in their respective seasons. And although you won't find key limes in the catalogs, if they're in stock, Cushman's will arrange to ship them to you. See Things to Order, page 338.

Calamondin Marmalade   MAKES ABOUT 3 PINTS

All I had to do was hear John Egerton say the word "calamondin" with that delicious slow Southern twang, and I knew this was a recipe I had to have. Alas, John fretted that you'd not be able to get there from here, since the calamondin—similar in appearance to a kumquat, but not really the same thing—is hard to come by. His potted plant was given to him by a friend, Tom Stovall, whose wife, Virginia, taught John how to make the marmalade. John suggests using smooth, thin-skinned tangerines as a substitute but notes that the result, while good, will not be "a classic calamondin delight."

Delight is what I felt, though, when, shortly after his recipe arrived, I came across a flyer from Edible Landscaping—a wonderful nursery in Afton, Virginia—with potted calamondins for sale. Calamondins grow excellently indoors in containers, and the folks at Edible Landscaping say the fruit also makes yummy lemonade. The plant is not listed in the regular catalog, but they do sell them. See Things to Order, page 338.

When you get your first crop, make the jam and plenty of biscuits. If you just can't wait, substitute 4 or 5 medium-sized tangerines for the calamondins in the recipe.

about 36 ripe calamondins
water
sugar
1 tablespoon fresh lemon or lime juice

Rinse the calamondins, remove the seeds and pulply membrane, and set aside. Cut the fruit and skin in slivers. (It should equal about 2 cups.)

Place the seeds and membrane in a small, nonreactive saucepan with ½ cup of water. Bring to a boil, then remove from the heat and let steep for a few minutes. Strain and set the liquid aside.

Add 1½ cups of water to the cut-up fruit, and measure the mixture. In a glass or crockery bowl, mix the fruit mixture with ¾ cup of sugar per cup of mixture, for marmalade with a characteristically sharp, almost bitter edge. (If you prefer it sweeter, add 1 cup of sugar per cup of fruit mixture). Stir to dissolve the sugar. Add the reserved liquid, cover, and leave to stand overnight, if convenient. (If you are in a hurry, you can go ahead and make the marmalade immediately, but allowing it to sit for a while gives it a stronger flavor.)

When you are ready to cook the marmalade, place it in a heavy, nonreactive saucepan. Bring it to a boil over high heat, then lower the heat, and continue to cook, stirring frequently, until the mixture begins to thicken and roll from the edge of a spoon, about 20 minutes. Pour the marmalade immediately into sterile jars and seal with new lids or paraffin.

ABOUT PEACHES, MAYHAWS, QUINCES, AND BANANAS

Camille's Best Peach Ice Cream

No-Cook Peach Ice Cream

Peach Cobbler

Jammy Biscuits

Peach and Dried-Cherry Chutney

Old-Fashioned Quince Butter

Black-Bottom Banana Cream Pie

Ultimate Banana Pudding

Banana Crunch Snack Cake

Don't like my peaches?
Don't shake my tree.
　　　—Sittin' On Top of the World

Few fruits are as purely associated with the South as sweet, dripping peaches. Georgia gets the lion's share of attention, but South Carolina is also a major producer, and great peaches thrive through all the Southern states.

Brought to North America by the Spanish in St. Augustine or the French along the Gulf Coast sometime in the mid-1500s, peaches became so prolific that one hundred years later many settlers assumed they were native. In 1676, Thomas Glover wrote of Virginia: "Here are likewise great Peach-Orchards, which bear such an infinite quantity of Peaches that at some Plantations they bear down to the Hoggs fourty bushels in a year."

The "Hoggs" do not get such bounty today, however. Southerners eat fresh peaches out of hand, cook them up in pies and cobblers, can them, brandy them, and spice them. Colonials made a potent drink called mobby, which could be distilled into brandy, and the early tradition of drying peaches for eating and cooking through the winter continues to this day. Best of all, perhaps, is peach ice cream, for which there is a recipe in Mary Randolph's *The Virginia Housewife* of 1824.

Thomas Jefferson had over thirty-nine varieties of peaches in his south orchard alone, and planted not only fruiting but also purely ornamental varieties. The Thomas Jefferson Center for Historic Plants is a good source for seedlings of the Indian Blood Peach, a deep-red-fleshed fruit with striped skin that is a hybrid of a French variety and the wild "black" peach of Georgia. The center's annual seed catalog also offers several varieties of fig and apple trees, and a range of seeds from Jefferson's era. (See Things to Order, page 338.) Mayhaws and quinces were among the odd fruits that Southerners sought out and prized for making jellies and preserves. And then there is the banana.

Yes, we have no bananas growing in the South, except for a few primarily ornamental ones, which crop up deep along the Gulf. But bananas entered this country at the port of New Orleans and made their way north along the same rail lines that carried passengers to and fro on the romantic City of New Orleans. Fulton, Kentucky, was a stopping point for those banana shipments—a good place to unload and send a share of the crops east and west. And that's why Fulton became home to the world's largest banana pudding, a part of the banana festival which was held in Fulton every year until 1992. Banana puddings are still as much a standard in the Southern larder as peach cobblers.

Camille's Best Peach Ice Cream
MAKES 1 GALLON PLUS

Camille Glenn, Queen Mother of Southern Food Writers, declares that peach ice cream is "one of the favorite summer desserts in the South, if not *the* favorite." Her recipe includes the mashed kernels of the peach pits, and she cautions that you must not forget them, since they are what adds the authentic hint of almond to the dish.

The other trick to this recipe is to have all the ingredients well-chilled before beginning the freezing.

This recipe works best using an old-fashioned bucket freezer with ice and rock salt (hand-crank or electric), since it makes over a gallon, more than a small hand-freezer like a Donvier can accommodate.

1 cup half and half
1½ cups milk
1½ cups sugar
4 egg yolks
8 large, ripe peaches
2 teaspoons lemon juice
¼ teaspoon kosher salt
2 cups heavy cream, cold

In the top of a double boiler, directly over medium-high heat, scald the half and half and milk, but don't allow them to boil. Have the bottom pan ready with hot water.

While they are heating, set ¾ cup of sugar aside. Add the other ¾ cup to the egg yolks, and mix thoroughly. When the milk is ready, slowly add it to the eggs, beating as you do. Return the mixture to the top of the double boiler and place it over—not in—boiling water in the bottom pan. Cook, stirring, until the custard just begins to thicken—enough to coat the back of a wooden spoon, but not too thick.

Remove the custard from the heat and immediately pour it into a cooled bowl or pan. Refrigerate until cold.

When the custard is cold, peel the peaches. Remove the pits, but keep them. Using a potato masher, mash the peaches thoroughly with the lemon juice. Leave no large lumps. Crack the peach pits (use a nutcracker or small hammer), and remove the kernels inside. Mash the kernels, and add them to the peaches, along with the remaining sugar and the salt. Mix well, cover tightly with plastic wrap, and refrigerate.

Mix the cold custard with the cold cream. Freeze according to your ice cream maker's instructions, just until the custard turns to soft ice cream. Stop turning, remove the cover of the freezer, and add the peaches, using a long spoon to mix well. Resume freezing to the proper ice cream consistency.

No-Cook Peach Ice Cream
SERVES 6

Sweetened condensed milk, invented by Gail Borden in the 1850s, became a Southern staple shortly after the Civil

War. It combined sugar with milk in a concentrate made by heating, which gave it both a slightly caramel taste and greater thickening power than unheated milk or cream. Because of these attributes, it soon became a preferred ingredient in a number of Southern desserts, including key lime pie.

It was also frequently used for ice cream. There are purists who object to the product's distinctive taste in plain vanilla or more delicate fruit flavors, but it's absolutely perfect paired with the fullness of very ripe peaches. I also like this recipe because it can be prepared on short notice. Cooked-custard bases must be chilled for a good eight hours for the cream to set up in my handy Donvier. This recipe can be thrown together and in the freezer in a few minutes.

Very ripe fruit is the secret to very good ice cream. Along about mid-July, we start to get *beaucoup* peaches in town, and the fruit market I frequent will sell big baskets of slightly bruised or super-ripe ones at a cut-rate price. I bring them home, and we have a peach party for a couple of days, moving from cobbler to shortcake to this delicious ice cream. The skins give the ice cream a rosy complexion.

This recipe is just the right size for a Donvier or other tabletop hand-freezer.

1 cup half and half
14 ounces sweetened condensed milk
1 cup pureed peaches (with skins)
½ cup chopped peaches (with skins)
¼ teaspoon almond extract

In a mixing bowl, combine all the ingredients. Place in an ice cream freezer with 1-quart capacity, and freeze according to directions.

"All ceremonies and rituals in the South seem to involve food. At the first mention of pregnancy, food becomes a direct link to the baby. And at death, well, of course there's food, great tables full of food brought to comfort those in grief. Whenever we heard somebody had died, we knew we were going to eat.

"There's even a difference between Death chicken and Homecoming chicken, you know. When somebody dies, you're thinking about them, you turn the heat down low while you do, and you get that nice, soft, tender fried skin. When it's Homecoming, though, it's two o'clock, and you're just home from church, and everybody's starved, and you're in a hurry. So you cook it fast, and it gets brown and crispy.

"There was a rite of passage in the kitchen, too, that marked a coming of age as sure as that in any culture. When you stopped being only a consumer but became a provider. When you got to help make the biscuits, string the beans, cut the peaches for the cobbler. That was something. That was a sign that you were growing up."

—Atlanta caterer and chef Tim Patridge

Peach Cobbler
SERVES 8

Blackberry cobbler is dark and delicious; rhubarb—with or without strawberries—is a celebration of spring; but the best cobbler of all, bar none, is peach, where the oozing sweetness of the gold and crimson slices cozies up just perfectly to the two types of crust.

Two types of crust is the secret to most great cobblers—one crisp and delectable on the outside, the other doughy (almost pudding-like) inside, where it mingles with the fruit.

This recipe combines two venerable family traditions. The crust comes from John Egerton's mom; the technique for putting the pieces together, from Emmylou Harris's mom, Eugenia. The result is scrumptious on its own but becomes a company's-coming treat if you serve it with Lemon Buttermilk Sorbet (page 258).

2 cups flour
1 teaspoon kosher salt
⅓ pound (1⅓ sticks) unsalted butter
ice water
6 cups peaches, sliced but not peeled
1 cup white sugar
½ cup brown sugar
2 cups water
4 tablespoons salted butter

Preheat the oven to 400°F. Liberally butter the inside of a 9-by-12-inch baking pan.

Mix the flour and salt, then use a pastry cutter or your fingers to lightly work in the butter until well blended and crumbly. Add ice water, a couple of tablespoons at a time, until the dough holds together. Divide it into 2 portions, pat them into balls, cover, and refrigerate while you prepare the fruit.

In a heavy saucepan, bring the peaches, sugars, water, and remaining butter to a boil over medium-high heat. Boil for 5 minutes, stirring often to prevent sticking. Remove from the heat and set aside.

Roll one ball of pastry to pie-crust thickness, and cut it into inch-wide strips. Pour half the fruit mixture into the baking pan, then cover it with the strips.

Roll out the second ball of pastry, and cut it the same way. Pour the rest of the fruit mixture into the pan, then lay the strips over it. Bake 45 minutes, until the top crust is golden, and peach filling is bubbling through. Serve warm.

"I don't know what the deal is. I've been through four pastry chefs, all graduates of culinary school, and not one of them can make a decent cobbler. They keep wanting to do something with it. I tell them, you don't do something with cobbler, you just slap it out. Forget the mixer. Cobbler is for hands. Get 'em in there and slap it out."

—Kathy Cary, owner/chef Lilly's

MAiL ORDeR

The craving for peach sweetness knows no season—particularly if the craving is defined as cobbler. While I would never, ever try to convince you that canned peaches can hold a candle to fresh, there is one canned variety that is nevertheless worthy not only of your attention but of mail order. Maybe it's the Shenandoah River Valley summers, or maybe they really do put them up just like Grandma used to, but Shawnee Springs Cannery in Cross Junction, Virginia, sells canned peaches that are superb.

These peaches are not mushy like most, and even though they come packed in heavy syrup, it doesn't drown out that crisp peach flavor. The peaches are put up at the cannery just outside Winchester, within sight of Whitacre Orchards, where the peaches are grown. The peaches are steam-peeled (some canneries use a lye solution) and prepared by hand. The result is a product that tastes delicious out of the can and cooks up perfectly. You can order peach halves for straight-ahead eating, or the less expensive irregular pieces, which cook up perfectly in pies and cobblers.

To use it in the cobbler recipe on page 276, simply substitute 2 cans of irregular pieces, juice and all, for the peaches, sugar, and water in the filling. Heat the peaches with butter before putting them in the cobbler pan. See Things to Order, page 338.

Jammy Biscuits
MAKES 8

Jammy Biscuits are a Southern interpretation of sticky buns, one which takes advantage of the light, fluffy quality of the soft winter wheat used in the South and the abundance of flavorful fruit jams. I like this best with chunky peach or apricot jam, but it also works very well with a tart, thick orange marmalade.

½ cup butter, plus some for the pan
1 cup peach or apricot jam, or marmalade
⅛ cup crystallized ginger, minced
2 cups flour (preferably soft-wheat, see page 107)
1 tablespoon baking powder
½ teaspoon kosher salt
¾ cup milk
¼ cup brown sugar
½ cup chopped pecans

Preheat the oven to 425°F. Grease an 8-inch square baking pan liberally with butter, and set it aside.

Melt ½ cup of butter in a small saucepan. Pour ¼ cup out of the pan, and set it aside. Add the jam and crystallized ginger to the pan, and stir over very low heat until mixed and of pouring consistency. Pour it into the bottom of the greased pan.

In a large bowl, mix together the flour, baking powder, and salt. Make a well in the middle, and pour in the remaining ¼ cup of melted butter and the milk. Use a wooden spoon or your floured fingers to quickly mix, until the dough holds together in a rough ball. Turn it out on a liberally floured flat surface, and roll it into a rectangle about a foot long and 8 or so inches wide.

Mix the brown sugar with the pecans, and sprinkle the mixture evenly over the surface of the dough. Roll the dough into a log 12 inches long. Use a sharp knife to cut every 1½ inches to make 8 biscuits. Place them with a cut side down in the jam, snugly. It's okay if they touch.

Bake for 15 minutes, until the tops of the biscuits are golden. Allow to cool for 3 minutes, then turn upside down onto a serving plate. Serve at once.

Peach and Dried-Cherry Chutney
MAKES 1 QUART

Chutneys were one of the most popular fruit spreads put up by Southern cooks. Served most often with pork, the sweet/sour marriage of flavors is also excellent with grilled chicken and butter beans or crowder peas.

Peaches make excellent chutney, and dried cherries add a nice visual accent in lieu of more traditional raisins. This recipe has been scaled back from most traditional chutney recipes, which were more apt to yield a gallon, all to be put up in Mason jars in the cupboard. The quart you get here can be easily consumed in a few weeks, and will keep nicely for that amount of time covered tightly in the refrigerator.

1½ pounds slightly underripe peaches
juice of 1 lime
1 cup white wine vinegar (or cider vinegar)
⅔ cup sugar
1 cup dried cherries
1 tablespoon minced fresh ginger
½ teaspoon ground cloves
1 teaspoon kosher salt
¼ teaspoon ground red chile
1 large garlic clove, minced

Rinse, but don't peel, the peaches. Cut them into ½-inch chunks. Add the lime juice and toss, then set aside.

In a heavy, noncorrosive pot, bring the vinegar and sugar to a boil over high heat, stirring until the sugar dissolves. When mixture boils, add the peaches and the remaining ingredients, except the garlic. Bring the mixture back to a boil, reduce the heat to low, and simmer uncovered for about 30 minutes, until the chutney thickens. Remove it from the heat and stir in the garlic.

Allow the chutney to cool, then transfer it to glass jars, and keep it tightly covered in the refrigerator. It will keep for several weeks. Serve on the side with grilled chicken breasts, Lime-Butter Fish (page 254), or Soup Beans (page 39).

Old-Fashioned Quince Butter MAKES 6 PINTS PLUS

When I asked John Egerton for a few recipes for this book, he was most eager to share this one for a tart, distinctive spread made from quince.

"Recipes like this were all over old Southern cookbooks," he said. But these days, the gnarled, ugly, pear-like fruit of the japonica (or, rarely, the quince) tree is ignored by modern cooks who think it too much trouble.

John says, however, "If you cut them up and squirrel away the barest meat, then put all the 'wasteful' stuff in a pan and boil it . . . if you extract the hard essence of the fruit, something miraculous happens.

"I'm telling you that this is *the* best, my favorite. It'll pucker your jaw. It makes that useless fruit something quite wonderful."

2 dozen egg-sized quinces
2 cups water
4 tablespoons fresh lemon or lime juice
¾ to 1 cup sugar

Rinse the quinces, then peel and core them. Set the meat of the fruit aside for the moment, and put all the leavings—peel, core, and seeds—in a noncorrosive pan with the water. Bring to a boil and boil about 15 minutes. Remove from the heat and set aside.

In a broad, shallow bowl, using a nut mill, chop the meat of the fruit until the

"Viz'tin. That's what the Ya-Yas called their impromptu get-togethers when Sidda was a girl. The four Walker kids crammed into the T-Bird with Vivi, bombing into town to Caro's or Teensy's or Necie's, pulling into the driveway, madly blowing the horn, shouting out, 'Yall better be home.' Then a batch of Bloody Marys appeared and cream cheese with Pickapeppa and crackers, a gallon of lemonade and Oreos for the kids, Sarah Vaughan on the stereo, and a party. No planning, no calls in advance."

—Rebecca Wells, *Divine Secrets of the Ya-Ya Sisterhood* (HarperPerennial, 1996).

Legendary Southern hospitality can't wait for somebody to run to the store but must rise spontaneously from the big chair on the screened-in porch, spread its arms wide, grin, and say, "Come on in. You all hungry?"

Consequently, few Southern hosts or hostesses would ever be caught dead without a brick of cream cheese in the fridge and a jar of spicy jelly or hot sauce in the pantry. Lay the former on a pretty plate, pour the latter gracefully over the top, and open a box of crackers. Voilà—instant party. Peach and Dried-Cherry Chutney (page 278) works superbly.

hard pieces become a soft and shapeless mass. It should equal 4 to 5 cups of pulp.

Put the pulp in a large pot along with the lemon or lime juice and sugar, using the larger amount only if astringent tartness bothers you. Strain the core and seed mixture and add the liquid to the pulp, discarding the solid matter. Stir to mix, then bring to a rapid boil over high heat. Reduce the heat and continue cooking at a lively simmer for approximately 30 minutes, until the mixture thickens like apple butter.

Remove from the heat and ladle into sterilized jars and seal with hot paraffin or new canning lids and seals.

Black-Bottom Banana Cream Pie
SERVES 8

Kathleen Castro met her cook-husband, Joe, when both were working in upscale hotel kitchens in Washington, D.C., in the late 1980s. They moved back to Joe's stomping grounds around Louisville, Kentucky, when Joe got the job of executive chef at one of Louisville's premier spots, the English Grill at the Brown Hotel. (See Places to Go, page 341.) Kathleen said they wanted a more relaxed pace, and believed Louisville was a great place to bring up kids. This they are doing, with two charmers, Eleanor and Max. Kathleen now bakes at home instead of professionally, but she is always willing to get out the rolling pin and come up with something scrumptious for parties—or to provide a little help

for a friend who is writing a cookbook. This simple and delectable pie is hers.

Kathleen says you can make it without the chocolate in the bottom and it's also tasty, but who would want to? If you're wondering just how delicious it is, I should tell you that our otherwise perfect dog, Gromit, actually sinned for the very first time for this pie, sneaking into the kitchen when no one was looking and scarfing down the last piece right from the table. He was punished, but the look he gave the whole time he was being hotly scolded let me know he thought the pie was worth it.

8-inch prebaked pie crust

1 cup milk

2 tablespoons cornstarch

¼ cup sugar

1 egg

3 tablespoons unsalted butter

3 ounces semi-sweet chocolate

4 firm but ripe bananas

1 cup whipping cream

3 tablespoons 10X confectioner's sugar

1 teaspoon vanilla

The crust needs to be completely cooled before filling.

To make a pastry cream, heat the milk in a heavy saucepan over medium heat. Mix together the cornstarch, sugar, and egg. When the milk is steaming, drizzle some into the egg mixture, whisking as you do. Then whisk the mixture into the remaining milk. Bring to a boil, and remove from the heat. Add 1 tablespoon of butter. Set aside to cool.

While the pastry cream is cooling, melt

the chocolate with the remaining butter over hot water. Pour it into the bottom of the cooled pie crust, spreading it with a spatula to cover the crust evenly. Place it in the refrigerator to chill.

When the chocolate is chilled and the pastry cream is cool, peel the bananas and slice them about ½ inch thick. Fold the bananas into the pastry cream, and pour it into the pie crust.

Cover tightly with plastic wrap, and refrigerate until ready to serve.

Take the pie from the refrigerator at least 15 minutes before you are ready to cut it. This allows the chocolate to soften enough to make cutting easy, and to bring out the full flavor. Whip the cream with the confectioner's sugar and vanilla until soft peaks form. Spread it over the top of the pie.

MAIL ORDER

Mayhaws are tiny, tart red fruits that grow in the swamps and bogs of southwestern Georgia, as well as some parts of Louisiana and Texas. Although they're called berries, they're actually a distant relative of the apple. The juice they produce is both sharp and sweet, intoxicating enough that for generations locals have gone to some pains to gather mayhaws by hand or by scooping them from the water in fishnets.

For generations, those precious mayhaws were put up in jelly to be eaten only by those lucky enough to live in mayhaw territory. But a couple of years ago, four enterprising women in the Colquitt, Georgia, area decided mayhaws were just too good not to share, so they started The Mayhaw Tree, Inc., a homegrown company which produced jelly and other products to sell in stores around the country and by mail order. The whole community got in on the act, and out of it came the annual Mayhaw festival in Colquitt the third Saturday in April. Along with arts and crafts and an antique car show, the festival offers plenty of mayhaw products and other Southern foods. See Places to Go, page 341.

Meanwhile, back at the cottage industry, The Mayhaw Tree, Inc., was sold to Carol and Mark Goodwin, who moved the base of operations to their hometown, Jefferson, in northern Georgia. (See Things to Order, page 338.) The Goodwins sell the same jelly and also offer mayhaw syrup, wine jelly, a line of salad dressings and sauces, peach preservers, and more.

That more includes a Vidalia onion mustard that's become the ingredient du jour in a number of gourmet Southern dining spots. Carol says that one chef in Sea Island, Georgia, orders cases to use as a glaze for pork roast. Her favorite trick is to boil tiny new potatoes in their jackets, then toss them with the mustard and serve warm.

Folks in zones 6 to 8 who want to try growing their own mayhaws can order the small trees (which can get up to 20 feet tall) from Edible Landscaping. See Things to Order, page 338.

Ultimate Banana Pudding · SERVES 12

Banana pudding is one of the supreme pleasures of the Southern picnic table. There are multiple recipes for it, including those which are baked and topped with meringue. My favorite, though, is this recipe, which requires no baking and is cool and creamy on the tongue. It really does have to sit overnight to reach its peak. Tempted as you may be, don't try some as soon as you put it together, or you will be disappointed.

The bananas should be ripe but not mushy.

4 cups half and half
1 cup sugar
½ cup cornstarch
pinch of salt
3 eggs
1 cup sour cream
12 ounces vanilla wafers
8 ripe bananas

Heat the half and half over medium heat until steamy but not bubbling. While it's heating, mix the sugar, cornstarch, and salt together in a medium-sized saucepan. When the half and half is hot, whisk it into the sugar mixture, then place it over medium heat and cook, stirring constantly. When the mixture just begins to thicken, remove it from the heat.

Beat the eggs until light and frothy. Slowly drizzle ¼ cup of the hot mixture into them, whisking constantly as you do.

Then slowly pour the warmed eggs into the remaining half and half mixture in the saucepan, again whisking as you do. Cook over medium heat, stirring constantly, until the mixture begins to gently boil. Remove from the heat and transfer immediately to a heavy glass or ceramic bowl to stop the cooking. Mix in the sour cream.

Assemble the pudding in a bowl or other glass or ceramic container with a 4-quart capacity, beginning with a single layer of vanilla wafers to cover the bottom. Slice the bananas about ⅛ inch thick and lay a single layer over the wafers. Cover with about ½ inch of custard. Repeat until all the wafers and bananas are used, ending with a layer of custard. Cover securely with plastic wrap and refrigerate overnight.

Banana Crunch Snack Cake · SERVES 6

This sort of quick delectable is something country cooks called a snack cake. Too sweet to be a bread, too simple to pass as a genuine dessert cake, it was just right for afternoon coffee or tea. I make mine in what we call a brownie pan, a 10¾-by-7-by-1-inch baking pan, which makes enough brownies, bar cookies, or cake for our small family to snack on of an evening and have some left for lunch the next day.

1 stick salted butter, softened
1 cup sugar
1 cup mashed bananas

1½ cups cake flour
½ cup coarsely chopped pecans
¾ teaspoon baking soda
½ cup shredded coconut
1 teaspoon vanilla

Preheat the oven to 325°F.

Grease a brownie pan with shortening, then dust it with flour, shaking out the excess.

Cream the butter and sugar until fluffy. Fold in the bananas. Sprinkle some of the flour on the pecans, just to dredge them, then sift the rest with the baking soda. Fold the flour into the creamed butter. Add the pecans, coconut, and vanilla, and stir just until mixed.

Pour the batter into the prepared pan and bake 50 minutes, until the sides pull away from the edge of the pan and a cake tester inserted in the middle comes out clean. Cool in the pan, then invert to remove, or cut in the pan and serve with a spatula.

About Apples

Autumn Apple and Black Walnut Cobbler

Apple-Walnut Cake with Ginger Cream

Fried Apples—Classic and Deluxe

Fried Pies

Dried-Apple Butter

Classic Apple Stack Cake

Bourbon-Apricot-Cherry Stack Cake

I don't wish to appear un-American, but the words "Mom" and "apple pie" have virtually never been uttered in the same breath in my home. My mother wasn't a big pie maker in the first place, but when she did sally forth with a rolling pin, it was apt to be one more stab at making a butterscotch pie as good as the ones she remembered from her youth. (She never did, her memory of foods past always outstripping the realities, which we, her present companions, found extraordinary.)

What's more, her contempt for the apple pies the rest of the country seemed to deem its birthright was harsh. The ones she'd buy for my dad at the grocery or bakery always earned a quick dismissal from her. "That's got nutmeg in it," she'd say with lips pursed and eyebrow cocked, the same expression that any pie with cinnamon earned. Even those pies that managed to squeak by her rigid "no spice" rule were found wanting in the taste and texture departments. "That filling's just mush," she'd say. "Watery," "cardboard," and "dull as dishwater" were also part of her apple-pie vocabulary.

This is not to say she'd never met an apple pie she didn't hate. In fact, she remembered exquisitely the apple pies that some aunt or cousin I'd not met made, back when she was a girl. She described them fiercely: "Just the apple slices with the peels on. Lots of 'em. Nothing but brown sugar and butter dots all over the top. And in a thin, crisp crust. Not all this old flakey, puffy stuff they think is so good these days."

Despite the recipe's simplicity, though, neither she nor I ever made an apple pie that could live up to that memory, so after a time we just didn't try.

This didn't mean we went lacking for apples in our lives, however. Fried apples were a recurring theme at dinnertime from autumn right through springtime. And when we had good, crisp apples with plenty of flavor in the house, she'd core and slice them and spread them out, fan-like, on a saucer to be passed at dinner like cucumbers or pickles. There was always a jar of apple butter in the refrigerator for biscuits or toast, and chilled cider in the fall. And my great aunts provided us with a bounty of delicious dried-apple stack cakes and fried pies whenever we went to see them or one of them came to stay with us for a while.

Such uses were common in the mountain South, where apples were grown in abundance. Although the crisp cold weather necessary for opening the nascent bud was unreliable in the Deep South, the winters of the southern Appalachians and the Ozarks provided an excellent environment for apple trees. Small orchards dotted the mountains and foothills, producing fruit that many swear is both sweeter and tarter than that grown elsewhere. Apples provided vitamins and flavor through the winter as "keepers" (apples which would store well in the root cellar) or in their "put-up" forms, ranging from dried apples to apple butter to applejack, a highly potent fermented cider that you might be lucky to get if you knew your local moonshiner well.

Apple customs were also a part of folklore. My great-aunts taught me at an early age that if you hold the stem of an apple between your fingers, then twist the fruit, saying a letter of the alphabet at each turn, the letter where the stem breaks will also be the first letter of the name of your true love. As usual, men seemed to get a better deal on the options: a piece of old Kentucky mountain wisdom held that a man who could pull apart an apple with his bare hands could get any girl he wanted.

In *Apples* (North Point, 1998) orchardist and expert Frank Browning notes that by the end of the Civil War, American nurseries listed more than eight hundred varieties of apples, although today only about thirty distinct varieties are offered. Of these only about ten are sold in quantity.

But there has been an apple renaissance of sorts in recent years. Drive through the Southern mountains in the fall and you are apt to come on apple stands by the side of the road or hand-lettered signs pointing you to an orchard just off the beaten path where tasty Cortlands, Mutsus, and Arkansas Blacks can be found. Locally made apple butter and cider are de rigueur at gift shops and country stores, and Monticello, Thomas Jefferson's home

in Virginia, hosts an apple tasting and workshop every fall.

Autumn Apple and Black Walnut Cobbler   SERVES 8

Black walnuts are native to America and beloved in the desserts of the South, particularly the mountain South, where they often end up brilliantly married with tart fall apples in recipes such as this easy cobbler.

6 cups thinly sliced tart apples
  (5 or 6 medium)
1 cup brown sugar
8 tablespoons unsalted butter, room
  temperature
1½ cups all-purpose flour
1 teaspoon baking powder
½ teaspoon baking soda
1 teaspoon kosher salt
½ cup white sugar
¼ to ½ cup buttermilk
½ cup black walnut pieces

Preheat the oven to 350°F.

Liberally grease a 3-quart baking dish. (I use a shallow, ovenproof pasta bowl.)

Mix the apples, brown sugar, and 4 tablespoons of the butter, cut in thumbnail-sized pieces. Spread the mixture evenly in the pan.

Sift together the flour, baking powder, baking soda, salt, and sugar. Cut the remaining butter into small pieces and use your fingers to lightly incorporate the pieces into the flour. Add ¼ cup of buttermilk, and lightly stir until the dough holds together in a ball. Add more buttermilk, if necessary, but don't let the dough become too wet.

Turn the dough out on a floured surface and sprinkle the black walnuts on, kneading to incorporate them into the dough. When the walnuts are mixed in, sprinkle flour on the dough and roll it into a circle about ¼ inch thick. Cut it into strips about 1 inch wide, and lay the strips over the apples. The dough should roughly cover the apples, with little gaps between the strips. Bake 45 minutes, until the dough is golden brown and the apples are moist and tender. Serve warm.

Apple-Walnut Cake with Ginger Cream
SERVES 8 TO 10

In this cake, the combination of apple and nut flavors is underscored by the tang of buttermilk. Served warm from the oven, with cool ginger custard spooned over it, it's a dramatic finish to any meal.

Prepare the custard the day before so that it has time to cool completely.

CUSTARD
2 ounces candied ginger
1 cup milk
2 egg yolks (reserve the whites)
½ cup sugar
2 cups half and half
salt

Mince the ginger. Heat the milk in a small saucepan until it begins to steam. In a blender, process the milk and ginger on high until the ginger is nearly liquefied. (If you don't have a blender, pulverize the ginger with a mortar and pestle, or mince it as finely as you possibly can and vigorously whisk it with the milk by hand. The end result will include small nuggets of ginger.)

Bring some water to a lively simmer in the bottom of a double boiler. In the top of the double boiler, off the heat, whisk the egg yolks lightly to blend. Have the sugar and half and half measured and near the stove. Place the top of the double boiler over the bottom, and begin whisking the yolks immediately and continuously. Add the sugar slowly, then the half and half. Add a pinch of salt.

Whisk until the sugar has dissolved and there are no lumps. Continue stirring constantly with a wooden spoon for several minutes, until the mixture thickly coats the back of the spoon.

Take the whole double boiler off the burner. Slowly pour in the ginger milk and stir for another minute. Transfer the mixture to a glass or ceramic container and allow it to cool almost to room temperature, then cover it with plastic wrap and refrigerate it overnight. The end product will be the consistency of thick cream. (This mixture also makes dynamite ice cream. Double the proportions, chill overnight, and freeze according to your ice cream maker's instructions.)

CAKE

½ cup canola oil

1 cup brown sugar

2 egg whites (from the custard)

1½ cups all-purpose flour

1 teaspoon kosher salt

1 teaspoon baking soda

1 cup buttermilk

1 cup crushed walnuts

2 cups tart apple chunks (peels may be left on)

Preheat the oven to 350°F.

Grease a Bundt pan with shortening, and flour it.

Use an electric mixer to cream the oil

ROAD NOTES

WAYNESVILLE, NORTH CAROLINA, OCTOBER 1994

The Smoky Mountains, shrouded in dewy mystery, are living up to their name on this cool fall morning. I have been too long a time from home and am looking for a little country comfort before getting on the highway for the last leg of my trip. I've found good country ham and short, crisp-crusted Southern-style biscuits at a diner, and now have stopped at a roadside stand for something to take back to Meghan and Ken.

The fella who runs the stand is younger than I am, but his voice sounds like my father's, still rolling with the mountain cadences that no amount of television or tourism can erase. The rocking chairs for sale on the porch were made by someone he knows who lives further up in the mountains; and the sorghum, jams, and honey he sells were put up in Mason jars by someone else. But the apples, in baskets which fill the parking lot just outside his door, are his. He grew them and harvested them. He knows them with the familiarity of a shepherd with his flock, resting his rough hand gently on the tender skin of this one and that, as he tells me their varied attributes.

I've got a basket of Arkansas Blacks already. (I'm crazy for their crisp and winey taste.) I am examining the brown paper bags of Mutsus when he steps up and tells me not to waste my time looking for a pretty peck.

"These Mutsus are like people," he says. "The uglier they are, the sweeter and better they get."

He is right, at least about the apples. Later, at home, when I come upon a particularly lopsided and mottled specimen, I set it aside for eating out of hand. It tastes like blossoms, tiny blossoms of sugar, followed by the drizzle of a sharp green wine.

and sugar together until there are no lumps. Add the egg whites and beat until the mixture is well blended and has begun to lighten.

Sift together the flour, salt, and baking soda. Add them in portions to the egg mixture, alternating with buttermilk, and mixing thoroughly after each addition.

Stir in the walnuts by hand, and then the apples. Turn the batter into the Bundt pan, shaking the pan lightly from side to side to settle the mixture. Bake on the center shelf of the oven for 45 minutes, until the top is dark gold and a cake tester comes out clean. Cool for 5 minutes in the pan on a rack, then turn the cake out onto a plate. Serve warm with spoonfuls of cold ginger cream ladled over each slice.

Fried Apples— Classic and Deluxe   SERVES 6

If you have ever chosen "fried apples" from a diner side-dish list and been served a little bowl with pale beige chunks of soggy peeled apples floating in tepid juice spiked with cinnamon, don't be discouraged. That is not the real thing—and if they ever make me Queen of Menus I will declare it illegal to ever call such a sorry mess fried apples again.

Fried apples is a vibrant dish with good texture and a lively flavor that juggles sweet and tart sensations. It's so easy to prepare—and the chances of having all the ingredients on hand in the fall or winter, when apples are best, are so good— that it has made appearances as "best

supporting side dish" at countless meals in both my mother's house and my own. Tasty with chicken and beef, it absolutely shines when paired with pork.

This recipe makes enough for six. If you don't have that many at the table, make it anyway. It keeps nicely in the refrigerator for a couple of days and is delicious warmed up. It is especially good slathered on hot biscuits or over pancakes for breakfast.

As with any of the apple recipes in this book, the more flavorful the variety, the better the dish. I like to use tart apples to make fried apples, particularly the down-right sour June apples which appear early in the season and cook up soft but sassy. Of common grocery varieties, Granny Smiths seem to do best, although it's also nice to mix them with the more delicate Gala or Fuji, if they're available.

6 medium-sized tart apples
2 tablespoons butter
¼ to ½ cup brown sugar

Cut the apples into quarters and remove the cores. Cut each quarter lengthwise into three or four slices. (Cut out any blemishes or brown spots, but leave the peel on.)

Melt the butter over low heat in a skillet with a cover. Add the apples, and stir lightly with a spatula to coat them with butter. Cover, and cook for about 5 minutes to soften.

Sprinkle the sugar over the apples. (Use the larger quantity if the apples are especially tart.) Turn them again with the spatula to spread the sugar around. Cook over medium-low heat for another 10 to 15 minutes, until the apples are soft and the sugar has begun to thicken into a light syrup. Serve warm.

VARIATION: *For a deluxe version of this dish, substitute 2 tablespoons of honey mixed with 2 tablespoons of freshly squeezed orange juice and a teaspoon of finely minced orange zest for the brown sugar.*

Fried Pies
MAKES 12

My great-aunt Minnie made the best fried pies in the world. During the time she lived with us, right after Uncle Finley died, I'd come home from elementary school on a cold winter afternoon to find the kitchen steamed up with the fragrance of dried apples that had cooked in brown sugar. Aunt Minnie would be waiting with a spatula in hand for me to sit down and have one of her crisp, golden half-moon pies straight from the skillet. That's the way to eat them, with an icy cold glass of milk, although they're not bad to find in your lunch box on the day after, either.

In the South, your preference in fried pie filling can place you geographically. Most folks from Alabama and Georgia, where fried pies are often the dessert du jour at a really good barbecue place, prefer dried peaches. Up in the southern Appalachians, where my family was from, dried apples are the choice. At Herbert's, an outstanding barbecue place just off the interstate in Franklin, Tennessee, the woman who makes the fried pies daily understands that her constituency is from a border state, and so she makes some of each. You may use either in this recipe and, as you'll see in the next, it's possible to substitute other dried fruits for a satisfying filling. It's not appropriate to use fresh-fruit pie filling, however, not only because it doesn't taste right but because it will make the pie too runny to eat out of hand.

I buy dried apples at the farm market in the fall or from our local health food store, because the fruit there has gumption. The apples available in plastic packs at the grocery usually have been treated to keep them pale white. They are also flaccid and tasteless. Apples dried the old-fashioned way (see page 294) are a ruddy beige and full of flavor.

PASTRY CRUST
2 cups all-purpose flour
1 teaspoon kosher salt
½ teaspoon baking powder
½ cup lard or vegetable shortening
¾ cup hot skim milk

FILLING
2 cups dried apples or peaches
2 cups water
½ cup brown sugar

lard, canola, or peanut oil for frying

Sift together the flour, salt, and baking powder. In a large bowl, mix the lard or shortening with the milk until some of it dissolves and some remains in small lumps. Add the flour a little at a time and mix lightly with a fork. (Use your fingers, floured, if it's easier toward the end.) When the flour and liquid are just blended, pat the dough into a ball, wrap it tightly in plastic wrap, and refrigerate it for at least 2 hours. It will keep overnight.

To make the filling, put the fruit and water in a saucepan, bring it to a boil, then turn it down to simmer for 1 hour. Add more water if necessary to keep the fruit from drying and sticking, but not too much. The fruit should have a thick, jammy consistency. When the fruit is softened and can be mashed with a fork, mix in the brown sugar, mashing the fruit as you do. This, too, can be refrigerated, but should be allowed to come to room temperature before frying the pies.

When you're ready to make the pies, divide the dough into 12 equal balls. Flatten each into a disk, and roll it out on a floured board into a circle about 6 inches in diameter.

Put about 2 heaping tablespoons of the filling on the lower half of the circle, near the center, leaving an edge for crimping. Fold the top half over the filling and down to meet the edge of the bottom, creating a half moon. Press the dough down on the edges, then turn a bit of the edge back and crimp it with your fingers or a fork to seal it. Use a little bit of cold water to secure the seal. (It's important to seal the edges well, and to repair any holes or tears in the crust before frying, or the filling will seep out and cause the oil to splatter dangerously.)

Repeat until all the crust is used. (If you have any filling left over, refrigerate it for biscuits the next day.)

In a wide, heavy skillet, heat about ½ inch of lard or oil until a little piece of dough dropped into it dances and turns golden. Lay the pies in carefully (I use a metal spatula), a few at a time. Don't overcrowd the skillet. When they turn golden on one side, turn them over carefully with the spatula and fry until golden on the other side. Drain on a rack set over paper towels. Allow to cool just enough to bite into them, then eat while warm.

My friend Wade Hall grew up in southern Alabama, squarely on the peach side of the fried-pie line. "We never called them fried pies down home," he confided. "We called them tarts. Don't you know that 'fried pies' just seems too common, too descriptive. But tarts. Now that has an edge, some excitement."

Dried-Apple Butter
MAKES ABOUT 1½ CUPS

Dried apples take some of the tedious cooking out of making homemade apple butter, and the resulting spread is moodier and more complicated than the commercial kind.

1 cup dried apples
water
¼ cup brown sugar, or more to taste
⅛ teaspoon freshly grated nutmeg (optional)

Place the apples in a heavy saucepan and add enough water to cover. Over high heat, bring the apples to a boil. Turn the heat to low, and simmer, uncovered, until the apples are soft enough to mash—40 minutes to 1 hour. (You may need to stir several times during the simmering to keep them from sticking.)

When the apples are soft enough, use a potato masher to make a lumpy puree. Add the sugar as you mash. Taste and add more sugar, if you like, but don't make the butter too sweet, or you'll lose some of the mystery of the apples. Add the nutmeg. Continue to cook for a few more minutes, until the consistency is thick enough to spread. Serve on hot buttered biscuits or with pancakes. Store covered in the refrigerator.

MAIL ORDER

Starting sometime in June, my great-aunts' house in Corbin took on the heady, flowery fragrance of apples, a scent that lingered right on into the late fall. First of the crop were the super-sour and ugly little green June apples my aunt Johnnie picked from a tree in the side yard. She would carry the few first ones around to the front porch, and we'd sit in the swing together as she peeled, cored, and sliced them into a pan, the long curls of apple skin slithering onto the newspaper spread in her lap. We'd eat these fried with butter and brown sugar for afternoon dinner, the perfect match for ham or pork.

Johnnie usually saved a good apple or two for herself, and after the cut ones were passed on to Aunt Rae or Aunt Minnie for cooking, we'd swing and talk, and she'd slice the apples, pour a little salt on a piece, and offer it to me. June apples were too potent for a little girl to eat out of hand, but Johnnie relished their bite.

By midsummer, the apples came in bushel baskets—not just the ones from the yard but those from Aunt Bert's place up in the country and from other relatives. The slicing got down to business, moved to the screened-in back porch and ladder-back chairs. Johnnie's fingers were long and gnarled, but she cut perfectly uniform pieces at lightning speed. These she spread on big window screens covered with clean white sheets, which she laid over sawhorses just outside the door. She monitored them as she went about her day's work, shooing away scavenging birds, and with one eye always cocked to the sky, where the first wisp of a cloud would occasion hauling the screens and sheets back onto the enclosed porch.

The apples dried in batches through the summer and into the fall. Johnnie turned them daily until they reached the appropriate state of leatheriness. Then she piled them into bags, washed the sheets (in a hand-cranked wringer-washer I was not allowed to stand close to, for fear of being suddenly sucked into the dreaded wringer), and started again.

It was tedious labor, and she did it almost as an aside to the hard chores of her daily life—tending to the house, garden, and chickens. But she grinned in the fall as she gave apples to neighbors and kin who had moved away, and as her stores provisioned the fried pies my Aunt Minnie was famous for and the stack cakes my Aunt Rae would make and serve all winter long. I love you a bushel and a peck, indeed.

Johnnie's was just one of the many methods mountain folks use to dry a season's bounty of apples for the year. The Native Americans who inhabited the region and the early European settlers cored and sliced the apples into even rings, which were then "beaded" on strings and hung in a dark, dry place—often in a chimney corner, where the smoke from the wood fire lent an unmistakably dusky fragrance and taste. Some folks built kilns for drying apples and the like on sheets of tin. These days, some enterprising people spread their apples on sheets inside of junked cars sitting in the sun, turning them into solar-powered drying ovens.

I sometimes dry small batches of especially flavorful apples at home in my oven on expandable metal window screens, and am fascinated at what a difference there is in the taste of varieties. Mutsus are delicate, almost like pears, while the Arkansas Black has a woodsy, powerful taste.

To dry apples in the oven on screens (you could, instead, use a baking sheet, but you'll need to turn the apples during the process so they dry evenly on both sides), preheat the oven to 250°F. Wash the apples and towel dry them. (As a rule of thumb, a pound of fresh apples will yield about a cup of dried ones.) Quarter them and cut out the cores. Then slice the quarters as evenly as possible about ⅛ inch to ¼ inch thick. The thicker slices will take longer to dry but are less apt to turn brown quickly near the end of the drying process. (You can peel the apples if you like. They will dry faster, but I prefer the rougher texture and more interesting taste of unpeeled apples.)

Lay the slices on the screens or baking sheets in a single layer, nestled close to one another but not overlapping. Put them in the oven, shut the door, and turn off the heat. Go to bed.

In the morning, turn the oven to a very low setting (120 to 140°F) for 5 minutes, then turn it off. Repeat through the day, every 3 or 4 hours. As the day wears on, check the apples to see what the texture is like. Set aside any that are browning faster than the rest of the batch or are turning crisp. You can add them back to the batch when it's done, but you don't want any to burn.

The apples are done when they turn a dark tan color and feel leathery but still somewhat supple to the touch. Let them come to room temperature, then pack them in tightly sealed containers or plastic bags. It's cheating, I know, but I keep mine in the freezer to avoid any chance of spoiling or infestation by pantry pests.

You can also dry apples in a commercial fruit dryer according to the manufacturer's directions. Mullins' Orchard in Wise, Virginia sells dried apples through mail order when they have them. Depending on the size of the harvest, that can be about nine months out of the year. Roy Mullins, his mother, and his aunt dry the apples they grow and provide them to produce markets in the region.

See Things to Order, page 338.

Classic Apple Stack Cake

SERVES 12

Fried pies can be found all around the South, but stack cakes made with a dried-apple filling are southern Appalachian food, pure and simple. My father loved stack cake more than any other dessert. He ate it for breakfast and lunch, as well as a treat after dinner. It is humble and nourishing, a sweet that wins the eater not with a surfeit of white sugar but with the more subtle fruit and molasses. It tastes like home, especially if that home was in the hills.

The layers of a stack cake are hardly more than flat, molasses-sweetened biscuits. Between them, frugal mountain cooks spread a thick, jam-like puree made from dried apples cooked slowly to tenderness with some brown sugar and maybe a pinch of spice. Take a taste of either during the assembly process, and chances are you won't be impressed. But, like any great couple, the two bring out the best in each other as they snuggle up over time.

Finished stack cakes must be wrapped securely (in plastic these days, in cheesecloth in the past), and then covered by a thick towel or blanket and left to sit for at least two, preferably three, days before serving. By that time, the moisture and fragrance from the apples will have permeated the cake layers, the molasses in the layers will have seeped over to the apples, and the whole will have become an exceptionally delectable sum of its parts.

Stack cakes should have a minimum of five layers, and sometimes boast as many as eight, although I find cakes that tall unwieldy to cut and serve.

Traditionally, the layers are baked in a cast-iron skillet, one layer at a time. I think that works best, but many cooks now use cake pans for the job. I use two skillets, baking a layer in one while the other one cools enough so I can pat the next layer of dough into it. The ritual of making a stack cake purely the old-fashioned way is as much a pleasure to me as the cake itself.

The recipe here is similar to the one in *Shuck Beans, Stack Cakes, and Honest Fried Chicken*, but with a few changes to clarify it and help beginners avoid the pitfalls. The first and most important thing to know is to use sorghum syrup (not sugarcane molasses and never, ever blackstrap) to make the cake. Sorghum has a light, tangy sweetness that is an absolute characteristic of stack cake. (For information on ordering sorghum, see page 339.)

The second thing you should do is find home-style dried apples for the filling. Most of those sold in groceries are treated chemically to keep them soft and white, and they'll cook up pasty. Health food stores often have untreated dried apples. They have turned light brown or reddish brown in the process, and have some gumption in the texture. They smell divine and will cook up sturdy and flavorful. For more on dried apples, see page 294.

Get the filling started cooking on the stove, and then begin making the cakes.

FILLING

5 cups dried apples, tightly packed
1 cup brown sugar
½ teaspoon freshly grated nutmeg

Put the apples in a heavy saucepan and add water to cover. Bring to a boil, then turn the heat down and simmer for an hour or so, until the apples are soft enough to be mashed. Stir frequently during the cooking to keep the apples from sticking, and add more water if needed.

When the apples are soft, mash them with a potato masher, adding the sugar and nutmeg as you do. The mixture should be a lumpy puree, like chunky apple butter. If it's too watery, continue to simmer and stir until thickened. Remove from the heat.

STACK CAKE LAYERS

5 to 6 cups soft-wheat flour
1 teaspoon baking soda
½ teaspoon kosher salt
⅔ cup salted butter, softened, or
  shortening
1 cup white sugar
1 cup sorghum syrup
2 large eggs, beaten
1 cup buttermilk

Preheat the oven to 350°F.

Liberally grease an 8- or 9-inch cast-iron skillet with shortening. Sprinkle a tablespoon of flour into the skillet and shake it to spread it evenly, smacking the sides with the palm of your hand to get the flour to coat about ⅛ inch up the sides. Turn the skillet upside down over the sink and smack the bottom with the palm of your hand to shake out the excess flour. (If you are using two skillets or pans, prepare the second one the same way.)

Sift 5 cups of flour with the baking soda and salt. Set aside. In a large mixing bowl, use a wooden spoon to cream together the butter and sugar. Add the sorghum syrup and beat to blend.

In a cup or small bowl, mix the beaten eggs and buttermilk. Add first some flour, then some buttermilk to the butter and sugar, stirring well after each addition to blend. Repeat until all the ingredients are added and the dough holds together in a very soft ball. If it's too moist to lightly pat together, add as much of the remaining cup of flour as necessary to get that texture.

Pat the dough into a ball, cover it with plastic wrap, and refrigerate it until the filling is ready.

When the filling is ready, place the ball of chilled dough on a floured board. Use your floured palms to lightly roll it into an even log 10 inches long. Use a sharp knife, which you have floured, to cut the log every 2 inches, into 5 equal pieces. Roll each piece lightly in flour to make a ball. Pat one ball into a disk and put the others, tightly covered, back in the refrigerator.

Place the disk in the greased and floured skillet and, pressing lightly with floured palms and fingers, flatten it evenly so it just touches the edges of the pan all around. Don't pat it too hard, and don't press it up against the sides of the pan or it will stick.

Bake for 15 minutes, until the top is

golden and the cake has pulled away slightly from the edges of the pan.

You may want to use a butter knife to lightly loosen the edges. Turn the layer out on a plate or a cake rack. (I do this by laying a rack with a handle over the top of the skillet, then, wearing oven mitts, carefully flipping the rack and skillet upside down so the layer falls right out. You can also lay a plate over the top of the skillet if you don't have a large enough rack.)

If the layer doesn't come away easily, or if part of the bottom sticks to the pan, don't despair. Simply use a metal spatula to get the remainder of the layer out in as intact a piece as possible, and fill in the gap. Then let the pan cool completely, scrape it clean with the spatula, and regrease and flour it, taking care to cover the surface well with both.

Carefully turn the layer over so the top is up, and lay it on a serving plate. Cover it with 1½ cups of the apple filling, spreading it evenly to the edges.

Prepare each successive layer as you did the first, using all the apples on the first 4 layers and leaving the 5th uncovered. Let the stack cake cool to room temperature, then cover it, plate and all, with plastic wrap. Wrap it in a thick towel, and let it sit for at least 48 hours, preferably for 3 days, before serving.

Notes: *Some more pointers: Because they are so short, the baked layers will sometimes break coming out of the pan or while you are handling them. Be very gentle to avoid breaking them, but if a break does occur on any layer except the top one, simply put the pieces together as neatly as possible and cover them with apple filling. Clever cooks will set aside an especially perfect early layer and use it as the top one.*

Also, try as you might, the layers will bake up unevenly, and your stack cake may begin to list after a layer or two. If one side is noticeably taller than the other, check the next layer to see if one side is thicker, and lay that on the short side to even things out.

Finally, most mountain cooks disdained using toothpicks to keep their stack cakes stable, but if it makes you feel more secure, anchor the first two layers with two toothpicks on opposite sides, then the next layer to the one below it, and so on.

STACK CAKE TALL TALE

There is a much-disputed legend that stack cakes were invented as wedding cakes for young mountain couples, with their poor kinfolks each bringing the single layer they could afford to make to the celebration and stacking them together to make a big cake for the party. But anyone who's made stack cakes knows full well that (1) the cakes and apples both need to be warm when they are assembled for the marrying of flavors to take place, and (2) that marriage (of flavors) takes at least two days to consummate. Anyone who tried to eat a stack cake on the day it was made would surely wonder what all the shouting was about.

Bourbon-Apricot-Cherry Stack Cake

SERVES 12

Stack cakes seem to enchant anyone who is introduced to them, but friends who are also pastry chefs have been particularly intrigued by the possibilities this simple dessert presents. Not long after they taste it, the "what ifs" start. Many options I reject out of hand: caramel icing would be overkill; whipped cream or ice cream is totally beside the point; and, no, it won't work with chocolate mousse between the layers. But suggestions for using different fruits, or dressing up the layers just a bit with nuts, or adding liquor to the mix began to intrigue me.

I had some success using a puree of dried strawberries and candied ginger, much like the filling for Fried Pies on page 292, but the cost of the strawberries seemed a bit prohibitive. Then I tried the apricot, cherry, and bourbon mix here. The first version was far too dry, teaching me that all dried fruits don't cook up to the same moist texture. Adding applesauce made a puree moist enough to permeate the cake but still dominated in taste by the apricots and cherries. Bourbon and pecans dressed things up perfectly for the Derby party at which the cake made its debut. Despite a vat of burgoo, a buffet table groaning with homemade goodies, and several of those signature pecan, chocolate, and bourbon pies, every crumb of the cake disappeared, including a wedge my friend Bill Boyd hid away for breakfast the next day.

I never thought I'd find a dessert so pleasing to the tastebuds and the soul as classic apple stack cake, but this one finishes second by only a nose.

STACK CAKE LAYERS
stack cake layers, page 296
1 cup pecan pieces

FILLING
10 ounces dried apricots
6 ounces dried cherries
1 cup brown sugar
1 cup water
2 cups applesauce
⅛ cup bourbon

Prepare the stack cake dough according to the directions on page 297, adding the pecan pieces after the final flour has been mixed in. Pat the dough into a ball, cover it tightly, and chill it while you prepare the fruit.

To make the filling, cut the apricots into slivers and place them in a heavy saucepan with the cherries, brown sugar, and water. Bring the mixture to a boil over high heat, stirring as you do, until the sugar is dissolved. Turn the heat very low and simmer, stirring occasionally to keep it from sticking, until the fruit is soft enough to mash, about 30 minutes. Remove from the heat and use a potato masher to mash the mixture coarsely, then add the applesauce and stir. Set aside, preferably in a warm place, such as the back of the stove.

Preheat the oven to 350°F, and bake the cake layers according to the instructions on page 296. When the first layer is done and you are ready to cover it with fruit puree, stir the bourbon into the fruit. Assemble the cake; store and serve it according to the directions on page 296.

Even a bad stack cake can be good, or so my friends and neighbors swore when the first, not-moist-enough apricot cake made the rounds. It was George Holmes, who lives across the street, who discovered the antidote for a piece of too-dry stack cake—something which occasionally can happen even to a perfect cake if the last piece is left-over long enough. George was having his cake for breakfast, just like my father liked to do, when he decided to put it in a bowl and pour a little of his hot, sweetened, creamy coffee over the top. Not enough to make soup, mind you, but just enough to steam and soften things up.

"It was really delicious," he told me later. "I ate it and then wiped the bowl clean with my finger." Pap Lundy would have been proud.

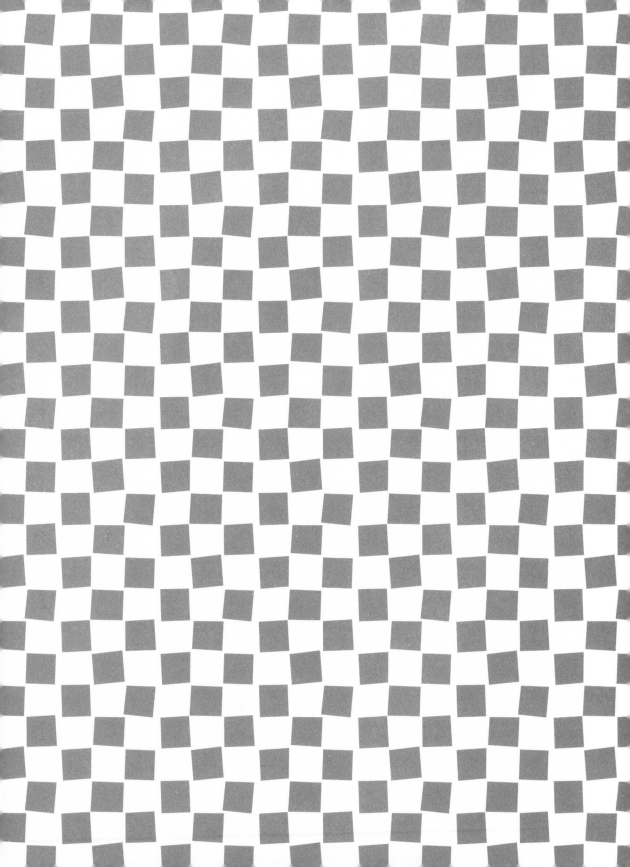

Figs, PLUMS, AND SCUPPERNONGS

Fig Cake

Carol's Red Plum Jam

Author Wade Hall lives down the street from me now, but he grew up in south Alabama, right in the thick of fig country. He and his four younger brothers would risk scrapes and breaks to climb out on perilous branches for the ripest fruit—fruit, he says, that "tasted like it was straight from the orchards of paradise."

My friend Craig Lege, an extraordinary piano player who grew up around Abbeville, Louisiana, also remembers the whole family getting in on the act at fig-picking time, some of them dressed in long-sleeved shirts and britches to protect them from an allergic reaction to the figs' skin. "It was worth it," he recalls, for the fabulous fig preserves his mother and grandmother would put up from the harvest, preserves he describes as "the best in the world."

Author? Piano player? Could there be a connection between figs and creativity? Indeed, when Wade made a pilgrimage a few years ago to the Jackson, Mississippi, home of legendary writer Eudora Welty, with whom he'd been corresponding for several years, it was a jar of his family's homemade fig preserves he took as a tribute and which Welty deemed "lovely."

Creativity is also at work in the delightful names the varieties of figs are given in the South. On the tiny North Carolina island of Ocracoke alone there are brown turkey figs, sweet celeste figs, sugar figs, green fingerleaf figs (also called Portsmouths after another nearby island where they flourish), pound figs, blue figs, yellow figs, lemon figs (which are not as yellow as yellow figs), and mystery figs.

Most Southerners put up whole figs in a silky syrup spiked with lemon slices, although a thick jam is also made with the fruit. These fig preserves might show up later in moon-shaped hand-pies, compote for a pork roast, or, as my friends in Cajun country taught me, simply folded in a piece of good white bread and eaten as a luscious sandwich.

Every cook in fig country had a signature cake (see page 306) made from fig jam, and a clever way of serving figs fresh as an appetizer or dessert. One of Wade's favorite things to do is to take plump figs ripe from the tree, chill them, sprinkle them lightly with sugar, then douse them liberally with cold, rich cream. It's a delight that can't be beat.

Equal to the frenzy of preserve-making at fig time was that which occurred a little farther north when the Damson plums came in. Damsons are small, dark-purple-skinned plums with tart flesh which turns from greenish yellow to deep crimson when fully ripe—or cooked. John Egerton grew up watching the local Damson harvest turned into delectable preserves, a tradition he continues every late August or September. He describes homemade Damson spread as "superior preserves—tart, rich, flavorful" and says the best part is that they are easy to make. Alas, the hard part in recent years has been finding Southern Damsons, so hard that John relies on the harvest from Michigan for the 20 pounds or so he needs to put up his 50 to 75 half-pints of preserves, most of which he gives away at Christmas.

The encouraging news, though, is that regionally grown Damsons are starting to make a very cautious reappearance at farm markets. One farmer at our local market has a stand of old Damson trees, and the fruit from it gets gobbled up as soon as he sets up shop. In lieu of Damsons, there are several delicious varieties of plums still available in the South. Carol Cassedy looks for red-fleshed plums for her jam (page 308).

The ultimate Southern jam or jelly, though, is that made from the native American wild grape, the muscadine. Muscadines and their most beloved variety, the scuppernong, grew in such abundance on the Carolina shore that early European sailors could smell the sweet, winey fragrance of America days before they saw land. Even now, you can find a patch of ripe muscadines by following your nose through the woods, where they still grow wild. Also called fox grapes, they can be either deep purple or a mottled yellow-white, and have thick skins. More and more, however, the grapes are being grown by enterprising farmers looking for a good cash crop, particularly to take the place of tobacco. Savvy entrepreneurs turn the grapes into signature jellies widely available by mail order, and there are those who venture to fulfill Thomas Jefferson's

early dream of creating a truly distinctive American wine from the wild grapes.

Fig Cake
SERVES 10

There are dozens and dozens of recipes for fig cakes throughout the South with very little variation from the one here. Some cooks use more spices—cloves, ginger, and allspice—but I prefer the purer taste of the figs. Some cakes are baked in layers and are served iced with a cream cheese frosting, like that frequently used for carrot cake, or the hard penuche frosting that is beloved in the South. That always seemed like overkill to me, though, since the figs are rich enough. In fact, I like this cake without the buttermilk glaze, but that puts me in the minority in my household and among the neighbors who helped us polish off the cakes we tested. You can decide for yourself. This cake is best served with cups of very hot and very, very strong dark coffee.

FIG CAKE
3 large eggs
1 cup sugar
1 cup vegetable oil
2 cups all-purpose flour
1 teaspoon baking soda
1 teaspoon kosher salt
1 teaspoon ground cinnamon
1 teaspoon ground nutmeg
½ cup buttermilk
1 teaspoon vanilla

2½ cups jam-like fig preserves
(see page 339)
1 cup chopped pecans

BUTTERMILK GLAZE
½ cup sugar
1½ teaspoons cornstarch
¼ cup buttermilk
¼ cup butter
1 teaspoon vanilla

Preheat the oven to 350°F. Liberally grease a Bundt pan with vegetable shortening and flour it. Turn the pan over and tap the bottom lightly to remove the extra flour.

Use an electric mixer on medium-high speed to beat the eggs, sugar, and oil until fluffy and pale yellow.

Sift together the flour, baking soda, salt, cinnamon, and nutmeg, and set aside.

Add the buttermilk and vanilla to the egg mixture and beat just to combine. Add the flour mixture and beat until smooth. Remove from the electric mixer and fold in the preserves by hand. Add the pecans and fold until mixed throughout.

Turn the batter out into the Bundt pan and bake 50 to 55 minutes, until a cake tester inserted in the middle comes out clean. Allow the cake to cool for 10 minutes in the pan, then invert it over a cake rack to remove it from the pan. (Use a blunt knife to loosen the edges first, if needed.)

While the cake is cooling, prepare the glaze. Combine the sugar and cornstarch in a small saucepan. Add the other ingredients and heat over medium heat, stirring constantly, until the mixture comes to a boil.

Boil for 1 minute without stirring, then remove from the heat. Turn the cake right side up on a large serving plate. Pour the warm glaze over the warm cake. Much of the glaze will soak into the cake or stick to the surface, but some may pool on the plate around the cake. You can wait until the cake and glaze cool, then use a spatula to scoop the pooled glaze up and onto the cake, or you can serve it the old-fashioned way, cutting wedges of cake and spooning a dollop of any extra glaze onto each piece.

MAIL ORDER

If you don't live in fig country, putting up your own fig preserves can be a pretty costly business, with fresh figs commanding a king's ransom even in season. Much better to spend your money ordering Mrs. Sassard's Fig Preserves, made from South Carolina sugar figs put up the old-fashioned way, with slivers of lemon, and available from the Lee Brothers of Charleston (see Things to Order, page 338). These preserves are delicate and delectable on biscuits or toast or just eaten with a spoon.

For fig cake, the preserves should be less like the traditional whole figs in syrup and more like a thick jam. You can get this consistency by mashing whole fig preserves, or you can buy good fig preserves already put up that way. A. M. Braswell Food Company makes just such a preserve. You'll need two jars for the Fig Cake recipe here. See Things to Order, page 338.

Carol Cassedy, her husband, Linn, and their seven children operate a 45-acre organic farm in Bagdad, Kentucky, where they grow heirloom vegetables, produce sorghum syrup, and raise Jersey cows, llamas, pigs, chickens, rabbits, bees, herbs, and more. Whitestone Organic Farm also has an on-site commercial kitchen, where the Cassedys prepare some of the tastiest pastries in the region, as well as limited batches of jams and preserves available by mail order. Much of their produce is sold through farm markets in Louisville and Lexington, and Carol and Linn have been strong supporters of the collaboration between small family farmers and urban restaurateurs and consumers in the area.

Carol makes quilt batting from the fleece of the llamas along with local alpaca and sheep to fill her handmade cotton, silk, and wool quilts.

Whitestone Farm's mail order is very limited: sorghum, jams and jellies in season, until they run out, and an exquisitely intense lemon tea bread are the primary items offered. If you are in the region, you can contact the farm to arrange a tour by appointment. While you're there, you can buy any of the jams, pickles, quilts, breads, or other items on hand.

See Things to Order, page 338, and Places to Go, page 341.

Carol's Red Plum Jam
MAKES APPROXIMATELY 7 PINTS

Carol Cassedy makes her jewel-like red plum jam as it was done in the old days, without commercial pectin and in small batches. ("Never more than seven pints at a time, or you risk losing control of the pot," she says.) For best results, Carol says, there are some rules of thumb.

First, she chooses red plums or black plums with deep-red flesh and leaves the peel on them for the best color. Don't fool with any fruit that has blemishes. And when you are picking plums, choose about one-third of the lot from soft, very ripe plums and the remaining two-thirds at the just-ripe stage, yielding to pressure but not soft. If your plums are too ripe overall, the natural pectin will be decreased and they will have to cook too long before setting up.

Carol sets her jam pot (a heavy copper-bottomed, stainless steel one) over high heat and stirs constantly. But she cautions that if the fruit starts to cook too quickly (a furious rolling boil, or if the fruit on the bottom begins to stick before the rest sets up) you should turn the heat down.

Humidity and altitude will have an effect on how long it takes the jam to set up, anywhere from 8 to 30 minutes. And finally, if you go through the entire process, allowing the jars to cool for 12 hours, only to discover the product is still too runny, you can unseal the jars and cook the mass down again—or declare it a batch of yummy pancake syrup.

6 cups pitted red plum pieces (about 4
    pounds)
4½ cups sugar
juice from 1 lemon

Put about 2 cups of the fruit in a large, heavy pan and use a potato masher to crush it. (This will provide more moisture in the early stage of cooking.) Add the rest of the fruit. Over high to moderately high heat, simmer the fruit, stirring as you do, until it is softened. Add the sugar (if you put it in sooner, you increase the chance of scorching) and lemon juice. Continue to simmer on high, stirring all the while, until the jam sheets off the back of a metal spoon. (This means instead of dripping off in single droplets, the fruit comes together in a "sheet" to drip.) If you are using a candy thermometer, the temperature should be 220°F.

Remove from the heat and immediately fill hot sterilized pint canning jars to within ½ inch of the top. Cover with new lids and seals.

FARM MARKETS AND FESTIVALS

For a one-stop extravaganza in Southern cooking, uptown style, you can't beat the annual Celebration of Southern Chefs. The event was the brainchild of Charleston chef extraordinaire Louis Osteen and his wife, Marlene, who wanted to bring together the best minds of their generation, as it were, in one big cooking gala. Participants read like a Who's Who of Southern kitchens, including Stephan Pyles of Star Canyon in Dallas, Emeril Lagasse of Emeril's in New Orleans, Marcel Desaulniers of The Trellis Restaurant in Williamsburg, Frank Stitt of Highland's Bar and Grill in Birmingham, Ben Barker of the Magnolia Grill in Durham, and more.

In 1998 the celebration left Charleston and settled in at the home base of one of its more innovative chefs, José Gutierrez of the Peabody Hotel in Memphis, Tennessee, and it looks as if Memphis will be its home in years to come. In addition to the all-star dinner, the weekend features a showcase of Southern products, meals in great restaurants in the surrounding area, Southern food seminars, and more. See Places to Go, page 341.

MAiL oRDeR

Lee Brothers (of boiled peanut fame) offer jars of small-batch scuppernong jelly among their other mail-order items. They can also put you in touch with a North Carolina firm which ships genuine scuppernong wine, and some growers who will gladly sell you muscadine vines so you can grow your own. Some restrictions apply regarding shipments of wines and vines to certain states, so call the Brothers before you get your hopes up and hoes out. See Things to Order, page 338.

Meanwhile, Callaway Gardens in Georgia has been selling muscadine products for more than fifty years, including jelly, preserves, and a sauce that's good poured over other stuff ranging from ice cream to venison steaks. You can mail-order, but this is one place where folks flock to the source. Callaway Gardens, a gorgeous resort on 2,500 acres, includes demonstration gardens, hiking trails, sports facilities, and a dining room where they serve Southern-style meals three times a day, starting with a breakfast that always includes piping-hot biscuits and muscadine preserves. Just 70 miles south of Atlanta, Callaway Gardens is a popular vacation destination.

See Things to Order, page 338, and Places to Go, page 341.

Butter Beans to Blackberries

STRAWBERRIES AND BLUEBERRIES

Freezer Jam

Strawberry-Mango Ice Cream

Drive-In Strawberry Pie

Strawberry Romanoff Icebox Tarts

Unfried Pies

Steel Magnolias

Fresh Blueberries with Intense Lemon Curd
and Lemon Cornmeal Cookies

"Stra-a-a-a-aw-ber-ries; *straw-berries*." The siren call of summer still thrills me, even if I hear it only in memory. The voice of the itinerant fruit seller was strong enough for me to pick up three blocks away. I would stand in the kitchen, pleading with my mother.

The fruit peddlers who popped up in our neighborhood all summer long were a mixed blessing for her. In season, their produce was as ripe and full-flavored as any she could get from someone's garden, especially the strawberries and blackberries, which are prolific in our region. But the savvy sellers knew well enough how berry-deprived we kids felt after a winter spent with apples, bananas, and oranges; and they always got a jump on the season with the less-tasty berries and peaches shipped from far away. Damaged in the process, and hence picked up at a hefty discount, the fruit could be hawked to unsuspecting housewives and their salivating children.

My mother was not unsuspecting. She knew full well when berry season arrived, and knew even better that if she went out before it and hailed the man with his bicycle cart loaded with cartons all topped with perfect crimson berries, that what she'd see is not what she'd get. Underneath the perfect ringers would be a near-quart of squashed, blemished, or unripe fruit; and she'd spend twenty minutes picking through it, cutting out the bad parts, and fussing under her breath, just to get me that one single bowl of strawberries and cream.

But, oh, the look of delight that must have been on my face when she sat that little crystal bowl of scarlet jewels in front of me. I can only imagine how it must have pleased her, because every late spring, fully against her will, she'd go out and buy a quart of those flawed, too-early strawberries just for me. Then, my psychic hunger sated, I would wait patiently with her the three or four weeks more before the local berries came in. Then there would be a great dishpan full to the brim in our kitchen, and my mother would hum to herself as she rinsed one plump, perfect berry after another, to make into her special company cake, jam, pies, and ice cream, or—best of all—just for eating.

I think about this every spring when the farmer's market up the street opens and one vendor in overalls and gimme cap suddenly appears with a tableful of seductively scented berries, about three weeks too early in the season. The by-laws of our market say the produce sold there must be "local" (grown within a 50-mile radius), and though this man swears his berries meet the mark, any of us with a knowledge of the regional climate and conditions know he's fibbing. My guess is his berries come from Florida, for they are sweeter and smaller, more intensely strawberry, than the fat, flavorless berries from the far coast we've been sniffing at disdainfully in the supermarket all year.

Most springs I pass him by with a knowing smile and a shake of the head. Occasionally the fever hits me, or I long to see that look of pure delight in my own daughter's eyes, and I buy a pint, only to be disappointed that they don't live up to my memory of the local berries from last season.

Those I have to wait for, but the anticipation does not exceed the reality once they come in. It's not just the abundance of the berries that turns the market into a festival, but the variety. I try to hit at least two vendors, sometimes as many as four, every visit during berry season, buying a pint or quart from each and marveling at the differences among them.

"These are from Shebby County," a grower says, giving the next-door county of Shelby its regional pronunciation. The pint is packed with juicy berries sweet and mild, and so red they are almost purple. They are the perfect whole berries for filling a Drive-In Strawberry Pie (page 318), but it needs the bite of the tarter, orangy Henry County berries to put the zip in the puree that surrounds them.

I have my pick of berries grown in Jeffersontown, Kentucky, or Jeffersonville, Indiana; berries from Okolona, to which our neighbor Bert drove every June to fill the dishpan in our kitchen. For years I thought the road sign to "Waddy Peytona" directed travelers to a single town with a singular name. Now, every June, I get to compare the berries from one of these communities to those of the other.

Sometimes Waddy's produce is sweetest, sometimes it's Peytona's, but always the fragile local berries are more intensely delicious than any grown for shipping.

Not long after the strawberry crop is exhausted, regional blueberries begin to show up at our local produce stand. Unlike strawberries, which seem to lose flavor as they are bred for resilience, blueberries can be both sturdy and delicious.

I've had blueberries in Maine, Michigan, and Oregon in season and all are superb, but I'd match berries we get around here from North Carolina to any of their more celebrated counterparts.

Freezer Jam MAKES ABOUT 5 CUPS

Such a mixed blessing, the fragrant jams and preserves put up from the bounty of summer berries. The product was divine, but making it meant steaming up the kitchen, and the cook, with big vats of berries a-bubble and pots of boiling water to scald the canning jars and lids. Even air conditioning couldn't take the edge off the process, and so most busy modern cooks have all but forsaken the art of putting by. But, joy of unexpected joys, one of the best ways to make fresh, fruity strawberry jam is virtually painless. Freezer jam is that uncommon combination: a recipe that is not only easy but unusually delicious. I love the translucent scarlet color of this jam set out in crystal bowls, bringing the glory of the summer garden to the table all through the winter.

Measurements should be adhered to strictly in this recipe, or the result may well be too runny—hardly a disaster, though, since what you get then is a wealth of fresh strawberry syrup for waffles and ice cream. If all the strawberries are perfect, you can get 2 cups from a single quart, but I find I usually have to discard a few and cut some soft spots out of others, so it's safer to start with 1½ quarts, measure out the 2 cups, and use any extra as described in the Note.

1½ quarts ripe strawberries
4 cups sugar
1¾ ounces powdered fruit pectin
¾ cup water

The strawberries should be room temperature. Rinse them, and discard any unripe berries. Remove the stems of the remaining berries and cut out any blemishes or soft spots. Put the berries in a large bowl and use a potato masher to coarsely mash them, leaving chunks of berry intact. (If you use a processor, pulse to chop, but don't puree the berries.)

Measure the sugar exactly, using the edge of a knife to level it in the measuring cup. Add it to the berries and stir to mix. Allow the berries to sit for 10 minutes, stirring once or twice.

Mix the powdered pectin with the water in a small saucepan. Place it over high heat and, stirring constantly, bring it to a boil. Boil for 1 minute, still stirring constantly. Remove it from the heat and immediately mix it with the fruit. Stir to dissolve the sugar, being sure to scrape the bottom of the bowl to bring all the sugar up and into the mixture. (I use a wide, flat-bottomed plastic mixing spoon.)

When the sugar is completely dissolved, pour the jam into clean plastic freezer containers (1- to 2-cup capacity), leaving ½ inch clear at the top. Wipe off the top edges to ensure a good seal, then cover the containers securely with lids, and allow them to sit at room temperature for 24 hours.

Store the containers in the freezer for up to one year; thaw them in the refrigerator before using. The jam can be stored in the refrigerator for up to 3 weeks.

Note: *Depending on the berries, you can have ¼ to ½ cup of berries left after mashing. For a quick drink, toss them into a blender with 2 cups of fresh orange juice, and blend just to mix. Serve immediately. Berries are also delicious as the base for a fruit smoothie made from any combination of seeded chunks of watermelon, cantaloupe, peaches, or other berries blended with ice and orange juice or plain yogurt. If you have at least ½ cup of leftover berries, they may be used in Strawberry-Mango Ice Cream (next recipe).*

Strawberry-Mango Ice Cream
SERVES 4 TO 6

The luscious, velvet-fleshed mangoes of Florida migrate north now with frequency, showing up in supermarkets and fruit markets, and pairing beautifully with their less exotic cousins, strawberries or blackberries and cantaloupe or honeydew melon. You can make a knockout fruit salad of chunks of fresh mango mixed with whichever berry is in season and whichever melon is ripest.

This ice cream melds berries and mango in a voluptuous combo. It's also a terrific spur-of-the-moment treat, since the mango juice can be sitting in the pantry, waiting for a party; and the berries can be either fresh or frozen.

½ cup pureed fresh or frozen ripe
　　strawberries
1½ cups mango juice
½ cup sugar (or more)
1 cup whipping cream

After you have pureed the berries in the blender, add the mango juice and sugar, and whir just to blend. Taste and add more sugar, if needed. Add the whipping cream and whir just to mix. Freeze in a 1-quart capacity Donvier-type freezer, according to directions.

"Saturday morning

Found me itching

To get on over

To my grandma's kitchen

Where the sweetest little berries

were cooking up right . . .

We was making jam.

Strawberry jam.

If you want the best jam,

You got to make your own."

　　　　—Michelle Shocked, "Strawberry Jam"

Drive-In Strawberry Pie　　SERVES 8

For all my daughter knows, the days before air conditioning may well have been in prehistoric times. I do not begrudge her the pleasure of living in a climate-controlled house or the luxury of driving to and from work in August without once breaking a bead of sweat.

But I do believe my daughter has lost something in exchange for this shelter from summer's torpor—a subtle but telling edge of pleasure that marked certain seasonal delights. She can savor the juicy sweetness of the first ripe watermelon of the season, but for me the beauty of that fruit was also tangled up in the arid ride across Corbin in my uncle Charlie's hot Buick, with the sticky straw seat, to the fruit market, which was always dark and a good ten degrees cooler inside. In the back were galvanized tins filled with melons, frigid water, and big velvety blocks of melting ice. I got to put my arms up to the elbow in the water to pat prospective melons, and could dangle my hands there while Charlie and the proprietor pulled a plug to check a prospect. The ride home was as good as air-conditioned, with my still-cold arm pressed against one cheek and the frosty melon full of promised pleasure clutched beside me on the seat.

Back home in Louisville, going to the drive-in restaurant was another summer respite. No steamy kitchen for my mother, and, hard as it is to imagine now, sitting in the car with windows rolled down under the drive-in's canopy seemed as cool as basking in an ocean breeze. We had burgers, onion rings, and if the temperature was hot enough, Cokes with dinner and shakes for dessert, cold enough to give you a headache.

But there were also times when dinner was not the destination. Instead, we made the trek simply for pieces of "in season" strawberry pie.

With huge, crunchy California strawberries at the grocery year-round, it's hard to remember the heady gluttony of real strawberry season, when every night you had ice cream or shortcake, every morning strawberries in cream, and the local drive-in restaurants put up signs proclaiming: "Yes! We have strawberry pie!"

That was the siren call to my mother, her best friend, Sarah, and my cousin Billie, all of whom loved beyond reason the flaky pastry crust filled with whole crimson tart berries, held together in a sweet strawberry gelatin, and topped with silky whipped cream. You can get poor imitations of these pies anytime you want, but I'm here to tell you that the out-of-season strawberries and factory-reddened goop that surrounds them don't hold a candle to the real thing.

Billie or Sarah would call, sometimes in the heat of the day, sometimes late at night, and tell my mother to get ready, they were coming by. Billie's son, Rocky, was just my age, and Sarah's boys, Larry and Keith, flanked us on either side by a year. While I loved them all, they did tend to be a bit rowdy. (I was perfect, of course.)

On the way to the Ranch House (the drive-in which made the best strawberry pie, in the connoisseurs' opinion), the women would balance their fear of embarrassment from wild children with the pure pleasure of eating the pie off a real plate instead of the paper plate it was served on outside.

We would hold our collective breath in the back seat, knowing from experience that a verbal urging from any of us could tip the balance in the wrong direction. Inevitably, though, by the time we got to the turquoise building they would have decided to go inside, "if you children can behave."

In fact, it was no problem. That first blast of arctic air as we stepped through the door ("Come on in. It's KOOL inside," proclaimed a sly blue penguin painted on the glass, exhaling a blast of white icicled air with his invitation) stunned us into absolute submission. It was so cold we had to hold our bare legs in shorts up off the plastic seats until they got accustomed to the chill. And then it was pleasure enough just to lean back, basking in the unaccustomed iciness.

The pie was the exquisite capper to the whole experience. We all got frosty glasses of milk and could not fathom why our mothers would opt for hot and bitter coffee. We compared pieces to see who got the largest whole berry, the winner gloating as he or she ate every bite all around that last luscious one. As long as we could contain ourselves afterwards, the mothers would sit and smoke and talk, letting themselves be soothed by the chilly pleasure. But, of course, the sugar from the strawberry confection usually took its toll, and like bugs brought back to life from hibernation, we'd begin to squirm and wiggle, pinch and whine—all of which got us evicted from the Garden of Eden in no time.

The recipe below should be made only with local strawberries in season. You will fill the pie better if you avoid the big show-offs and use berries no bigger than an inch at the stem end. The pie must be served cold, and is best served in air conditioning to guests sitting on cold vinyl.

9-inch prebaked pie crust
1 quart ripe strawberries
1 cup plus 4 tablespoons sugar
3 tablespoons cornstarch
⅛ teaspoon kosher salt
1 cup water
2 cups whipping cream
⅛ teaspoon almond extract (or vanilla)

The crust must be completely cooled before filling.

Cut the stems from the berries, leaving a relatively flat top, and arrange the whole berries in the pie crust with points sticking up, enough to fill the crust. Set aside any berries from which you have cut bruises or unripe spots, and those which are larger than the rest. The set-aside berries should equal at least 1 cup. Puree them in a blender.

In a heavy saucepan, mix 1 cup of sugar with the cornstarch and salt. Add the pureed berries and the water, swirling

the water in the blender first to get all of the berry puree out.

Set the saucepan over medium heat and, stirring all the time, heat it until the syrup thickens and just begins to boil. When bubbles start to break the surface, count to 15, then remove the pan from the heat. The syrup should be very thick, but still pourable. Pour it evenly over the berries in the pie crust.

Allow the pie to cool to room temperature, then cover it securely with plastic wrap, and refrigerate it for 1 hour.

When you are ready to serve, whip the cream with the remaining sugar and the almond or vanilla extract until soft peaks form. Serve with a generous dollop of whipped cream on each piece.

Strawberry Romanoff Icebox Tarts
SERVES 6

When I was growing up in the 1950s, icebox pie—simply made of egg yolks, sweetened condensed milk, and pureed fruit or juice in a graham cracker crust—was a classic in family kitchens as well as on diner menus. But a host of new products, from prewhipped "cremes" to instant pudding, changed the very definition of icebox pie through the 1960s, and what was once not only an easy but wholesome dessert became an object of scorn.

This recipe uses the slightly caramel flavor of sweetened condensed milk (I use fat-free because it thickens a little better) to good end but is dressy enough to serve for a company supper.

CRUST

vanilla wafers to make ¾ cups of fine crumbs (about 18)

⅛ cup blanched almond pieces

⅛ cup sugar

2 tablespoons salted butter, melted

Preheat the oven to 350°F.

Arrange six 1-cup custard cups on a baking sheet.

In a blender, using the pulser, process the vanilla wafers and the almond pieces on high to make fine crumbs. Transfer them to a bowl and mix in the sugar. Drizzle the butter over the crumbs and mix with a wooden spoon until all the crumbs are moistened. Place 2 heaping tablespoons of the crumb mixture in each custard cup and press gently but firmly with your fingers to evenly cover the bottom of the cup. Bake 5 minutes, until the crust is set. Remove from the oven, and cool completely on a rack before filling.

FILLING

12 large, ripe strawberries

1 lime

14 ounces fat-free sweetened condensed milk

1 cup sour cream

Rinse the strawberries and set aside 6 perfect ones. Remove the caps from the remaining 6, and puree them in a blender. You should have at least ½ cup of liquid.

Zest the lime and mince the zest. Extract the juice.

In a large mixing bowl, mix the sweetened condensed milk, strawberry puree, lime juice, and lime zest until blended. Fold in the sour cream until just blended. Spoon the mixture into the crust-lined custard cups. Place a strawberry on top of each. Set on a tray and cover securely with plastic wrap. Chill for 2 hours.

Unfried Pies   SERVES 8

The pioneer necessity of drying fruits for sustenance through the winter lasted right up through this century in much of the mountain South. For the rest of us, though, the art has been neglected; and for many years, such products—outside of raisins, prunes, apples, and apricots—were relatively unavailable in the marketplace.

Recently there has been a resurgence of culinary interest in dried fruit, particularly as a gourmet ingredient in pilafs, salads, and the like. Dried cherries, blueberries, and cranberries are common supermarket fare these days; and dried strawberries are becoming increasingly easy to find, if not at the local grocery, then at health food and specialty food stores. The strawberries are usually expensive, but you get a lot of bang for your buck, since each one is packed with intense flavor. I had a hard time testing this recipe, simply because my daughter and her friends, home from college on vacation, couldn't resist raiding the stash in the pantry for snacking.

The first time I made these pies, I mixed the strawberries with very thin and crispy pieces of dried persimmon, another premium-priced dried fruit. But any flavor the persimmon may have had was overwhelmed by the strawberries. Dried peaches, apples, or (my favorite) pears are much less expensive and easier to come by, so that is what I use here.

Finally, although the pastry recipe is the same as that for fried pies, I opted to bake these, not only for calories' sake, but also for ease in serving them at a dinner party. Later we compared the baked versions to some which I fried the traditional way, and found that the frying, which works well with the more robust flavors of dried apples or peaches, overwhelmed the berries and the ginger.

1 recipe pastry crust for Fried Pies (page 292)
2 cups dried peaches, apples, or pears
1 cup water
1 cup dried strawberries
½ cup sugar
1 tablespoon minced candied ginger
melted butter

Prepare the pastry crust dough and refrigerate it, tightly covered, while you cook the filling.

Simmer the dried peaches, apples, or pears in the water over very low heat for 25 minutes, or until moist enough to mash with a potato masher. (The time can vary as much as 30 minutes or more, depending on how moist the dried fruit is to begin with.)

Mash the fruit into a very coarse puree. Cut the strawberries into small pieces and add them to the puree along with the sugar. Stir to mix, then let it steep for 20 minutes.

While it's steeping, preheat the oven to 450°F. Have 2 baking sheets ready. Lightly flour a flat surface and rolling pin for rolling out the crust.

When the fruit has steeped, stir in the minced ginger.

Remove the dough from the refrigerator, and break off a piece a little smaller than a golf ball. Lightly roll it in your palms to make it round, then press to flatten it. Lay it on the floured surface and roll it a few times lightly with a rolling pin to make a circle about 2½ inches in diameter.

Place a heaping dessert-spoonful of fruit filling in the center of the dough, and fold it over to make a half-moon shape. Use a fork dipped in water to crimp the edges tightly shut; pierce the top once with the fork.

Continue doing this until you have used all of the dough, or filling. You should have 2 dozen pies.

Lay them on the baking sheets, leaving at least an inch of space between them. Brush the tops lightly with melted butter, then bake 8 minutes, until they are turning golden on top. Allow them to cool for a few minutes, then serve warm.

Steel Magnolias

MAKES 4 TO 5 DOZEN

I found the flavor of dried strawberries so intoxicating that I started looking for favorite recipes to put them in. The original version of these cookies is a recipe given to me some years ago by my friend Lee Hutchison, a woman who exemplified for me the very spirit of Southern womanhood.

Lee raised three extraordinary children on her own in the 1940s and '50s, when such a thing just wasn't done. She was strong and independent, level-headed and competent, and one of the most beautiful and gracious women I have ever known. Before she died in 1998, she had passed on her recipes, her kitchen secrets, her hospitality, and her indomitable spirit to her children, a whole new generation of grandchildren, and a few of us privileged friends. This version of her cookies, with the heady sweetness of the strawberries balanced by the zing of ginger, is named in her honor.

1 cup salted butter, softened
1 cup firmly packed brown sugar
1 cup granulated sugar
2 large eggs
½ teaspoon kosher salt
½ teaspoon vanilla extract
1 teaspoon freshly ground cardamom
1 tablespoon milk
½ cup chopped pecans
½ cup chopped dried strawberries
¼ cup minced crystallized ginger

1¼ cups all-purpose flour
1 teaspoon baking soda
3 cups rolled oats

Preheat the oven to 350°F. Lightly grease 2 cookie sheets.

In an electric mixer, cream the butter and sugars until light and fluffy. Add the eggs, salt, vanilla, cardamom, and milk, and blend. Remove the bowl from the mixer and, using a wooden spoon, mix in the pecans, strawberries, and ginger.

Sift together the flour and baking soda, and fold them into the rest. Add the oats, and mix until just blended. Spoon out in tablespoon-sized dollops on the baking sheets, leaving about 1 inch space between cookies. Press each lightly with the back of a fork to flatten it. Bake 12 minutes, until lightly browned. Cool for 2 minutes before removing from the cookie sheets with a spatula.

These are delicious slightly warm. If you are going to store them, allow the cookies to cool completely before packing them in air-tight containers.

If this were a romance, I'd tell you about my whole family piling in our '56 Chevy and heading out to a nearby you-pick strawberry farm for a day spent picking and eating. But the '56 Chevy didn't come along in my family until 1961, and even when we got the car, I don't recall ever using it to go strawberry picking. We didn't have to pick strawberries, because our neighbor Bert did.

Every June, regular as thunderstorms

and sunshine, Bert would show up on our doorstep some Saturday evening with a pan full of strawberries from her cousin's Okolona farm.

The frangipane fragrance of that wealth of berries made my mother giddy with delight. She would begin washing berries on the spot, slicing them into little square glass bowls with pebbled sides, for anyone who might be in the house when supper-time rolled around. All got doused liberally with sugar, then set in the refrigerator "to sweeten." When supper was finished and it was time for dessert, my mother would pour a little pool of milk into each dish, and we would daintily eat those first real berries of the season, heart-shaped slices of crimson in cold milk just ever so slightly turned pink.

My mother popped whole sugar-crusted berries into the mouth of every neighbor child who stepped onto our porch. Once it was Johnny, who lived down the street and who I had the most merciless crush on. He'd come to the door to fetch me for a neigh-borhood ball game called peggy. While I was tying my tennis shoes, my mom told Johnny to close his eyes, then rolled the biggest berry she could lay her hands on in the sugar bowl and popped the whole thing into his open and waiting mouth. He was too startled to do anything but gulp, an act that triggered his furious allergy and turned him red as the fruit. The offending straw-berry sent him to bed for the better part of that early-summer week, and dashed all hopes I'd had of summer romance.

My mother's best berry trick was an unbelievably easy but outrageous-looking (and tasting) strawberry shortcake she could whip together when unexpected company showed up. She'd carefully slice the top off an angel-food cake from the A&P, about a half-inch worth, keeping it intact. This she'd set aside. Then she'd use a small sharp knife to hollow a trench out of the inside of the remaining cake. She'd fill it with sweetened berry slices mixed with the crumbled pieces of the cake she'd just extracted. Then she'd place the top back on carefully and "ice" the whole thing with fresh-whipped mounds of sweetened cream. Whole berries deco-rated the top of the cake, and toothpicks kept the Saran Wrap from smooshing the creamy peaks as it sat in the refrigerator for the requisite couple of hours so all the fla-vors could mingle.

Guests always oohed and aahhed when the cake was carried triumphantly to the table, telling my mother repeatedly that she shouldn't have gone to such trouble on account of them. She hadn't, of course. It was the berries that made her do it.

Fresh Blueberries with Intense Lemon Curd and Lemon Cornmeal Cookies
SERVES 4

Miles James says the Ozark strawberries are delicious, but you just won't believe the blueberries! He serves them in season at his Johnson, Arkansas, restaurant, James at the Mill, with a zesty lemon cus-tard, which sets off their sweetness per-fectly. When the blueberries are all gone and small, sugary raspberries are in, the lemon custard cozies up to them. Meanwhile, the cornmeal in the cookies gives them a unique texture that is at once both chewy and crunchy, and is absolutely, divinely delicious.

BLUEBERRIES AND LEMON CURD
3 lemons
4½ tablespoons salted butter
8 tablespoons sugar
1 large egg
2 egg yolks
3 cups fresh blueberries

Rinse the lemons, zest them, and chop the zest fine. Extract the juice from the lemons. In a heavy, nonreactive saucepan over medium heat, stir the juice, zest, butter, and sugar until the butter melts. Continue to heat until the mixture comes to a boil.

Meanwhile, whisk together the egg and additional yolks until blended. When the lemon mixture begins to boil, remove it from the heat and slowly pour about half of it into the beaten eggs, whisking as you do. Once the two are blended, pour them into the remaining lemon mixture in the pan, also whisking as you do. Continue to whisk over medium-high heat until the mixture begins to thicken and bubble at the edges.

Remove from the heat and chill immediately. (To do this, either set the hot pan in a sink with ice water halfway up the sides of the pan until the pan is cool, or transfer the curd immediately from the hot pan to a cool bowl.) Cover the pan or bowl, and refrigerate.

Rinse the berries, divide them evenly in four wine glasses, and chill while the custard cools and you prepare the cookies.

LEMON CORNMEAL COOKIES
zest of 1 lemon
¼ pound salted butter, soft
1 cup sugar
¼ teaspoon kosher salt
1 egg
¼ teaspoon vanilla
1 cup flour
1 cup finely ground white cornmeal
¼ teaspoon baking powder

Preheat the oven to 325°F.

Mince the lemon zest. In an electric mixer, cream it with the butter, sugar, and salt. Add the egg and vanilla, and blend.

Combine the flour, cornmeal, and baking powder, and mix them into the creamed ingredients by hand. Mix until the ingredients are well blended and the dough holds together in a ball.

You can roll the dough out on a floured surface to ½-inch thickness and cut it into uniform shapes with cookie cutters, or you can roll the dough into a cylinder about 2 inches in diameter, and cut rounds ½ inch thick.

Lay the cookies on a cookie sheet with an inch of space between them. Bake in the center of the oven until the edges turn golden, 10 to 12 minutes. Remove the cookies from the pans and cool them on racks before serving. Makes one dozen.

When the cookies are cooled and the lemon curd is chilled, spoon the curd over the berries and serve, passing a plate of cookies on the side.

BLACKBERRIES

Blackberry-Bourbon Vinaigrette

Seared Chicken Salad with Blackberries
and Heirloom Tomatoes

Blackberry-Bourbon Custard Pie

Blackberry Cobbler à la Maud

Fresh Blackberry Trifle

> *"I came across excellent blackberries and ate of them heartily. It was mid-day, and when I left the brambles, I found that I had a sufficient meal that there was no need to get to an inn. Of a sudden it struck me as an extraordinary thing. Here had I satisfied my hunger, without payment, without indebtedness to any man."*
> —George Gissing, *Commonplace Book* (1903)

Maybe it's the streak of mountain independence in me, but there's something about the sheer wild abundance of blackberries that's as heady as wine—almost as heady as their dark and sugary tang. Blackberries were the fruit of the very first Southerners. The local Indian tribes foraged for wild varieties, which grew in profusion all across the region, from the mountains to the shore. The settlers who came after followed suit. Wines and tonic drinks were made from the juice; jams and jellies, pies, puddings, trifles, ice creams, and that ultimate dessert of Southern country kitchens, blackberry cobbler, from the fruit.

Countless generations of Southern children, black and white, were tempted and tortured by the berry patch. Brambles tore our flesh, the sun beat down relentlessly, the chiggers lived happily every after—or so it seemed it would be—right under our skin. Nevertheless, we plunged in every year for the remembered tang of warm berries pulled from the stem, and the promise of all the goodies later to come from the kitchen.

There still is no taste like that of a wild blackberry, and you will know it by the premium price they sell for at the farmer's market. They are easily transplanted—too easily, and if you coax a couple of brambles up in the yard one year, you may end up burning off a field full the next. Blackberries are audacious, but the taste is bodacious, so worth the trouble.

Worth the trouble of seeds, too, most old-timers swear. Wild berries always have them, and the domestic berries bred without them seem to have lost some flavor in the process as well. If you can't abide the seeds, it's really not that much effort to use a wooden spoon to rub the berries through a sieve to extract them. The resulting pulp can be combined with whole seedless berries, so you get the best of both worlds.

Blackberries freeze very well, so you can make many of the recipes here year-round. But here's what you must do when you get that first quart home, still warm from the field or the farm market: Rinse them lightly and pull off any leaves or stems. Pile them into a cut-glass bowl, or an antique soup dish with little flowers painted on the edges. Sprinkle a heaping spoon or three of granulated sugar over them, stirring lightly to make sure every berry gets some. Let it sit until the sugar is melted. Pour half and half about halfway up the berry pile. Eat it with a spoon and grin.

Blackberry-Bourbon Vinaigrette   MAKES ABOUT 2 CUPS

This salad dressing is intoxicating, literally and figuratively. Kentucky chef Sara Gibbs created it as the essential binding element in Seared Chicken Salad (next recipe), but it's a versatile player and lends itself well to a number of uses, particularly as a tart topping for cold sliced cantaloupe, avocados, or a salad of fresh, ripe fruit.

You can buy blackberry vinegar in some specialty stores, but it's easy enough to make your own. You will need to do that three days in advance, however. Once the vinegar is made, you can store it, tightly covered, in the refrigerator.

BLACKBERRY VINEGAR
¾ cup mashed fresh blackberries
1½ cups rice vinegar

VINAIGRETTE
1 cup olive oil
1 tablespoon Dijon-style mustard
¼ cup seedless blackberry jam
¼ cup blackberry vinegar

¼ teaspoon white pepper
2 tablespoons brown sugar
¼ teaspoon kosher salt
2 garlic cloves, minced
¼ cup bourbon

Make the vinegar at least 3 days before you make the vinaigrette. In a glass jar with a lid, mix the mashed berries and rice vinegar together. Refrigerate, covered, for 3 days. Strain before using. This recipe uses ¼ cup. The remainder can be used in any recipe calling for a fruity, flavored vinegar.

To make the vinaigrette, whisk together the olive oil, mustard, and jam. When blended, whisk in the blackberry vinegar, the rest of the seasonings, and the bourbon. Let sit for at least 30 minutes.

Use immediately or store in a tightly covered container in the refrigerator, and use within a week. Some separation may occur. Simply whisk together before using. This makes enough for 1 recipe of Seared Chicken Salad.

Seared Chicken Salad with Blackberries and Heirloom Tomatoes   SERVES 4

Created by Sara Gibbs when she was chef at the Cottage Café in Middletown, Kentucky, this recipe may seem a bit daunting at first glance. But in practice, it breaks down into several simple parts. The result is a single dish which serves as a meal in itself. It is also breathtaking to look at, with the deep purple of the berries set off by the dramatic reds of heirloom tomatoes (see page 332). All you have to add is a loaf of bread and wine.

Note: *If you are making the vinegar for the vinaigrette, it takes 3 days to ferment.*

MARINATED CHICKEN

1 teaspoon minced garlic

1 tablespoon minced fresh sage

juice and minced zest of 1 lemon

2 tablespoons olive oil

salt

pepper

4 boneless, skinless chicken breasts

GRILLED ONIONS

1 sweet white onion

1½ teaspoons olive oil

1 teaspoon minced mint sage or sage

dash of salt

dash of freshly ground pepper

SALAD

mesclun or mixed greens for 4 salads

2 medium heirloom tomatoes

1 cup fresh blackberries

1 recipe Blackberry-Bourbon Vinaigrette
   (page 330)

To marinate the chicken: In a shallow glass bowl, blend together the garlic, sage, lemon juice and zest, and olive oil. Add salt and pepper to taste. Lay the chicken breasts in the marinade, turning them once to coat both sides. Cover snugly with plastic wrap and marinate in the refrigerator for 1 hour.

About 20 minutes before the hour is up, preheat the oven to 350°F.

About 10 minutes before the hour is up, slice the onion into 4 rounds about ¼ inch thick. Mix together the olive oil, sage, salt, and pepper. Toss the onion slices in the oil to coat. (Keeping the rounds whole until after cooking makes browning them easier.)

Heat a griddle or heavy skillet over medium-high heat. Add the onion rounds and oil, and brown the onion for about 1 minute on each side. Remove from the griddle and set aside, preferably somewhere where it can stay warm while you prepare the chicken.

Now place the marinated chicken breasts on the same hot griddle, still seasoned with the onion juice and oil. Sear them for 4 minutes on each side, then transfer them to a lightly oiled casserole or baking dish. Cover tightly with a lid or aluminum foil and bake 20 minutes.

While the chicken breasts are baking, rinse and dry the mesclun and arrange it on four large plates. Chop the tomatoes into pieces about the size of the berries. (If you are using really ripe heirloom tomatoes, you won't need to peel them.) Scatter the tomato pieces and berries evenly over the mesclun. Break the onion rounds into individual rings and scatter them evenly over the berries and tomatoes.

When the chicken is ready, remove it from the oven and cut it in thin slices. Lay these over the onions, and pour vinaigrette over all. Serve immediately.

Sara Gibbs lived most of her life in West Virginia or western Maryland, right on the border. There she developed a taste for fully sun-ripe, juice-oozing tomatoes. She did her culinary training in Louisville, Kentucky, and it was there that she started learning about locally grown heirloom tomatoes.

"There are so many kinds, and each one has a distinctive taste and texture. I love them all, but especially the pinks, and most especially the Eva purple balls.

"When I got my first commercial cooking job, one of the other students warned me not to use those odd kinds of heirloom tomatoes at the restaurant, because you can't control the texture of the slice, or how much juice they'll ooze. It was all for appearance, but I wanted to cook for taste."

Which is not to say that the visual isn't important to Sara, as well.

"There's nothing so striking as a plate of different kinds of heirloom tomato slices. My husband says that when you've got a bowl of Eva purple balls sitting on the counter, they look exactly like Christmas balls."

Sara and her husband grow their own heirlooms on their 18-acre farm near Taylorsville, Kentucky, from seed she buys from Southern Exposure Seed Exchange. See Things to Order, page 338.

Blackberry-Bourbon Custard Pie
SERVES 8

Blackberries, walnuts, and bourbon are a truly wicked combination, particularly in this sinfully delicious pie.

9-inch prebaked pie crust
2½ cups fresh blackberries
1½ cups granulated sugar
6 tablespoons cornstarch
¼ teaspoon kosher salt
2 tablespoons unsalted butter
4 egg yolks, beaten
½ cup broken walnut pieces
1 cup chilled whipping cream
2 tablespoons brown sugar
1 tablespoon bourbon

The pie crust must be thoroughly cooled before filling.

Use a wooden spoon to press the berries through a sieve or strainer to remove the seeds. Discard the seeds and put the puree in a heavy saucepan over medium-low heat.

Sift together the sugar, cornstarch, and salt. Add them to the puree, and stir. Add the butter. Continue to stir until the sugar and butter are melted and the mixture is steamy but not boiling. Whisk several spoonfuls of the hot berry puree into the beaten egg yolks to temper them, then whisk the yolks into the puree in the pan. Continue to stir and cook until the mixture boils. Reduce the heat and simmer 1 minute.

Pour the berry mixture into the prebaked pie crust. Cool it to room temperature. Sprinkle the walnuts over the top. Using the back of a large spoon or the palm of your hand, very lightly press them into the custard just enough to set. Cover tightly with plastic wrap and refrigerate for at least 1 hour before serving.

When you are ready to serve, whip the cream with the brown sugar and bourbon until light peaks form. Serve slices of pie with a generous dollop of bourbon whipped cream on each.

Blackberry Cobbler à la Maud

SERVES 10

Maud Fernandez was an exchange student from France who lived with us for a month the summer I started work on this book. Maud grew up in Cannes, and I wondered how my concoctions of Southern vegetables, old-fashioned fruits, and humble cornbread would compare to the French Mediterranean fare she was accustomed to.

I need not have worried. Though she could be quite firm about what she did not like (the tiny celery slivers I'd so painstakingly cut for a cool rice salad appeared in a neat pile on the side of her plate after one dinner), she was passionate in her appreciation for the foods that generations of Southerners had grown up eating.

Toward the end of the visit, when I asked if there was any particular dish she wanted to eat again before going home,

she thought for a moment, then won my heart completely when she answered, "Cornbread."

One of her favorite discoveries in our "new world" were the blackberries we had in abundance that summer. She was intrigued by their glistening darkness and winey scent, and I wanted to create a dessert in her honor which accentuated the berries' distinctive beauty.

To get there, I used two varieties of berries: tiny, tart, wild ones, which cooked up into a flavorful puree, and whole, plump, sweet Navahos, which floated like jewels in it.

Maud, Meghan, and I dipped into the still-warm dish one evening and, with stout glasses of cold milk, did in half the copious pan in one sitting. Later, before heading up to the attic room the girls shared, Maud confided that she just might sleepwalk that night "down the stairs and to the kitchen, where I will eat all the rest without anyone knowing."

2 cups soft-wheat flour
1 teaspoon baking powder
½ teaspoon baking soda
1 teaspoon kosher salt
2 cups sugar
8 tablespoons unsalted butter
½ to ¾ cup buttermilk
4 cups small, tart blackberries
2 cups large, plump blackberries

Preheat the oven to 350°F.

To make the dough, sift the flour, baking powder, baking soda, and salt together, then mix in 1 cup of sugar until

GREENBRIER, ARKANSAS, APRIL 1995

U.S. 65 snakes through small Arkansas towns with evocative names—Damascus, Bee Branch, Choctaw. Framed between the low ridges of the Ozark foothills, they remind me of the south-central Kentucky towns we drove through on the way to my family's hometown, Corbin, when I was a child. Feeling a little homesick and in need of comfort, I decide to pull into Katie's Kitchen and Tea Room in Greenbrier for something cold to drink.

The iced tea is offered sweetened or not, as sure a sign as I know that we are below the Mason-Dixon Restaurant Line. Katie herself brings it out to me and wants to know if I don't want a homemade biscuit just out of the oven to go with it. She brings two on a pretty little saucer decorated with flowers, and plops a jar of deep-purple jam down next to it. It is blackberry, so full and tart there's no mistaking the flavor, though there's not a telltale seed to be found.

"Sure enough," Katie says when I ask if she made the heady concoction. "Grew the berries, too. We grow them without any pesticides. That way you know you're just getting berries in the jam." Her husband picks them in the summer and she freezes them whole in plastic bags. "Then one cold day in November or December, I fire up the pot and make jars and jars of jam. It's too hot to think about it in July and August when the berries are ripe, but it's perfect in the winter. Makes the house smell great, too."

She asks where I'm from, and when I say Kentucky, we talk the other common B's, basketball and bluegrass. It's almost like being home, a fact underscored when I start to leave and Katie frets that I haven't eaten nearly enough. She offers another biscuit, gratis, for the road, her generosity as much a trait of the Southern table as sweet tea and biscuits.

Katie's idea of freezing berries for jam later is a good one. Even if you never get around to the jam, you'll savor the summer scent and taste of frozen berries in pies, cobblers, and pancakes all winter long.

Any berries can be frozen. Don't rinse raspberries, but all others can take a quick spritz in a colander, then spread them out on paper towels and lightly pat them dry. Place the berries in a single layer on cookie sheets, and put them in the freezer for 20 minutes. The berries will be hard enough then to be tossed into plastic bags or containers without sticking or clumping together. You can keep them for a year, until the next crop comes in, although I find they tend to lose some intensity after six months.

thoroughly blended. Cut the butter into small pieces. Spread them into the flour mixture so they aren't all in one clump. Use your fingers to incorporate them until mostly blended. Sprinkle ½ cup of buttermilk over the mixture, and use a large spatula to incorporate it into the dough, until it sticks together in a ball. Add more buttermilk in small amounts if needed.

Liberally butter a shallow 2-quart baking dish (I use a stoneware pasta dish). Mix the small berries with 1 cup of sugar and pour them into the baking dish. Spread the plump berries over them.

Pinch off golf-ball-sized pieces of the dough, and place them on top of the berries, close together but not quite touching. The dough should cover the top, with little openings between the pieces. Bake 45 to 50 minutes, until the crust is puffy and a deep golden color on top. (The bottom of the crust will not be completely firm, giving a little bit of a pudding texture where the fruit meets the crust.) Allow to cool.

This dessert is best served just a little warm, but not hot. Because of the richness of the crust, ice cream or whipping cream is superfluous, and may actually detract from the flavor.

Fresh Blackberry Trifle
SERVES 10 TO 12

This eighteenth-century English dessert came to the colonies along with its characteristic bowl—a deep, wide glass cylinder set on a pedestal to perfectly display its many colored and textured layers of cake, fruit, and custard. It became a favorite in the South, where its air of truly sinful indulgence was offset by the surprising ease of preparation—and where a surfeit of succulent fruits in the summer made for a heady concoction indeed.

I like the contrast between rich, dusky blackberries and the tart strawberry-orange sauce, although you may prefer to use red raspberries. Strawberry and blackberry seasons don't quite overlap, so instead of using the tough, flavorless California berries we get in the grocery almost year-round, I use headier, sweeter locally grown berries which I have frozen. (I have also found commercially frozen berries more flavorful than out-of-season store berries.)

Thomas Jefferson made his trifle with crumbled Italian cookies as the cake base. Most Southern cooks preferred either ladyfingers or strips of leftover pound cake or white cake. You can use any of these to assemble a trifle quickly, but if tossing those leftover egg whites is going to make you a little crazy, I suggest you make Orange Blossom Special Cake layers (page 260).

The cake was often soaked in sherry, brandy, or a fruit liqueur—or one of the fruit layers was augmented by spirits—giving the dish one of its more charming colloquial names, Tipsy Parson. The version here is parson-safe, having no alcohol, but feel free to add a tablespoon or two of orange liqueur to the strawberries, or to sprinkle the blackberries with a shot of very good bourbon, if you so desire.

Most trifles have a plain pastry cream between layers, but to add extra oomph to this one, I use an orange pastry cream from Shirley Corriher's *Cookwise: The Hows and Whys of Successful Cooking* (William Morrow and Co., 1997).

You don't have to have a trifle bowl to make this—any bowl about 8 inches in diameter and 4½ inches deep will do—but I think you will find it a good investment when you hear the ooohs and ahhhs of guests as you bring a filled trifle bowl to the table. Decorate the top of the trifle with plump berries or beautiful edible flowers.

The trifle needs to sit, refrigerated, for about an hour for the flavors to blend, but is best eaten the same day it is made.

PASTRY CREAM

2 cups half and half

zest of one orange, in strips

1 cup sugar

¼ cup all-purpose flour

⅛ teaspoon salt

6 large egg yolks

STRAWBERRY SAUCE

1½ cups sliced fresh or frozen
   strawberries

¾ cup sugar

½ cup fresh orange juice

1 tablespoon cornstarch

water

WHIPPED CREAM

1 pint whipping cream

¼ cup sugar

BLACKBERRY LAYER

2 pints fresh, seedless blackberries

⅛ cup sugar

CAKE

1 recipe Orange Blossom Special Cake
   (page 260), baked as two layers, or 36
   ladyfingers, or 1 pound cake

Prepare the pastry cream by heating the half and half with the orange zest in a medium-sized, heavy saucepan over medium heat until just steaming. Remove from the heat.

In a bowl, mix the sugar, flour, and salt, then whisk in the egg yolks. Strain the hot half and half to remove the zest, and slowly add about 1 cup of the liquid to the yolks, whisking all the while. When blended, put the yolks and the rest of the hot half and half in the saucepan. Cook over medium heat, stirring constantly, until the pastry cream begins to thicken. Immediately transfer it to a bowl, cover it with plastic wrap touching the top of the pastry cream to prevent a film from forming, and refrigerate.

Prepare the strawberry sauce by bringing the berries, sugar, and juice to a boil, stirring. Remove from the heat. Mix the cornstarch with just enough water to make a paste, and stir it into the hot fruit mixture. Transfer to a bowl and allow to cool completely before assembling the trifle.

When you are ready to assemble the trifle, prepare the whipped cream by beating the cream and sugar together until soft peaks form. Prepare the blackberries by rinsing them, patting them dry, and sprinkling them with the sugar. If you are using cake, slice it into strips about one inch wide.

Place about an inch of pastry cream in the bottom of the trifle bowl. Cover it with a layer of cake or ladyfingers. Pour half the strawberry sauce over this.

Add another inch of pastry cream, a layer of cake, and the rest of the strawberry sauce. Drizzle the remaining pastry cream over the strawberry sauce then add a thin layer of whipped cream. Add a final layer of cake, leaving a ½-inch margin around the rim. Spread the blackberries over the cake, and use them to fill in the margin so they are clearly visible through the glass. Spread the remaining whipped cream over the top.

Decorate with extra berries or edible flowers, if you want. You can serve the trifle immediately, or chill it for no more than 2 hours in the refrigerator, tightly covered with plastic wrap.

"When I picked a berry,
I didn't miss the blossom.
The blackberry blossom was white
  as the snow,
But the berry that it brings is sweeter than
  molasses
And black as the wings of an Arkansas
  Crow."
"Blackberry Blossom," Traditional

Adams Milling Company of Alabama, Route 6, Box 148, Dothan, Alabama 36303; 800-239-4233: Famous for its tasty "whole heart" grits.

A. M. Braswell Food Company, P.O. Box 485, Statesboro, Georgia 30458; 912-764-6191: Good fig and pear preserves, a savory artichoke relish from an old family recipe, pepper jellies, and more.

A. S. Margraf's Fine Foods, Brevard, North Carolina; 888-468-3003; http://www.brm.org/margraf: A line of gourmet items, such as salad dressing, featuring ramps.

A Southern Season, Eastgate Shopping Center, P.O. Box 2678, Chapel Hill, North Carolina 27515-2678; 800-253-3663: Gourmet products with a Southern accent.

Berea College Agricultural Department, Berea, Kentucky: The college is attempting to grow and market some heirloom beans, including the elusive greasy or creasy beans, through its agricultural department. Supplies will be limited. Call 606-986-9341 ext. 5590 and ask for Sean Clark for information.

Blenheim Bottlers, P.O. Box 452, Hamer, South Carolina 29547; 800-270-9344: The pluperfect super-spicy ginger ale comes in hot, not-so-hot, clear, and diet varieties.

Blue Moon Farm, 3584 Poosey Ridge, Richmond, Kentucky 40475-9780: A variety of distinctively flavored garlics are available by mail order from this small family farm. Send $2 for their annual catalog, which describes the garlic and other garlic products available.

Cajun Power Sauce Manufacturing, 318-893-3856: Cajun Power Original Recipe Garlic Sauce and other products.

Callaway Gardens, Highway 27, Pine Mountain, Georgia 31822; 706-663-2281: Muscadine jelly, preserves, and sauces are among the large assortment of Southern-style food items sold at this popular resort and demonstration gardens.

Cherry River Food Land, Cherry River Plaza, Richwood, West Virginia 26261; 304-846-6238: Fresh ramps shipped throughout the U.S. in season. They sponsor the annual April Ramp Feed in town.

Colony South Products, 843-762-4151: Holy City Heat, Charleston hot pepper sauce, and other South Carolina products.

Comeaux's Cajun Corner, 4519 W. Congress, Lafayette, Louisiana 70506; 318-983-2080: Tasso, andouille, and other products for Cajun cooking.

Cushman Fruit Company, 3325 Forest Hill Boulevard, West Palm Beach, Florida; 800-776-7575 or fax 800-776-4329: Super-sweet Honey-Bells, a cross between a Dancy tangerine and Duncan grapefruit, are so juicy the Cushman's will send you a bib with every box. Available only in January, but you need to order in November to be sure to get in on the stock. Other fruits are available all year. They have two other Florida retail outlets, at 223 Ocean Avenue in Lantana, and 204 U.S. Highway 1 in North Palm Beach.

Edible Landscaping, 361 Spirit Ridge

Lane, P.O. Box 77, Afton, Virginia 22920; 800-524-4156: Beautiful trees and plants with edible fruits and berries, including the elusive calamondin and mayhaw.

Falls Mill and Country Store, Route 1, Box 44, Belvidere, Tennessee 37306; 931-469-7161: Fine grits and stone-ground cornmeal.

Frank Lewis Alamo Fruits, 800-477-4773: Frank Lewis's Royal Ruby red grapefruits have fans who swear they are the best you can get. Available November through December; other fruits are available all year.

Garber Farms, 3405 Des Cannes Highway, Iota, Louisiana 70543; 318-824-6328: Superb "Cajun" yams by mail order in season. The Garbers also grow and sell deliciously aromatic Creole Rose rice.

Gatton Farms Father's Country Ham, Bremen, Kentucky 42325; 502-525-3554; GAT-FARM@muhlon.com: First-rate commercial long-cured country ham in whole hams or slices.

Gazin's Specialty Foods, New Orleans, 800-262-6410: Regional foods shipped nationally, including Camellia-brand dried lady cream peas, which must be ordered by the case.

Hoppin' John's, 30 Pinckney Street, Charleston, South Carolina 20401; 800-828-4412: Truly excellent grits and cornmeal, and a select line of delicious Low Country products. Also a full-service cookbook store, which can help you find the hard-to-get.

Kentucky Sweet Sorghum Producers Association, Danny Ray Townsend, Townsend's Sorghum Mill; 606-498-4142: Real sorghum syrup in season and in limited supply.

King Cotton Produce, 9100 Atlanta Highway, Montgomery, Alabama 36117; 334-272-1040: Will ship fresh butter beans, including speckled butter beans, and a variety of fresh crowder peas, including lady cream peas, purple-hull peas, and black-eyed peas, in season, which starts midsummer. Other produce may be available throughout the year.

Knox County Co-operative Extension, Ken-

tucky; 606-546-3447: Real sorghum syrup sold in attractive gift packages.

Kurz Meat Shoppe, 2206 Dundee Road, Louisville, Kentucky 40205; 502-451-6328: Handmade sausages low in fat and large in flavor, including rosemary lamb links.

Lee Brothers Boiled Peanuts Catalog, P.O. Box 315, Charleston, South Carolina 29402; 843-720-8890; www.boiledpeanuts.com: You have to send a dollar to get a catalog, which is something of a collectors' item. Great boiled peanuts and an eclectic assortment of Southern products, including fig preserves and scuppernong jam. They will also connect interested parties with a North Carolina firm that sells scuppernong wine and grape vines, although restrictions may apply in certain states.

L'Esprit de Campagne, P.O. Box 3130, Winchester, Virginia 22604; 540-955-1014: Hand-picked, sun-ripened Shenandoah Valley tomatoes, dried and sold in bags and jars, or marinated in olive oil with herbs. Also dried apples, blueberries, cherries, and cranberries. No sulphur. Certified kosher.

Long Creek Herb Farm, Route 4, Box 730, Oak Grove, Arkansas 72660; 417-779-5450; www.longcreekherbs.com: Jim Long raises herbs and teas available by mail order. Also an excellent small cookbook describing foods and cooking practices during the Civil War.

The Mayhaw Tree, Inc., 129 Washington Street, Jefferson, Georgia; 800-2MAYHAW: Jellies, preserves, and syrup made from south Georgia's special mayhaws, plus other Southern-style products.

McIlhenny's Tabasco, Avery Island, Louisiana; 800-634-9599: Classic Tabasco sauce and other Tabasco products, ranging from salsa to cups to posters.

Mullins' Orchard, c/o Roy Mullins, Route 2, Box 644, Wise, Virginia 24293; 540-328-3575: Dried apples seasonally.

Nora Mills Granary, 7107 S. Main St., Helen,

Georgia 30545; 706-878-2375 or 800-927-2375; NoraMill@aol.com: Stone-ground cornmeal and first-rate grits.

Mr. Alan Overholzer, HC 65, Box 128, Liberty, Kentucky 42539: Mr. Overholzer's sorghum is worth the trouble of writing to find out if any is available and how much it costs.

Panola Pepper Corp., 318-559-1774: Bat's Brew (Melange de la Chauve-Souris) and other hot-pepper products.

Ramps, From the Seed to the Weed, G and N Ramp Farm Specialties, P.O. Box 48, Richwood, West Virginia 26261; 304-846-4235: Fresh ramps during the short early-spring season, and ramp products such as jelly, bulbs, and seeds the rest of the year.

Route 11 Potato Chips, Middletown, Virginia; 800-294-SPUD (7783): The regular chips are a cut above excellent; the salt-and-vinegar variety are superb, and the sweet potato chips with cinnamon and sugar are beyond superlatives.

Serendipity of the Valley, San Benito, Texas; 956-399-0924; SEREND@aol.com: Jalapeño Orange Jelly, made from wild Rio Grande oranges, and Ruby Red grapefruit jelly.

Shawnee Springs Cannery, Cross Junction, Virginia; 800-713-1414: Canned Shenandoah Valley peaches which are exceptional for cobblers.

Some Say Tomato, c/o Mariflo Stephens, 108 2nd Street, SW, No. 5, Charlottesville, Virginia 22902: A collection of poetry about tomatoes.

Southern Exposure Seed Exchange, P.O. Box 170, Earlysville, Virginia 22936; 804-973-4703: Unusual and heirloom seeds, with an emphasis on traditional Southern varieties. Catalog includes helpful growing tips and information on the history of many of the plants.

Thomas Jefferson Center for Historic Plants, Monticello, P.O. Box 316, Charlottesville, Virginia 22902; 804-984-9816: The annual seed catalog offers seeds, plants, and small trees of the same varieties found in Thomas Jefferson's extraordinary gardens.

White Lily Foods Co., Knoxville, Tennessee; 800-264-5459: Soft-wheat flour perfect for making Southern-style biscuits, pies, and cobbler crusts. Also a good source of finely ground white cornmeal for cornbread.

Whitestone Organic Farm, 1420 Cedarmore Road, Bagdad, Kentucky 40003; 502-747-5822: Limited batches of farm-made jams and preserves, sorghum, and tart lemon tea cake.

PLACES TO GO

ALABAMA

The Bright Star, 304 19th Street, Bessemer; 205-424-9444. (p. 184)

John's, 112 N. 21st Street, Birmingham; 205-322-6014. (p. 184)

King Cotton Produce and Restaurant, 9100 Atlanta Highway, Montgomery; 334-272-1040. (p. 5)

ARKANSAS

Dairy Hollow House, 515 Spring Street, Eureka Springs; 501-253-7444. (p. 239)

James at the Mill, 3906 Great House Springs Rd., Johnson; 501-443-1400. (p. 245)

Long Creek Herb Farm, Route 4, Box 730, Oak Grove, 72660; 417-779-5450 (by appointment); www.longcreekherbs.com. (p. 240)

FLORIDA

Florida Citrus Showcase, 211 Avenue G. SW, Winter Haven, 33881; 941-292-9810. (p. 299)

Tarpon Springs, Chamber of Commerce; 727-937-6109. (p. 184)

GEORGIA

Betty's Country Store, Main Street, Helen; 706-878-2943. (p. 107)

Callaway Gardens, Highway 27, Pine Mountain; 706-663-2281. (p. 310)

Farmer's Market Café, 63 Chattahoochee Street, Helen; 706-878-3705. (p. 107)

The Georgia Peanut Festival, P.O. Box 60, Sylvester (actually in Possum Poke in Poulan); 912-776-7718. (p. 48)

Horseradish Grill, 4320 Powers Ferry Road, Atlanta; 404-255-7277; www.horseradishgrill.com. (p. 228)

The Mayhaw Festival, Colquitt/Miller County Chamber of Commerce, P.O. Box 253, Colquitt; 912-758-2400. (p. 281)

Nora Mills Granary, 7107 S. Main St., Helen, 706-878-2375 or 800-927-2375 or NoraMill@aol.com. (p. 107)

Sorghum Festival, Blairsville Jaycees, P.O. Box 701, Blairsville; 706-745-4745; www.blairsvillechamber.com. (p. 220)

KENTUCKY

The Cottage Café, 11609 Main Street, Middletown; 502-244-9497. (p. 154)

Dudley's Restaurant, 380 S. Mill Street, Lexington; 606-252-1010. (p. 206)

The English Grill, The Camberley Brown Hotel, 4th and Broadway, Louisville; 502-583-1234. (p. 280)

Lilly's, 1147 Bardstown Road, Louisville; 502-451-0447. (p. 262)

Lynn's Paradise Café, 984 Barrett Avenue, Louisville; 502-583-3447. (p. 14)

The Morgan County Annual Sorghum Festival, West Liberty; 606-743-3330. (p. 220)

The Ohio Valley Harvest Festival, Louisville Convention and Visitors Bureau, 400 S. First Street, Louisville; 502-584-2121. (p. 219)

The Rudyard Kipling, 422 West Oak Street, Louisville; 502-636-1311. (p. 40)

Shariat's Restaurant, 2901 Brownsboro Road, Louisville; 502-899-7878. (p. 102)

Whitestone Organic Farm Tours (by appointment), 1420 Cedarmore Road, Bagdad; 502-747-5822. (p. 308)

LOUISIANA

Comeaux's Cajun Corner, 4519 W. Congress, Lafayette; 318-983-2080. (p. 43)

Dupuy's Oyster Shop, 108 S. Main Street, Abbeville; 318-893-2336. (p. 28)

McIlhenny Company's Tabasco Factory and Country Store, off SR 329, Avery Island; 800-634-9599. (p. 28)

New Orleans Jazz and Heritage Festival, The Fairgrounds, New Orleans; 504-522-4786. (p. 231)

Plaquemines Parish Fair and Orange Festival, Box 309, Port Sulphur, 70083; 504-564-2951. (p. 255)

The Praline Connection, 542 Frenchman Street, New Orleans; 504-943-3934. (p. 232)

MISSISSIPPI

Jocelyn's, Highway 90 East, Ocean Springs; 228-875-1925. (p. xvii)

Smitty's, 208 S. Lamar Street, Oxford; 601-234-9111.

NORTH CAROLINA

A Southern Season, Eastgate Shopping Center, Chapel Hill, 27514; 800-253-3663. (p. 338)

Bum's Restaurant, 115 E. Third Street, Ayden; 252-746-6880. (p. 86)

Collard Festival, Ayden Chamber of Commerce, Ayden; 252-746-2266. (p. 86)

Crook's Corner, 610 West Franklin Street, Chapel Hill; 919-929-7643. (p. 338)

Fearrington House Restaurant, Fearrington Village, Pittsboro; 919-542-2121. (p. 27)

The Inn at Celebrity Dairy, 2106 Mount Vernon–Hickory Mountain Road, Siler City, 27344; 919-742-5176. (p. 278)

The Moose Café, at the Western North Carolina Farmers Market, I-40 exit #47, Asheville; 828-255-0920. (p. 67)

Ramp Convention, first Sunday in May, Waynesville; 800-334-9036. (p. 124)

Sourwood Honey Festival, mid-August, Black Mountain/Swanannoa Chamber of Commerce, Black Mountain; 828-669-2300. (p. 67)

SOUTH CAROLINA

The Beacon Drive-In, 225 Reidsville Road, Greenville; 864-585-9387. (p. 155)

Hoppin' John's, 30 Pinckney Street, Charleston; 800-828-4412. (p. 112)

Louis's Restaurant and Bar, 200 Meeting Street, Suite 8, Charleston; 843-853-2550. (p. xvii)

Limehouse Produce, 6168 Wappoo Road, Charleston; 843-556-3400. (p. 8)

World Grits Festival, P.O. Box 787, St. George; 843-563-9091. (p. 115)

TENNESSEE

A Celebration of Southern Chefs, The Peabody Hotel, Memphis; c/o Marlene Osteen, 28 Wentworth Street, Charleston, South Carolina, 29401; 843-722-6274. (p. 309)

Falls Mill and Country Store, Route 1, Box 44, Belvidere; 931-469-7161. (p. 112)

Herbert's, 111 North Royal Oaks Boulevard, Franklin; 615-791-0700. (p. 292)

The Peabody Hotel, 149 Union Avenue, Memphis; 901-529-4000. (p. 194)

TEXAS

Bryce's Cafeteria, I-30, exit 222, Texarkana; 903-792-1611. (p. 17)

Texas Citrus Festival, P.O. Box 407, Mission, 78572; 956-585-9724. (p. 255)

VIRGINIA

The Inn at Grist Mill Square, Box 359, Warm Springs, 24484; 540-839-2231. (p. 173)

Metropolitain, 214 West Water Street, Charlottesville; 804-977-1043. (p. 116)

Monticello, Route 53, Charlottesville; 804-984-9822; http://www.monticello.org. (p. 125, 115)

Museum of American Frontier Culture, U.S. 250 off I-81 at exit 222, Staunton; 540-332-7850. (p. 69)

The Pork, Peanut and Pine Festival, Chippokes Plantation State Park, 695 Chippokes Park Rd., Surry, 23883; 757-294-3625. (p. 48)

WEST VIRGINIA

Richwood Ramp Feed, Cherry River Food Land, Cherry River Plaza, Richwood; 304-846-6238. (p. 129)

FARM MARKETS

If I'm traveling somewhere and want to know where to find a good farm market, I try the agricultural extension service for the area, the local chamber of commerce or visitor's center, or the food editor of the nearest good-sized newspaper. I also ask where the food comes from anytime I run into something good and fresh at a restaurant.

Farm market hours and days vary with the seasons. Some operate year-round, others only in summer. Saturdays are a good bet for finding a market open in any region, and remember, it's the early bird who gets the greasy beans.

Here's a list of the markets mentioned in this book, and a few other outstanding Southern farm markets.

Carrboro Farm Market, Carrboro, North Carolina, town square: Local produce in season and other products, including first-rate goat cheese from the Celebrity Goat Dairy outside of nearby Siler City.

Charlotte Regional Farmer's Market, 1801 Yorkmont Road, Charlotte, North Carolina; 704-357-1269: Two buildings full of locally grown produce, crafts, and baked goods.

Columbia Farmer's Market, 1001 Bluff Road, Columbia, South Carolina; 803-737-4664: Some 200 vendors set up across the street from the University of South Carolina football stadium 364 days of the year. Diversity of goods is the hallmark of this market, which is at a major crossroads in the region.

Highlands Farmer's Market, parking lot of Bardstown Road Presbyterian Church, 1722 Bardstown Road, Louisville, Kentucky: Louisville has farm markets in various places around the city Tuesday through Saturday. This one offers an interesting medley of organic "designer" vegetables, heirloom tomatoes and plants, fresh mint, and country favorites like white half-runner beans. Open Saturday mornings by Derby Day; also open Thursday evenings during the peak growing season.

King Cotton Produce, 9100 Atlanta Highway, Montgomery, Alabama 36117; 334-272-1040: Fresh produce in season, including local strawberries, which are the talk of the town. Lunch is served daily, featuring Chef Wylie Poundstone's Southern specialties.

Limehouse Produce, 6168 Wappoo Road, Charleston, South Carolina: Excellent source for hand-shelled sivvy beans in season (June–August and September–November). No mail order.

Little Rock River Market, 400 E. Market, Little Rock, Arkansas 72201; 501-375-2552: Only a few years old, this downtown market has already established a reputation for good food. Year-round indoor facility, with a butcher, baker, and gourmet shop open daily. Outdoor stalls open May–November, featuring some 40 regional farmers and more than a dozen artists and craftsmen; Tuesday and Saturday, 7 a.m.–3 p.m.

Matthews Regional Farmer's Market, South Trade Street, Matthews, North Carolina: Lots of organic produce as well as fresh flowers and art.

Montgomery Curb Market, 1004

Madison Avenue, Montgomery, Alabama: 334-263-6445: Year-round farm market open every Tuesday, Thursday, and Saturday. Great seasonal produce, including fresh lady cream peas in summer. Homemade cakes and goodies at Christmas.

Pink and George's Produce, Edisto Island, South Carolina. A little ways off S.C. 174, up a red clay road. Ask for directions in Edisto.

Western North Carolina Farmer's Market, I-40 exit 47, Asheville, North Carolina; Year-round produce market with regional specialties, including sorghum, greasy or creasy beans in midsummer, and sourwood honey along about August. While you're there, visit the Moose Café next door, where Southern vegetable dishes made from the market's produce are the specialty.

accompaniments: black-eyed pea relish, 33; freezer pickles, 152; peach and dried-cherry chutney, 278; sorghum pepper relish, 164; *see also* sauces and gravies

ajvar: and corn custard, 102

appetizers: boiled peanuts, 45–46; bolitos, 31–33; Creole eggplant dip, 183–84; sweet potato guacamole, 31–33; toasted and spiced peanuts, 50–51

apples: about, 287–88; apple and black walnut cobbler, 288–89; apple stack cake, 296–98; apple-walnut cake with ginger cream, 289–91; dried-apple butter, 293–94; drying, 294–95; fried apples, 291–92; in fried pies, 292–93

asparagus: benne-coated, 121–22; in Green and Gold, 123–25; steaming, 122–23

bananas: about, 273; in black-bottom cream pie, 280–81; pudding, 282; snack cake, 282–83

bean cakes, *see* bolitos

bean pies, 44–45

beans: *see* butter beans; crowder peas; green beans; navy beans; pinto beans; red beans

beets: ginger, 228–29

bell peppers, *see* peppers, bell

berries: about, 315–16; freezer jam, 316–17; fresh blueberries with lemon curd, 324–25; *see also* blackberries; strawberries

biscuits: fruit jam, 277–78; pepper cheese, 139; served with English peas, 125–26; *see also* cornbread

blackberries: about, 329–30; in chicken salad with tomatoes, 330–31; in cobbler, 333, 335; in custard pie, 332–33; in trifle, 335–37; in vinaigrette, 330

black-eyed peas: about, 23; in bolitos, 31–33; and goat cheese in salad, 27–30; in Hoppin' John, 25–26; in relish for pecan-crusted trout, 33–34; in succotash, 16; *see also* crowder peas

bolitos, 31–33

boudin, 43–44

bourbon: blackberry-bourbon custard pie, 332–33; blackberry-bourbon vinaigrette, 330; bourbon-apricot-cherry stack cake, 299–300

breads, *see* biscuits; cornbread

butter beans: about, 5–6; classic recipe, 6; and green beans with coddled egg sauce, 61–63; in ragout, 14–15; with shoepeg corn, 11–12; speckled, 5, 7, 9, 16; in succotash, 13, 15–16

Cajun cooking, *see* Maque Choux stuffed peppers

Cakes: apple stack, 296–98; apple-walnut, with ginger cream, 289–91; banana crunch snack, 282–83; bourbon-apricot-cherry stack, 299–300; fig, 306–7; lemon pound cake pudding with hot toddy sauce, 262–64; Orange Blossom Special, 260–62

calamondin marmalade, 268–69

candy, *see* fudge, peanut butter

carrots: broth for corn risotto, 230–31; and grits, 229

chayote, lime, 205; *see also* mirliton

cheese: goat, 27, 29–30; mizithra, in grits casserole, 116; in pepper cheese biscuits, 139; white cheddar and roasted red pepper, 196–98

chicken salad, 330–31

chutney, peach and dried-cherry, 278

citrus fruits: about, 253–54; calamondin marmalade, 268–69; drinks, 264–67; grapefruit gelatin, 256; lemon buttermilk sorbet, 258; lemon cornmeal cookies, 324–25; lemon curd with fresh blueberries, 324–25; lemon curd for pound cake pudding, 262–64; lemon okra soup, 165; lime-butter fish, 254–55; lime chayote, 205; lime pie, 259–60; Orange Blossom Special cake, 260–62

citrus julep, 266–67

cobblers: apple and black walnut, 288–89; blackberry, 333, 335; peach, 276

colcannon, 88–89

collards with cornmeal dumplings, 85–86

cookies: dried-strawberry, 323; lemon cornmeal, 324–25

corn: about, 97; and ajvar custard, 102; on the cob, 97–98; milking, 101–2; picking, 98–99; pone, 106–7; pudding with crab, 101; in risotto with fresh carrot broth, 230–31; roasted in shuck, 99–100; shoepeg, 11–12, 16; in succotash, 13, 15–16; *see also* grits; hominy

cornbread: basic, 103–4; in Green and Gold, 123–25

corn cakes: with butter bean ragout, 14–15; crawfish, with smoked tomato sauce, 102–3

corn fritters: basic, 105; okra, with sorghum pepper relish, 164–65

cornmeal: dumplings with collards, 85–86; lemon cookies, 324–25

crab: in corn pudding, 101

crawfish: in corn cakes with smoked tomato sauce, 102–3

cream peas, *see* lady cream peas

Creole eggplant dip, 183–84

crookneck squash casserole, 208–9

crowder peas: about, 23–25; cooking fresh, 25; in Limpin' Susan Edisto, 26–27; and macaroni in salad with charred green-tomato dressing, 143–44; with mustard greens, 86–87; *see also* black-eyed peas; lady cream peas; purple-hull peas

cucumbers: about, 151; for freezer pickles, 152; in mousse, 152–53

custard, savory: corn and ajvar, 102; turnip, 227–28

custard pie, blackberry-bourbon, 332–33

desserts: banana pudding, 282; dried-strawberry cookies, 323; fresh blackberry trifle, 335–37; fresh blueberries with lemon curd, 324–25; lemon cornmeal cookies, 324–25; lemon pound cake pudding, 262–64;

desserts (*cont.*)
strawberry Romanoff icebox tarts, 320–21; *see also* cakes; cobblers; ice cream; pies; sorbet
drinks: citrus julep, 266–67; iced tea, 264–66

eggplant: about, 181; Creole dip and pudding, 183–84; and green tomatoes, grilled, in sandwich, 181–83; moussaka, 184–85
English peas, *see* peas

figs: about, 305; cake made from jam, 306–7
fish and seafood: crab in corn pudding, 101; crawfish corn cakes, 102–3; Frogmore soup, 175–76; hush puppies stuffed with shrimp, 193; lime-butter fish, 254–55; pecan-crusted trout, 33–34
freezer jam, 316–17
freezer pickles, 152
fried apples, 291–92
fried green tomatoes, 142–43
fried pies, 292–93
Frogmore soup, 175–76
fruits: about, 273; bourbon-apricot-cherry stack cake, 299–300; fig cake, 306–7; ginger grapefruit gelatin, 256; honeydew dessert, 154; peach and dried-cherry chutney, 278; red plum jam, 308–9; in unfried pies, 322; watermelon salsa, 154–55; *see also* apples; bananas; berries; peaches
fudge, peanut butter, 49–50

German potato salad, 174–75
ginger: in beets, 228–29; in grapefruit gelatin, 256; in sweet potato pie, 219–21
ginger ale, 256–58
goat cheese: about, 30; and black-eyed pea salad, 27–30
gravy, *see* sauces and gravies
Green and Gold (asparagus in cheese sauce), 123–25
green beans: about, 55–56; and butter beans with coddled egg sauce, 61–63; classic Southern-style, 56–57; deviled, 66; McCaslan variety, 68; stringing and snapping, 57–59; and tomatoes in salad, 59–60; zydeco, 66–67; *see also* shuck beans
greens, *see* sallet greens
green tomatoes: charred, in salad dressing, 143–44; and eggplant, grilled, in sandwiches, 181–83; fried, with cream gravy, 142–43; in mincemeat pie, 145–46

grits: about, 111; cakes, 113–15; carrot, 229; classic, 111–13; mizithra, in casserole, 116; okra, with winter tomato gravy, 163–64; pumpkin, in pudding, 209–10; roasted garlic, 117; *see also* hominy
guacamole, sweet potato, 31, 32
Gumbo Z'Herbes , 90–92

ham broth, 162–63
hominy: and winter squash in soup, 209
Hoppin' John, 25–26
hot sauces, 28–29
huevos rancheros, 61–62
hush puppies, stuffed with shrimp, 193

ice cream: peach, 274–75; sorghum and sweet potato, 221; strawberry-mango, 317–18
iced tea, 264–66

jammy biscuits, 277–78
jams and jellies: calamondin marmalade, 268–69; dried-apple butter, 293–94; freezer jam, 316–17; quince butter, 279–80; red plum jam, 308–9; *see also* jammy biscuits
julep, citrus, 266–67

kale, 88–89

lady cream peas: about, 23–25; and buttermilk in stew, 34–35
lamb: in stuffed peppers with rice, 192–93
lemon: in buttermilk sorbet, 258; in cornmeal cookies, 324–25; in okra soup, 165; *see also* lemon curd
lemon curd: for fresh blueberries, 324–25; for pound cake pudding, 262–64
lima beans, *see* butter beans
lime: with chayote, 205; fish in lime butter, 254–55; pie, 259–60
Limpin' Susan Edisto, 26–27

macaroni: and crowder pea salad, 143–44
Maque Choux stuffed peppers, 193
mayhaws, 281
McCaslan beans, 68
melon: about, 151–52; watermelon salsa, 154–55; zippity honeydew, 154
mirliton, stuffed, 204–5; *see also* chayote
mizithra grits casserole, 116
molasses vs. sorghum, 220
morel mushrooms, 237–38, 243–44
moussaka, 184–85
mousse, cucumber, 152–53

muscadines, 306, 310
mushrooms: fixing morels, 237–38, 243–44; wild, and potato hash, 247–48
mustard greens with crowder peas, 86–87

navy beans: in soup, 41–42

okra: about, 161–62; in Bibb lettuce salad, 166–67; braised, 161–62; cooked with tomatoes, 163; in corn fritters, 164–65; in grits, 163–64; in Limpin' Susan Edisto, 26–27; soup with lemon, 165
Orange Blossom Special cake, 260–62

pattypan and leek buttermilk soup, 203–4
peaches: about, 273; in cobbler, 276; and dried-cherry chutney, 278; in fried pies, 292–93; in ice cream, 274–75
peanut butter: fudge, 49–50; sandwiches, 49
peanuts: boiled, 45–46; green, 45–46; in soup, 47–49; spiced, 50–51; sweet potatoes with, 216–18; toasted, 50–51
peas: about, 125–26; cooked with lettuce, 127; and new potatoes, 128–29; served over biscuits, 125–26; *see also* black-eyed peas; crowder peas; lady cream peas
pecan-crusted trout, 33–34
pepper cheese biscuits, 139
peppers, bell: about, 191–92; creamy red pepper soup, 195; in hush puppies, 193; in potato salad, 195–96; stuffed, Maque Choux–style, 193; stuffed with lamb and rice, 192–93; *see also* pimientos
peppers, hot, 28–29
pickles: freezer, 152; in peanut butter sandwiches, 49
pies: bean, 44–45; blackberry-bourbon custard, 332–33; black-bottom banana cream, 280–81; fried, 292–93; ginger sorghum sweet potato, 219, 221; Kentucky lime, 259–60; strawberry, 318–20; strawberry Romanoff icebox tarts, 320–21; unfried, 321–22
pimientos: and corn custard, 102; making paste, 102
pinto beans: in soup, 39–41; *see also* red beans
plums: about Damsons, 305–6; red plum jam, 308–9
poke, 82–83
pork: and purple-hull peas in stew, 30–31
potatoes: about, 171; hash with wild mushrooms, 247–48; mashed, 171–72; new, and sweet peas, 128–29; *see also* potato salad; sweet potatoes

potato salad: with bell peppers, 195–96; German, 174–75
pot likker, greens with, 84
preserves, *see* jams and jellies
pudding, dessert: banana, 282; lemon pound cake, 262–64
pudding, savory: corn with crab, 101; eggplant, 183–84; pumpkin grits, 209–10
pumpkin grits pudding, 209–10
purple-hull peas: about, 17, 23; and pork in stew, 30–31

quince butter, 279–80

radishes, 129–30
ramps, mountain, 124–25
ratatouille, 207–8
red beans: in bean pies, 44–45; and rice, 42
red plum jam, 308–9
rice: corn risotto with fresh carrot broth, 230–31; and lamb in stuffed peppers, 192–93; and red beans, 42
roots, 227–31

salad dressings: blackberry-bourbon vinaigrette, 330; buttermilk, 166–67; charred green-tomato, 143–44
salads: Bibb lettuce with okra croutons, 166–67; butter beans and shoepeg corn, 11–12; German potato, 174–75; goat cheese and black-eyed peas, 27–30; macaroni and crowder peas, 143–44; potato, with bell peppers, 195–96; seared chicken with blackberries and heirloom tomatoes, 330–31; tomatoes stuffed with egg salad, 138; warm green beans and tomatoes, 59–60
sallet greens: about, 79–81; colcannon, 88–89; collards with cornmeal dumplings, 85–86; in Gumbo Z'Herbes, 90–92; kale, 88–89; mustard greens with crowder peas, 86–87; poke, 82–83; and pot likker,

84; spring greens soup, 89–90; winter greens soup, 90
salsa, watermelon, 154–55
sandwiches: grilled eggplant and green tomato, 181–83; peanut butter, 49; tomatoes in, 137–38
sauces and gravies: with canned tomatoes, 141–42, 163–64; cream gravy for fried green tomatoes, 142–43; with fresh tomatoes, 141–42; lemon velouté, 9; smoked tomato sauce for crawfish corn cakes, 102–3; *see also* accompaniments
scuppernongs, 306, 310
shrimp Provençal: hush puppies stuffed with, 193
shuck beans: about, 69–70; cooking, 73–74; drying, 71–73
sieva beans, 5, 8
skillet corn, 100–1
sorbet: lemon buttermilk, 258
sorghum: vs. molasses, 220; in pepper relish, 164; in sweet potato ice cream, 221; in sweet potato pie, 219, 221
soup beans, 39–41
soups and stews: pinto bean soups, 39–41; creamy red pepper soup, 195; Frogmore stew, 175–76; golden gazpacho, 139–40; Gumbo Z'Herbes, 90–92; lady cream pea buttermilk stew, 34–35; navy bean soup, 42; pattypan and leek buttermilk soup, 203–4; pork and purple-hull pea stew, 30–31; spring greens soup, 89–90; sweet potato and corn chowder, 218; winter greens soup, 90; winter squash and hominy soup, 209
spaghetti squash, 205–7
speckled butter beans, 5, 7, 9
spring greens soup, 89–90
squash: about, 203; crookneck squash casserole, 208–9; lime chayote, 205; pattypan and leek buttermilk soup, 203–4; in ratatouille, 207–8; spaghetti squash with spicy peanut sauce,

205–7; stuffed mirliton, 204–5; winter squash and hominy soup, 209
stack cakes: about, 296; apple stack cake, 296–98; bourbon-apricot-cherry stack cake, 299–300
Steel Magnolias, 323
stews, *see* soups and stews
sticky buns, *see* jammy biscuits
strawberries: about, 315–16; dried-strawberry cookies, 323; icebox tarts, 320–21; pie, 318–20; strawberry-mango ice cream, 317–18
stuffed peppers: lamb and rice, 192–93; Maque Choux, 193
succotash, 13, 15–16
sun-dried tomatoes, 18–19
sweet peppers, *see* peppers, bell
sweet potatoes: about, 215–16; and corn chowder, 218; guacamole, 31–33; hash, 216; ice cream with sorghum, 221; with peanuts, 216–18; pie with ginger sorghum, 219, 221
sweet potato squash, 208, 209
sweets, *see* desserts; fudge, peanut butter

Tabasco, 28–29
tomatoes: about, 135–36; cherry, 59–60; in golden gazpacho, 139–40; gravy using canned tomatoes, 141–42, 163–64; gravy using fresh tomatoes, 141–42; and green beans in warm salad, 59–60; and okra, 163; in sandwiches, 137–38; smoked tomato sauce for crawfish corn cakes, 102–3; stuffed with garden egg salad, 138; sun-dried, 18–19; *see also* green tomatoes
trout, pecan-crusted, 33–34
turnip custard, 227–28

unfried pies, 321–22

watermelon salsa, 154–55
winter greens soup, 90

zydeco beans, 66–67